Managing Open Innovation Technologies

Jenny S. Z. Eriksson Lundström
Mikael Wiberg • Stefan Hrastinski
Mats Edenius • Pär J. Ågerfalk
Editors

Managing Open Innovation Technologies

Editors
Jenny S. Z. Eriksson Lundström
Stefan Hrastinski
Mats Edenius
Pär J. Ågerfalk
Uppsala University
Uppsala
Sweden

Mikael Wiberg
Department of Informatics and Media
Uppsala University
Uppsala
Sweden

ISBN 978-3-642-31649-4 ISBN 978-3-642-31650-0 (eBook)
DOI 10.1007/978-3-642-31650-0
Springer Heidelberg New York Dordrecht London

Library of Congress Control Number: 2012952144

ACM Computing Classification (1998): K.4, K.6, H.1, D.2

© Springer-Verlag Berlin Heidelberg 2013
This work is subject to copyright. All rights are reserved by the Publisher, whether the whole or part of the material is concerned, specifically the rights of translation, reprinting, reuse of illustrations, recitation, broadcasting, reproduction on microfilms or in any other physical way, and transmission or information storage and retrieval, electronic adaptation, computer software, or by similar or dissimilar methodology now known or hereafter developed. Exempted from this legal reservation are brief excerpts in connection with reviews or scholarly analysis or material supplied specifically for the purpose of being entered and executed on a computer system, for exclusive use by the purchaser of the work. Duplication of this publication or parts thereof is permitted only under the provisions of the Copyright Law of the Publisher's location, in its current version, and permission for use must always be obtained from Springer. Permissions for use may be obtained through RightsLink at the Copyright Clearance Center. Violations are liable to prosecution under the respective Copyright Law.
The use of general descriptive names, registered names, trademarks, service marks, etc. in this publication does not imply, even in the absence of a specific statement, that such names are exempt from the relevant protective laws and regulations and therefore free for general use.
While the advice and information in this book are believed to be true and accurate at the date of publication, neither the authors nor the editors nor the publisher can accept any legal responsibility for any errors or omissions that may be made. The publisher makes no warranty, express or implied, with respect to the material contained herein.

Printed on acid-free paper

Springer is part of Springer Science+Business Media (www.springer.com)

Foreword

"There are too few information boards at this airport", the traveller explained. "Get more information boards and you will address the biggest challenge for travellers at your airport". Many travellers "liked" this solution. Going about getting more information boards still did not solve the issue. How come?

Open innovation could bring profit to companies and organisations via the inflow of a multitude of new ideas that are put into action as new products, services and solutions. Accessing the distributed knowledge of global inventors and users becomes the way to go forth, in a competitive era driven by globalisation, new technology and changes in user requirements. But as open innovation is not a panacea for solving any particular problem and addressing changing user demands, how are we to ensure that the adopters of open innovation are focusing on the "right" problems and with the "right" methods? What are the challenges of open innovation, and how are industries and organisations to capitalise on the distributed knowledge and inventions and successfully bring these inventions, via the manufacturing process flows, on to the market place? With valuable learnings from research and industrial settings like Intel, Nokia, Philips Healthcare, small municipality approaches, innovation intermediaries, e-learning platforms and user communities, this book focuses on some of the key dimensions to open innovation and open innovation technologies and how we may address them by asking the question, how are we to manage open innovation technologies?

Stockholm 2012
Håkan Ozan

Acknowledgements

We gratefully acknowledge that this anthology is part of the Open Innovation Frameworks project—a collaborative effort between National Swedish IT-user Centre (NITA) at Uppsala University, Computer Sciences Corporation (CSC) and Centre for Information and Communication Research (CIC) at Stockholm School of Economics. The project is funded by VINNOVA, the Swedish Governmental Agency for Innovation Systems.

Contents

Theme I   Motivations

1   Open Source Software as Open Innovation: *Experiences from the Medical Domain*   3
Björn Lundell and Frank van der Linden

2   "It's the Conversation, Stupid!"   17
Aldo de Moor and Mark Aakhus

3   Organisational Participation in Open Innovation Communities   35
Matt Germonprez and Brian Warner

4   Open Innovation Technologies and Exploitative and Explorative Learning   53
Mats Edenius and Ali Yakhlef

5   Open Innovation in Inter-Organisational Networks in the IT Industry   67
Karlheinz Kautz, Sameen M. Rab, and Michael Sinnet

Theme II   Best Practices

6   Encouraging Open Community Innovation: *Outils-Réseaux*'s Modular Approach   93
Lorna Heaton, Florence Millerand, David Delon, Florian Schmitt, Laurent Marseault, and Jessica Deschamps

7   Open Source Technology in Intra-Organisational Software Development—Private Markets or Local Libraries   107
Juho Lindman, Mikko Riepula, Matti Rossi, and Pentti Marttiin

8 Open Innovation in Practice: The Development of the IT Capability Maturity Framework 123
Brian Donnellan and Gabriel J. Costello

9 Voluntary Contributors in Open Innovation Processes 133
Anna Ståhlbröst and Birgitta Bergvall-Kåreborn

10 Creating Value Through Open Innovation in Social E-Learning 151
Per Andersson, Pierre Jarméus, Simone Masog, Christopher Rosenqvist, and Carl Sundberg

Theme III   Moving Forward

11 Overcoming Industrial Inertia by Use of Open Innovation Technologies 165
Juho Lindman, Tuija Heikura, and Petra Turkama

12 Using Information Technology to Manage Diverse Knowledge Sources in Open Innovation Processes 179
Vincenzo Corvello, Davide Gitto, Sven Carlsson, and Piero Migliarese

13 Pico-Jobs as an Open Innovation Tool for Utilising Crowdsourcing 199
Jens Fähling, Ivo Blohm, Jan Marco Leimeister, Helmut Krcmar, and Jan Fischer

14 Open Strengths and Weaknesses of IT User Innovation: Evidence from Three Cases 215
Matthias Hürlimann and Ali Yakhlef

15 Open Service Innovation in Health Care: What Can We Learn from Open Innovation Communities? 239
Christina Keller, Mats Edenius, and Staffan Lindblad

16 How Open Is Open Innovation? Considering, Adapting and Adopting User Knowledge and Competence in the Solution Space 253
Oscar Persson Ridell, Jimmie G. Röndell, and David Sörhammar

The Future of Open Innovation Technologies and its Management 275
Mikael Wiberg and Jenny Eriksson Lundström

Postludium 279

List of Contributors 281

Index 291

Managing Open Innovation Technologies

The objectives of this book are to advance and disseminate research on systematic practical open innovation, and make research results available to practitioners. The intended target audience is both international academic community and industry community partners, including civil society.

In particular, with the book we aim to

- Motivate and analyse the benefits of open innovation
- Present challenges in adopting open innovation technologies
- Capture best practices in the management of open innovation technologies
- Offer experiences from real-life open innovation projects

Topics addressed in this book include:

- Open innovation as in use today—theoretical underpinnings and lessons from related research fields
- Analysis of the use of open innovation in organisations today in order to extract best practices
- Forward-looking theoretical as well as practical future use of open innovation

The chapters address the particular topics by experiences/results gained in real-life projects and/or other empirical research. Each chapter clearly states its purpose and how readers are supposed to benefit from it by means of experience reports and easy-to-grasp practical advice.

Jenny Eriksson Lundström
Mikael Wiberg
Stefan Hrastinski
Mats Edenius
Pär J. Ågerfalk

Managing Open Innovation Technologies—Contemporary Best Practices

Precursors

In addressing how to successfully manage open innovation and open innovation technologies we first need to define what we mean with "innovation" and "open". While invention is the first occurrence of an idea that changes thinking, things, processes or services (McKeown 2008), innovation means an invention that was implemented and taken to market (Brown 2006). Hence, in our view, innovation means enabling an increase in value for producer and/or consumer. Such enabling may come in the form of new offerings such as new or improved products or services; new processes of how products or services are created; new business models, or via changes in structuring the organisation or its value chain.

Usually the incentives of open innovation are the limitations inherent in the closed. Open means removing boundaries (Chesbrough 2003). As the world is getting more competitive, organisations find themselves in an era of innovation, distinguished by its availability of venture capital. Today, expertise is less scarce, and more people are educated. The mobility of knowledge workers, to new job opportunities outside of the organisation, means that desired knowledge and experience are more frequently available outside of the organisation than within. Locking in the best knowledge is no longer possible. Often the source of valuable offerings is to be found outside of the organisation, stemming from individuals; consumers or users who initially created value for themselves (von Hippel 2005), and refined in collaborative innovation communities to viable offerings (Baldwin et al. 2006), or via (networks of) external experts. With new technologies for communication, the transaction costs of tapping into this knowledge are decreasing, thus resulting in a shift to user-centred innovation processes, leaving traditional in-house innovation processes lagging behind.

xiii

Open Innovation and Open Innovation Technologies

Looking around the landscape of existing open innovation technologies we notice their multitude and their multifaceted nature: brainstorming, idea management, technology scouting, innovation marketplaces, prototyping sandboxes, market intelligence and test beds for innovation, just to mention a few. Not requiring high technology, innovation is still relative to the prevailing infrastructure and market maturity. Hence, IT presents itself as an enabler for both. Internet technology lends itself well to connecting large groups of customers, seamlessly interfacing with existing technology in the manufacturing line. Customer studies are bygones when direct customer interaction becomes possible, enabling learning from the customer as well as educating the customer of the offerings and the potentials of their use. Hence, at the time of internet technology and the maturity of the users, Web 2.0 applications present a great opportunity for innovation. From working hard to getting the top brains to work for us, we are instead able to tap into the vast and diversified knowledge of the world. Clearly, innovation policies are now turning from closed in-house innovation processes into open innovation ecosystems.

Managing Open Innovation Technologies

Due to the unstructured nature of these open innovation ecosystems, strategic management is the means of providing structure and direction, and hence value from the interaction. Managing open innovation technologies is about structured methods for identifying, finding, collecting and incorporating the resulting creativity and new thinking of open innovation into the existing organisation's business strategy, processes or structures. Even more importantly, management deals with political, social and cultural issues that have an impact on rethinking social structures and on the mind-sets of the employees.

This means that managing open innovation technologies touches upon changes of planning, processes, people, technical infrastructure and performance. It is about finding strategies and processes of innovation and to align these to other processes of the organisation, through implementation and maintenance of current methods and tools of innovation.

Potential Issues and Challenges

Going about open innovation is never solely about theories nor best practices. It is through implementation and the use of new thinking in the existing organisation that realises the potential of open innovation. Any platform set up for collecting ideas cannot by itself transform the wisdom of the crowd into business advantage for the organisation. Additionally, the incentives and means to invest in open innovation are essential. Organisations embracing open innovation are presumed to do so for its proven ability to maintain and advance business innovation, but not all organisations that desire to adapt to customers' demands are businesses or have the aim of generating profit. Drawing on open innovation is possible if management of the open innovation technology is fitted for its purpose and the organisational goals are clear. Undoubtedly, a mere reinterpretation of open innovation on to old concepts to fit the existing organisational structure or business models may cause the potential of open innovation to be left unexplored. Here lies the challenge.

Coming back to our initial story, the airport refined their understanding of the traveller's solution by a root cause analysis. At a closer look, the issue was not about information boards at all, it was about the difficulty of finding the way at the airport. Clear management of any type of technology, including open innovation technologies, is the way to create value for the organisation and its customers. Doing so is all about learning the essential lessons from others, what the challenges are, to understand how this would create benefits for the organisation and push it to completion. In this book, we offer you an aggregated view of benefits and challenges of open innovation technologies, and present experiences from managing real-life open innovation projects.

Target Audience and the Objectives of the Book

The objectives of this book are to advance and disseminate research on systematic practical open innovation and make research results available to practitioners. The intended target audience is both international academic community and industry community partners, including civil society.

Overall, the book addresses the particular topics by experiences gained from real-life projects and other empirical research. The experiences recorded are drawn from sound empirical studies conducted at the particular sites described, and include observations of practitioners as well as other observations from various sources. Each chapter clearly states its purpose and how readers are supposed to benefit from it by means of experience reports and easy-to-grasp practical advice. Together, they provide existing state-of-art and state-of-best-practice of the facets addressed of managing open innovation technologies.

Book Overview

Topics addressed in this book are presented in the following three themes and a concluding section:

Theme 1 deals with open innovation as in use today—theoretical underpinnings and lessons from related research fields. This theme comprises five chapters that develop the theoretical underpinnings of open innovation as they elaborate on theories from adjacent fields. The results are exemplified by empirical findings. They discuss precursors of open innovation and provide valuable insight on how and why organisations are to position themselves to benefit from technology and openness.

Theme 2 concerns analysis of the use of open innovation in organisations today in order to extract best practices. The five chapters of this theme present contemporary best practices derived from industrial applications of open innovation technologies. The chapters of this theme provide industrial experiences of open innovation. The overall focus is set on the collective, collaborative nature of open innovation, the role of networking and how the underlying technical infrastructures and the application of open innovation technology change the organisation. The chapters provide practical advice on the coordination and management of diffusing opportunities for innovation, the motivations of the users of open innovation outcomes themselves as well as aspects of open innovation in digital platforms for learning.

Theme 3 presents forward-looking theoretical as well as practical future use of open innovation. In this theme the chapters deal with prerequisites of open innovation, how various sources of knowledge for open innovation are to be approached and how open innovation technologies may be employed for smaller tasks. Two of these chapters deal with the potential and barriers of open innovation, and poses a final question on how open, open innovation really is.

The concluding section is written as a conceptual exercise, reflecting on the phenomenon of open innovation. It works as material for further reflections and as a starting point for further explorations into future challenges of open innovation.

References

Baldwin, C. Y., Hienerth, C. & von Hippel. E. (2006) How user innovations become commercial products: A theoretical investigation and a case study. *Research Policy* (35)9:1291-1313.

Brown, J.S. (2006) Foreword: Innovating innovation. In Chesbrough, H.W. *Open Innovation: The New Imperative for Creating and Profiting from Technology*. Harvard Business School Press, Boston, MA, ix–xii.

Chesbrough, H. W. (2003). *Open innovation: the new imperative for creating and profiting from technology*. Harvard Business School Press.

McKeown, M., (2008) *The truth about innovation*, Pearson, Financial Times.

von Hippel, E. (2005) *Democratizing Innovation*. Cambridge, MA: MIT Press.

Theme I
Motivations

Open Innovation in Use Today: Theoretical Underpinnings and Lessons Learnt from Related Research Fields

The chapters of this section provide an overview of recent open innovation technology applications. The authors develop theoretical underpinnings of open innovation, by adapting theories from related fields, and also illustrate their findings by presenting case studies.

In the first chapter, Björn Lundell and Frank van der Linden address some of the premises of open innovation by using open source software as an exemplar. They specifically address "commodification" and how various degrees of openness can be situated in a continuum that spans from technology that differentiates a company from its competition to commodities that provide no business advantage in itself. The study draws on experiences from software development in the medical imaging domain at Philips Healthcare with lessons potentially applicable to a broad array of industries.

In the second chapter, Aldo de Moor and Mark Aakhus elaborate on the role of conversation for successful open innovation. More specifically, they provide a framework based on linguistics and language philosophy and use this to propose a social media tool system that could be used by the Intergovernmental Panel on Climate Change (IPCC) to improve their interaction with stakeholders. In the spirit of Kurt Lewin's "there is nothing so practical as a good theory", they provide a useful set of advice for anybody aiming to approach the social media space to engage with the crowd in product and service innovation.

The third chapter, by Matt Germonprez and Brian Warner, explores how and why organisations may participate in open innovation communities. To address these questions, the authors analyse participation in the open innovation community associated with the design and development of the Linux operating system—again using open source software as an exemplar of open innovation technology. Participation in terms of contributions and differentiation is investigated within the context of two large international organisations involved in the development of the Linux kernel. The findings contribute to our understanding not only of open innovation but also more generally of agile development in a contemporary development context.

The fourth chapter, by Mats Edenius and Ali Yaklef, continues the exploration of organisational adoption of open innovation technologies, specifically investigating how and why organisations are managing feedback from their customers and how this contributes to processes of organisational learning. The study draws on experiences from ten different organisations that have used the Kundo application to engage with their customers. The results show that the specific technology under study can contribute to an organisation's understanding of their customers, but that its implementation has to factor in the dynamics involved when trying to control learning processes that transcend the border of the firm.

In the fifth and final chapter, Karlheinz Kautz, Sameen M. Rab and Michael Sinnet turn to open innovation in inter-organisational networks in the IT industry, specifically following how a software development company developed over time through partnership, outsourcing and merger. The analysis shows the decisive role that open innovation technology may serve in turbulent contemporary business environments, which more often than not include globalisation, customisation and large-scale collaboration.

The five chapters clearly show that although technology is important to open innovation, understanding the social interactions, conversations, politics and knowledge processes involved is key to successfully managing these technologies and to reaping the most benefit from them. By doing this they summarise the comprehensive theme of all the papers; we need to identify and understand both the barriers and drivers to practice open innovation.

Pär J. Ågerfalk

Chapter 1
Open Source Software as Open Innovation:
Experiences from the Medical Domain

Björn Lundell and Frank van der Linden

Abstract In the past decade, we have witnessed an increased interest amongst commercial and public sector organisations for Open Source Software (OSS). As any individual and organisation has the right to freely read, use, improve and redistribute the source code for software that is developed and released under an OSS licence, it creates new opportunities for Open Innovation. In this chapter, we report on how companies collaborate on production of software artefacts in an OSS project, thereby showing how a form of Open Innovation can be utilised by a large company that goes beyond collaborative development of ideas. In doing so, we report on company decisions and development practices concerning how a software project evolved from proprietary to an open collaborative software development project that is released under an OSS licence (LGPLv2).

1.1 Introduction

Open Source Software (OSS) is software that is licenced and made available under certain "open" conditions, which inherently stimulates a collaborative development of ideas and software artefacts. Anyone who has developed, obtained or adopted such software has the right to freely read, use, improve and redistribute the source code for such software. Over the years, collaboration based on (or stemming from) OSS has influenced many individuals and organisations who have adopted new work practices, and in some cases, even fundamentally changed their way of working.

This chapter gives an illustration of how development of OSS, as an example of Open Innovation, has been adopted by a large company in the secondary software

---

B. Lundell (✉)
University of Skövde, Informatics Research Centre, Skövde, Sweden

F. van der Linden
Philips Healthcare, Best, The Netherlands

J.S.Z. Eriksson Lundström et al. (eds.), *Managing Open Innovation Technologies*,
DOI 10.1007/978-3-642-31650-0_1, © Springer-Verlag Berlin Heidelberg 2013

sector. We discuss challenges in software development and present a framework, the commodification diagram, in order to conceptualise experiences from a case study of OSS development in the medical domain. By drawing from the case, we discuss emerging trends and relate these to Open Innovation. The case study was conducted in a large European company and illustrates how emerging commodification trends in the software domain have impacted on company decisions and development practices.

With the adoption of OSS and development practices in companies, the practice for development and deployment of software systems is changing. When companies collaborate on OSS projects, the Open Innovation goes beyond collaborative development of ideas and also includes collaborative production of software artefacts in Open Source projects outside the traditional organisational boundaries. This trend of open collaboration can be seen as an implication of the ongoing trend of contemporary commodification of software which inevitably has consequences for companies leading to new forms of collaborative development.

In the secondary software sector, we have recently seen an increased interest in new forms of development practices, such as inner and open source development of software systems. This form of new development models can be seen as one way by which companies in this sector can deal with the contemporary commodification of software. However, for large companies, it may not be so easy to change established traditions and current work practices. Consequently, adoption of new principles and practices for software development certainly imposes new challenges. In this chapter, we comment on these by drawing from a specific case, which we then relate to the broader picture of Open Innovation. Our case study, stemming from the medical domain, gives insights into how organisational and development practices have evolved over time with a resulting increased "openness". Today, our case constitutes an interesting exemplar of how a large company can utilise a form of Open Innovation to collaborate on the production of software systems.

1.2 Open Source Software as an Exemplar of Open Innovation

Since the late 1960s, researchers and practitioners have struggled with how to cope with an ever increasing complexity in the development of software systems. One way by which companies have sought to address challenges in various projects has been to utilise new development models, including OSS and its associated collaborative model for development (Bonaccorsi and Rossi 2006; Fitzgerald 2006; Lundell et al. 2010).

Open Source is the widely used term for a type of software licence that Richard Stallman referred to as "Free Software" when he founded the Free Software

1 Open Source Software as Open Innovation: *Experiences from the Medical Domain*

Foundation (FSF[1]). The term "Open Source" was coined in 1998 to give the phenomenon a more "business-friendly" association. The definition is controlled by the Open Source Initiative (OSI[2]) and the term "Open Source Software" is today more widely used in company contexts than "Free Software". The definition of such software used by the FSF states that it is "a matter of the users' freedom to run, copy, distribute, study, change and improve the software". More specifically, the definition refers to "four kinds of freedom, for the users of the software", namely the freedom to:

- Run the program, for any purpose
- Study how the program works, and adapt it to need
- Redistribute copies
- Improve the program, and release the improvements

Although there are differences in terms of value between OSI and FSF, both organisations refer to the essentially same type of software. Today, both organisations have much in common with collaboration on many practical issues. For example, OSI accepts almost all of the licences defined by FSF, and vice versa. For OSI, the "openness" of source code for any piece of software is primarily a practical issue that allows an open form of collaborative development, whereas for FSF the "freedom" is primarily an ethical issue.

Sometimes, the term "FOSS" is used to stress the similarities rather than the differences between the two. Further, the term "Libre Software" is also used for this type of software, especially in the Latin speaking countries. The term "Libre" avoids the ambiguity of the word "free" in the English language (i.e. "free" as in no-cost vs. "free" as in freedom) and sometimes the term "FLOSS" (Free, Libre and Open Source Software) is used when referring to the collective phenomenon whilst trying to avoid an ideological debate. However, when referring to such software for the purpose of this chapter, we adhere to the term Open Source Software (OSS), which is commonly used in industry.

Irrespective of which term is used for denoting software systems that have been developed using this open form of collaboration, it is essential to recognise that a number of industrial strength software systems have been developed as a result of this form of collaborative development over the years. For example, the operating system kernel Linux (Moon and Sproull 2000), the web server Apache (Mockus et al. 2002) and the web browser Mozilla/Firefox (Mockus et al. 2002) are all being developed, maintained and made available by their respective communities as OSS. Such communities, typically, involve a variety of different stakeholder groups that collectively contribute to OSS projects. It should be noted that there are a range of different motivations, including pure self-interest, that encourage stakeholders to contribute to an OSS project (e.g. Bonaccorsi and Rossi 2006). For many years now, it is clear that a "significant amount of software developed by commercial

---

[1] http://www.fsf.org/

[2] http://www.opensource.org/

firms is also being released under open source licences" (von Hippel 2005, p. 99). In fact, many companies have experienced that open collaboration in OSS projects, which involve a number of different active users and developers representing a variety of different organisations, can together bring the software to high value and quality.

Today, all the above-mentioned examples of OSS projects are being used in a range of different usage contexts, including mission critical applications in many different organisations. In doing so, it is clear that OSS development shares some fundamental ideas with Open Innovation, such as "greater external sources of information to create value" (Chesbrough 2006). It is therefore, perhaps, not surprising that embedded Linux has been ascribed as a prominent success story of Open Innovation (Henkel 2006).

Collaboration in OSS projects represents a novel way for open collaboration on both ideas and production of software artefacts. As stated by von Hippel (2005), "open source software communities do not allow contributing innovators to use their intellectual property rights to control the use of their code. Instead, contributors use their authors' copyright to assign their code to a common pool to which all—contributors and non-contributors alike—are granted equal access. Despite this regime, innovation seems to be flourishing" (p. 113).

> **Practical Tip**
>
> Collaboration is beneficial for you, especially if you do not break your own added value. Collaboration with the competition may be useful, as you both improve without harming each other. A healthy competition is good for your market, as being the monopolist implies that you have to do any innovation on your own.

In fact, many of the successful OSS projects attract interest and contributions from a range of different individual contributors and commercial organisations. According to von Hippel (2005), "Open source software projects are object lessons that teach us that users can create, produce, diffuse, provide user field support for, update, and use complex products by and for themselves in the context of user innovation communities" (p. 14). Further, it has been noted that there are also similarities between communities related to physical products and OSS communities, in that "complex communities devoted to the development of physical products often look similar to open source software development communities in terms of tools and infrastructure" (von Hippel 2005, p. 103).

It should be noted that adoption of Open Source and Open Innovation principles in company contexts is not always without problems, as experienced by Wallin and von Krogh (2010). They identified tensions in a company between top- and middle-level management concerning its adoption of an Open Source strategy, and report that "While top management embraced an open source policy, middle-level managers who supervised the internal developers were negative toward it. Perhaps the use of external developers undermined their power or prestige, or created concerns about the quality of the products in other ways. Political forces may make it difficult to open up the innovation process to outsiders" (p. 419).

However, a recent study conducted in 13 companies in the secondary software sector, involving senior decision makers with experience of assessing OSS adoption, found that "open innovation practices are already in operation in all of the companies studied" (Morgan and Finnegan 2010, p. 91). Further, the study revealed "the need to increase innovativeness by opening up internal software innovation processes" (p. 91).

1.3 Software Commodification and Its Implications for Software Development

In the past decade, there has been an increasing trend towards changing established software development processes in many organisations. Many companies in the secondary software sector have experienced an increasing amount of complex software systems which are no longer providing a competitive advantage to the company, and it is clear that organisations need to adapt to a new situation which involves an increasing amount of commoditised software systems. With a broader recognition of this commodification trend amongst different stakeholder groups within companies, and with the availability of an increasing amount of complex commodity software, it is clear that organisations need to strategically consider their own development practices in light of their own business goals.

Many companies in the secondary software sector need to deal with how to obtain best leverage from the changing conditions which affects their own established practices. In fact, "only a small part (5–10 %) of the software is differentiating" (van der Linden et al. 2009), and it is this part of the software (which constitutes only parts of a product in this market) that "provides added value over the competitors" (van der Linden et al. 2009). This implies that it is only this small part of the software that helps distinguish a company's own developed product "from competitors' products" (van der Linden et al. 2009). Hence, there is potential for collaboration amongst competitors over large (non-differentiating) parts of the software, and many companies have realised that new development models, including different Open Source development models, may be beneficial for addressing challenges in developing and maintaining complex software systems in many situations in this sector.

When utilising such, network-enabled collaboration in developing the software is jointly developed by stakeholders representing different concerns, both within a single company and beyond its organisational borders. Typically, the software may be produced by a group of designated developers that share a common vision for the Open Source development project. However, for individual companies in

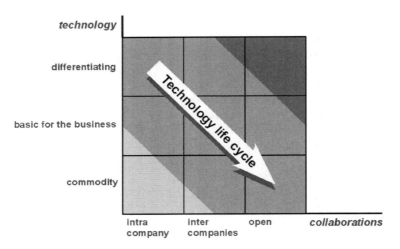

Fig. 1.1 The commodification diagram

this domain, it is important to strategically consider how a company's business and development strategies are congruent and reinforce each other. Obviously, business goals must be in line with development practices, and it is critical for any company to strategically consider what (and when) to initiate and engage in Open Source development related to any specific software systems. In general, the advantages and drawbacks of utilising OSS and its methodology in software intensive systems are not by and large completely understood. However, there are many companies in this sector which engage in Open Source development and "utilise commodity software in order to free resources for innovation" (Lundell et al. 2011).

A significant amount of all software being developed in the secondary software domain does not provide any added value for an individual company over its competitors, as it is more or less common to the product domain. It may even be the case that specific software is a commodity across different domains. Hence, for achieving efficiency and effectiveness in software development, it makes sense for any company to only focus on producing the differentiating parts, i.e. those with the highest added value, in the in-house development. For the remainder, collaboration between different companies and individuals in Open Source development projects is a viable option.

Figure 1.1 shows the commodification diagram for software development (see also van der Linden et al. 2009). It illustrates the landscape of technology versus business decisions on how to develop (or acquire) software. There are two corner areas to be avoided in producing technology. The upper right-hand (red coloured) corner should be avoided, since it would mean exposing (and passing) added value to competitors. For example, a company has reasons to diversify before opening up a unique software system for which they have to spend considerable resources on development in a highly specialised niche market, and as it therefore can be envisaged that the pool of potential contributors from external organisations will be very limited. The lower left-hand (yellow coloured) corner should also be avoided in order to minimise development costs, since commodity technology can be obtained cheaper by adopting (buying) existing technology instead of making it. Hence, healthy software development is characterised by the middle (green coloured) area, from top left to bottom right. Differentiating software, with high added value, is developed within the organisation (top left corner). Commodity software, with low added value, is bought at the market or even available at low (or no) costs (OSS).

Over time, all software is moving from top to bottom in Fig. 1.1. Most (innovative) software development starts out as being differentiating software for some party. At a certain moment, the specific software will not provide a competitive advantage for the company that initiated its development. In such a situation, it can be considered as basic for the business. Further, at a later stage, the software even moves towards commodity. Healthy software development is characterised by combining this vertical movement with the move, for any software, from left to right, from in-house to (open) collaborations. In order to avoid the top right-hand and the lower left-hand corners, companies need to consider strategically when to change their existing development model for any specific software, in order to change the development model at the right pace.

In essence, any company needs to analyse carefully its software with respect to Fig. 1.1 in order to know when to change their development model and approach for collaboration. Further, it is essential to realise that different companies have different business objectives, which affects the interpretation of the status of their software. It is clear that a specific software, which may be a commodity software for company A, may at the same time, for example, be a software which is "basic for the business" for company B. For example, where an integration platform may be seen as commodity for a company offering specific hardware which uses this platform, it may not be for a vendor offering integration platforms as part of its proprietary products. Implications of the commodification of software (i.e. the move from top to bottom in Fig. 1.1) mean that an increasing amount of the software stack in a company is commoditised over time. Hence, it is essential to realise that each company needs to understand these shifts and consider its own software in light of its own business objectives in order to make the right decisions concerning choice of collaboration. In summary, each individual company needs to stay on the "green" in Fig. 1.1 in order for them to stay competitive.

> **Practical Tip**
>
> All organisations must continuously consider technology shifts and assess their own development and adoption of software systems in light of the commodification diagram. In order to obtain leverage from opportunities with open collaboration, an organisation must fully understand technology shifts and how prerequisites for open collaboration evolve over time in different business scenarios and contexts.

In addition to "pure" Open Source software development, some companies also utilise the development model from Open Source. This has been referred to as inner source development, and it involves a set of teams which collaborate in a cooperative ecosystem (Stellman and Greene 2009). Its scope is more restricted compared to "pure" Open Source software development and relates only to the first two vertical columns of Fig. 1.1. Similar to open source development, inner source development applies an open, concurrent, model of collaboration. However, for the rest of this chapter we will focus on Open Source software development.

Currently, a number of companies are utilising open and inner source development to address the commodification of industrial software. In the next section, we draw from a case study in order to illustrate how a large European company has addressed the software shift towards open collaborations, using Open Source software development. In particular, we comment on the evolution through the landscape of Fig. 1.1 and show how the case has moved from a closed to an Open Source software development model which is freely provided on an open platform.

1.4 Open Source Software Development in the Medical Domain

This section gives an example of an endeavour originating from Philips Healthcare[3] in increasing the amount of open innovation of parts of its software, by opening up software in an open source community (Engelfriet 2007). This endeavour was partly based on business reasons—the software was becoming commodity—and partly it was a test case to discover the consequences of starting an open source community. The company should spend most effort on the most business-relevant technology. For the rest, it should cooperate with others. In cases when software becomes a commodity, this means that one should consider opening up software. It will be successful if it attracts enough external collaboration that relieves the company from part of its development costs. It becomes even better when contributors from a large community that are affiliated to other external organisations provide fresh new ideas to innovate the software for the benefit of all involved. Several measures were taken to improve the motivation of participants in the community. The company found that this endeavour of utilising an Open Source community as a strategy for Open Innovation can be profitable, and the conclusion from this experience was that it is profitable. This example is further discussed in van der Linden et al. (2009).

Exchange of medical information has been subject to standardisation and standards since the end of the 1980s, and we have seen an increasing number of standards in this area over the last decades. One such standard is the DICOM standard (Digital Imaging and Communications in Medicine), which is used as a basis for the exchange of medical images. Over the years, different companies have

---

[3] Formerly called Philips Medical Systems

developed various implementations of the standard. Therefore, conformance to the standard has become important, leading to a need for having a validation tool that can check conformance to the standard. This, in turn, leads to less field problems in interoperability and reduced field support costs.

Since 2000, Philips Healthcare and AGFA Healthcare have been distributing a free binary DICOM validation tool. To make this tool independent of the companies and to improve an open collaboration on the topic, it was decided in 2005 to release the tool as an Open Source software project. The Open Source software DVTk[4] is made available under the GNU Lesser General Public Licence (LGPL v2[5]) and the Open Source project is hosted on the SourceForge.net platform.

The success for the two initiating companies of this transition was based on the community that uses and contributes to the tool. The scope of the open source tool is extended towards the creation of state-of-the-art standard tools to prevent and solve integration problems of systems in the medical imaging domain.

By opening up the software, the initiating parties aimed to create worldwide acceptance of DVTk as an independent (de facto standard) and trustworthy tool, involving a large base of users. By initiating an open collaborative development of the tool, the initiators expected to get the best value out of the development cost. Further, it was also expected that a large user and developer group would result in higher quality and fewer overhead costs. To support these goals, the initiators have remained active in providing community mechanisms that address different motivations for participation in the open collaboration amongst individuals and companies.

A number of initiatives to stimulate collaboration with (and within) the project have been undertaken by the initiators of the project, including:

- Creating DVTk website with forum and registration
- Organising and executing timely User Events
- Implementing the concept of "trainee project"
- Participating in IHE Gazelle Open Source project
- Responding to tenders for Test SW development

The latter two initiatives illustrate the extension of the scope towards other interoperability standards in healthcare. To measure the achievement of the goals, the company has monitored the Open Source project since its start, and in doing so continuously measured a number of aspects which indicate project activity:

- The number of downloads of the tool per year; indicating whether the tool, which is updated regularly, is still useful for a wide community
- The number of comments on the tool received per year; indicating the active interest of the users in improving the tool

---

[4] http://www.dvtk.org/; http://en.wikipedia.org/wiki/DVTk
[5] http://www.opensource.org/licenses/LGPL-2.1

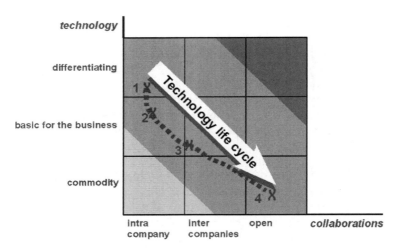

Fig. 1.2 The DVTk project and DICOM in the commodification diagram

- The number of companies participating in the development of the tools; indicating whether there is enough sharing of development

Figure 1.2 shows an overview of four important stages in the history of the DVTk project, clearly illustrating how different company decisions have resulted in an evolution of the project through the commodification diagram (additional details of the project can be found in van der Linden et al. (2009)). Figure 1.2 shows how the project has evolved, via four stages, into a "commodity" project for which there is open collaboration.

Briefly, the four stages in the evolution of the project can be characterised as follows:

1. In 1995, DICOM was a quality interface, only available as a system option for those that really needed interoperability on medical images. Several vendors provided their own solutions, and this was part of the competition. DICOM support was an added value for medical equipment companies.
2. In 1999, DICOM was no longer differentiating. The clients all needed interoperability and they just expected DICOM support and Philips Healthcare decided to provide the DVTk application binary freely downloadable via their own website.
3. In 2001, to share development costs and increase adoption of DVTk, a joint development started with another company (AGFA). The development of DVTk was still developed and provided under a proprietary licence. The functionality is necessary for each company that supports DICOM interoperability.
4. In 2005, it was decided to create an open platform to ensure uniformity. The software is still domain specific, but for the companies involved it is regarded as commodity.

The DVTk project is very ambitious in its objective and strives for global acceptance and more co-developing partners. The project has several different types of participants and users, which can be characterised as: the common user, the interested collaborator and the dedicated developer (O'Reilly 1999). Over time, some users eventually migrate and become more involved, so a common user could become a future dedicated developer. The DVTk project decided to implement some mechanisms which address the motivational factors of developers to promote contributions. These are to:

- Implement User Registration on the website to address the "reputation among peers" motivation. The idea is that when people can have a virtual face when communicating with the community they are more likely to communicate more actively.
- Implement the concept of "trainee project" in the DVTk project to address the "learning" motivation. Co-developing on DVTk is positioned as a way to learn the standard. By having a set of trainee projects, people can select a work item which helps them in understanding the standard.
- Organise and execute timely User Events to motivate the "sense of belonging to the community". If you can meet your co-developers face to face in timely events people tend to feel more committed to the co-developers and thus to the project.

After User Registration was implemented, the number of posts on the discussion forum increased, indicating growing activity and involvement. About ten trainee projects were defined in December 2006. Several of these project assignments led to new developers in the project. In February 2007, the user event attracted 40 participants from 30 companies. After the workshop, five parties were considering participation, of which three eventually became involved. The event resulted in a new collaboration with the IHE organisation which is a leading organisation in the healthcare domain.

The user registration has a positive impact on motivating users to post questions and provide problem reports. It is not a burden for people to register, since it provides the ability for people to gain reputation. For DVTk it seems as it is better to have a smaller group providing a lot of feedback than having a large group of users only posting a small set of comments. The User Event is an effective mechanism to meet potential new parties. Having the training projects is a controlled and effective mechanism to get the potential parties really involved.

The number of downloads has increased enormously since the project was provided as Open Source software. In the first two years, the number of downloads increased from 1,000 to 14,000 per year and the number of comments increased from 5 to 80 per year. The number of users increased by 1,200 % within the same time period. The number of companies and initiatives that work together with the project has grown from 2 to 9. This means that sharing the maintenance and

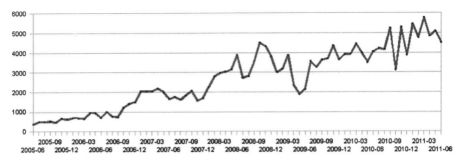

Fig. 1.3 Number of downloads of the software per month

development of the DVTk tool is of value for a large community. It suggests that the project is becoming the de facto standard. More recently, since July 2009, the number of downloads for the software per month has exceeded 3,000 downloads per month (which may be considered significant, given the specific nature of the software). Figure 1.3 shows an overview of the evolution for the number of downloads for the software (until the end of June 2011). From this, it is evident that the overarching trend has been an increased number of downloads of the software each month, ranging from around 500 downloads each month (for the last 6 months during 2005), whereas there have been more than 4,000 downloads each month (for the first 6 months during 2011).

In order to extend the community and the funding base of the project, it successfully applied to a commercial software tool development tender for the IHE-Radiation Oncology Test software and the IHE Gazelle Open Source tooling project. This extends the scope of the community, but stays within the healthcare interoperability domain.

It should be noted that the results reported in this example are not restricted to the medical domain. Instead, the experiences should be useful to the entire secondary software domain. Further, an additional important aspect of this example is that there is a standard that can be used by many companies in the domain. At first the provision of support for the standard gives a significant added value for the provider of an implementation which supports the standard. However, over time, as several competitors will implement the standard, the associated added value stemming from support for the standard becomes reduced as it becomes expected by the clients. Therefore, despite competition on the market, it is wise to open up the supporting software as a strategy for sharing development costs between companies. However, an important prerequisite for success is that the knowledge of the standard is not restricted to one (or a few) companies. In addition, when it becomes successful, it might be attractive for both the company and other external contributors to extend the scope of the open collaboration in the OSS project.

1.5 Discussion and Conclusions

In this chapter, we have presented an illustration of how the development of Open Source Software, as an example of Open Innovation, has been adopted by a large company in the secondary software sector. We have discussed challenges in software development and presented a framework, the commodification diagram, as a means for conceptualisation. We have used this framework as a basis for our presentation of experiences from a case study of Open Source Software development in the medical domain. In doing so, we have elaborated on company decisions and development practices in a software development project that is central for the company and openly provided under the LGPL software licence.

By drawing from the case study conducted in a large international company, we have discussed emerging trends and thereby presented how software development—when conducted as Open Source Software development—constitutes a novel exemplar of how Open Innovation can be conducted. Open Source Software development goes beyond collaborating on ideas, as it also includes collaboration on software artefacts, therefore it can potentially constitute an inspiration for how other areas can adopt an open development beyond the established form of open development as we have seen in the software domain in the form of Open Source Software.

It is envisaged by many that new forms of more open collaborations between different types of communities, as well as large and small companies, will emerge. It remains to be seen which of these collaboration models will be sustainable in the long term.

References

Bonaccorsi, A., & Rossi, C. (2006). Comparing motivations of individual programmers and firms to take part in the open source movement: from community to business knowledge, technology & policy. *Winter, 18*(4), 40–64.

Chesbrough, H. W. (2006). *Open innovation: A new paradigm for understanding Industrial Innovation, Chapter 1 in open innovation: Researching a new paradigm.* Oxford: Oxford University Press.

Engelfriet, A. (2007) Open Source and Open Innovation, Koninklijke Philips Electronics NV, handout: *LinuxWorld Open Summit 2007*, Stockholm, at http://www.idc.com/nordic/downloads/events/linuxworld07/9%20-Arnoud%20Engelfriet.pdf, accessed 7 July 2011.

Fitzgerald, B. (2006a). The Transformation of open source software. *MIS Quarterly, 30*(3), 587–598.

Henkel, J. (2006). Selective revealing in open innovation processes: The case of embedded Linux. *Research Policy, 35*(7), 953–969.

Lundell, B., Lings, B., & Lindqvist, E. (2010). Open source in Swedish companies: where are we? *Information Systems Journal, 20*(6), 519–535.

Lundell, B., Lings, B., & Syberfeldt, A. (2011). Practitioner perceptions of open source software in the embedded systems area. *Journal of Systems and Software, 84*(9), 1540–1549.

Mockus, A., Fielding, R. T., & Herbsleb, J. D. (2002). Two case studies of open source software development: Apache and Mozilla. *ACM Transactions on Software Engineering and Methodology, 11*(3), 309–346.

Moon, Y. J. & Sproull, L. (2000) Essence of distributed work: The case of the Linux kernel, *First Monday*, 5(11) http://firstmonday.org/htbin/cgiwrap/bin/ojs/index.php/fm/article/view/1479

Morgan, L., & Finnegan, P. (2010). Open innovation in secondary software firms: an exploration of managers' perceptions of open source software. *SIGMIS Database, 41*(1), 76–95.

O'Reilly, T. (1999) Ten Myths about Open Source Software, http://www.oreillynet.com/pub/a/oreilly/opensource/news/myths_1199.html, accessed 7 July 2011.

Stellman, A. & Greene, J., 2009. Inner source 'An interview with Auke Jilderda', Chapter 8 in. O'Reilly, T. (2009) *Beautiful Teams*, 103–111.

von Hippel, E. (2005). *Democratizing Innovation*. Cambridge, MA: MIT Press (April).

van der Linden, F., Lundell, B., & Marttiin, P. (2009). Commodification of industrial software: a case for open source. *IEEE Software, 26*(4), 77–83.

Wallin, M. W., & von Krogh, G. (2010). Organizing for open innovation: focus on the integration of knowledge. *Organisational Dynamics, 39*(2), 145–154.

Further Reading

Dedrick, J. & West, J. (2003) Why firms adopt open source platforms: A Grounded Theory of Innovation and Standards Adoption, Proceedings of MISQ Special Issue Workshop on Standard Making: A Critical Frontier for Information Systems. Minneapolis: *MIS Quarterly*, pp. 236–257.

Fitzgerald, B. (2006b). The transformation of open source software. *MIS Quarterly, 30*(3), 587–598.

Jaaksi, A. (2007) Experiences on Product Development with Open Source Software, in: Feller, J. Fitzgerald, B. Scacchi, W., Sillitti, A. (Eds.), *IFIP International Federation for Information Processing*, Vol. 234, Open Source Development, Adoption and Innovation, Boston: Springer, 85-96.

Jilderda, A. A. (2004) *Inner Source Software Engineering at MIP Fostering a Meritocracy of Peers*, Research report, Philips Research.

Wesselius, J. (2008). The bazaar inside the Cathedral: Business models for internal markets. *IEEE Software, 25*(3), 60–66.

Chapter 2
"It's the Conversation, Stupid!"

Social Media Systems Design for Open Innovation Communities

Aldo de Moor and Mark Aakhus

Abstract Open innovation is about crossing boundaries to create networked synergies in/across collaborative communities. Conversations are the lifeblood of communities, building the common ground of shared meanings, beliefs, interests, norms, goals, trust and social capital. A fundamental challenge for open innovation lies in the successful *crafting* of the social media *systems* supporting the community conversations. Innovation communities (which are not limited to business interests but also include public and civic organisations and communities) therefore need to continuously make sense of the conversation context of the tools they use. We provide a conceptual lens with which to examine this sociotechnical conversation context. We illustrate the use of this lens with a plausible scenario of open innovation in the societal stakeholder networks around climate change research.

2.1 Introduction

Open innovation is about crossing boundaries to create networked synergies in/ across collaborative communities. Such communities are no longer small, informal groups of individuals sharing an interest. Instead, they are collaborative communities comprising complex, interconnected webs of interacting individuals and organisations focused on producing knowledge-intensive innovative outputs (West and Lakhani 2008).

A. de Moor (✉)
CommunitySense, Tilburg, The Netherlands
e-mail: ademoor@communitysense.nl

M. Aakhus
School of Communication & Information, Rutgers University, New Brunswick, NJ, USA
e-mail: aakhus@rutgers.edu

J.S.Z. Eriksson Lundström et al. (eds.), *Managing Open Innovation Technologies*,
DOI 10.1007/978-3-642-31650-0_2, © Springer-Verlag Berlin Heidelberg 2013

Conversations are the lifeblood of communities, building the common ground of shared meanings, beliefs, interests, norms, goals, trust and social capital, which are all essential for successful communities. This "grounding" consists of many conversations over time, determined by both the purpose and the medium of the communication. In doing so, the costs of using various communications media need to be carefully balanced with the way they contribute to accomplishing the goals of the community (Clark and Brennan 1991).

Popular collaborative innovation approaches like "Wikinomics" and "We-Think" (Leadbeater 2009; Tapscott and Williams 2008) propose smart combinations of Web-mediated content, social media, context and conversations to drive and scale such mass collaboration forms of open innovation communities. For instance, We-Think argues that each open innovation community should have a core of good ideas around which to start creative conversations in which people can contribute, connect, collaborate and create. Wikinomics argues that by being open, interacting with peers, sharing and "acting global", new conversation-based Enterprise 2.0 business models, such as "peer pioneers", "Ideagoras" and "Open Platforms" can emerge.

So, how should social media-supported conversations in open innovation processes be positioned exactly? Central to the open innovation paradigm, as introduced by Chesbrough (2003), is the understanding that the boundaries of the firm are semipermeable. Indeed, Chesbrough and Appelyard (2007) argue that the successful open innovation firms in the technology environment have figured out solutions to four key issues for changing from the classic closed innovation approach to an open innovation approach: (1) attracting the participation of a broad community of contributors and sustaining it over time; (2) successfully competing for contributors because potential contributors have many choices about where to exercise their talents; (3) leading and coordinating the open innovation project and the evolution of its agenda; (4) generating outcomes that sustain the open innovation initiative over time.

Implementing such an open-innovation philosophy in practice is very communication-intensive. Emerging, multi-layered webs of conversations by stakeholders both within and outside the firm generate, connect and coordinate the required ideas, processes and outputs (Fig. 2.1). Social media can be a major enabler of the transformative change needed in and around these emerging knowledge-intensive organisations and networks (Manlow et al. 2010). Often, however, the focus is on single tools ("The 10 best ways to use Twitter for your corporate marketing"; "How to expand your business network with LinkedIn", and so on). Furthermore, the attitude is one of "let's just talk and connect and then things will change". Talk, however, has to be organised into action and the supporting media carefully tailored to business needs. Although useful, laissez-faire, insular social media approaches are often insufficient to support stratified, purposeful collaborative communities, with their many interdependent stakeholders, objectives and tools. An irony is that even though open innovation communities are "open" they are still governed by implicit (and explicit) rules and the actions are afforded and constrained by technology. One underlying tension is the wish between communities being

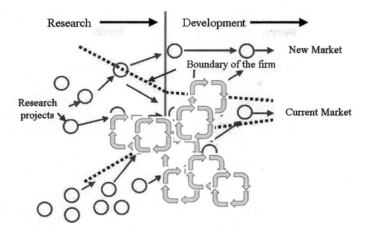

Fig. 2.1 Open Innovation through Webs of Conversations (adapted from Chesbrough 2003)

naturally emergent around the organic desires and values of the community, and the community being directed to address some specific goal such as a business or policy outcome, which often leads to conflicts between community and organisation (West and Lakhani 2008).

We contend that a fundamental challenge for open innovation lies in the successful *crafting* of the social media *systems* supporting the conversations. Innovation communities (which are not limited to business interests but also include public and civic organisations and communities) need to continuously make sense of the conversation context of the tools they use (De Moor and Aakhus 2006). It is the properties and design of these sociotechnical conversation webs that we explore and elaborate on in this chapter with the aim of a more expansive concept of open innovation and the role of conversation. Our goal in this chapter is not to conduct an empirical analysis of a particular case and come up with a practical set of *do*s and *don't*s for open innovation, nor to come up with the theoretical critical success factors for open innovation. Rather, we hope to provide a lens with which to see more clearly an understudied, but key enabler of open innovation: webs of focused conversation supported by tailored systems of social media that provide the substrate within which open innovation can flourish. By illustrating the use of this lens with a concrete, plausible scenario of open innovation in societal stakeholder networks, we hope to inspire open innovation researchers and practitioners to take up the challenge of applying this framework to their concrete cases.

Section 2.2 introduces our social media systems design perspective. This perspective is illustrated by a hypothetical but plausible scenario of the design of such social media systems in Sect. 2.3. We then offer practical design recommendations and implications for research in Sect. 2.4 before concluding the chapter.

2.2 Enabling Open Innovation Conversations: A Social Media Systems Design Perspective

Information systems are no longer static, monolithic behemoths. Instead, organisations, networks and communities increasingly make use of tools (including parts of those information systems) that compete, evolve, are mashed up and are continuously replaced. In order to make sense of what tools they need, and even more important, how to effectively use them, the members of collaborative communities themselves need to continuously capture and reflect upon their way of working in a collaborative sensemaking process.

This sensemaking process is often triggered by breakdowns in collaboration ("why is nobody contributing any ideas to this forum?") and can result in context specifications of different degrees of formality—ranging from informal stories to formal software design patterns. This captured context information can be used to design (select, link and configure) social media and the information systems they make accessible. The aim of this sensemaking exercise is not so much the detailed specification of the content, but to understand and design what interconnected conversations between stakeholders are needed and which combinations of tools can best support these conversation webs (de Moor and Aakhus 2006).

2.2.1 Towards Social Media Systems Design

Design is typically understood as creating artefacts like buildings, software and appliances. Within this conventional understanding, communication is typically seen as part of the design process—that is, through communication, designers, design teams and clients discover how to build what is needed for the purposes at hand. Communication, however, must also be understood as an object of design— that is, through the arrangement of features of interactivity (e.g. turns, roles, sequences of turns, topics) that particular forms of communication, such as conversation, can be constructed or articulated in particular circumstances (e.g. where quarrels can be turned into negotiations; chat into problem solving) (Aakhus 2007). A central issue for understanding the nature of conversation facilitated through social media for the purpose of accomplishing a large-scale goal is to understand how conversation is an object of design.

First, taking a design stance towards conversation requires attending to the *features of interactivity* and *norms for interaction* evident in the way members of groups, organisations and communities interact with each other (or could interact with each other). Features of interactivity, such as mentioned earlier, are organised in patterned, normative ways relative to the demands of communication the community faces. For instance, many online communities exist to provide social support to people with illnesses and their caregivers. Each community develops its unique patterns and norms of interacting with each other to provide support. This includes the roles taken up, the preferred speech acts offered and preferred ways of responding to others. The features of interactivity and norms for interaction that these communities develop are the basis for what the members come to know about their disease and to understand how to cope with it. These aspects of interaction are fundamental to the sustainability of a community as Aakhus and Rumsey (2010) revealed in an analysis of a cancer support group. The community's ability to offer mutual support to each other broke down because of differing interpretations and beliefs about the norms of interaction and the preferred features of interactivity necessary to communicating social support. The community broke down and rebuilt itself over preferences for acts, sequences of acts and the epistemic aims of interaction. The design of conversation is a dynamic, evolving aspect of community sustainability and the form of the conversation is consequential for what content is developed.

Second, taking a design stance toward conversation requires attending to the *web of interactivity*. The particular focal conversations that constitute a community also presuppose and contribute to other conversations within and at the boundaries of the community. For instance, group decision-making can often be broken down into key conversations and the flow of these conversations into each other. Brainstorming conversation that seeks the development of many ideas at some point turns into a convergent conversation where arguments are made to choose one idea over another (de Moor and Aakhus 2006). It is in the development and sequencing of differing kinds of conversations that intellectual and imaginative labour can be successfully organised and through which stakeholders can be effectively and legitimately involved. Aakhus' (1999) analysis of Science Court provides an illuminating example of how the arrangement and sequencing of conversations had consequences for how stakeholders participate in science policy formation. The formation of a court-like proceeding to resolve questions of scientific fact required preparatory conversations to define the question, select case managers and to select judges. The adversarial logic of the web of interactivity affected the very way parties could argue about and make sense of the science for the purposes of policy formation. Alternative ways of coordinating conversations could lead to a different kind of sensemaking about scientific information in policy making. The content of interactions is influenced by the way some content becomes input for subsequent conversations.

Third, taking a design stance towards conversation requires attending to the material affordances for interacting, which includes the circumstances and technologies. Groups, organisations and communities evolve socially and in their capacity for communication among, and between, their members. In some cases, as members work together over time, they can expand their capacity for more sophisticated, nuanced communication, which, in turn, enables the group, organisation or community to deal with increasingly complicated circumstances and matters. This is best exemplified in the emergence of scientific communities where the capacity to engage and improve scientific argumentation co-evolves with the technologies for conducting their scientific work. But this can also be seen in other domains of practice. For instance, de Moor and Aakhus (2006) illustrate how a grass roots

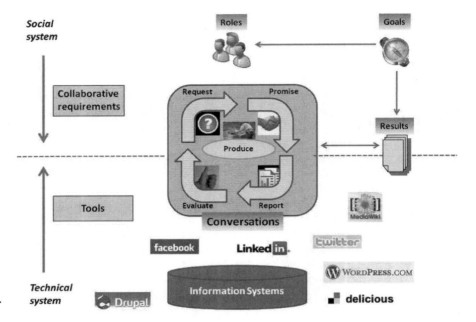

Fig. 2.2 The sociotechnical conversation context framework

policy community co-evolves with its technologies for communication. As the community persisted, it not only incorporated more stakeholders and developed greater sophistication in arguing about the complexities of the environmental and political circumstances, it also incorporated increasingly sophisticated information and communication technology to support its conversational activity. As communities evolve so too can their capacities for new conversational practices.

These key points of a design stance thus provide perspective for understanding the role of conversation and its support through social media in achieving large-scale goals. Realising these broader points about design in the context of social media has been taken up in de Moor (2010) and is explained in the next section.

2.2.2 Analysing Conversation Practices and Purposes

For communities to better understand, design and reuse the sociotechnical building blocks of such communities, we have adopted a sociotechnical conversation context framework (de Moor 2010). This framework (Fig. 2.2) can be used by communities as an instrument for reflection on which sociotechnical design decisions should be made. The framework matches the collaborative requirements of the community with the support affordances and constraints provided by the system of tools available to the community. The starting point is the goals that determine the roles community members play as well as the results that need to be accomplished to realise the goals. The system of tools consists of both (legacy) information systems which form the backbone of most organisations and networks, as well as the constellation of social media that the community members use to create, discover and share content in these information systems and other social media. The way this content is created is by community members, who play particular roles, getting involved in a series of interlinked conversations, while being supported by specific functionalities of the tool system.

These conversations are not just held for their own sake, but are conversations for action, in which collaboration to produce certain results are coordinated. One of the most basic forms of conversation is a *communicative workflow loop*. In such a loop, some community member typically requests another member to produce something, say a document. This member then promises to create this document. After having written the document, she reports to the requester that it has been completed, who can then inspect it and evaluate its quality. If satisfied, the requester closes the loop. Of course, in real life, much more complex communicative workflow situations occur: instead of two participants, many people can be involved, some of them unknown. Each workflow loop can spawn new loops, leading to misunderstandings and problematic delegation of responsibilities. Conflicts and breakdowns can happen, where multiple, partially overlapping tools support the conversations, and so on.

Each community has a unique, continuously evolving sociotechnical system. To understand which tools to select, how to link and configure them in a particular conversation context, communities should understand more about them than their technical functionalities. They should also understand, by trial-and-error and careful case analysis, which are the conversational practices they naturally support. Often, similar functions (e.g. posting a reply) may have totally different effects in how they can be effectively used in supporting collaboration. For instance, a reply to a post on somebody's (closed) Facebook Wall enables very different behaviours than the reply made by somebody to a tweet on an organisation's public Twitter timeline.

There are many ways to analyse such tool-mediated conversation practices. In de Moor (2010), we showed how to compare functionalities and conversation practices of social media like blogs and Twitter. Choosing the right set of tools is especially important for mediating and generating open innovation conversations. Blogs are very useful as distributed knowledge bases, but also have their weaknesses in terms of supporting conversations: they are fragmented, lack the bidirectional link and lack tracking technologies (Efimova and de Moor 2005). Twitter, however, creates less conversation fragmentation than blogs, because it is run on a single server as compared to hard-to-trace conversations that can spread to the vast blogosphere. It is also strong in generating tangential conversations, in which new topics are spawned with very little effort through follow-up tweets. In an open innovation conversation, blogs would typically be used to work out and link the ideas in detail, whereas Twitter can be used to generate the buzz and attention around these ideas. This is a good example of a tool system where the whole is more than the sum of its parts.

To match the practices social media enable with the collaborative requirements, we need to map them to the main conversation purposes they can satisfy though these practices. Four important *conversation purposes* particularly useful in growing collaborative communities include: information exchange, coordination of (inter)actions, collaborative sensemaking and relationship building (de Moor 2010). Twitter, for instance, is particularly good for information exchange and relationship building purposes, but weak in supporting the coordination of interactions over time and many participants. Through the sociotechnical conversation context framework, community managers can map the available tools to the collaborative conversation requirements of a particular community, then use these mappings to set community governance policies, configure tools, create documentation, and so on.

To illustrate what social media systems design means in practice, we expand on a scenario of a hypothetical but plausible scenario on climate change research assessment.

2.3 Scenario: Open Innovation in Societal Stakeholder Networks

Climate change is one of the greatest challenges facing humanity. Addressing it requires the concerted effort of scientists, governments, businesses, non-governmental organisations and citizens from all across the globe. The Intergovernmental Panel on Climate Change (IPCC) has as its mission to provide the world with a clear scientific view on the current state of climate change and its potential environmental and socioeconomic consequences. Thus, IPCC provides a case for reflecting on social media systems design.

One of the main results of the IPCC is its assessment reports. Producing these reports is a massive undertaking. To get an idea, for the fifth report (AR5), 831 highly qualified researchers have been selected to contribute.[1] Given the complexity of the theme and the numerous, often opposing points of view, the production process of these reports is extremely difficult and the results are often controversial, illustrated by the InterAcademy Council, a multi-national organisation of the world's science academies having been requested to conduct an independent review of the IPCC processes and procedures.[2]

The goal is clear: to conduct an independent review of the procedures. For the review to be trusted it is essential to get enough and timely input from stakeholders from all over the world. However, how to do this, given the very limited resources available? In this section we illustrate how our conversation-based social media systems design approach could be used to help the InterAcademy make sense of

---

[1] http://www.ipcc.ch, accessed June 29, 2010.

[2] http://www.interacademycouncil.net/?id=12852

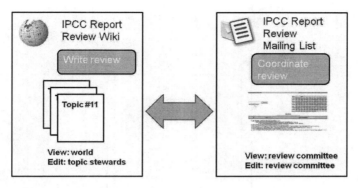

Fig. 2.3 IPCC social media subsystem for drafting the review

their requirements and design their tool system. The following scenario sketches a practical way the InterAcademy Council could reorganise its review procedures with a well-designed social media system, to increase participation by the larger community, the quality of the reviews and ultimately trust in the IPCC reports.

To draft the review, the review committee decides to use a wiki and a mailing list (Fig. 2.3). To write the review, each review topic gets a separate page on the wiki. Each topic (page) has at least one "topic steward" assigned to it, i.e. somebody responsible for documenting all knowledge related to that topic. Each page also gets its own, unique tag, like "IPCC_T11" designating topic #11 of the list of review topics, say about the impacts of climate change on the Arctic regions. The topic pages are visible to the whole world, but can only be edited by the review committee members. Unlike in Wikipedia, it is decided that wiki editing rights cannot be given to the general public, given the strict report focus, the quality required and fear of vandalism.

The review report is written in several rounds. For overall coordination of the review, including making sense of how to organise the review process, the review committee uses a private, archived mailing list. At the micro-level, the wiki is also used to support coordination of topic page editing, since wiki revision histories ensure that no separate meta-communication is needed about who changed what and changes can always be rolled back.

Now, how to open up this process? How to scale the web of conversation in order to check the review and get creative suggestions for improvement? A mailing list is not suitable for soliciting input from the world, as such communication does not scale because participation by more than a limited number of members would flood subscribers' inboxes. The committee is considering the use of Twitter as a tool for scaling up the conversation (Fig. 2.4). To communicate with the world, an "@ipcc_review" Twitter account is created. Any topic steward can use this account to request comments, find relevant experts, announce new updates of the wiki page, etc. To ensure that interested people get only the Twitter updates of the pages they

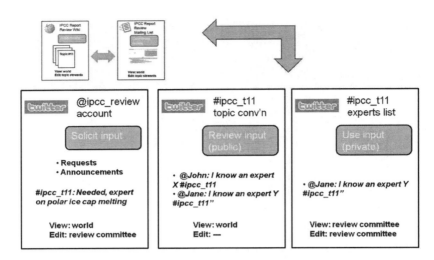

Fig. 2.4 IPPC social media subsystem for soliciting input and handling input

are interested in, each tweet includes a hashtag with the proper topic. Such a tweet could be about the review committee looking for an expert on polar ice cap melting to review topic #11. Such a tweet could look like this:

"**ipcc_review** #ipcc_t11 Needed: expert on polar ice cap melting".

Now, anybody interested in this topic may reply. For instance, somebody called John working for an environmental organisation (or perhaps an oil company) may reply:

"**John** I know an expert X #ipcc_t11"

Whereas well-known climate change researcher Jane answers with

"**Jane** I know an expert Y #ipcc_t11"

Some topics may attract thousands of replies. Each of these replies can spawn new conversations, many of them outside the view of the IPCC review committee. These invisible ripple effects are key to grounding the work of the IPCC in society, however, as each conversation web involves different stakeholders, with different conversation needs and impacts. For example, a few "replies down the line", a network of environmental organisations might be triggered to launch an Arctic exploratory mission, while a totally different conversation web is centred on high school kids discussing a science assignment.

There is no need for the topic steward to get involved in a discussion of each reply or tweet containing the topic hashtag #ipcc_t11 (let alone of the spawned conversations), as this may simply not be feasible timewise and plenty of followers will discuss amongst themselves. To ensure that the topic steward sees all the replies of those people most relevant to her, she can create an ipcc_t11 *Twitter list* (a list of Twitter users that shows their combined tweets) with a selection of Twitter users the @ipcc_review account follows who are most into this topic. This list could consist of, for example, the Twitter users who are her official collaborators plus those users whose replies over time she finds most insightful.

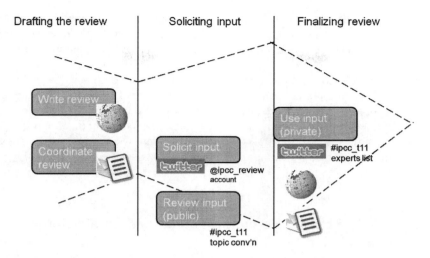

Fig. 2.5 The IPCC social media system from an open innovation perspective

The created list contains Jane, but not John, as he is somebody not known to or trusted by, the review committee and hence not being followed on Twitter. By just monitoring this list, she sees the tweet by Jane, and decides to contact the suggested expert Y.

To summarise, what has happened here in terms of social media systems design? Collaborative communities these days make use of an ever growing palette of online tools: social networking sites like Facebook and LinkedIn, Twitter, wikis, blogs, and so on. However, typically the adoption of these tools happens ad hoc and without much reflection. This results in undesired effects like collaborative fragmentation, unclear responsibilities, privacy losses[3] and so on. The systematic systems design approach we propose can help think through these issues systematically. The focus is on conversation, since this defines and fosters communities. *Whereas in traditional information systems development methodologies, the focus was on information analysis, in the twenty-first century, communication analysis should be primary.* Conversations as purposeful, interrelated acts of communication are about making sense of what a community is about, building its relations, sharing information among possibly numerous stakeholders and coordinating their actions.

Finally, how to frame the social media system just designed in open innovation terms? Whereas Chesbrough's (2003) paradigm for open innovation R&D has a funnel shape (from many unspecified ideas to the selected, refined outcome), the flow in our case at least follows a different pattern (Fig. 2.5): the initial drafting of the core ideas (what Leadbeater (2009) would call creating "the core") is followed

---

[3] Many cases of this continue to be reported on sites like Facebook, e.g. http://mashable.com/2010/05/04/facebook-privacy-report/ Given the impact on, for instance, trust of users, carefully considering such settings in social media systems design is essential.

by a massive influx of ideas from contributors from all over the world, which are finally narrowed down by means of the Twitter list, revisions by the topic stewards on their wiki pages and concluding discussions by the review committee on their mailing list.

In open innovation communities, there needs to be a continuous balancing of social, professional, political and technological interests. Our sociotechnical conversation context provides a practical framework for a collaborative community to make informed design decisions that go beyond merely taking into account technical functionalities. It also illustrates an analysis guided by a design stance with an interest in designing conversations to support mass collaboration.

2.4 Practical Design Recommendations and Implications for Research

Engaging stakeholders creates risks and has transaction costs, but it can also bring innovation and sustainability to solve large-scale and "wicked problems". So, then, there is a natural interest in doing open innovation well and for community managers and leaders, in particular, to attend to the emergent communication systems design and to engage in explicit conversational design in order to foster goal-oriented communities. In this chapter, we have only outlined the scaffolding of social media systems design, but in doing so we highlight a simple yet central point about open innovation: conversations are key. That central point was the basis for articulating a design stance and highlighting aspects of conversational design. Several implications for practice and research follow from the idea that conversations are key.

In terms of practice, awareness that conversations can be designed suggests that communities, especially community managers and leaders, should endeavour to:

Develop a focus on stakeholders that includes close attention to the conversations that involve stakeholders and how those conversations should be interconnected. This includes determining how stakeholders will need to be involved in shaping and supporting the purpose and form of the conversations. The stakeholders should be determined by their relationship to the problem to be solved more than their relation to the central organisation or sponsor, otherwise the collaborative enterprise will lose sight of producing common goods such as knowledge, support and practices needed to address the problem. These are most centrally problems of crafting conversations that generate joint action.

> **Practical Tip**
>
> Make a thematic topic map to break down problems in main deliverables and process steps to realise these deliverables. For example, (1) coordinate research review, (2) solicit inputs from research community.

> **Practical Tip**
>
> Use this mind map to make a stakeholder interaction matrix for each of these process steps. To do so, outline all possible combinations of stakeholders who ought to be involved in that step and the nature of their specific interactions. For example, soliciting input for the research review requires addressing the international scientific subcommunities working on climate change subtopics.

Pay continuous attention to the analysis of conversation practices as afforded by (combinations of) tools. The purpose is to inform sociotechnical systems design for the community or inter-community collaboration. This could be enhanced through: the development of libraries/knowledge bases that illustrate genres of conversation for various purposes; assessment and evaluation geared towards understanding the effectiveness and legitimacy of various genres of conversation available in the community and provision of access to knowledge about various formats. The aim is to reuse sociotechnical lessons learnt for social media systems design.

> **Practical Tip**
>
> Build up a conversation support pattern base of best/good/bad conversation practices combined with practical design/configurations of the social media systems supporting these practices. Make this pattern base as customised as possible for the open innovation community targeted. For example, the pattern "address an open-ended research sub community" could be to (1) identify the report topic(s) most relevant for that subcommunity, (2) write a blog post outlining the review questions the subcommunity could help out with, (3) send a regular stream of tweets including both the specific report topic hashtag and the link to the blog post, (4) find Twitter hashtags for current subcommunity conferences and retweet the call-for-participation tweets with the hashtag of those conferences to increase exposure.[4]
>
> For each cell in the stakeholder interaction matrix, select the most relevant patterns from the conversation support patterns base and act on them. Do this at key milestones in the project, but preferably on a regular basis, so that a conversation rhythm can emerge. It may be useful to assign a specific "conversation manager" role for this purpose.[5]

---

[4] It is customary nowadays that research conferences announce a unique hashtag at the start of the event, so that participants can easily exchange conference tweets. Since many conference participants (and persons interested in the theme) intensively monitor this stream, injecting related tweets (such as on a research review) with the same hashtag generates many extra potentially interested "eyeballs" for the cause.

[5] http://www.theconversationmanager.com/

Learn how to balance implementing ready-made tools from "the cloud" versus customising tools for specific purposes. These different interests should be a key factor in any community design decision. Implementing complex tool systems becomes, on the one hand, easier to do in "the cloud", since implementation details of the tool system are taken care of by hosting companies. On the other hand, customising the tool system to the particular needs of communities becomes more difficult since the communities have less control over the configuration parameters of their tools. In other words, the *generativity* of these hosted tools tends to become less (Zittrain 2009), increasing the constraints and reducing the affordances of social interactivity.

Practical Tip

Make a conversation tool inventory outlining all tools currently or potentially available to the community. Include not only online tools, but also those supporting all forms of physical interaction. A face-to-face meeting is also a conversation tool: a powerful, yet expensive one!

Define a set of quality aspects, including their metrics, on which to assess the fit of the conversation tools in the inventory with the conversation purposes of the community. Include not only conversation tool requirements (e.g. ease of interaction, control over conversation processes and content, user-familiarity), but also conversation tool costs (e.g. in-house expertise required, hosting costs, development costs). Assign weights to these aspects indicating their relative importance to the community.

Assess the value of each (existing or proposed) tool in the conversation tool inventory by assigning scores on each quality aspect. Use the resulting ranking, combined with an assessment of in-house development and hosting capacity to make decisions on which tools to self-develop and host and which ones to use from the cloud.[6]

In terms of research, there is considerable need for understanding the pragmatics of web-based communication that could facilitate socio-technical conversation design. Researchers should endeavour to:

Develop typologies of mediated conversations that illustrate the context of use and what the conversational format enabled the community to achieve. A descriptive orientation such as this would enable the development of deeper theory about the design of conversation in the social media space. It would also identify the multiple communicative demands of open innovation enterprises and how forms of conversation enabled or exacerbated the dilemmas of managing those multiple demands.

---

[6] See (de Moor 2007) for a related, practical approach.

Advance knowledge about the interactions in a complex web of conversation (e.g. numerous stakeholders, multilevel spawns of new loops, conflicts and failures). In open settings there is greater ability to move in and out of conversations. Yet, even open innovation settings will lead to the emergence of social structure that facilitates and inhibits participation. Here, then, is a need for a better understanding of the way that implicit social structures that arise in the web of conversation shape the flow of communication.

Improve understanding of governing open innovation processes. The Social Media Conversation Context framework makes concrete the problem being addressed—how to make sense of communicative workflows and to support them. The next level of challenge is how to incorporate this analysis and support it in an organic, emergent community for which there is no central designer as there might be for a business organisation's use of social media. Typically, there is an interplay between the community manager and the community. This is a continuous process, often driven by breakdowns, which needs to be supported by practical community management guidelines, conversation and tool usage practices in order to be successful. This interplay between innovation (conversation) requirements and community management principles is still a wide open area of research.

2.5 Conclusions

Open innovation is about crossing boundaries to create networked synergies in/ across collaborative communities. Open innovation communities need smart combinations of web-mediated content, context and conversations to drive and scale the mass collaboration required. Just providing access to social media and information systems is not sufficient for successful communities and collaboration to emerge, however. The engine of innovation stems from well-connected and supported webs of conversations. These conversation webs do not appear spontaneously. Instead, innovation communities need to continuously make sense of their evolving requirements, relevant tool functionalities and how to design these into customised sociotechnical systems needed so that collaboration can flourish.

In this chapter, we outlined an approach for using a sociotechnical conversation context model as a lens for focusing emerging systems design efforts in collaborative communities. We illustrated our approach with a scenario showing how it could help in designing the tool systems enabling focused mass collaboration on climate change research. Our main point is that, although necessary, it is not sufficient to develop ever more powerful collaboration tools, such as social media. Equally needed for collaborative communities, such as open innovation communities, to become successful, is for them to continuously reflect in a focused way on how to effectively match their collaborative needs with the functionalities to which they have access—that is, how to craft conversation.

References

Aakhus, M. (1999). Science court: A case study in designing discourse to manage policy controversy. *Knowledge, Technology & Society, 12*(2), 20–37.

Aakhus, M. (2007). Communication as design. *Communication Monographs, 74*(1), 112–117.

Aakhus, M., & Rumsey, E. (2010). Crafting supportive communication online A communication design analysis of conflict in an online support group. *Journal of Applied Communication Research, 38*(1), 65–84.

Chesbrough, H. W. (2003). *Open innovation: the new imperative for creating and profiting from technology*. Boston, MA: Harvard Business Press.

Chesbrough, H. W., & Appleyard, M. M. (2007). Open innovation and strategy. *California management review, 50*(1), 57–76.

Clark, H. H., & Brennan, S. E. (1991). Grounding in communication. *Perspectives on Socially Shared Cognition, 13*, 127–149.

Efimova, L., & de Moor, A. (2005). Beyond Personal Webpublishing: An Exploratory Study of Conversational Blogging Practices. In Proceedings of the 38th Hawaii International Conference on System Sciences (HICSS-38), Hawaii, January 2005. IEEE.

Leadbeater, C. (2009). *We-think: mass innovation, not mass production*. London: Profile Books.

Manlow, V., Friedman, H., & Friedman, L. (2010). Inventing the future: using social media to transform a university from a teaching organisation to a learning organisation. *Journal of Interactive Learning Research, 21*(1), 47–64.

de Moor, A (2007). A Practical Method for Courseware Evaluation. In *Proceedings of the 2nd International Conference on the Pragmatic Web (PragWeb 2007), Tilburg, the Netherlands, October 22–23, 2007*. ACM International Conference Proceedings Series, 280: 57–63.

de Moor, A. (2010). Conversations in Context: A Twitter Case for Social Media Systems Design. In *Proceedings of I-SEMANTICS 2010, September 1–3, Graz, Austria*. ACM, 1–8.

De Moor, A., & Aakhus, M. (2006). Argument support: From technologies to tools. *Communications of the ACM, 49*(3), 93–98.

Tapscott, D., & Williams, A. D. (2008). *Wikinomics: how mass collaboration changes everything*. London: Atlantic Books.

West, J., & Lakhani, K. R. (2008). Getting clear about communities in open innovation. *Industry & Innovation, 15*(2), 223–231.

Zittrain, J. (2009). *The future of the internet–and how to stop it*. New Haven & London: Yale University Press.

Further Reading

Aakhus, M., & Jackson, S. (2005). Technology, interaction, and design. In K. Fitch & R. Sanders (Eds.), *Handbook of language and social interaction* (pp. 411–437). Mahwah, NJ: Lawrence Erlbaum.

Dixon, D. 2009. Pattern Languages for CMC Design. In: Whitworth, B. and De Moor *Handbook of Research on Socio-Technical Design and Social Networking Systems.*, A. Hershey, PA: IGI, 402–415.

Fraser, M., & Dutta, S. (2008). *Throwing sheep in the boardroom: How online social networking will transform your life, work and world*. West Sussex: John Wiley & Sons, Ltd.

Hunter, M., Menestral, M., & Bettignies. (2008). Beyond control: Crisis strategies and stakeholder media in the Danone Boycott of *2001*. *Corporate Reputation Review, 11*(4), 335–350.

Li, C., & Bernoff, J. (2008). *Groundswell: Winning in a world transformed by social technologies*. Boston: Harvard Business Press.

Shum, B. (2006),. Sensemaking on the Pragmatic Web: a Hypermedia Discourse Perspective. *In Proceedings of the 1st International Conference on the Pragmatic Web, Stuttgart*. Germany, 21–23 September, 2006, 22–37.

Taylor, J., Groleau, C., Heaton, L., & van Every, E. (2001). *The computerization of work: A communication perspective*. Newbury Park, CA: Sage.

Winograd, T., & Flores, F. (1986). *Understanding computers and cognition a new foundation for design*. New York, NY: Ablex Publishing Corporation.

Chapter 3
Organisational Participation in Open Innovation Communities

Matt Germonprez and Brian Warner

Abstract Organisational participation is a critical consideration in the examination of open communities. Many open communities are no longer the domain of solitary individuals but have come to include organisations representing many of the largest financial interests across a variety of economic interests. Organisations seek to participate in open communities for reasons of leveraged development, economics and flexibility but participation is not a simple task. In this chapter, we explore what the primary motivations are for organisational participation in open communities. We follow this with considerations of how organisations participate once they have determined to engage with open communities. This chapter provides a glimpse of *why* and *how* organisations participate in open innovation communities and provide insights valuable for both practical and academic interests.

3.1 Introduction

Open innovation communities create complicated issues for organisations and researchers because they are more multifaceted than simply technology-enabled groups; they are a mix of power and knowledge, liberty and enlightenment, progress and intervention (Kelty 2009). Open innovation communities adapt to dynamically changing situations, accommodate altered plans and engage in non-typical, cooperative work in which there is an emergence, never a guarantee, of

---

This project was funded through the National Science Foundation VOSS—IOS Grant: 1122642, Organisational Participation in Open Communities.

M. Germonprez (✉)
University of Nebraska at Omaha, Omaha, NE, USA
e-mail: germonprez@gmail.com

B. Warner
Linux Foundation, San Francisco, CA, USA
e-mail: brian.warner@linuxfoundation.org

J.S.Z. Eriksson Lundström et al. (eds.), *Managing Open Innovation Technologies*,
DOI 10.1007/978-3-642-31650-0_3, © Springer-Verlag Berlin Heidelberg 2013

stability (Germonprez et al. 2007). In our chapter, we define an open innovation community as a collection of varied organisational members where organisations approach the community as a strategic motivation and seek to leverage the community for organisational benefit (West and Lakhani 2008).

The technology used in an open innovation community is only one-half of the design process. The other, equally important half includes the reflective, active and interactive practices that community members engage in. Within open innovation communities, members create new structural couplings in alignment with their domain of action in coordinating efforts, eliminating redundancy, pursuing options and sequencing activities (Germonprez et al. 2007). As design and development evolve within open innovation communities, new affordances present new possibilities and organisations must balance "contributions to" and "differentiation from" the open innovation community for reasons of cost, resource management and time to market. These considerations are instilled in both practice and academe, and in this chapter we aim to contribute to the advancement of both organisational participation and research inquiry in open innovation communities.

We build on principles of public sharing and collaboration using the Linux *open-source* community as our basis for understanding (see Fitzgerald 2006). The Linux Foundation estimated the value of Linux to be $10.8 billion in 2008 with the number of participants surpassing 3,500, illustrating that the Linux open innovation community is both viable and important for study. While open source is strictly a licensing distinction that does not necessarily define an open innovation community, it is often used to describe permissively licenced software developed by an open innovation community (Fitzgerald 2006; Ågerfalk et al. 2009). The focus of this chapter is not on Linux per se; rather it is on open innovation community participation associated with the design and development of Linux.

We explore primary features of organisational participation with the Linux open innovation community including leverage, contribution and differentiation. Leverage constitutes the power of open innovation community to benefit all participants: How does the community provide advantages for participants? Contributions constitute the degree to which community participants play a part in the open innovation community: Do they actively engage in the design and development of Linux? Differentiation constitutes the degree to which participants follow the primary release of the artefact: Do they use Linux as publicly released or do they differentiate it for internal reasons? Practice and research are beginning to address these issues through frameworks, theories, methods and contributions of open innovation communities (von Hippel and von Krogh 2003; Henkel 2006; Ågerfalk et al. 2009). To extend literature on open innovation community participation, we used reference literature and the Linux open innovation community to create frameworks relevant to both our problem and research domains. To begin, we understand the interaction between the open innovation community and the corporate organisation and consider what characteristics foster a relationship. In doing this, we address why organisations participate with the Linux open innovation community, leading us to our first of two research questions:

- Why do organisations participate with the Linux open innovation community?

Determining the *why* of participation leads to the second research question.

- How do organisations participate with the Linux open innovation community?

We expect these patterns to be varying as members balance commercial and community responsibilities and knowledge sharing at the interface between the participating organisation and the Linux open innovation community (Henkel 2006). We investigate how organisational decisions determine and are determined by participation with the Linux open innovation community. This understanding can act as a roadmap for both organisations considering open innovation communities as a viable systems development option and researchers seeking to expand organisational theory around open innovation community participation.

In addressing both research questions, we investigate the growing research streams associated with open innovation communities. As open innovation communities represent an emerging and fast growing consideration for organisations, it is incumbent on practitioners and researchers to better understand this domain and to learn how the findings apply to a generalised study of open innovation communities.

3.2 Open Innovation Communities

> "Whenever possible, design the system to run with open content, on open protocols, to be potentially available to the largest possible number of users, and to accept the widest possible range of experimental modifications from users who can themselves determine the development of the technology."

- James Boyle (2006) quoted in The Cultural Significance of Free Software (Kelty 2009)

Open innovation communities have clearly reached a business-critical tipping point as organisations strive to better understand them in order to participate with them (von Hippel and von Krogh 2003; Fitzgerald 2006). Open innovation communities have become media darlings, garnering considerable recognition and success. Linux continues to make strong gains as a viable business option (Kelty 2009). Twitter's market cap has surpassed $1billion in 2009 as reported by *The New York Times*. Flickr claims over four billion images and Wikipedia over 16 million articles as reported on their respective Wikipedia pages. These are all tremendous successes where openness and adaptability are valued over management and control (Kelty 2009). In these cases, coordination, contribution and compliance in open innovation communities become the processes of design for new and emergent systems. Organisations must look to balance their knowledge of property, their styles of management and their notions of control within open innovation communities made up of non-developers, casual participants and corporations. This balancing act is not an easy task in this apparent "Wild West" of development, but it is a necessary one in order to participate in open innovation communities and leverage their advantages.

Many open source research publications have focused exclusively on a single open innovation community and not its interface with participating organisations. For example, Sowe et al. (2008) examine knowledge sharing internal to the Debian open innovation community and Kuk (2006) explores interactions within the KDE open innovation community. In each of these cases, the focus is on the open innovation community itself and not the relationship between the open innovation community and organisational participants. This is an important point, as our aim is to squarely examine why and how organisations participate in open innovation communities; therefore, our chapter is positioned at the interface of participating organisations and existing open innovation communities. To address this, we provide an iterative process of literature investigation and applied considerations as the research team members represent both academe and practice regarding organisational participation with the open innovation communities.

Through the research questions we consider all participants in an open innovation community to be of equal importance and do not predetermine organisations to be better or worse participants. We aim to understand *why and how* they participate in open innovation communities and issues associated with the critical requirements, motivations and challenges of participants. In doing so, we assume that the ecosystem of an open innovation community supports a variety of participants and that quite likely, a vibrant ecosystem needs much variety. In the next section, we introduce action research as an important approach for contributing to these goals, using it to frame our quantitative field study of organisational participation in the Linux open innovation community.

3.3 Research Approach

We apply action research as a methodological approach within which a qualitative study is conducted (Chiasson et al. 2009). Action research allows us to specifically address practice and research cycles, providing critical structure in defining our project. Action research supports our dual goal of developing a solution to a practical problem which is of value to the people with whom we are working, while at the same time developing theoretical knowledge of value to a research community involved in research and pedagogy (Mathiassen et al. 2009). A dominant approach of action research is used to frame our study within which other, more localised research methods are applied (Chiasson et al. 2009). Action research requires specification of an area of concern under investigation, a problem-solving context, research frameworks, problem-solving and research methods and their respective contributions (Mathiassen et al. 2009). Table 3.1 highlights these action research elements and their application in our project.

3 Organisational Participation in Open Innovation Communities

Table 3.1 Action research elements (Mathiassen et al. 2009)

Action Research Elements	Action Research Elements in Project	Description
Area-of-Concern	The Organisational Value of IS IS Management	Why organisations participate in leveraged models and how organisations manage the interface with the Linux open innovation community.
Real World Problem Setting	Linux Open Innovation Community	Organisational participant types are differentiated by contributions and differentiation. A practical examination of organisational participation in the Linux open innovation community.
Framing Based on Area-of-Concern	Open Innovation Community Participation	Structure to the applied issues associated with open innovation community participation (von Hippel and von Krogh 2003; Neus and Scherf 2005)
Framing Independent of Area-of-Concern	Communities of Practice Open Innovation Community Interaction	Participation in open innovation communities of practice (Brown and Duguid 1991; Wenger 1999) and open innovation community theory (Chesbrough 2003)
Problem Solving Method	Leveraged Models	A 'leveraged' system that has shared value for all members with lower costs for each participant than if they developed on their own (Neus and Scherf 2005).
Research Method	Interviews	Action research as a dominant approach, including interviews (Chiasson et al. 2009).

Action research was used to achieve two outcomes. First was a developmental round of data collection to establish grounding for the project. To achieve this outcome, the investigation was rooted in practice, not academe, to foster a strong problem-solving connection. Rooting in practice provides an opportunity to embed practical concepts from the Linux open innovation community into our researched areas of concern. A similar approach was used by Davison and Martinsons (2002) to investigate how the practical use of GSS could inform organisational culture. As such, industry participants were interviewed regarding the broad issues of why and how organisations participate in open innovation communities. The primary outcome associated with this phase of the action research was the *development of the interview questions*. In all, three organisations were involved in the development of the interview questions, iterating over the course of 6 months. The interview questions have a strong practice orientation, and their high applicability to a variety of open innovation community participants provided traction for our second outcome.

The second outcome of the action research approach was to discover the characteristics associated with why and how organisations participate in open innovation communities. Interviews with members of participating organisations were conducted in the *execution of the interview questions.* Participating organisations were identified through personal contacts, Linux Foundation membership and online media. Each interview lasted approximately 1 h depending on the depth of the answers. To date, 15 interviews have been performed and analysed thematically. The interviewees were both developers and managers directly associated with Linux open innovation community participation. The 15 interviewees represented 9 different organisations, all rooted in the technology industry.

Evidencing participation within the Linux open innovation community provided a mechanism for generalising from descriptive observations to our studied areas of concern (Lee and Baskerville 2003). Generalisation from the Linux community to a similar community (see the Apache community) was not done as community-to-community comparisons can prove problematic. Instead, we generalise to our within-case areas of concern (Lee and Baskerville 2003). The findings constituted the progression through one action research cycle. Through this cycle, we grounded our project in the practice of the Linux open innovation community and we engaged academe in the dissemination of our findings to the aforementioned areas of concern (Brown and Duguid 1991; Wenger 1999; von Hippel and von Krogh 2003; Chesbrough 2003; Neus and Scherf 2005). The findings represent the first phases of a long-term research project to engage organisations and provide tractable findings to better understand and describe organisational participation in open innovation communities.

3.4 Why Organisations Participate in Open Innovation Communities

Open innovation community participation is not a solution to all design and development projects. However, open innovation communities and their supported leverage, economics and flexibility represent viable approaches to why organisations participate (Fitzgerald 2006). Table 3.2 provides illustrative quotes from our interviews based on why organisations participate in the Linux open innovation community.

Open innovation communities provide flexibility and adaptability as a *real option* through this fundamental principle: we all give a little; we all get a lot. This has the benefit of enabling "leveraged design" of a system that has shared value for all participants. A system is built through a model where design and development are leveraged through participants, value is provided for all and prediction, planning and control are the domain of an open innovation community.

3 Organisational Participation in Open Innovation Communities

Table 3.2 Why organisations participate in open innovation communities

Issue	Summary	Illustrative Quote
Leveraged Development and Support	Organisations can leverage the open innovation community for both development and support needs.	*What we get is [. . .]90 per cent of the Linux system, so we do less than 10 per cent of the work. We then leverage that investment to provide client value to make money off a broad set of things. If we were doing Linux on our own, we would have to do that other 90 per cent and that other 90 per cent of work can be used instead to do other things for our clients and stockholders. One of the things we get from the community is that leverage.*
Economics	Organisations can realise economic improvement through both the use of free artefacts and the use of leveraged development and support.	*The royalty-free is a factor, I'm not sure if it's the biggest one, but certainly it's a low entry cost. The cost of admission [with Linux] is very low. To even get started, even to explore a path with Linux, is quite accessible rather than going to make some big commitment to some other embedded platform that has all of these upfront costs and then you're kind of committed and locked in.*
Flexibility	Organisations can tailor the open innovation community artefact to suit distinct strategic and technical needs.	*In some respect our large systems have more in common with embedded computers than general purpose computers. So what this means for us is that we need to make modifications [as allowed by the GPL] to the Linux kernel so that it can boot on one of our compute nodes that does not have a commodity chipset.*

3.4.1 Leveraged Development and Support

With the leveraged development model, systems can be developed through the "leveraging" of the open innovation community where participants contribute portions of a completed system (von Hippel and von Krogh 2003). A complete system can be developed by leveraging the rest of the open innovation community.

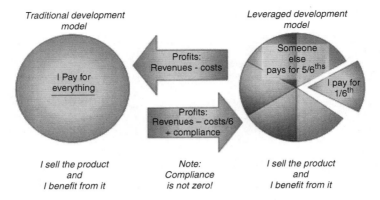

Fig. 3.1 Leveraged development model

For example, the Linux open innovation community can develop "5/6ths" of the Linux kernel to a new chipset. A single organisation must then only contribute the remaining "1/6th" of development costs to produce an artefact that they, as well as the rest of the community, can benefit from. The complexities and costs of developing are distributed throughout the open innovation community, not a single organisation, where all organisations play crucial roles in providing a leveraged development model (Fitzgerald 2006) (Fig. 3.1).

Participating organisations also leverage the open innovation community for support. Organisations aim to have their contributions to the community accepted and subsequently released in future versions of the Linux kernel. This allows the original, participating organisation to receive support from the open innovation community through testing, bug reporting and patches to the contribution. Organisations are also able to leverage the Linux open innovation community when entering third-party contracts. A contracted organisation can perform development work for an organisation that is not a community participant. A contracted organisation can then actively participate with the Linux open innovation community, aiming to have contracted work accepted upstream. In doing this, they are able to return successfully contracted development work back to a client, while shifting support to the Linux open innovation community. The consultant becomes "free and clear" of the maintenance of the contribution, while at the same time maintaining their own strong citizenship within the open innovation community.

In both leveraged development and leveraged support, organisations are responsible for maintaining compliance with the open innovation community. Compliance includes social interaction and expectations of participating in the community and also includes the more pragmatic licence compliance. The Linux open innovation community is primarily compliant to the General Public Licence (GPL) which defines the rules of engagement. Compliance includes organisational responsibilities for providing authored source code to defining code authorship. In all cases, organisational costs are incurred in *how* to maintain compliant participation within the community.

3.4.2 Economics

Open innovation communities represent a shift in how systems are designed and developed (Neus and Scherf 2005; Kelty 2009). The economics of open innovation communities have been well established in literature (Henkel 2006; Lerner and Schankerman 2010; Aksulu and Wade 2011) and include the free artefact costs often associated with open communities. The artefacts created in these communities (see Linux, Apache, Mozilla) are often a free and viable economic alternative to proprietary solutions.

In addition to the free costs of an artefact, it is widespread to consider open innovation community participation for developing and supporting systems used for organisational profit (see leveraged development). We have traditionally designed systems in proprietary ways, so why shift to an open innovation community model? The answer lies in the financial reality that the costs of developing an open innovation community are reduced as a result of the leveraged development model ("I pay for 1/6"). As such, the economics of participation also include reduced costs of development and support stemming from community leverage (Triole and Lerner 2002).

3.4.3 Flexibility

Participation in the Linux open innovation community is legally defined by the aforementioned GPL which accepts flexibility in how organisations participate. The GPL allows organisational participation to include differentiation and embedding of the Linux artefact to suit specific organisational goals and strategies. Flexibility is largely evident in embedded devices which are fuelling the growth of the Linux open innovation community. As specific and tailored computing devices become more prevalent in the form of television menus, navigation systems and router interfaces, differentiating embedded Linux has become a primary way to engage the Linux open innovation community and deploy the Linux artefact.

In adherence to the GPL, participating organisations are responsible for making a differentiated Linux code publicly available when a Linux-based system is sold for profit. However, organisations are not responsible for sharing the proceeds from the sale of the Linux-based system. The nuances of the GPL constitute a study in their own right. In our case, the licence flexibility of the GPL requires that participation with the Linux open innovation community balances organisational strategic and technical objectives with the necessary compliance imbued in the GPL.

3.5 How Organisations Participate in Open Innovation Communities

Once organisations realise *why* they should participate with open innovation communities, the following issue becomes *how* they should participate. Understanding the incentives to participate does not entail the knowledge of participation on a regular basis. Table 3.3 highlights the key issues of how organisations participate in the Linux open innovation community with illustrative quotes from our interviews.

As an organisation addresses how to participate, a sufficient argument must exist that compliance is a necessary part of participation with the open innovation community. As an example, a team may receive pushback regarding a contribution because the organisation does not want to expose the nature of particular intellectual property as a key differentiating factor in selling a product. The team must successfully demonstrate the leverage and financial benefits and the legal necessity of contributing changes. For an individual organisation, it is a balance of intellectual property, community compliance and organisational gains realised from participation in the open innovation community.

3.5.1 Contributions and Differentiation

Open innovation communities require the commitment of participants dedicated to common goals. Commitment as *contributions* comes in a variety of forms. Contributions are the degree to which participants supply committed changes to a product (Lakhani and Wolf 2005; Crowston et al. 2006). Contributions are also the engagement with an open innovation community to share, trade, test and develop ideas (Wenger 1999). In the context of our research, we identified contributions to the Linux open innovation community as *high contributions* and *low contributions*. A high contributor is a participant actively engaging in the community by developing "1/6" in the leveraged models. A low contributor is a participant far less active with respect to contributions to the leveraged development model. Both types of contributors, high and low, are necessary in the ecology of open innovation communities as the goals and applications of open innovation community systems vary from participant to participant.

We also found organisational participation to be defined by the adherence to, or differentiation from the open innovation community. *Differentiation* is the degree to which participants modify a stable, publicly available product for specific organisational requirements. Differentiation requires participating with the open innovation community, understanding changes and differentiating a product away from the open innovation community. Differentiation does not have a zero cost (Wenger 1999); it requires internal development support from the differentiating organisation but is expected to cost consistently less than non-leveraged development. Like the contributions, differentiation is viewed in two forms: *high differentiation* and *low differentiation*. Low differentiators are participants

3 Organisational Participation in Open Innovation Communities

Table 3.3 How organisations participate in open innovation communities

Issue	Summary	Illustrative Quote
Contributions	Organisations can participate in the open innovation community through the contribution of source code changes to the Linux kernel.	*From our position it was probably not so much of a concern that we would think too highly about what the community was thinking about our contributions. In some sense the community was interested in what we would do. So if for example, in the message passing interface, the libraries for doing highly parallel computing, if we found an issue with those or we contributed an enhancement, people would be all over that like flies to honey and they would love it. But in some sense, some of the contributions we were providing may have been more or less interesting to people.*
Differentiation	Organisations participating in the open innovation community can modify the Linux kernel to suit business and strategic needs.	*Over time Linux has become good enough for the heart of the enterprise. The community has broadened; there's many more companies, many more people. The sophistication of the differentiation we want with Linux has become more. We continue to have substantial efforts around the architecture to make Linux better for everybody, but a bulk of our work now is about making sure Linux fully exploits our hardware/software, is ready for our services, works on our cloud.*
Compliance	Organisations must consider how they adhere to the licensing associated with open innovation community participation.	*It's certainly a compliance with GPL, LGPL, and all of that is something that originally took a while for our corporate council to get their heads around. I think it's been a challenge in terms of ensuring that we try and maintain a very clean run approach to our codebase so that we're ensuring that we're not unintentionally putting our intellectual property into whatever source code we would be required to share. We are required to share. We have a desire to be good citizens of this community and therefore as part of our effort to reach out to the Linux Foundation, to help us get informed of how we could improve anything that we currently have underway and looking forward to the future.*

Table 3.4 Contributions and differentiation

		Differentiation	
		Low	High
Contributions	High	– Industry standard, commodity (or close to it) system – Large participant base outside of the company driving the innovation *Examples: Linux open innovation community example: x86 chip vendors, Linux consultancy*	– Highly specialised system developed by one company – Feature exploitation requires very detailed and specialised knowledge *Examples: Linux open innovation community example: Mainframes, UNIX-class systems, high end databases*
	Low	– Uses industry standard parts, with little specific differentiation – Large and savvy user base – Open system stack *Examples: Linux open innovation community example: Commodity x86 server vendors, "hackable" embedded devices like routers*	– Highly specialised system/service meant to operate as a black box – Interface is (intended to be) closed to the consumer/hacker *Examples: Linux open innovation community example: Flat screen TV, DVR, cars, appliances*

engaged in ways generally prescribed by the open innovation community. As an example in the Linux open innovation community, chip manufactures could be low differentiating participants as their processors should work with the largest, most stable release of the Linux kernel. High differentiators are participants engaged in specialised and tailored ways that are not necessarily in compliance with the majority of participants. As an example, manufacturers of embedded devices may differentiate a product in the development of tailored or customised devices specific to organisational strategies. High differentiating participants create new or "forked" systems that are quite different from their open innovation community. Table 3.4 presents a matrix of contributions and differentiation.

3.5.2 High Contributor/Low Differentiator

High contributors/low differentiators supply contributions that are compliant within the respective open innovation community. They can be paid as IBM employees or volunteers contributing to the Linux kernel (Lakhani and Wolf 2005). High contributors/low differentiators have the ability to help define and maintain a strategic roadmap for the open innovation community. They focus on lowering overall community development costs, improving system time to market and increasing the adoption of the system for a broad public. As a high contributor/ low differentiator, effective communication, strong external relationship management and internal organisation structure for fostering contributions are expected (Gambardella and Hall 2006).

3.5.3 High Contributor/High Differentiator

High contributors/high differentiators are contributors yet choose to differentiate their application of the common or "mainline" system. This is done when a mainline system is applied in a system-specific manner with knowledge concentrated and applied strategically within the organisation. High contributors/high differentiators are active participants in their open innovation communities to maintain an understanding of community processes and future integration in an existing organisational innovation stream. Like the high contributors/low differentiators, the high contributors/high differentiators are interested in lowering development costs and improving time to market. They are also interested in differentiating in an otherwise commodity market and maintaining ties to an existing innovation stream to work with skilled individuals for internal design and development needs (Gambardella and Hall 2006). Challenges for high contributors/high differentiators come from earning and maintaining trust with the open innovation community and communicating and aligning the internal and external motivations associated with the respective system of the open innovation community (Henkel 2006).

3.5.4 Low Contributor/Low Differentiator

Low contributors/low differentiators do not actively contribute to the open innovation community, but mainly participate by viewing the open innovation community in a commodity-like role, considering the community responsible for the design and development of systems to run on top of or underneath a private solution. Perhaps in working with the "mainline" system of the open innovation community there is a potential for contributions through testing and use, but the overall participation is limited. Low contributors/low differentiators have a heavy reliance on industry standards and organisational product innovation is driven from elsewhere in the value chain (Henkel 2006). The low contributor/low differentiator is a common role for organisations as the open innovation community supports a broad range of solutions with little internal effort; "a rising tide floats all boats" irrespective of their role within an open innovation community. Rightfully, the low contributors/low differentiators have little influence on the open innovation community design decisions and much less opportunity for specialisation within the community.

3.5.5 Low Contributor/High Differentiator

Similarly, low contributors/high differentiators do not contribute back to the open innovation community in a consistent way. They differentiate the mainline system of the open innovation community, creating a black box around the new, differentiated and private system. Instances could include the need to build systems or services with very specific needs, but this comes at the expense of having to singularly maintain the differentiated or forked system and sacrificing much of the leveraged development model (Neus and Scherf 2005). At a minimum, low contributors/high differentiators must adhere to the open innovation community GPL licensing requirements. The low contributor/high differentiator is a model for embedded applications and can result in major competitive advantages, using the open innovation community as a launch pad for the differentiated system. It is difficult for the differentiated consumer to create a strong image within the open innovation community, and maintaining and synchronising parallel lines of similar systems can become onerous and expensive.

The aforementioned participant types regarding contributions and differentiation are community-based perspectives on how organisations participate with open innovation communities. Within an organisation, *how* questions remain regarding the more pragmatic, daily relationships with an open innovation community in the management of property, knowledge and power, leading to the second issue of organisational compliance with the open innovation community.

3.5.6 Compliance

Compliance has been alluded to as a characteristic of *why* organisations participate in open innovation communities. Henkel (2006) provides an examination of managing intellectual property through organisational licensing and contracting, illustrating complexities of the process. Complying with the GPL to effectively participate with the open innovation community has the aforementioned advantages of leverage, economics and flexibility. However, with compliance come certain risks of exposing intellectual property. Organisations require compliance considerations when participating with the open innovation community. These include both technical and legal considerations. First, technical considerations consist of solutions that the open innovation community could benefit and include new drivers or improved kernel performance. In these cases, the hurdle of compliance is relatively low as the contributions are primarily in support of the leveraged development model. Technical considerations also include contributions that must be made available to the community when the use of the Linux kernel is for organisational profit. In this, the GPL requires that specific guidelines be followed: display of appropriate copyright and warranty notices and a record of the differentiation from the original Linux kernel.

3.6 Discussion

The findings from this research contribute to our areas of concern within our specific study (Lee and Baskerville 2003). We speak to open innovation community participation as one of strategic motivation, seeking to leverage the community for organisational benefit (West and Lakhani 2008). From our findings, we draw two conclusions regarding organisational participation in the Linux open innovation community: conclusions of deference and distinction.

Participation remains an organisational decision of leverage, economics and flexibility, but the nature and design of organisational participation in the open innovation community is influenced by the community's history and technical meritocracy. Being a participant requires *organisational learning* to understand the combined nature of organisational needs and design of the community being participated with (Brown and Duguid 1991; Wenger 1999). As highlighted in the following interview quote, deference is paid *from* a participating organisation *to* the community:

The [Linux] community favours good code over bad code. If you work yourself into the web of trust over time and you produce code, your code will go in. It doesn't make any difference if you're from [a large technology company] or a high school student in Bulgaria. Initially there was a worry that the community would disfavour companies/corporations, that wasn't true. The community, we talk about it as a meritocracy. It's an imperfect meritocracy, it's filled with human beings, but by and large you get fair treatment and even treatment if you're at a company and it depends on the code. You write good code, you'll get it in; you write bad code, you won't get it in.

Deference to the community is a necessary, learned consideration in organisational participation when engaging the open innovation community. Additionally, deference is paid *from* a participating organisation *to* the GPL or similar open source licences:

If we want our code to be accepted, you've got to write the code in the licence the community uses whether it's GPL, or Mozilla, or APACHE, or whatever. The senior executives said that makes a lot of sense, so therefore, if we're going to do Linux we have to be able to provide GPL code. Therefore, legal [had to] figure it out, which they did. But the key notion is there, that you have to use the licence that the community uses and that's part of adapting to the community.

Under the GPL, deference is to the legal structure that, in part, defines participation in the open innovation community. Deference to the licence requires continued organisational learning around the legal aspects of participating in the Linux open innovation community (Brown and Duguid 1991), but the GPL also provides an avenue for distinction.

The GPL allows, and even encourages, organisations to create distinction within the community. In the findings, we identified four participant types as unique categories that define an organisation participating in an open innovation community. Distinction extends how we consider the participation types. It recognises that organisations are not solitary participants, residing in isolation, but are collaborative and contributive participants, part of their open innovation community:

[Flexibility] is certainly something that affects us more because we're a high performance computing organisation. So it's being able to allocate very large continuous and contiguous portions of memory for applications, and that's actually one of the more successful areas where my organisation has been working with the

community to push code back out to the general public, and it's not necessarily a differentiation. It's improving a portion of the kernel or a portion of the libraries that definitely affects us to a great degree but also has the added benefit of benefiting everybody else in the community too.

Distinction is evident through contributions to the community (*benefiting everyone else in the community*) as well as a differentiation of the Linux kernel (*improving the kernel for high performance computing*). Distinction highlights an appreciative approach towards an open innovation community, recognising that it takes all types of organisations to build a community:

Well, by definition, I mean there's always a tragedy in the commons. So, yes, there's bad code, people don't know what they're doing, people just going on this stuff and taking it, but I really think the deeper community, they just consider that it's the cost of citizenship in a free society and in that free society of Linux development, so be it.

Distinction is also evident as organisations realise a change in their participation with the open innovation community. Distinguishing as a new participant type is not simply deciding to be a stronger contributor or a conscious differentiator; distinction is an organisation learning to involve the open innovation community as a new type of participant:

For a brief time [we] could have been considered [a free-rider of the community] because [we were] grabbing from the community any solution to get my project done and [we weren't] contributing much at all. [We] did it because we had no budget and we really had a real good idea, and we could get there by reaching out to the community for some support. Ultimately when we were successful, we had no way of putting money back in, so the only thing that we could do was contribute back in and that converted [us] to being a contributor. Ultimately I think if you're a constant freeloader and you're not contributing back, pretty soon your ideas are going to run amuck and nobody's going to help you and you're going to be going down a path of burnt bridges and roads to nowhere. For the people that do turn around and start contributing, all of a sudden the user forums and the open source environment becomes a garden to kind of walk around in freely, and I think that we've kind of gotten to that point.

Distinction was seen to vary and evolve from the contributions and differentiation that can establish an organisation as a unique participant within the open innovation community. Finally, distinction can be applied outward, away from the community, to the marketplace that an organisation is a member of:

Something we definitely espouse is that we are involved in open-source and open-standards. It somewhat differentiates us in the marketplace. We embed Python interpreters in our product so that people can write their own controls, we publish our control protocol, we use open sound control, we work IEEE groups for open-standards, and Linux fits right into that. So it's a whole package in which Linux plays a very large part.

We do not provide a precise mapping of how deference and distinction precisely relate to the findings of *why* and *how* organisations participate in open innovation communities. We expect participation to vary across organisations and communities, and prescription is premature. Participation in the Linux community is not likely to be the same as the Apache community as leverage, economics, flexibility, contributions, differentiation and compliance vary. As such, the evident deference and available distinction will also vary. This does not preclude us from drawing more generalisable and transferable conclusions based on our findings (Lee and Baskerville 2003). We believe organisations can facilitate, and even accelerate, their learning for successful participation in open innovation communities. The evolution of organisation participation in open innovation communities is actively unfolding and this domain is far from understood, in spite of the considerable research done in this area to date (Aksulu and Wade 2011).

> **Practical Tip**
>
> Organisations participate in open communities for reasons of leveraged development, cost savings and improved developer flexibility. However, knowing why an organisation participates in open communities is only half of the equation. Organisations must also consider how they participate through contributions to the community, compliance with the community and differentiation from the community. Realising these issues can aid organisations in future open community engagements.

References

Ågerfalk, P., Fitzgerald, B., & Slaughter, S. (2009). Introduction to the special issue, flexible and distributed information systems development: state of the art and research challenges. *Information Systems Research, 20*(3), 317–328.

Aksulu, A., & Wade, M. (2011). A comprehensive review and synthesis of open source research. *Journal of Association for Information Systems, 11*, 576–656.

Brown, J., & Duguid, P. (1991). Organisational learning and communities-of-practice: Toward a unified view of working, learning, and innovation. *Organisation Science, 2*(1), 40–57.

Boyle, J. (2006). Mertonianism unbound? imagining free, decentralised access to most cultural and scientific material. In C. Hess & E. Ostrom (Eds.), *Understanding knowledge as a common: from theory to practice*. Cambridge, MA: MIT Press.

Chesbrough, H. W. (2003). *Open innovation: the new imperative for creating and profiting from technology*. Boston: Harvard Business School Press.

Chiasson, M., Germonprez, M., & Mathiassen, L. (2009). The conventional role of research methods in information systems action research. *Information Systems Journal, 19*, 31–54.

Crowston, K., Wei, K., Li, Q. & Howison, J. (2006). Core and Periphery in Free/Libre and Open Source Software Team Communications, *In Proceedings of the 39th Annual Hawaii International Conference on System Sciences, 6*, 118a.

Davison, R., & Martinsons, M. (2002). Empowerment or enslavement? A case of process-based change in Hong Kong. *Information Technology & People, 15*(1), 42–59.

Fitzgerald, B. (2006). The transformation of open source software. *MIS Quarterly, 30*(3), 587–598.

Gambardella, A., & Hall, B. (2006). Proprietary versus public domain licensing of software and research projects. *Research Policy, 35*, 875–892.

Germonprez, M., Hovorka, D., & Collopy, F. (2007). A theory of tailorable technology design. *Journal of the Association for Information Systems (JAIS), 8*(6), 315–367.

Henkel, J. (2006). Selective revealing in open innovation processes: The case of embedded linux. *Research Policy, 35*(7), 953–969.

Kelty, C. (2009). *Two bits: The cultural significance of free software.* Durham, NC: Duke University Press.

Kuk, G. (2006). Strategic interaction and knowledge sharing in the KDE developer mailing list. *Organisation Science, 52*(7), 1031–1042.

Lakhani, K., & Wolf, R. (2005). Why hackers do what they do: understanding motivation and effort in free/open source software projects. In J. Feller, B. Fitzgerald, S. Hissam, & K. Lakhani (Eds.), *Perspectives on free and open source software.* Cambridge, MA: MIT Press.

Lee, A., & Baskerville, R. L. (2003). Generalizing generalizability in information systems research. *Information Systems Research, 14*(3), 221–243.

Mathiassen, L., Chiasson, M., & Germonprez, M. (2009). Compositional styles in action research: a critical analysis of leading information systems journals sprouts. *Working Papers on Information Systems, 9*(35).

Neus, A., & Scherf, P. (2005). Opening minds: cultural change with the introduction of open-source collaboration methods. *IBM Systems Journal, 44*(2), 215–225.

Sowe, S., Stamelos, I., & Angelis, L. (2008). Understanding knowledge sharing activities in free/open source software projects: an empirical study. *The Journal of Systems and Software, 81*(3), 431–446.

Triole, J., & Lerner, J. (2002). Some simple economics of open source. *Journal of Industrial Economics, 52*, 197–234.

von Hippel, E., & von Krogh, G. (2003). Open source software and the 'private-collective' innovation model: issues for organisation science. *Organisation Science, 14*(2), 209–223.

Wenger, E. (1999). *Communities of practice: learning, meaning, and identity.* New York: Cambridge University Press.

West, J., & Lakhani, K. (2008). Getting clear about communities in open innovation. *Industry & Innovation, 15*(2), 223–231.

Further Reading

Lee, G., & Cole, R. (2003). From a firm-based to a community-based model of knowledge creation: The case of the Linux Kernel Development. *Organisation Science, 14*(6), 633–649.

Lerner, J., & Schankerman, M. (2010). *The comingled code: Open source and economic development.* Cambridge, MA: The MIT Press.

Torker, R., Minoves, P., & Garrigós, J. (2011). Adopting free/libre/open source software practices, techniques and methods for industrial use. *Journal of the Association for Information Systems, 12*(1), 88–122.

Chapter 4
Open Innovation Technologies and Exploitative and Explorative Learning

Mats Edenius and Ali Yakhlef

Abstract Many organisations are embracing the open innovation approach. However, becoming open to ideas coming from outside requires a revision of their innovation processes in order to integrate external and internal ideas effectively. The aim of this chapter is to explore why and how firms are coping with managing new external ideas from their customers and what they are learning from these ideas. Using information gleaned from interviews with ten organisations which have set up IT application for eliciting feedback from their customers, we found that much of the ideas obtained have led to exploitative learning. Only small firms (with fewer than ten employees) have learned ideas from their customers that have led to exploratory activities. Theoretical and practical implications are discussed.

4.1 Introduction

Based on an almost axiomatic belief on which innovations are seen as a foundation for prosperity and sustainable growth (cf. Grant 1996; Volberda et al. 2010), Chesbrough (2003) has suggested that many contemporary firms have shifted to an open innovation model, becoming increasingly reliant, for their innovation, on a wide range of external actors and sources outside their hierarchical boundaries and ownership control. Open innovation pays attention to both external and internal sources for innovation and knowledge processes. If cross-fertilisation of internal and external knowledge and ideas are to generate new ideas, integrative

---

A previous version of this chapter has been published at ISPIM in Hamburg 2011.

M. Edenius (✉)
Department of Informatics and Media, Uppsala University, Uppsala, Sweden
e-mail: mats.edenius@im.uu.se

A. Yakhlef
Stockholm University School of Business, Stockholm, Sweden
e-mail: aya@fek.su.se

J.S.Z. Eriksson Lundström et al. (eds.), *Managing Open Innovation Technologies*,
DOI 10.1007/978-3-642-31650-0_4, © Springer-Verlag Berlin Heidelberg 2013

mechanisms need to be set up in order to combine internal and external knowledge assets (Chesbrough 2003; Lichtenthaler 2008). Nevertheless, building such external thinking in combination with internal thinking into the firm requires a radical change, as aptly put by Witzeman et al. (2006, p. 27): "The firm must review [learn] the new product development processes, the supply chain, the strategic planning process, the reward system, the technology roadmap, and many other systems for their ability to incorporate external innovation...in employee thinking". Most of all, the 'Not Invented Here' syndrome needs to be replaced with the 'Invented Anywhere' approach.

This shift to 'openness' can be studied from many different perspectives and be linked to many different developments such as globalisation processes, advances in information technology (IT) as well as the availability of new and sophisticated IT tools (cf. Gassmann 2006). Witzeman et al. (2006) maintains that open innovation processes require that a host organisation invest resources in open innovation processes that go far beyond the efforts to invest and set up different IT support systems processes. The present exploratory study seeks to investigate how firms are coping with integrating external ideas within their own processes. Although we know that many firms have implemented IT application aiming at eliciting ideas and feedback from their customers, we know less about what they do with those ideas and feedback. Whereas current research into IT-enabled innovations has focused on success stories (such as P&G with its application *connect and develop*, Dell's *Idea Storm,* etc.) there is a lack of research into how and why open innovation-related technologies are used (Hrastinski et al. 2011). More specifically, we put forward the question of what kind of knowledge and learning processes are generated by such systems and how they can be managed by organisations. Our aim is thus to explore why and how firms are seeking feedback from their customers, what they are doing with the bulk of information they receive from their customers and how and if they can manage these learning processes. In order to answer these questions we conducted 14 interviews with organisations that have set up an IT-based application called "Kundo" featuring a *Let-us-know-what-you-think!* button.

The remainder of the chapter is organised as follows: The next section (Sect. 4.2) will present the theoretical framework outlining our argument, taking a knowledge perspective (Grant 1996) on ICT-based open innovation IT tools. Section 4.3 presents the method and the material used to illustrate our argument. Section 4.4 is devoted to a discussion of the material elicited from our informants. Finally, the chapter ends with a further discussion, concluding remarks, implications and suggestions for further research.

4.2 Theoretical Framework

The relationship between technology in general and knowledge processes, and outcomes in particular, has long been of interest in scholarly literature (for an overview, see e.g. Robey and Bourdreau 1999). However, during the last three decades, this interest has moved from understanding technology as a determinant of organisational structures and channels for information distribution, to perspectives where researchers apply notions to social phenomena, such as innovations and learning processes, to account both for more dynamic perspectives, as well as to understandings of business and organisational implications of new technologies (Orlikowski 1996, 2000).

The application of open innovation systems could be regarded as part of an emerging research area in the information systems field. The overall purpose is to determine how information and communication technology (ICT) tools can support knowledge and innovation processes (cf. Kane and Alavi 2007) in organisations. An emerging research area in this connection is focused on the application of advanced ICT tools to support the underlying process of knowledge sharing and organisational memory (Alavi and Leidner 2001). ICT tools enable knowledge processes in synchronic (e.g. chat groups, mobile calls, etc.) (Orlikowksi 1996) or asynchronic ways (such as systems for knowledge storage and retrieval, El Sawy and Bowles 1997).

Previous research indicates that knowledge acquisition is important for innovation processes (cf. Fiol and Lyles 1985; Mom et al. 2007). Knowledge processes are not linear and may be the outcome of many different simultaneously ongoing processes. For that reason, we conceptualise knowledge acquisition in terms of knowledge flows. This may allow us a greater precision about the directionality of the knowledge being transferred (cf. Mom et al. 2007). A firm's knowledge flow and knowledge stock can be regarded as necessary for facilitating organisational learning and innovation processes (Teece et al. 1997).

Maybe two of the most widely recognised concepts in connection with (individual) knowledge and innovation are "knowledge exploration" and "knowledge exploitation" (March 1991, p.71). Knowledge exploration refers to the search for new knowledge and is usually signalled by such terms as "search", "variation", "risk taking", "experimentation", "play", "flexibility", "discovery", "innovation", etc. By contrast, exploitation includes such things as refinement, choice, production, efficiency, selection, implementation, execution, etc. Exploration refers to the search for new useful adaptations and exploitation refers to the use of propagation of known adaptations (Fang et al. 2010a, b; see also Mom et al. 2007).

Most research suggests that firms tend to overemphasise exploitation at the expense of exploration because exploitation provides more immediate and certain results (Fang et al. 2010a, b; Denrell and March 2001). However, irrespective of how the optimal balance can be reached, our knowledge about learning practices and how they can be managed and organised is of crucial importance.

Hence, in light of this classic distinction between exploration and exploitation, it is relevant to pose the question how ICT applications can influence an organisational learning process and how, if at all, this learning affects organisational activities. Previous research has pointed out that the nature of learning resulting from knowledge that flows between entities is dependent upon the nature of the relationship between the parties involved (Kang et al. 2007).

Social relation is usually understood in terms of three dimensions: structural, cognitive and affective (as captured in Table 4.1). Following the framework put forth by Kang et al. (2007), it is suggested that these dimensions can be linked to

Table 4.1 Forms of knowledge that are exchanged depending on the features of the relationships between the cognising units

	Structural	Affective	Cognitive
Explorative	Sparse network	Dyadic trust	Component knowledge
Exploitative	Dense network	Generalised trust	Architectural knowledge

different characteristics of learning processes in terms of explorative and exploitative learning.

Strong and dense social connections are efficient at sharing fine-grained and in-depth knowledge, supporting exploitative learning. However, we might also argue that the nature ties (strong or weak ties) may have a negative effect on explorative learning, because strong and dense interconnections may limit an organisation's opportunity to explore varied knowledge domains.

The affective dimension defines the cultural values and norms that the knowledge entities share. Among the salient features of this dimension are (1) "generalised trust", which refers to a kind of impersonal or institutional trust, and is usually accorded to members of a social unit; and (2) "resilient dyadic trust", which refers specifically to trust between two parties having direct experience with each other. Generalised trust may be regarded as instrumental but does not support exploration, because this kind of trust is accorded based on the norms and expectations of the broader community and might even limit the range for new ideas. Dyadic trust, on the other hand, may deliver more advantages, in facilitating explorative learning.

Along the cognitive dimension, two forms of knowledge are discerned. First is "component knowledge", which refers to the knowledge of "parts", rather than the whole. Second, "architectural knowledge", is related to the whole or firm-wide routines for coordinating various components of the firm and putting them to productive use. Kang et al. (2007) argue that architectural knowledge allows individuals to recognise deeper understanding of the whole picture, thereby helping them to pursue exploitative knowledge. Component knowledge, on the other hand, allows the knowledge entity to be in a better position to understand and interpret new, explorative, knowledge.

This framework will be used as an analytical template to analyse the bulk of information (in the form of feedback) received from customers of Kundo, thereby seeking to answer the questions posed above, namely (1) what is the nature of learning (exploratory or exploitative) an open innovation technology like Kundo generates, and (2) how are these learning processes managed. The framework will guide us in structuring and analysing the information generated from our informants, as described in the next section.

4 Open Innovation Technologies and Exploitative and Explorative Learning

Table 4.2 Names and sizes of firms that have taken part in the study

Type of organisation	Size (numbers of employees)
Public Transportation Company (SL)	>1000
Borås municipality	>1000
Linnaeus University	>1000
	(2000)
Folk University	>1000
(adult education all over Sweden)	(7000)
Business Region Skåne	<100
Real Estate Company	<100
Web book shop	<100
Health Care Company	<10
Storytel (audiobooks)	<10
Weather site	<10

4.3 Method and Material

4.3.1 Data Generation

As noted earlier, the target of analysis consists in a body of information generated during interviews with informants of firms that adopted a website tool called Kundo in order to elicit feedback from their customers. A number of firms have adopted Kundo as part of their website strategy. It is an application that is linked to firms' websites. By clicking the button "Add comments" customers can access a site where comments and opinions about the website of a given firm can be made. Users have a menu of four choices from a dashboard: ask a question, give a suggestion, report a problem or give positive feedback. Users fill in a heading and write down their comments. The users must also fill in their proper names and e-mail addresses. Subsequent users can comment upon previous users' comments textually. This creates a transparent environment. The users can also pick up popular and shared comments, read them and lend support to previous comments by others. The users can add another comment or just glance through others' comments.

A series of interview questions were developed and 14 interviews were performed within ten different firms that were providing the service Kundo designed to elicit feedback from users on the website of the respective companies. We returned to four of the companies to deepen our knowledge. Each person was contacted by phone or email to set up a time for the interview. Each interview lasted between 30 and 100 min. A questionnaire was used as a guide for the conversation, rather than as a strict question-and-answer tool. In this way, the interviewer was able to structure the conversation in such a way so as to obtain the most relevant information about how the respondents perceived the innovation. Each interview was recorded and transcribed.

Table 4.2 summarises the names and sizes of firms that have taken part in the study.

4.3.2 Mode of Analysis

The research process has proceeded in an iterative fashion (cf. Glaser and Strauss 1967). The interview material was first transcribed and translated from Swedish into English. In a second step, the data were constructed around patterns, forming different themes that are related to our theoretical framework. In practice, it means that we have formed themes according to the typology of exploring and exploiting activities and the three different dimensions of social relations. Subsequently, the analysis proceeded by focusing on each interview separately. Finally, cross interview analysis was conducted to generate overall themes.

In this way, the interviews were treated as multiple experiments, providing us with some empirical evidence (Yin 2009; Eisenhardt and Graebner 2007). This approach is suitable, given the explorative character of this study, whose purpose it is to highlight constructs, by showing their operation in an ongoing organisational context (cf. Yin 2009).

The present approach may fall prey to criticism due to its inability to provide generalising conclusions. However, as Yin (2009) notes, there is a difference between *analytical generalisation* and statistical generalisation, where in the case of the latter, the aim is to use previously developed theory as a template to compare empirical results (Yin 2009, p. 15).

4.4 Results

4.4.1 Why Do the Organisations Use Kundo?

As noted earlier, the organisations we are studying have adopted Kundo in order to elicit from their "customer" feedbacks on the site. Kundo consists of a button—Tell-us-what-do-you-think!—that prompts customers to make comments, give suggestions, criticise or pose questions, etc. Since Kundo aims to improve the functionality of websites, the decision to implement it in all cases was taken by website managers.

Our findings show that customers use the application Kundo in almost the same way in all the organisations under consideration. However, the amount of feedback and comments has varied from few to many messages a day. In general, the respondents find the service easy to use, requiring insignificant technical skills. The organisations are satisfied with its functions, finding that Kundo has exceeded their expectations. In explaining why the organisations have implemented Kundo, here are some of the answers:

We regarded Kundo as part of our strategy, to open up our innovation processes, to be better at eliciting new ideas, thoughts, comments and problems coming from outside our organisation. . .to go from working as megaphones to conducting a dialogue, it is a new way of working, so we started using Kundo on a small scale with Kundo. (SL).

At an earlier stage we worked with web questionnaires, but the method was a kind of one-way communication. It was difficult to find adequate e-mail-addresses and to provide appropriate answers. By contrast, Kundo is a simple way of getting feedback rapidly; it is also easy to manage. It is transparent so everybody could see everything (Borås Municipality).

Openness, timely response and ease of communication and management were important criteria for the interviewees. Transparency *and rapid responses are also crucial. Getting feedback from customers amounts to embarking upon a dialogue* with them. However, this is a demanding process. The *interviewees stressed the importance of timeliness in responding to customers' questions and requests.* They emphasised the *importance of giving feedback on a continuous basis, for once you enter into a dialogue with them, they say, they cannot afford breaking that dialogue.*

From the beginning, we have decided to be an open university. The web is, you know, the first aspect of the university that was made visible to the great mass of people, and to start a dialogue with the people was very important—you know. We wanted feedback...but we have to communicate back too, customers must feel that we, at the university, treat them as flesh-and-blood human beings, who are worthy of our attention. Their opinions are given utmost consideration (Linnaeus University).

...it is absolutely important that we answer everything...it is important to confirm that we have taken part of the ideas and comments and to give speedy replies to our customers. (SL)

However, as the interviewees say, handling the customers' requests can also be regarded as a demanding process. The problem is that people in charge of the websites at the companies feel that they have set in motion a process that span out of their control. They seem to be quite busy handling the many customers who are willing to enter into a dialogue with the companies and to give feedback. Such feedback seems to yield two categories of ideas involving explorative and exploitative learning.

4.4.2 Exploitative Learning

In general, our interviewees maintain that through Kundo they learn about things they already know. In other words, the feedback they get deepens their knowledge but does not provide new knowledge:

A lot of things do happen in small steps, we are not so radical...I must say that most of the users are not so visionary, when we get a question it is often about glitches they found in our application. What they actually do is that they tell us about things that they saw on other sites and ask us to implement them on ours too. But we do not get so many 'out-of-the-box' questions... customers are quite down to earth in their thinking. (Borås Municipality)

When we classify a book in the wrong category, the customer communicates to us the mistake, so we correct that. We receive quite a lot of good suggestions about details like that. But we take seriously all the suggestions and discuss them at meetings. However, we hardly receive breakthrough ideas (Bokus)

Kundo has enabled the organisations to obtain ample advice which is often linked to short-term goals that are aligned with the firms' different strategies, framework and institutionalised way of thinking. The organisations seem to regard the learning resulting from the feedback they got through Kundo is exploitative in nature. Subsequently, these ideas are incorporated into their everyday work processes in order to correct and improve them.

If you fail to categorise a book correctly, this is a plain mistake that has to be corrected; customers are helpful if they can notify that to you. We receive quite a lot of small and good suggestions, which we discuss at several meetings, but we do not get totally new ideas (Bokus).

In our case we have chosen to limit the feedback on our website—because we know we do not get new ideas. For instance, we are focusing on the problems that are to be found in our web application, such as on how to fix dead links, to correct navigation, to further improve our "find" application. (Borås Municipality).

What seems to emerge is that most of the organisations under consideration are using the feedback in order to modify, in small steps, their homepages and services, based on deeper understanding of general cultural values.

We also got a lot of [general] criticism, it has been quite unpleasant to handle all the different opinions about the new university, because there are a lot of people that do not like the fact that the new university is a merger between two universities (Linnaeus University).

They hardly use the feedback to change their routines and practices. For them, Kundo (primarily) generates exploitative learning that helps them make small improvements in their extant routines and processes, but not to change any of these.

However, there are some exceptions. One such exception is "Beautiful Weather", a small company owned by two brothers. The business idea of the firm is to import weather reports from well-known sites, reorganise them and customise them according to individual needs and linked to local circumstances. The site has become quite popular. Although the motives behind the firm's implementation of Kundo are similar to the other organisations, the outcomes turned out to be different. Says one of the owners:

At the outset, our expectations were low. Of course, we hoped it would work, but our business is based on working close to our customers. We don't think we have the proper and adequate answers all the time, what works and what doesn't, . . .we were able to make the first version of "Beautiful Weather" very quickly, launched it and got feedback from users. We got quite positive feedback that inspired us to improve the site, but we also realised from the comments, that we made a lot of mistakes that could be corrected, and a new version was launched within a month. That is the way we work.

4 Open Innovation Technologies and Exploitative and Explorative Learning

Windsurfers, too, are requesting other information specific to surfing. We are trying to keep apace of developments and learning the whole time how to meet their requests.

On our site, there is a lively activity thanks to this dialogue. We try to answer all the questions we get and say why we go in a certain direction rather than another, or make some decisions. Of course, we cannot respond to everybody's questions and implement all the ideas we get, but if we receive some ideas and suggestions that point in the same direction, we try to implement it.

The firm is at the moment in the process of translating its site into other languages. Via Kundo, the firm got in touch with somebody who is willing to translate the language of the site from Swedish into Turkish for free. It is thanks to this student's suggestion that the site is available in more than Swedish, which in turn implies that the firm is now turning its eyes to the international market. Of course, the owners understood that this was an opportunity to extend their business to reach foreign customers. Consequently, the two brothers are now on the lookout for new ideas and new knowledge from their external customers. For instance, customers are taking the lead and asking for increasingly sophisticated services:

Many of our customers demand a personalised version that would suit their smart phones. We realised that we have to prioritise this kind of solution. Recently we got a mail from someone who wanted a special forecast related to certain circumstances and different needs. Another customer asked to get more information about the height of the waves and particular details that we cannot provide today, but we should think of incorporating them in the future. We are challenged to explore new areas that our customers are suggesting to us.

Other examples of firms that have received exploratory feedback are Storytell and Daycare. Both of these firms are also small in size therefore enjoying swift and flexible decision-making processes.

...If our customers would like us to start selling new audiobooks in another genre or ... If our customers need something else that we do not have, I just have to ask the CEO of the firm and start doing it. (Storytell)

"We answer every request...if we get some more extensive and pervasive ideas we put them into a "suggestion box" ... we try to pick out the ideas and talk them over with other colleagues, exploring how to implement them. (Daycare)"

These companies are prompted by their customers' feedback to search for new possibilities and explore new paths. They are using Kundo for both exploitative as well as explorative reasons.

4.5 Discussion

The result from the empirical material is too limited to draw clear conclusions. Nevertheless, the empirical material generates some tentative results about factors influencing different learning processes in line with the explorative purpose of this chapter and also gives us some indications about how to manage these processes.

Table 4.3 Companies and the type of feedback received

Type of organisation	Exploration-related feedback	Exploitation-related feedback
Public Transportation Company (SL)		X
Borås municipality		X
Linnaeus University		X
Folk University (adult education all over Sweden)		X
Business Region Skåne		X
Real Estate Company		X
Web book shop		X
Health Care Company	(x)	X
Storytel (audiobooks)	(x)	X
Weather site	X	X

This chapter has focused on the information flow and learning processes that are generated by a quite limited and simple open innovation technology. The results in this chapter show that open innovation processes go far beyond the efforts of investment and setting up different IT support systems. To manage and take advantage of different open innovation technologies is to focus on both internal and external demands, balancing what organisations can do and what their customers require from them. The empirical material illustrates how IT-enabled applications, such as the knowledge flow via Kundo, may generate both exploitative and explorative learning.

Table 4.3 presents the companies and the type of feedback they received.

The analysis and framework put forth illustrate the types of learning that organisations may obtain by setting up open innovation technologies. Among other things, it appears that the structural, affective and cognitive dimensions of relationships between firms and their customers affect the type of learning that results from implementing the application. Exploitative learning manifested itself in almost all the organisations. And this is consistent with previous research relating learning and the structural, affective and cognitive dimensions of the relationship. Given that many of the organisations have fairly dense connections, featuring generalised trust and possessing largely elements of architectural knowledge, most learning has proven to be exploitative in nature.

However, in the few cases where explorative learning appears to prevail, it is interesting to notice that the organisations are all small (fewer than ten employees), flexible and non-hierarchical. Furthermore, all the organisations have plenty of customers, but just a few of them maintained a more dyadic, one-to-one, trust relationship with their customers. In addition, these organisations have a lot in common with their customers who appear to be what may be called "lead users" (Franke et al. 2006). On that count, we can say that these customers are more focused on specific components of the service, such as the service related to their particular concerns (i.e. wave height). There is reciprocity between the hobbies and

4 Open Innovation Technologies and Exploitative and Explorative Learning

Table 4.4 Obtained learning processes related to structural, affective and cognitive features

Explorative	**Sparse network** Spending time on investigating different individual ideas wherever they turn up. Flexibility.	**Dyadic trust** Having an individual perspective in mind and focus on lead users.	**Component knowledge** Interested in individual ideas and suggestions related to different circumstances.
Exploitative	**Dense network** Bringing together comments and ideas from the generalised population and aligning the ideas with the existing company policy.	**Generalised trust** Working as a support function for general issues shared by the users.	**Architectural knowledge** Limiting the service to rather common and already prepared and known issues.

interests of the customers and the organisation; they are both on the same wavelength. Such a relationship is bound to lead to explorative learning.

Table 4.4 relates the type of learning processes obtained to the structural, affective and cognitive features of the relationship created by setting the open innovation technology, processes that also may be managed.

Finally, it is worth mentioning Gangi and Wasko (2009) who, among others, argue that it is difficult to control distributed learning processes outside the walls of the firms. Difficult indeed, as most of the organisations under consideration cannot help the kind of feedback (and the learning ensuing from it) they have received. Nevertheless, our framework can be the initial means to answering whether a firm can or cannot control what it can learn from external sources. As noticed earlier, small-sized organisations, personalised trust between the parties, and common specialised interest would yield explorative learning. Future research should continue to explore the impact of micro-foundations of open innovation practices and new technologies to uncover more nuanced underpinnings between structure, learning processes and performance.

4.5.1 Practical Advice

Our chapter provides a fairly optimistic answer to the practical challenge of managing and balancing the opposing forces of exploration and exploitation.

An organisation that is pursuing explorative learning may attempt to adopt features the small organisations in the study enjoy. In that way, it increases its chances of controlling its learning processes (see the arrows in Table 4.4). They can structure themselves in small and flexible units so as to get closer to their customers. On the other hand, an organisation that is pursuing exploitative learning may strive to maintain strong interdependent communication structures with their customers and environment. Furthermore, they can enhance activities that strengthen shared goals and values linked to already known issues.

> **Practical Tip**
>
> An organisation that is pursuing explorative learning may structure itself in small and flexible units to get closer to their customers. An organisation that is pursuing exploitative learning may strive to maintain strong interdependent communication structures with its customers and environment and enhance activities that strengthen shared goals and values linked to (almost) already known issues.

References

Alavi, M., & Leidner, D. E. (2001). Review: Knowledge management and knowledge management systems: Conceptual foundations and research issues. *MIS Quarterly, 25*(1), 107–136.

Chesbrough, H. W. (2003). *Open innovation: The new imperative for creating and profiting from technology*. Boston: Harvard Business School Press.

Denrell, J., & March, J. (2001). Adaptation as information restriction: the hot stove effect. *Organisations Science, 12*(5), 523–538.

Eisenhardt, K. M., & Graebner, M. E. (2007). Theory building from cases: Opportunities and challenges. *Academy of Management Journal, 50*(1), 25–32.

El Sawy, O., & Bowles, G. (1997). Redesigning the customer support process for the electronic economy: insights from storage dimensions. *MIS Quarterly, 21*(4), 457–483.

Fang, C., Jeho, J., & Schilling, M. (2010a). Balancing exploration and exploitation through structural design: The isolation of subgroups and organisational learning. *Organisation Science, 21*(3), 625–642.

Fiol, C., & Lyles, M. (1985). Organisational learning. *Academy of Management Review, 10*(4), 803–813.

Franke, N., von Hippel, E., & Schreier, M. (2006). Finding commercially attractive user innovations: A test of lead-user theory. *Journal of Product Innovation Management, 23*(4), 301–315.

Gangi, P., & Wasko, M. (2009). Steal my idea! Organisational adoption of user innovation from a user innovation community: A case study of Dell IdeaStorm. *Decision support Systems, 48*, 303–312.

Gassmann, O. (2006). Open up the innovation process. *R & D Management, 36*(3), 223–228.

Glaser, B., & Strauss, L. (1967). *The discovery of grounded theory: Strategies for qualitative research*. London: Wiedenfeld and Nicholson.

Grant, R. (1996). Toward a knowledge-based theory of the firm. *Strategic Management Journal, 17*, 109–122.

Hrastinski, S., Edenius, M. & Kviselius, N. (Eds.) (2011) "Collaboration systems for open innovation" *International Journal of Networking and Virtual Organisations, 9*(2).

Kane, G., & Alavi, M. (2007). Information technology and organisational learning: An investigation of exploration and exploitation processes. *Organisation Science, 18*(5), 796–812.

Kang, S.-C., Morris, S., & Scott, S. (2007). Relational archetypes organisational learning and value creation: Extending the human resource architecture. *Academy of Management Review, 32*(1), 236–256.

Lichtenthaler, U. (2008). Open innovation in practice: an analysis of strategic approaches to technology transactions. *IEEE Transactions on Engineering Management, 55*(1), 148–157.

March, J. G. (1991). Exploration and exploitation in organisational learning. *Organisation Science, 2*(1), 71–87.

Mom, T., Van Den Bosch, F., & Volberda, H. (2007a). Investigating managers' exploration and exploitation activities: The influences of top-down, bottom-up, and horizontal knowledge inflows. *Journal of Management Studies, 44*(6), 910–931.

Orlikowski, W. (1996). Improvising organisational transformation over time: A situated change perspective. *Information System Research, 7*(1), 63–92.

Orlikowski, W. (2000). Using technology and constituting structures: A practice lens for studying technology in organisation. *Organisation Science, 11*(4), 404–428.

Robey, D., & Bourdreau, M.-C. (1999). Accounting for the contradictory organisational consequences of information technology: Theoretical directions and methodological implication. *Information Systems Research, 10*(2), 167–185.

Teece, D., Pisano, G., & Shuen, A. (1997). Dynamic capabilities and strategic management. *Strategic Management Journal, 18*(7), 509–533.

Volberda, H., Foss, N., & Lyles, M. (2010). Absorbing the concept of absorptive capacity: How to realise is potential on the organisation field. *Organisation Science, 21*, 931–951.

Witzeman, S., Slowinski, G., Dirkx, R., Gollob, L., Tao, J., Ward, S., & Miraglia, S. (2006). Harnessing external technology for innovation. *Research-Technology Management, 49*, 19–27.

Yin, R.K. (2009), Case study research: Design and methods, 4th edition, Sage Publications, Thousand Oaks, CA.

Further Reading

Fang, C., Jeho, J., & Schilling, M. (2010b). Balancing exploration and exploitation through structural design: The isolation of subgroups and organizational learning. *Organization Science, 21*(3), 625–642.

Hrastinski, S., Edenius, M. & Kviselius, N. (2012) (Eds) Collaboration systems for open innovation. International. *Journal of Networking and Virtual Organisations*, 9(2).

Nambisan, S., & Baron, R. A. (2009). Virtual customer environments: Testing a model of voluntary participation in value co-creation activities. *The Journal of Product Innovation Management, 26*(4), 388–406.

Pitt, L., Watson, P., Berthon, P., Wynn, D., & Zinkhan, G. (2006). The Penguin's window: Corporate brands from an open source perspective. *Journal of the Academy of Marketing Science, 34*(Spring), 115–127.

Xie, C., Bagozzi, R., & Troye, S. (2008). Trying to prosume: Toward a theory of consumers as co-creators of value. *Journal of the Academy of Marketing Science, 36*(1), 109–122.

Chapter 5
Open Innovation in Inter-Organisational Networks in the IT Industry

Karlheinz Kautz, Sameen M. Rab, and Michael Sinnet

Abstract Open innovation has been recognised by the IT industry as a novel way to create innovation, where organisations open their innovation processes and cooperate with others to develop new products and services. We study open innovation by looking at another new trend, innovation through customising standard software as a business model. We investigate the open innovation activities of an inter-organisational network which consists of a small customising company, a large global software producer and other involved companies. We integrate formally separate aspects of open innovation and inter-organisational networks, broaden the view from one focal firm to the relations in a network of companies and underline the importance of balanced formal and informal relations, and 'coopetive' and opportunistic behaviour for the open innovation process.

5.1 Introduction

Many organisations have the attitude that innovative work and the generation of new ideas are an internal affair which should be closed to the surrounding world. This has changed during recent years and more and more organisations see benefits

---

K. Kautz (✉)
Copenhagen Business School, Operations Management, Copenhagen, Denmark
e-mail: kk.om@cbs.dk

S.M. Rab
NNIT Management Consulting, Søborg, Denmark
e-mail: Sameen.M.Rab@gmail.com

M. Sinnet
Danske Capital, Kgs., Lyngby, Denmark
e-mail: michael@sinnet.dk

J.S.Z. Eriksson Lundström et al. (eds.), *Managing Open Innovation Technologies*,
DOI 10.1007/978-3-642-31650-0_5, © Springer-Verlag Berlin Heidelberg 2013

in opening up their innovation process. Open innovation has also been recognised by the IT industry as a novel way to create innovation, where organisations open their innovation processes and cooperate with others to develop new products and services. However, beyond work on open source development (West and Gallagher 2006) little insight on open IT innovation exists. We study open innovation by looking at another new trend, namely innovation through customising standard software as a business model (Pollock et al. 2003).

Software customisation has mainly been discussed in the literature as an activity which takes place within the development organisation. Another view, however, looks at customisation as a specialised business activity performed by an independent software customiser. This view implies some interaction in inter-organisational networks between the customiser and the developer to effectively customise the software (Pollock et al. 2003).

Vanhaverbeke (2006) makes a strong argument that open innovation takes place in inter-organisational networks and Feller et al. (2009) demonstrate inter-organisational relationships in open innovation based on whether these relationships are mediated or direct, and whether they seek to exchange intellectual property or innovation capability, and call for more research that takes into account an inter-organisational perspective on facilitating open innovation.

Thus, inter-organisational relationships and networks are both decisive for open innovation and software customisation. Against this background, we empirically investigate the open innovation activities of an inter-organisational network which consists of a small customising company, a large global software producer and other companies involved in the innovation process. Our research question then is how open innovation takes place in inter-organisational networks in the IT industry. We contribute to the development of a theory of open IT innovation with a theoretical framework which integrates formally separate aspects of open innovation and inter-organisational networks. We extend the literature on open innovation by broadening the view from one focal firm to the relations in a network of companies which mutually contribute to innovation occurring in the different companies. Our research underlines the importance of balanced formal and informal relations, and 'coopetive' and opportunistic behaviour for the open innovation process.

The remainder of this chapter is structured as follows: in the next section we provide the theoretical background for our research and present a theoretical framework which integrates concepts of open innovation with concepts of inter-organisational networks (summarised in Table 5.1) to study standard software customisation as an instance of open innovation in our case setting. We then introduce our case study research approach and the case description. This is followed by our case analysis and the presentation and discussion of our findings. We finish with a summary of our contributions and some conclusions.

Table 5.1 A framework for open innovation in inter-organisational networks

Open Innovation	Inter-organisational Networks
Idea Flow	Formal Relations
Knowledge Sharing Opportunities	Market, Product life, Shared destiny, Minority shareholding, Strategic alliance, Joint venture, Merger/Acquisition
Product Access	Informal Relations/Social capital
Flexible Development Context	Commitments, Expectations, Trust,
Active Partner Search	Performance of favours, Reciprocity, Admission to less accessible information
Stimuli	Norms, Sanctions, Behaviour governed by unwritten rules
	Coopetition/opportunistic behavior
	Close integration/open innovation process,
	Rules/caring for cooperation

5.2 Theoretical Background

5.2.1 Open Innovation

Close inter-organisational relations facilitate organisations' capability and willingness to open their innovation process and let innovation happen across organisational boundaries (Simard and West 2006).

Organisations have long had relations with other organisations, but these relations did not go beyond using others as suppliers or as sales channels and thus did not break with the paradigm behind closed innovation (Vanhaverbeke 2006).

Open innovation according to Chesbrough (2003) means that valuable ideas can come from inside or outside the company and can go to the market from inside and outside the company. Organisations committing to open innovation view the outside world as a source of inspiration and accept the strategic potential of letting other organisations contribute to the innovation process.

While in closed innovation, principles prevail such as (1) the smart people in our field work for us; (2) to profit from R&D, we must discover it, develop it and ship it ourselves; (3) if we discover it ourselves, we will get it to market first; (4) the company that gets an innovation to market first will win; (5) if we create the most and the best ideas in the industry, we will win and (6) we should control our intellectual properties, so that our competitors don't profit from our ideas.

Open innovation emphasises that (1) not all the smart people work for us; we need to work with smart people inside and outside our company; (2) external R&D can create significant value; internal R&D is needed to claim some portion of that value; (3) we don't have to originate the research to profit from it; (4) building a better business model is better than getting to market first; (5) if we make the best use of internal and external ideas, we will win and (6) we should profit from others' use of our intellectual properties, and we should buy others' intellectual properties whenever it advances our own business model.

Heavy exchange of ideas and easy access to products is a prerequisite for open innovation (Vanhaverbeke 2006). Vanhaverbeke and Cloodt (2006) argue that an organisation which is highly dependent on other organisations' support or deliverables strives to open its innovation processes to its cooperation partners. Open innovation is not only linked to openness with regard to access to a product, but is an overall strategy to provide stimuli and improve the conditions for companies which contribute to the innovation process. This, for example, can mean to provide capital for start-up companies which want to further develop their products. These spin-off companies can function as laboratories for which a large organisation sponsors a smaller one to contribute to the innovation process.

Organisations have to understand their role with regard to other parties when engaging in open innovation (Vanhaverbeke and Cloodt 2006). This includes searching for new partners, providing opportunities for innovators to effectively share their knowledge and their ideas (Vanhaverbeke and Cloodt 2006). An example is knowledge sharing forums in which the developers use each other as mutual inspiration to support the creation of innovations (von Hippel 2005), which provides an appropriate development context. An example of this is suitable development tools and a product of high quality with a flexible product architecture as well as other incentives in the form of new markets (Chesbrough 2003) where the customised solutions attract attention, but also create additional business value for the original product.

Vanhaverbeke and Cloodt (2006) underline the significance of nursing and steering an open innovation network to develop or use innovations. The composition of the network can also have an impact on the innovative processes. Simard and West (2006) argue that it is important not to be satisfied with tying together some established inter-organisational cooperation partners, but to build up a network which consists of many broad relationships instead of a network with a few and deep relations. This approach utilises innovative opportunities better as the generation of ideas becomes much more unpredictable. The knowledge and product flow between organisations in open innovation however does not necessarily have to happen in the open, unlimited public space, but can take place in hierarchical relationships (Feller et al. 2009) or on a dyadic level (Vanhaverbeke and Cloodt 2006).

Chesbrough (2003) distinguishes innovative processes in research and development. In the research processes, initial analysis and design tasks are performed, while the construction of the product takes place in the development phase. This allows for a clear distinction between the processes, but also leads to coordination and communication problems when creating new products as it does not consider their mutual dependency. This problem is solved through continuous mutual adjustment which is a much more complex task compared to closed innovation when performed across organisational boundaries. However according to Chesbrough (2003) the advantages of letting other organisations contribute to the development of new products often outweigh the difficulties of coordinating inter-organisational processes. In contrast to closed innovation where the organisational boundaries lock out any participation of external organisations, there are different ways how external organisations can contribute to the open innovation process (see Fig. 5.1). They can participate in the research and development of the product,

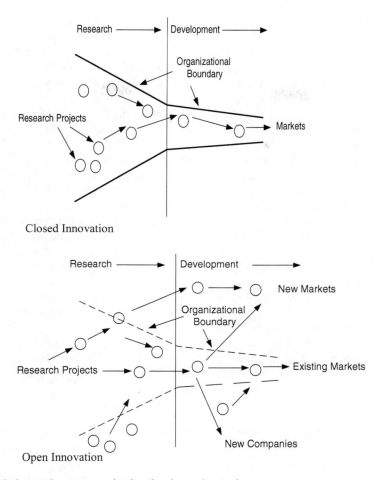

Fig. 5.1 Innovative processes in closed and open innovation

resell the product, promote the product or build upon the existing product (Chesbrough 2006). This is what companies which customise standard software products do.

5.2.2 Standard Software Customisation

Standard software has existed since the early 1960s (Sawyer 2000). The aim is to create a common comprehensive solution which can be implemented for a broad range of customers. As standard software however hardly ever satisfies all customer needs, customers tend to adapt or customise the standard software for their own needs (Scott and Kaindl 2000).

Software customisation is a creative task which goes far beyond adjusting pre-defined settings. Light (2001) argues that "Customisation is meant to describe changes or additions to the functionality available in the standard software. It does not refer to the switching on and off of functionality that is part of the blueprint of the software, sometimes referred to as software configuration." He distinguishes between the creation of reports, amendment of existing reports and/or displays, automation of existing processes, addition of functionality and change of existing functionality, a categorisation which allows for a more fine-grained analysis of the actual customisation practice.

We consider customisation here as a dedicated business activity performed by an independent business (Pollock et al. 2003) which is different from tailoring information systems by customers and end users (Germonprez et al. 2007). With regard to the business model of a company which solely bases its business on customising standard software, Kuitunen et al. (2005) categorise software businesses according to two parameters: (1) how tailored or standardised a software company's products and services are (tailored offerings vs. standardised offerings) and (2) the company's earnings primarily based on the sales of products or performance of services (product-based business vs. service-based business). This categorisation allows us to analyse the business model for software customisation in the case setting more precisely. It is, however, difficult to discuss business models for standard software customisation without analysing the role of the producer of the original software, the customers and other business partners and interested parties. Therefore, the concept of inter-organisational networks is relevant here; their composition, as stated earlier, is also important for open innovation (Vanhaverbeke and Cloodt 2006).

5.2.3 Inter-Organisational Networks

The concept of inter-organisational networks describes a specific type of relation which binds organisations closely together (Harland 1996). The concept does not just deal with the communication between different organisations, but also comprises their interaction and cooperation (Håkansson and Snehota 1995). This interaction and cooperation occurs across organisations and provides the organisations with competitive advantages they could not have achieved on their own (Dyer and Singh 1998). Dyer and Singh (1998) also argue that the development of organisations depends not only on their industry sector and their internal resources, but also on the networks they are part of Williamson (1991) illustrates that a network reduces the transaction costs for the exchange of information, minimises uncertainty and limits opportunistic behaviour.

The inter-organisational relations depend on the degree of cooperation between the organisations. Harland (1996) provides a taxonomy for formal relationships between organisations, ranging from a situation where organisations have no shared objectives, deal with each other on the market and communicate through purchase orders, to a situation where organisations merge, or where one organisation acquires

5 Open Innovation in Inter-Organisational Networks in the IT Industry 73

the other. In between these poles, Harland (1996) distinguishes between joint ventures, strategic alliances, minority shareholding, shared destiny and product life relationships. The last two are considered close partnerships where the partners share their vision and cooperate either with the organisations as a whole or with individual products.

Håkansson and Snehota (1995), however, argue that formalised contracts do not play the most important role in close inter-organisational relationships. Formal contracts are often inhibiting when problems arise or unexpected conflicts or crises have to be resolved. Then informal and emergent approaches are more usable, but it is a prerequisite that the organisations know each other well and have mutual trust.

In this context, Coleman (1988) has defined the concept of social capital which, like human or economic capital, contributes to organisations' competitive capacities. Inter-organisational networks consist of social structure and the concept helps to understand how inter-organisational relations are shaped by the social relations of the employees across the different organisations. Social capital consists of the following three elements: (1) commitments, expectations and trust which relate to the performance of favours and services without payment based on the believe that they will be returned, (2) information channels which provide access to less accessible information through personal relations to trusted employees in other organisations and (3) norms and sanctions which are the unwritten rules that exist between people and which govern how they act and behave.

Formal and informal relations in inter-organisational networks do not cover all aspects of interaction. An important aspect in such networks is that these relations can take a complex form where organisations cooperate while they simultaneously compete with each other. Ganguli (2007) has in this context coined the term 'coopetition'. The objective of coopetive relations is to achieve a joint competitive advantage by competing on some parameters while at the same time jointly striving for better quality in other areas. von Hippel (1987) found that it is often informal knowledge which is exchanged in these relationships, benefiting organisations in coopetive relations. Therefore, such relationships are difficult to manage and control and invite opportunistic behaviour (von Hippel 1987). Limiting opportunistic behaviour is important because it has a significant impact on the course and outcome of cooperation. Opportunistic behaviour can be reduced through close integration and nursing the cooperation between partners. One way to pursue close integration is for organisations to open up their innovation processes for their cooperation partners to contribute to this process.

Table 5.1 summarises the key concepts of our integrated framework for open innovation in inter-organisational networks.

5.3 Research Approach

Our research follows the approach of engaged scholarship (Van de Ven 2007) which is a participative form of research for seeking advice and perspectives of key stakeholders to understand and theorise about a complex problem. Given the limited literature concerning our topic, our investigation is based on an exploratory, qualitative, single case study (Creswell 2003) of a small Danish development company called

Alpha[1] which customises a standard product originally developed by a large global software producer called Zeta. Our research approach is inspired by Walsham (1995), who stresses that in all types of research, including case study research, theory is important as an initial guide to data collection, during the iterative process of data analysis, and as a final product of the research. While it is often stated that it is not possible to generalise and certainly not to theorise from a single case study, Walsham (1995) suggests that it is possible to generalise case study findings among others in the form of a contribution of rich insight. So inspired, we have used the theoretical background concerning open innovation, inter-organisational networks and software customisation to guide our data collection and analysis, in order to contribute to the existing body of knowledge with rich insight about open innovation in the IT industry.

The empirical data for the study was collected in semi-structured, open-ended interviews conducted by a team of two researchers. The team performed six interviews with the founders of Alpha and key personnel in the organisation which covers more than half of the organisation's staff and with their partner account manager at Zeta. The interview data were supplemented with publically available and internal company documents, especially about Zeta's partnership programme. The interviews were tape recorded and transcribed. Subsequently, the data was coded independently by two researchers. The few differences in the researchers' conceptions were discussed and resolved. A detailed narrative of the case organisation was written in order to move from observations towards theory building and from description to explanation. In a narrative theory, the story provides a progress or sequence of events and builds a conceptual model which serves as a frame of reference for the further analysis and interpretation of the data (Van de Ven 2007). In this process, the third researcher acted as a facilitator. The combination of interpretation and collaboration between three researchers with different levels of involvement brought interpretive rigor to the project. Figure 5.2 summarises the research approach.

5.4 The Case

In the following, we describe the case setting and take company Alpha as a point of origin. As the basis for the subsequent analysis, we describe how relations were formed, changed and disbanded in different phases the organisation went through. We identified seven such phases which were separated by significant events. Our narrative thus has seven subsections (see Table 5.2).

---

[1] On request of the parties involved, all company and product names have been anonymised in this chapter.

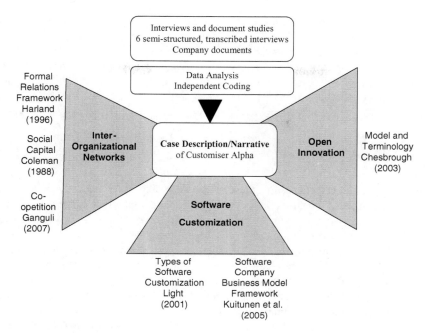

Fig. 5.2 The research approach

Table 5.2 The seven phases of the case narrative

Freelance work at Omega	Summer 2005
Launch of Alpha	Autumn 2005
Partnership with Zeta	Spring 2006
From Consultancy to Product Development	Early 2007
Organisational Growth	Spring 2007
Outsourcing to Asia	Autumn 2007
Merger with Omega	Spring 2008

5.4.1 Freelance Work at Omega

The narrative takes its starting point in the company Omega which was established in early 2005 as a consultancy company with a focus on a CRM (Customer Relationship Management) product. The CRM product was developed in 2004 by the large global software producer Zeta and is used by companies which exploit the advantage that the product is compatible with other Zeta products. The two founders of Omega were former Zeta employees and held positions there as product managers. Omega focuses on reselling Zeta's CRM product. Omega is a partner of Zeta, but experiences that its business domain is not sustainable without the technical competencies which are a prerequisite for reselling and implementing the product. As they lack the technical competencies at this point, Omega hires a freelance IT professional in the summer 2005, to support the technical domain and to take care of any tasks related to the configuration of the product. Subsequently, business develops very fast and as requests from customers grow, another freelancer is hired. In this early phase, the cooperation between Omega and the freelancers is characterised as a friendly turn without any direct payment for the work performed. The assignments are largely related to system configuration and customer specific adjustments, where some customers, for example, wish to import data from other existing systems to the CRM.

5.4.2 Launch of Alpha

When the two freelancers recognise that their work consists of repetitive tasks, they see a possibility for a business in their work and create Alpha in autumn 2005. In the beginning, their assignments are largely consultancy tasks where the two founders of Alpha adjust the CRM for their customers whom they get through Omega's contacts. The particular need for more flexibility to import customer data is the main focus of Alpha, and with Omega as strategic partner in their network, they continuously solve this problem for different customers. The cooperation with the customers is in the beginning characterised by informal agreements where the involved parties do not see the necessity for tight guidelines or more formal development methods.

These agreements concern the different stakeholders' interests in the solution. The customers want a cheap solution and Alpha wants to reuse parts of these solutions, so that they can resell them to other customers. The agreements create stability which provides Alpha with the firm ground for their first standard product. As the assignments from different customers concerning the import of data become more and more similar, the two founders of Alpha decide to develop the standardised solution DataImporter which Omega can resell to their customers. DataImporter plays an important role for Alpha as it is primarily this product which creates Alpha's initial earnings.

5.4.3 Partnership with Zeta: New Contacts

The standardised, adjusted solution DataImporter becomes a successful product which also satisfies the certification requirements in Zeta's partnership programme. With the partnership programme Zeta tries to enrol IT companies to act and work in accordance to Zeta's standards and interests. Through the relationship between Zeta and the IT companies the latter receive a certificate, get better access to Zeta's products and achieve a better recognition through their products.

Already at the start of Alpha its founders choose to register as partners in Zeta's partnership programme. Everyone can become a registered Zeta partner, but this form of partnership had only very limited advantages for Alpha. In the beginning of 2006, Alpha becomes a certified partner, which means that they can officially offer Zeta-based IT-services, products and know-how as an independent company. As a certified partner a company needs two Zeta certified products and has to pay a basic fee. Alpha becomes a Gold partner in April 2006, based on fulfilling further partnership requirements. This means that beyond getting more general attention, Alpha also receives support, licences and knowledge from Zeta. They can also preview much earlier, experiment with and test the beta versions of the product which Zeta continuously releases. However, through the partnership programme and its inscribed set of rules, Zeta also dictates its demands to their partners.

A partnership is accompanied by a 'partner account manager'. Alpha's founders perceive the relation to Zeta through their account manager as being bureaucratic and inconvenient. Thus, in the beginning there is a hint of minor conflict in the formal cooperation between the two partners. Alpha has a need for technical knowledge more than their account manager, who knows much about Zeta in general, can provide. In contrast to other Zeta partners, Alpha focuses on adapting the CRM product instead of focusing on selling Zeta licences. They, however, feel that they indirectly contribute to increased sales as their solutions make the CRM more attractive for potential users.

As Alpha does not feel that the formal communication channels are sufficient, they look for new possibilities to get information about the product they adjust. In spring 2006 here the relationship to Omega comes in again. As former Zeta product managers, the Omega founders create a number of informal relations between Alpha and some Zeta developers, where the parties support each other by mutually exchanging information about the CRM product. As Alpha and Omega are not in a competitive relation, it is only in Omega's interest that Alpha strengthens their business so that they can develop solutions which will benefit their collaboration. Despite their different business focus, the two companies act in agreement with each other's interests. Their informal relations are soon apparent to be advantageous for Alpha. These advantages, among others, reveal that Alpha no longer needs to go through all the bureaucratic information channels. This, according to the Alpha founders, leads to a good yield of their relationship with Zeta.

Alpha learns more about the CRM product and in June 2006 appears at an annual Zeta conference in the USA to present their standardised DataImporter to various Zeta partners. This is the first of many international conferences where Alpha presents and strengthens its network. Many interested parties, among them representatives from Zeta and actual developers of Zeta's CRM product, find the DataImporter appealing, contact Alpha and discuss the product with them as it closes obvious holes in Zeta's CRM product. The conferences thus become important events for Alpha in their striving to create relations between them and other Zeta partners. They tie first bonds to partners who want to resell the adjusted product to their own customers. This quickly creates a favourable market for Alpha. The new partnerships consist primarily of distribution contracts with existing CRM vendors, who see an advantage in including Alpha's solutions in their product portfolio. In autumn 2006, Alpha succeeds in interesting several local Danish CRM vendors in their products who increasingly take over the contact with potential customers. This leads to the end of Omega's role as link between Alpha and new partners because Alpha now itself handles the contact with these partners. Although customers can still buy Alpha's products from the company's website, Alpha chooses to change their focus from customers to distribution partners who thus become links in Alpha's already quite complex network.

5.4.4 From Consultancy to Product Development

The new focus on partners opens new opportunities for Alpha, as they now can sell their products to a larger range of customers. Until the end of 2006, Alpha's work assignments consist both of consultancy services and the development of their own standardised solutions. The success of the DataImporter however leads to the insight that there is a larger potential in dedicated product development, and the company thus chooses to standardise their own adjusted solutions. The change in focus results in developing a number of new off-the-shelf products of which both the new version of the DataImporter and a system to import business data from the Yellow Pages achieve Zeta certification. During 2007, the company develops a further three products based on the CRM system; one of the products automates searching the CRM product; another one provides document handling and the third provides a new interface to the CRM product.

All three solutions meet the demands of a broad user group and again fill some gaps in the original CRM product. There is an alignment of Zeta's and Alpha's interests as Zeta's solutions hit a broader group of customers. This gives Alpha the opportunity to develop solutions which are outside Zeta's interest to be included in new versions of the CRM product. However, over time, Alpha experiences that updates from Zeta include functionalities which correspond to their solutions as they lack legal protection of their ideas. This pushes Alpha to continuously develop new products, among others, another new version of the DataImporter, which again appears to be the bearing standard solution of the company.

5.4.5 Organisational Growth

Being conscious of the limited life time of most their products, in January 2007, Alpha starts to develop more products. This leads to an increased need for resources, and in February 2007, the two founders hire an employee to develop user documentation for all their products with the aim of enabling their new partners to support the products and to solve problems for their customers. To supplement the technical products with user friendly descriptions thus is the first step in the direction of a broader positive reputation of Alpha.

To further improve this reputation in the same period, Alpha hires another person to look after their sales related and promotion activities, such as the development of promotion material. In March 2007, Alpha employs a developer who takes care of the company's home page through which they distribute their promotion materials, offer their products and through which their partners can handle their customers. Even if Alpha has chosen not to focus on their customers, their home page becomes an important distribution channel and creates an image of their existing products. In the same period, the Alpha founders use their personal network and hire another developer, who is assigned an important role in the future development of the DataImporter.

5 Open Innovation in Inter-Organisational Networks in the IT Industry

In September 2007, the two founders decide to headhunt their partner account manager at Zeta, who has been very enthusiastic about the company. He is employed as a sales manager—a business domain to which Alpha so far has given a low priority, and assumes a very important role: he brings both knowledge about the industry sector and more contacts to Zeta and Zeta partners with him, which strengthens Alpha's position.

5.4.6 Outsourcing to Asia

In autumn 2007, a number of international companies start to show interest in the DataImporter. In this context, Alpha chooses to cooperate with the largest CRM vendor in the USA, Delta, and launches the product Delta DataImporter. As Delta insists on using its own two software testers in India, the collaboration with Delta becomes Alpha's first step in the direction of outsourcing. The positive experience with these IT professionals results in the company's decision to continue to use the services of the testers in India instead of performing tests internally at home in Denmark.

In this period, Alpha also starts to define their own processes including the use of development methods for their software development. They see the opportunity to let parts of their product development be performed outside the organisation and thereby achieve some financial savings. Therefore, in November 2007, they contact the Danish company Gamma which specialises in outsourcing of IT-related work tasks. Gamma offers them a solution where three developers from Pakistan are assigned to product development in Alpha. The three developers are highly educated, have experience with CRM and incur only low salary costs.

As a relatively young company, Alpha tries to keep the prices down for their products in order to obtain a greater market share. Their network is therefore characterised by a strong international aspect, both with regard to their sales, and their development activities. Despite some challenges related to the different time zones, culture and communication, the founders of Alpha state that the decision to outsource has been favourable for the company. The Pakistani developers are highly proficient in setting themselves in the already existing Alpha products and to take responsibility for their assignments which are handed over to them in daily telephone meetings. During the first meetings, Alpha, however, experiences the problem that the existing products have been developed without any technical documentation. This had not been a problem so far, as all developers had the necessary knowledge to further develop the software.

This problem and the lacking descriptions of Alpha's technical knowledge about their products leads to an intensified effort to help the foreign developers understand and adopt the way Alpha customises Zeta's CRM. At the same time, all code which is developed abroad is reviewed to ensure that the developers in Pakistan follow Alpha's guidelines. The Danish developers thus get the new task to specify assignments and to explain and document their code, which decreases their time to develop the products themselves. To perform the analysis and design in Denmark and the programming in Pakistan, thus, is a decision which puts an increased focus on documentation and governance.

5.4.7 Merger with Omega

Over time, Alpha's close alliance with Omega has resulted in a fruitful cooperation, where both companies continuously exchange experiences. The two organisations are also located in the same building. The two organisations have never been in any competitive relation to each other, but have taken care of each other's interests both on a professional and business level, as well as on a social level where the employees regularly mingle.

In March 2008, Alpha and Omega opt to merge. However, with the exception of redistributing the companies' capital, the owners decide that the merger should not have any immediate consequences for the original organisations' work processes, and they continue their businesses as before. Alpha sees an advantage in the merger as they want to increase their market share and extend their network. The merger provides them with access to more than 100 new partners worldwide.

5.5 Case Analysis and Discussion

The case narrative provides evidence of a company's successful business model for customising standard software in an open innovation milieu. Alpha closes gaps in the original CRM product. As they do not have the right to directly change the functionality of the CRM product, they add extra functionality. Alpha has moved from tailoring individual solutions for customers to product development (Kuitunen et al. 2005). Their primary product DataImporter represents a classical functional extension of the original CRM product. Their other products either fall in this category, or they are process automations like the search system or amendments of existing reports (Light 2001).

Since the early 1990s, Zeta has had a focus on the opportunities related to opening up their innovation processes. Zeta follows the premise of Chesbrough's (2003) model of open innovation that valuable ideas and knowledge both enter and leave the organisation when it commits to open innovation. This happens both in the research and the development stages where external companies contribute with competence, ideas and newly developed products. To gain rich insight about open innovation in our case setting, we focus in the following on the relationship between Zeta and Alpha in the inter-organisational open innovation network on a dyadic level (Vanhaverbeke and Cloodt 2006). Our findings are summarised in Table 5.3.

We find an open innovation process where external knowledge and technologies are acquired from outside a company, and where internal knowledge and technologies are introduced to the outside. This is a coupled process where both focal companies innovate as a result of their mutual relationship; innovation takes place inside both companies and analogically also outside of them (Gassmann and Enkel 2004).

Our case innovation network shows many traits of an innovation network that is based on homogeneous knowledge sources and a distributed mode of control and

5 Open Innovation in Inter-Organisational Networks in the IT Industry 81

Table 5.3 Characteristics of the inter-organisational open innovation network in the case

Idea Flow	Coupled Process—outside -in/inside-out
Knowledge Sharing Opportunities	Developer communities conferences Online developer forums
Product Access	Access e.g. through beta tests
Flexible Development Context	Provision of tools Flexible product architecture
Active Partner Search	Proactive search for partners Technical counselling for non-certified partners
Stimuli	Spin-off support Cheap partner programme Partner solutions promotion on company page
Formal Relations	Mostly formal partnerships Product life: Zeta/Alpha partners (Delta & other CRM vendors) Shared destiny: Zeta/Alpha/Gamma Strategic alliance: Alpha/Omega Merger/Acquisition: Alpha/Omega Market: Customers
Informal Relations/Social capital	Commitments, trust, performance of favours - Alpha/Omega/Zeta: Personal, trusting relationships based on friendly turns Admission to less accessible information - Alpha/Omega: Omega staff provides information about customer and business needs - Zeta/Alpha: Zeta staff provides access to product information Norms & sanctions - Zeta/Alpha: Continuous proof of worthiness of Zeta's staff trust
Coopetition/opportunistic behaviour	Close integration/open innovation process Rules/caring for cooperation - Formal contract - Defined scope of customisation/innovation Rules are broken - Updates and compatibility - Copying of solutions Limiting feedback on functionality in original product

coordination such as can be found in open source innovation (Yoo et al. 2008). However, we can also argue that Zeta, to a large extent, controls the network and thus the network shows traits of a centralised market with heterogeneous knowledge sources, or that Alpha much more independently follows its own path to innovation, pointing towards a doubly distributed network with heterogeneous sources and distributed control. We find a complex net of multiple relations which cannot be categorised neatly. Feller et al. (2009) distinguish inter-organisational relationships in open innovation into direct and mediated relations in markets and hierarchies to seek either innovation capabilities or intellectual property. With regard to this categorisation, both focal companies seek for knowledge in hierarchical and market relations and brokers such as Omega provide knowledge of potential solvers and solutions.

A direct consequence of the development and diffusion of Zeta's CRM product is the launch of Alpha which can thus be considered as a spin-off company. Alpha focused on this standard product from its very start. Through Omega's customer network they got ideas for customisations and adjustments which were lacking in the original product. Omega's close relationship to Zeta contributed to development knowledge from Zeta being shared with Alpha across Zeta's boundaries. This knowledge then contributed to Alpha's idea of building the DataImporter which could import data from different sources into the CRM product. The DataImporter then had decisive influence on Alpha's certification as Gold Partner. As a consequence, this gave Alpha access to knowledge which is produced in Zeta's research process.

Zeta is interested in ideas for extending their products and collects these kinds of ideas through dedicated interviews with their partners who have put their stamp on the future product already in the research phase. As Alpha has detailed knowledge about the CRM product, they contribute with development ideas which they believe are important to get implemented in the original product. Alpha has, for example, promoted the idea that the CRM product can interact with other vendors' database systems. This feature is in the interest of Alpha as they themselves cannot introduce this aspect into the original product. Beyond providing ideas the customised solutions which Alpha creates are also a direct source of inspiration for Zeta's products. The dilemma that the software producer creates solutions which correspond to those which the customising company has developed is a serious problem in open innovation environments (Graham and Mowery 2006), which we will discuss later.

As ideas enter Zeta's open innovation environment, Zeta also provides inspiration to Alpha's product development early in their process. Alpha has been accepted as a member of Zeta's early adopter program which provides them with front edge information about new CRM product features. Thus, Alpha gets ideas both from Zeta's research and development stages. That Alpha gets early access and insight into the new versions of Zeta's CRM is important, because, according to Alpha's developers, the original product is a source of inspiration in itself. As Alpha also participates in the early beta tests of the CRM product they get insight into those areas where they can develop new customised solutions for their customers. These solutions aim at closing the gaps which are in the original product and which will secure their customers a better utilisation of the CRM product. Beyond improving the original product, Alpha's solutions also contribute to the further sales of the CRM product to new markets. According to Vanhaverbeke (2006) a focus on open innovation emerges often when companies such as Zeta try to promote and sell their products on new markets. In our case, Zeta is relying and dependant on other companies' contribution to their product as they themselves cannot cover all markets; this is in particular valid for niche markets with special needs. They try to continuously provide new versions of the original product which their partners can customise and further develop. Alpha has a very positive perception of their placing in this environment.

Zeta works actively to identify companies which are interested in innovating their standard software. Beyond a significant effort to promote their partnership

5 Open Innovation in Inter-Organisational Networks in the IT Industry

programme with a minimal participation fee, Zeta helps minor non-certified companies by providing free support and technical advice to develop solutions which will allow them to achieve partner certification. Alpha uses this programme to build up a strong inter-organisational network where they draw from Omega's and Zeta's knowledge.

Zeta has created forums where people who customise their products can ask technical questions and extent their knowledge about the products. Zeta has an online forum for developers who customise their standard software. Even if the online forum only plays a small role in Alpha's work, it provides evidence for Zeta's attempts to create an effective information flow between its own, internal and external developers. In Alpha's case, the Zeta conferences played a more important role for building competences and relations. At the conferences where Alpha provided and received knowledge about Zeta's technologies, Alpha presented their solutions and experienced Zeta's technology in different contexts. In addition to product information, the conferences also support the formation of informal relationships which provide informal knowledge which official information channels such as online forums cannot always give.

According to Alpha, Zeta provides an appropriate development environment including interfaces and tools, as well as a suitable product architecture as a basis for their work to customise the CRM product. Zeta strongly focuses on making development work easier for the companies which customise their products. They provide a flexible product architecture so that the companies can reduce their resources as they easily can adjust and adapt components of the original product. For Alpha, it was critical that Zeta in version 4 of the CRM product made the technical architecture more flexible so that they themselves could host their customers' solutions and thus much easier maintain the software. The CRM product version 3 was a product where the user interface and the system functionality were closely interlinked and hard to separate. Zeta therefore based version 4 on a separation of these system layers. This made it easier for Alpha to customise the original product and to change and shift modules and functions, where necessary. The modular architecture of the CRM product allowed Alpha to change, add and remove functionality without larger compatibility problems.

Zeta supports the promotion of their partners' customised products to attract new markets. Through the certification process and other measures such as using approved testing personnel Alpha has ensured that their products satisfy Zeta's prerequisites and quality criteria for product promotion. With Zeta's permission, Alpha thus promotes their product directly on Zeta's home page where Zeta's own customers often look for new products and product information.

In addition to placing product information on Zeta's company web portal, Alpha has also been allowed to present their products at various conferences.

These conferences have provided Alpha with the opportunity to render their existence visible for numerous partners who could be interested in using or reselling Alpha's products. In particular, this initiative has been decisive for the extension of Alpha's inter-organisational network where they found new partners and customers.

The formal relations in the inter-organisational network are mostly made up by partners who have entered into a number of close alliances and less by customers.

The first links between Zeta and Alpha are created with the launch of the DataImporter. Alpha becomes a registered partner, which makes it easier for them to customise Zeta's CRM solution. This is beneficial for Zeta which gets its product promoted through an increase of its business value. The partnership with Zeta is advantageous for Alpha. Alpha cooperates with Zeta on the CRM product, but there is no other formal binding between them. Still there is a dependency as the rise or fall of Zeta will have a crucial impact on Alpha's existence. On the other hand, Zeta's reputation is, to some extent, particularly on the CRM market, now also bound to Alpha's products, and exhibits some characteristics of a shared destiny based on both companies' mutual dependency.

Alpha's product development also leads to partnerships with two of Zeta's Danish CRM vendors. Alpha has entered these relationships to secure an increased sale of licences for their products which are distributed through these partners. The partnerships are primarily a sales channel for Alpha where the two vendors resell and implement Alpha's solution to various customers. In a similar way, Alpha has a relationship to one of Zeta's US distributors, Delta, which however is limited to their DataImporter product. Delta had been interested in the product and Alpha had had a wish to enter the huge US market which Delta opens for them. Their mutual interest in the further development and promotion of the product results in a contract where Alpha develops a specific product for Delta which then owns and supports this solution.

Alpha also forms a partnership with Gamma to satisfy the company's need for more CRM competent staff. The contract between the two organisations incorporates a cooperation concerning resources from abroad. This cooperation is beneficial for both parts where Gamma utilises its business model which creates and administers relations between local, Danish companies and global suppliers and Alpha's need for resources is covered by the foreign developers. The partnership forms a reciprocal dependency and can be considered as shared destiny where both partners have an interest in a mutual progress. The closest relationship for Alpha is formed through the merger with Omega. In addition to the economical fusion, this step strengthens both parts' position in their individual networks. According to Harland (1996) this is an important strategic reason for a merger.

The social structures with other organisations within the network are strongly marked by the personal bonds of Zeta, Alpha and Omega employees. While Omega has provided advice free of charge for Alpha in its start-up phase about their customers' needs, Alpha mostly as a favour has helped Omega to overcome technical problems in Omega's work with the CRM product. Through these friendly terms Alpha and Omega have strengthened their mutual trust which has been beneficial in situations where there was a lack of resources, knowledge or competence. This trust has increased the social capital between the two organisations and decreased the need for formal rules and regulations in their cooperation.

With Omega's initial support Alpha has also created strong personal links with a number of Zeta employees. Especially the company's sales manager who has been a Zeta employee contributed and created a number of informal commitments between these two organisations. Alpha carefully nurses these links and commitments, e.g.

they are determined to providing technical help in situations where Zeta employees are not able to solve some tasks themselves. The personal links between Zeta and Alpha employees enable direct contact with relevant people and knowledge, thus bypassing bureaucratic information channels. Omega has also been an important source of information concerning business and customer needs, which has been decisive in the company's start-up phase.

With regard to informal agreements and unwritten laws which define a cooperation, Alpha's founders felt that they had to earn the trust of their personal Zeta relationships by rendering themselves visible and promoting their work at the various conferences. They also felt that they had to constantly meet the expectations which Zeta's employees had of them. By satisfying these expectations they believe that they have a much stronger position than other Zeta partners as they no longer have to go through the bureaucratic channels to obtain technical information. These activities of appearing at Zeta conferences and launching and promoting new Zeta-based products are a prerequisite to a quick access to information and a social norm where a partner profits from the unwritten rule that its activity is rewarded in the form of easy access to product information.

Trust has been identified as a premise for some forms of open innovation (Ågerfalk and Fitzgerald 2008). A broad innovation network, as in our case, with many partners in many forms of relations carries the risk of superficial, insufficient trust; nonetheless it is considered as having the best potential for innovation (Simard and West 2006). We observe a network where the central partners evidently found the right level of trust.

But we also find a number of examples for coopetive behaviour in the inter-organisational open innovation network. Zeta has placed Alpha under certain rules which determine which parts of the software they are allowed to customise and change in the original product. This limits their actions, but ensures that their solutions are functional and compatible even after larger changes in the versions of the standard software. Such rules delimit the implications of coopetive relationships as they state the boundaries between competition and cooperation, but these boundaries sometimes are hard to keep. Zeta has defined these boundaries in a formal, written contract which provides both sides with some certainty. However, no formal agreement exists which describes what Alpha can customise to prevent Zeta copying their customised solution; there exists only an informal agreement that Zeta does not update their software with a solution Alpha has already developed. This is however not always the case and has consequences for the life span of Alpha's products. Based on its experience with Zeta's development of identical solutions, Alpha estimates that most of its products have a lifetime of 18–24 months. Alpha therefore constantly develops new customised versions in order to survive in the market. Zeta's attempt to not develop matching solutions immediately is essential for Alpha's survival on the market and creates the kind of trust which characterises informal contracts. At the same time, Zeta expects Alpha to promote Zeta's products and contribute to Zeta's good reputation as a brand.

Opportunistic behaviour and the right balance is a challenge for the relationship of Zeta and Alpha. Zeta does not always stay within the limits of their changes when they update the original product. This creates a challenge as Alpha has to put an extra effort into their customised solutions. Alpha is aware of the risk, but they do not feel particularly negative about the situation; rather they accept it because they are conscious of the power balance which exists when they customise a larger software producer's product. So far, the situation has not had any pronounced consequences as Alpha had only to use some extra hours to secure compatibility again. Alpha sees this as a part of their living conditions. Alpha also has a dilemma: deficiencies in the CRM product are opportunities for new customised solutions which are the basis for their business. Thus, at times they delay and limit their feedback about the CRM product which Zeta asks for before they release a new version to their customers. However, given the power balance between Alpha and Zeta, mutual opportunistic behaviour will have more serious consequences for Alpha in the long term. Thus, cooperation which is beneficial for all involved parties prevails.

5.6 Conclusions and Practical Advice

Most research on open innovation focuses on one firm (Grøtnes 2009). We extend the literature on open innovation as an inter-organisational phenomenon by broadening the view from one focal firm to the relations in a network of companies which mutually contribute to the innovations which occur in the different companies. As such we contribute to the development of a theory of open IT innovation with a theoretical framework which integrates formally separate aspects of open innovation and inter-organisational networks.

This research presents an empirically grounded account and analyses a concrete case of open innovation in the IT industry.

Open innovation as enacted by the producer and customiser of the original standard software is the backbone of the customiser's existence. We demonstrate how both the original producer and the customiser innovate as a result of their mutual relationship.

In our case setting the focus has been on creating and caring for a broad network with many partners in many different forms of relations. This form of building a network despite the dangers of being short of deeper trust has the best potential for innovation in organisations (Simard and West 2006). Our practical advice thus is that this strategy is worth following.

> **Practical Tip**
>
> Open innovation takes place in inter-organisational networks. It is therefore important to
>
> 1. Create and care for a broad network with many partners in many different forms of relations
> 2. Support and nurture the informal relations of employees within and beyond organisational boundaries

5 Open Innovation in Inter-Organisational Networks in the IT Industry 87

> 3. Monitor the balance of formal contracts, informal relations and opportunistic behaviour; intervene if necessary
> 4. Search proactively for new partners
> 5. Provide occasions for knowledge sharing and community building
> 6. Afford a suitable development context with tools and an accommodating product architecture
> 7. Make stimuli available in form of partner promotion and/or financial resources

Inter-organisational networks have a significant influence on open innovation processes of the cooperating organisations. The studies of the formal and informal relations supplement each other as the formal relations in the inter-organisational network only provide limited information about the interaction which actually takes place. In our case setting the network has primarily been built on formal partnerships with a number of different companies, but the informal relations within the network are invaluable sources of knowledge. Companies should nurture the informal relations of their employees both within and beyond organisational boundaries.

We also find a complex network where, opportunistic behaviour occurs, despite formal contracts. While the mutual interest largely outweighs this behaviour, and has not led to any negative consequences for the cooperation, it has an influence on the case companies' inter-organisational network and innovation processes. Because of the limited life of its products the customising company constantly seeks and collaborates with new partners which provide it with information about new business opportunities. This pushes the company to continuously develop their solution to always be one step ahead of the producer of the original standard software. A sensible piece of advice is therefore to monitor the balance of formal contracts, informal relations and opportunistic behaviour and to intervene if necessary in order to not jeopardise open innovation initiatives.

Ways of supporting open innovation are to proactively search for new partners, provide occasions for developers to share knowledge and build communities, create a suitable development context with tools, accommodate product architecture and make stimuli available in the form of promoting innovation partners and/or financial resources. These are all schemes which successfully support open innovation, as our case setting has convincingly shown.

References

Ägerfalk, P., & Fitzgerald, B. (2008a). Outsourcing to an unknown workforce: Exploring opensourcing as a global sourcing strategy. *MIS Quarterly, 32*(2), 385–410.

Chesbrough, H. W. (2003). Open Innovation: The new imperative for creating and profiting from technology. *Boston: Harvard Business School Publishing., 20*, 888.

Chesbrough, H. W. (2006). Open innovation: A new paradigm for understanding industrial innovation. In H. Chesbrough, W. Vanhaverbeke, & J. West (Eds.), *Open innovation: Researching a new paradigm* (pp. 1–14). New York: Oxford University Press.

Coleman, J. S. (1988). Social capital in the creation of human capital. *American Journal of Sociology, 94*(6), 95–120.

Creswell, J. W. (2003). *Research design—qualitative, quantitative and mixed methods approaches* (p. 7, 69, 72, 73, 74). Thousand Oak, CA: Sage Publications.

Dyer, J., & Singh, H. (1998). The relational view: cooperative strategy and sources of inter-organisational competitive advantage. *Academy of Management Review, 23*, 660–679.

Ganguli, S. (2007). Coopetition models in the context of modern business. *Journal of Marketing Management, 6*(4), 6–16.

Feller, J., Finnegan, P., Hayes, J., & O'Reilly, P. (2009a). Information *Institutionalising information asymmetry: governance structures for open innovation. Technology & People, 22*(4), 297–316.

Gassmann, O.& Enkel, E. (2004). Towards a theory of open innovation: three core process archetypes. *In Proceedings of the R&D Management Conference*, Lisbon, Portugal, July 6–9, 2004.

Graham, S. J. H., & Mowery, D. C. (2006). The use of intellectual property in software: Implications for open innovation. In H. Chesbrough, W. Vanhaverbeke, & J. West (Eds.), *Open innovation: Researching a new paradigm* (pp. 184–204). New York: Oxford University Press.

Harland, C. M. (1996). Supply chain management: Relationships, chains and networks. *British Journal of Management, 7*, 63–80.

Germonprez, M., Hovorka, D. S., & Collopy, F. (2007). A theory of tailorable technology design. *Journal of the Association of Information Systems, 8*(6), 351–367.

Håkansson, H., & Snehota, I. (1995). *Developing relationships in business networks* (p. 1). New York: Routledge.

Grøtnes, E. (2009). Standardization as open innovation: two cases from the mobile industry. *Information Technology & People, 22*(4), 367–381.

Kuitunen, H., Jokinen, J.-P., Lassila, A., Mäkelä, M., Huurinainen, P., Maula, M., Ahokas, M., & Kontio, J. (2005). *Finnish Software Product Business: Results from the National Software Industry Survey 2005*. Centre of Expertise for Software Product Business, Tekes, Helsinki, Finland.14, 65, 67

Light, B. (2001). The maintenance implications of the customisation of ERP software. *Journal of Software Maintenance and Evolution: Research and Practice, 13*, 415–429. 63, 64.

Pollock, N., Williams, R., & Procter, R. (2003). Fitting standard software packages to non-standard organisations: The 'biography' of an enterprise-wide system. *Technology Analysis and Strategic Management, 15*(3), 317–332. 6, 11, 12.

Sawyer, S. (2000). Packaged software: Implications of the differences from custom approaches to software development. *European Journal of Information Systems, 9*, 47–58.

Scott, J. E., & Kaindl, L. (2000). Enhancing functionality in an enterprise software package. *Information and Management, 37*, 111–122.

Simard, C., & West, J. (2006). Knowledge networks and the geographic locus of innovation. In H. Chesbrough, W. Vanhaverbeke, & J. West (Eds.), *Open innovation: Researching a new paradigm* (pp. 220–240). New York: Oxford University Press.

Vanhaverbeke, W. (2006a). The interorganisational context of open innovation. In H. Chesbrough, W. Vanhaverbeke, & J. West (Eds.), *Open innovation: Researching a new paradigm* (pp. 205–219). New York: Oxford University Press.

Vanhaverbeke, W., & Cloodt, M. (2006). Open innovation in value networks. In H. Chesbrough, W. Vanhaverbeke, & J. West (Eds.), *Open innovation: Researching a new paradigm* (pp. 258–284). New York: Oxford University Press.

Van de Ven, H. A. (2007). *Engaged scholarship a guide for organisational and social research*. New York: Oxford University Press.

von Hippel, E. (1987). Cooperation between rivals: Informal knowhow trading. *Research Policy, 16*(6), 291–302. 18.

von Hippel, E. (2005). *Democratizing Innovation*. Cambridge: MIT Press, USA.

Walsham, G. (1995). Interpretive case studies in IS research: Nature and method. *European Journal of Information Systems, 4*, 74–81. 13, 90.

West, J., & Gallagher, S. (2006). Patterns of open innovation in open source software. In H. Chesbrough, W. Vanhaverbeke, & J. West (Eds.), *Open innovation: Researching a new paradigm* (pp. 82–108). New York: Oxford University Press.

Williamson, O. E. (1991). Comparative economic organisation: The analysis of discrete structural alternatives. *Administrative Science Quarterly, 36*(2), 269–296.

Yoo, Y., Lyytinen, K.& Boland, R. J. (2008). Distributed Innovation in Classes of Networks. *In Proceedings of the 41st Annual Hawaii International Conference on System Sciences.*

Theme II
Best Practices

Analysis of the Use of Open Innovation in Organisations Today in Order to Extract Best Practices

This section of the book comprises five chapters devoted to contemporary best practices derived from industrial applications of open innovation technologies. Each chapter provides different angles on open innovation and represents different industrial domains.

In the first chapter, Chap. 6, *Encouraging Open Community Innovation: Outils-Réseaux's modular approach*, Heaton et al. present a case study of Outils-Réseaux, a French group, whose mission is to encourage the development and use of collaborative tools. The aim of the chapter is to reflect on Outils-Réseaux's actions and approach to participate in community innovation, in which the community itself is an essential element of the innovation. Heaton et al. explore the co-evolution of both technical infrastructure (tools for collaboration) and the community and show how Outils-Réseaux mediates between the (social) world of users and the technical world of software developers. The success stories presented in this chapter illustrate the collective, collaborative nature of open innovation. Heaton et al. also show how innovation may emerge from local, everyday practices that produce incremental changes rather than major inventions.

The second chapter, Chap. 7, *Open Source Technology in Intra-Organisational Software Development: Private Markets or Local Libraries?* by Lindman et al., explores how two traditional software development organisations have changed their software development practices by introducing Open Source technology. The focus is on how open innovation technology, rather than open innovation as such, changes an organisation. The objective of the chapter is to understand the institutional changes that are needed and emerge from this process. Lindman et al. identify the links between the (1) emerging, yet embedded technology and (2) the underlying institutional decision-making, reward and communication structures.

The third chapter, Chap. 8, *Open Innovation: The Development of the IT Capability Maturity Framework* by Donnellan, provides insights into how the Innovation

Value Institute open innovation community (http://www.ivi.ie) has successfully implemented open innovation principles to develop a new IT Management framework. The institute has developed a framework for managing IT for business value, The IT Capability Mature Framework. This framework is being tested with leading organisations around the world. In the chapter, the framework is applied to the Intel Corporation IT organisation. The usefulness of the framework lies in its potential to organise and structure a complex portfolio of IT innovation activities in a manner that enables continuous improvement.

In the fourth chapter, Chap. 9, *Voluntary Contributors in Open Innovation Processes*, Ståhlbröst and Bergvall-Kåreborn investigate what motivates the public to participate in open innovation activities and how their participation influenced them. They found that involving contributors in innovation processes led to more knowledgeable and educated contributors keen to start using innovations. Notably, their willingness to buy, market, try or use innovations increased.

The final chapter, Chap. 10, *Creating Value through Open Innovation in Social E-learning*, by Andersson et al., explores social media-based e-learning at the Stockholm School of Economics. The project can be seen as a form of open innovation, as it combines the efforts of students, teachers, and external parties. The authors discuss how value can be created in such networks and how social media-based e-learning can be implemented and conclude by providing practical advice about how to implement social media-based e-learning.

In all, the chapters of this section underline that collaborating and networking between people, and technology infrastructures as support for these activities, are the key elements of open innovation. We can also learn that a small number of uniquely skilled innovation brokers are typically responsible for diffusing opportunities for innovation. They are essential in mediating between the users and the software developers. The use of open innovation technologies is dependent on many social factors, such as institutional decision-making, reward and communication structures. It is also evident that not only those organising open innovation projects, but also the users themselves, have become more knowledgeable and eager to start using innovations. Finally, a new perspective on open innovation is presented, labelled social media-based e-learning.

Stefan Hrastinski

Chapter 6
Encouraging Open Community Innovation: *Outils-Réseaux*'s Modular Approach

Lorna Heaton, Florence Millerand, David Delon, Florian Schmitt, Laurent Marseault, and Jessica Deschamps

Abstract Increasingly, individuals, groups and communities are participating actively in the process of technological innovation. Indeed, the novelty of Web 2.0 technologies and platforms appears to lie in the fact that the user has the possibility to produce—and not just consult—a vast array of content and tools. Users are more and more aware of their capacity for making and changing technologies, but participation does not happen automatically for most people. This chapter is a case study of *Outils-Réseaux*, a French group whose mission is to encourage the development and use of collaborative tools by associative movements. Drawing on interviews and an analysis of the content of various Wiki pages, we reflect on how *Outils-Réseaux*'s actions and approach participate in community innovation, in which the community itself is an essential element of the innovation. We explore the coevolution of both technical infrastructure (tools for collaboration) and the community, and show how *Outils-Réseaux* mediates between the (social) world of users and the technical world of software developers. We place particular emphasis on the modularity of the group's approach to illustrate how it helps reconfigure boundaries for innovation and collaboration. First, we outline *Outils-Réseaux*'s general approach and several guiding principles. We then describe several "success stories" that illustrate key elements of the approach: simplicity, modularity, user-driven innovation. We conclude with reflections on emergent, community innovation and relate our experiences to academic literature on open, collaborative innovation.

L. Heaton (✉)
Département de communication, Université de Montréal, Montréal, Québec, Canada
e-mail: lorna.heaton@umontreal.ca

F. Millerand
UQAM, Communication sociale et publique, Montreal, Quebec, Canada
e-mail: millerand.florence@uqam.ca

D. Delon • F. Schmitt • L. Marseault • J. Deschamps
Outils-Réseaux, TelaBotanica, Institut de Botanique, Montpellier, Héreault, France
e-mail: accueil@outils-reseaux.org

J.S.Z. Eriksson Lundström et al. (eds.), *Managing Open Innovation Technologies*,
DOI 10.1007/978-3-642-31650-0_6, © Springer-Verlag Berlin Heidelberg 2013

Table 6.1 Comparison of three success stories

	Saga pedo inquiry	Garrigues debates	"AnimaCoop" course
Tool(s) used	Wikini	Conceptual map	A toolbox of collaborative tools Wikini collaborative workspaces
Type of collaboration	Distributed, asynchronous	Face-to-face, real time	Both face-to-face and distant
Role of Outils-Réseaux	Development and installation of a collaborative tool	Guiding users' experience, followed by mini-training sessions	Presentation of tools Facilitating discussions Providing skeleton of workspace to be fleshed out by participants
Users' actions	Experiencing and experimenting	Experiencing Transposing the experience to reuse in other contexts	Experiencing and experimenting Transfer between projects tools used in new combinations
O-R/user interaction	Interaction with end-users mediated by the Wikini interface	Meeting facilitation, presentation of the collaborative tool	Workshops, online presence for support to participants
Outcomes	• Larger dataset of observations • Greater environmental awareness • Model for subsequent inquiries (20 underway) • Greater possibilities for individual participation and development of a shared sense of purpose	• Appreciation of other points of view • Mobilisation around the issue • Community building	• Users/trainees become designers • Multiplier effect
Key points	Simple tools enlarge the range of possibilities for individual participation	Demand-driven approach	• Modular approach assembling existing applications into a customised whole • Users are empowered to customise as their situation changes

6.1 Introduction

Open Innovation (Chesbrough 2003) is based on the premise that knowledge is widely distributed and often collaboratively produced. In order to innovate, it thus becomes important to actively scout for and use the discoveries of others. Not only

6 Encouraging Open Community Innovation: *Outils-Réseaux*'s Modular Approach

Fig. 6.1 Map of Saga observations in 2010

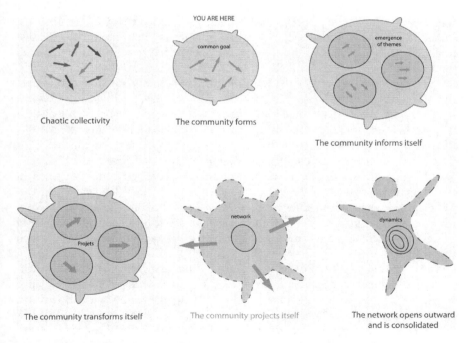

Fig. 6.2 Stages in community development

can knowledge be shared openly and freely without cost, it actually benefits from being passed around since users continually improve on it. The idea that copying, reusing and transferring collaborative tools from one situation to another will make them more robust is at the heart of the actions of Outils-Réseaux. This chapter shows how this philosophy, coupled with sustained attention to interaction with their user clients, enables the groups they work with to attract the participation of a broad community of contributors and to sustain that participation over time. Like a ripple effect with its ever-widening circles, we use three examples to show how Outils-Réseaux plants the seeds of innovation that communities then take up and sustain.

Following an ethnographic approach, we conducted 11 interviews with *Outils-Réseaux* staff and participants in the three success stories described below. We did a content analysis of various Wiki pages, documents and tools, and engaged in punctual participant observations (e.g. attending meetings) in order to understand *Outils-Réseaux*'s actions and approach to open community innovation. The association places strong emphasis on the need for reflexivity and critical reflection upon its own practices, thus four co-authors of this chapter are also members of *Outils-Réseaux*.

6.2 Outils-Réseaux: Activities and Approach

The French association *Outils-Réseaux* (http://outils-reseaux.org) began in 2003 in response to increasing demand for collaborative network tools from scientific and non-scientific communities in the fields of ecology and the environment. In 2010, *Outils-Réseaux* was at the centre of a constellation of innovative collaborative community projects, ranging from e-government projects to networks of artists to nanotechnologies.

The association has offices in Montpellier, France, and its mission is to initiate and accompany Internet-based cooperation, primarily not-for-profit associations. The five staff members provide software development services and technical support, but also training sessions on the use of collaborative tools. Most of its client organisations have been in the fields of ecology and the environment.

Drawing on elements of participatory design (Schuler and Namioka 2003), agile programming (Beck 2000; Dittrich 2002), and active pedagogy from environmental education (Perrenoud 1983), the *Outils-Réseaux* approach to development has several particularities. First and foremost, it focuses on accompanying the groups it works with, rather than simply providing technical solutions. Use of collaborative tools by a group is viewed as secondary, and subsequent, to a group's experience with cooperation.

The team is guided by its client associations' needs and group dynamics throughout the development and appropriation process. The goal is twofold: on the one hand, to help people imagine the field of possibilities and enlarge this inventory, and on the other, to put the accent on cooperation. Another defining characteristic of the *Outils-Réseaux* way is its accent on accessibility and simplicity. The team explicitly gears its actions to the "lowest common denominator" in any group, so that everyone can participate. This implies proposing the simplest possible configurations of collaborative tools and may involve masking certain functionalities, at least temporarily. Being attentive to clients' capabilities and their evolution also requires a gradual approach to increasing technical skill, as well as to learning how to work together. *Outils-*

Réseaux will typically begin by introducing a few, simple collaborative tools, and will propose more complex tools only once the people they are working with have become comfortable with the first ones. They also insist on dissociating the experience of cooperation from that of learning how to use computer applications. Thus, they will ensure that the groups they accompany acquire "small, irreversible experiences of cooperation", independently of the use of collaborative tools.

Outils-Réseaux operates according to the logic of assembling a variety of tools into custom packages that best suit the needs of particular groups. This modular "LEGO approach" allows them to customise their offer. From one group to another, *Outils-Réseaux* draws from the same general toolkit of primarily, but not exclusively, free and open source tools: wiki spaces, templates, mapping tools, shared agenda, etc. A bare-bones Wiki, called a Wikini, is used as the integrating mechanism to hold everything together. The Wikini is integrated with the Bazaar (the name is a reference to Raymond's (1999) work on the Cathedral and Bazaar), an easy-to-use relational database manager that enables management of histories and facilitates linking of resources across the Web, and thus scalability. Finally, despite this pick-and-choose approach, *Outils-Réseaux* insists on a graphic identity and the integration of the various modules, so that users are not immediately conscious of switching between applications. Use and user experience become the primary considerations.

> **Practical Tip**
>
> A clear graphic identity will ensure the fluidity and coherence between various modules or applications and limit confusion by users. An attractive interface will also help motivate users to want to use and explore the various parts of the site.

In short, *Outils-Réseaux* works from a *logic of attention* rather than a *logic of intention*. Staff propose conceptual and technical tools in ways that promote sustainability: starting small and simple, encouraging their clients to reflect on their practices and to ask questions, enlarging the inventory of possibilities gradually, facilitating use and appropriation.

6.3 Three "Success Stories"

This section contains examples of *Outils-Réseaux*'s actions in three different projects. Each of them highlights a particular aspect of the organisation's approach: keeping things simple, dissociating the experience of cooperation from learning about collaborative tools and modularity.

6.3.1 Focus on Simplicity: Observing the Cricket Saga

The Observatoire Naturaliste des Ecosystèmes Méditerranéens (ONEM) is a highly decentralised non-profit association based on the principles of open access and collective action. Founded in 2003 with the goal of providing a space in which to bring together anyone and everyone interested in the Mediterranean environment, ONEM's first concrete action (in 2004) was to launch an inquiry and call for observations of the *Saga pedo,* a very large, carnivorous cricket, also known as the predatory bush cricket. This insect is on the French, European and IUCN lists of threatened species, but largely unknown in France (a 2003 atlas edited by the French National Natural History Museum (MNHN) had reported only 72 sightings in France). ONEM printed and distributed 4,000 leaflets and established an Internet site for collecting and sharing observations (http://saga.onem-france.org). In just a year, the number of observations reported increased fivefold. Still active in 2010, the inquiry has gathered over 1,000 observations from more than 500 different contributors, principally in the French Mediterranean region.

The project is run on a voluntary basis, with a coordinator and a scientific and technical committee of about ten people. It requires very little money and a limited amount of technical know-how by contributors. *Outils-Réseaux* helped ONEM establish the Internet site, which is based on a Wikini with a cartography module. They also organised a database manager and a system for managing the photo gallery. The inquiry also uses email and a Yahoo discussion list.

Beyond the interest of the data it generated, which has been integrated into several biodiversity inventories, ONEM's *Saga* inquiry has been important in raising citizens' awareness of their natural surroundings. It allows them to participate directly in an interactive science program (dynamic mapping and database on a wiki platform). The system of data editing allows ongoing, permanent visualisation of all the information transmitted by contributors. Users write directly on the page and they see their contribution immediately, both in textual form and transposed onto a map. Data validation is thus permanent and collective: any user or participant can question information that he or she considers doubtful by adding a commentary to the observation or by contacting the inquiry's coordinator. It takes place upstream of traditional scientific validation of data (steering committee or validation criteria specific to the species).

The *Saga* inquiry has served as a model for other inquiries by ONEM (about 20 inquiries on various species of insect, animal or plant are underway). This innovative manner of collecting and validating data has proved to be a powerful enabling mechanism. While citizen science sites are becoming increasingly popular, the vast majority of them ask citizens to contribute observations that are validated by a committee before being accepted and posted. The *Saga* inquiry shows how putting technologies in the hands of ordinary people enlarges the range of possibilities for individual participation. Collaborative technologies can also help develop a shared sense of purpose and even a sense of community, as the next success story illustrates.

6.3.2 Small Irreversible Experiences of Cooperation: "Where Have All the Garrigues Gone?"

The garrigues in the south of France near Nîmes and Montpellier is a region of hundreds of thousands of hectares of arid land threatened by urban expansion, the abandonment of agriculture and fire. Despite a high degree of biodiversity and fantastic scenery, there has been little discussion about how to guarantee a future for this region. The Ecologistes de l'Euzière, an environmental education association, decided to raise this question through an itinerant exhibition coupled with field expeditions and a series of public debates.

In organising these debates on "Where have all the garrigues gone?" the facilitators sought a way to go beyond traditional oppositions between hunters and ecologists, newcomers to the region and natives, scientists and poets. *Outils-Réseaux* suggested that they record the comments of all participants in real time, using FreePlane to note them in mind maps (heuristic maps) and displaying them for everyone to see on a large screen. Over 500 people took part in more than 80 debates.

After a few minutes of initial surprise, a number of "map effects" started to take form:

- Ideas were not repeated: they were now visible on screen and formed a sort of collective memory of what had been said.
- Seen side by side, oppositions were highlighted.
- The branches of the map that could be opened up or collapsed allowed participants to focus on one or another aspect of the debate, without fear of losing the rest of the larger picture.
- Regular syntheses by looking back over the emerging collectively produced map enabled the debates to progress.
- As concepts were organised, arguments and problems became visible.
- With everyone's positions and ideas visible at a glance to all, groups started working on what unites them, rather than focusing on their differences.

At the end of a debate, participants were often proud of what they had produced together: "we did a good job", "finally, a productive debate", "we have some pretty good ideas". They had undergone a "small irreversible experience of cooperation". They had thought in a different way, collectively, and had learned something without initially realising it. What is more, they had appreciated the experience and wanted to repeat it.

Then came the inevitable question: what tool was it that enabled the facilitators to take notes in spider form like that, and could they learn to use it? It transpired that:

- The mayor would like to use it in the municipal council meetings
- The association president saw its potential for making association meetings more dynamic
- Some would like to use it for brainstorming
- Others saw its possibilities for organising a more complex project

The facilitators were waiting for this. With the advantages of a collaborative approach accepted, and the recognition that expertise is not always individual, participants were ready to learn how to repeat the experience in other situations. It was the facilitators' cue to provide a mini-training session on four basic functions of the FreePlane software that would let participants start using this free, open source software.

> **Practical Tip**
>
> Whet the appetite of the people you want to train. Start simply and wait for participants to ask for more. They will be more motivated to learn if they have not only seen what can be done with a particular tool, but are also convinced of its usefulness to them.

The garrigues debates clearly illustrate *Outils-Réseaux*'s on-demand approach and its sensitivity to group dynamics.

6.3.3 Modularity: Networking Local Pockets of Innovation

In 2010, *Outils-Réseaux* prepared an "education in action" programme on facilitating collaborative projects. Funded primarily by the French government, the programme was first delivered in Brest[1] to a group of 12 participants, all of whom were working as community organisers in local communities or with special groups such as youth or various social movements. Many were already exploring computer applications on their own and were seeking to consolidate or acquire more systematic knowledge of collaborative applications, particularly how these tools could be brought to bear in their work. Beyond their interest in collaboration and collaborative tools, one of the prerequisites for participation was to have a specific project in mind that would serve as a test bed for applying the course content.

The programme proposed an original delivery format—a combination of periodic two-day face-to-face workshops, online support and time and space for experimentation, and was held together with a Wiki platform. In terms of content, the course was designed so that participants would learn about cooperation and collaboration, with or without collaborative tools. They experienced all the stages in the life cycle of a network as they themselves worked together over several

---

[1] Brest is well known for its focus on local capacity building, project-based organisation of community development initiatives and an extended network of multimedia and IT animators and facilitators.

6 Encouraging Open Community Innovation: *Outils-Réseaux*'s Modular Approach

months. They learned about collaborative tools by trying to collaborate in real situations using them. In particular, they learned about:

- Forming the community: individual presentations and definition of what brings them together—in this case facilitating collaborative projects
- Informing the community: exchanges around each other's projects, leading to the emergence of common experiences and problems
- Transforming the community: working collaboratively, either in small groups or as one group
- Making the community visible: diffusing the results of cooperative work outside the community
- Consolidating community: evaluating and reflecting on how to keep the dynamics going and on opening it to others

The first two-day workshop took participants through stages 1 and 2 as they explored notions of cooperation, making each other's and the group's actions visible, as well as several collaborative tools. Participants then organised themselves into four small groups. These groups worked together on common themes using various collaborative tools for about 3 h per week with online support as required from the facilitators. Each participant also spent several hours each week transposing and testing the week's content in his or her particular project. This experience nourished the group discussions and the negotiation of shared understandings. In working together to try out different tools and apply various concepts, and in sharing their experiences in their respective individual projects, participants tested their assumptions and thought through the different ways that a given collaborative application might help a group. Sharing of experiences served to multiply tacit knowledge across projects as well as to anchor it more deeply. Each group posted a weekly progress report detailing what they had explored, how they had organised themselves and any difficulties they had experienced.

> **Practical Tip**
>
> Groups working together for the first time should ideally meet face-to-face. They need time to get to know each other and feel comfortable. This group feeling can then be carried over into online environments.

The course was held together by an online group space, organised with a Wikini. The AnimaCoop space (http://www.animacoop.net) integrated the course components and resources: content, calendar, instructions, interns' and facilitators' self-presentations, etc., all of which were visible to the entire group. There were also links to various tools and examples of their use in other situations, and spaces that were *constructed collectively* during the course: a concept box (for developing a common understanding of key concepts), jargon box (glossary), idea box, question box (FAQ), etc. The site was thus organised according to principles of transparency (anyone could view any page of either the standard course content or the production of other groups and participants), modularity and flattened hierarchy. Each group also developed a workspace that was accessible through the Wikini and modifiable by anyone. Particular attention was paid to supporting and recording the group process (posting meeting notes taken on Etherpad, heuristic maps or the collaborative construction of shared vocabularies, for example). Thus, in addition to learning about cooperation, the participants were also learning how to use collaborative tools effectively.

Participants' individual projects were a major component of the programme. Through the AnimaCoop site, *Outils-Réseaux* installed some simple collaborative tools—or links to tools—in order to encourage experimentation. Participants were able to select the most relevant or most interesting and combine them in various ways to fit the needs of their specific projects. This allowed them to apply what they were learning in the programme to their projects immediately, and to be able to ask the training staff questions as they arose. They were thus involved in action at the same time as they were learning concepts, thus facilitating the consolidation of the experience. This back and forth between action and reflection is a key element of active pedagogy, which stresses autonomy, reflexivity and collaboration.

Modularity is in evidence in the AnimaCoop training at several levels. First, there is the modularity of combinations of simple tools that formed both the course content and its delivery method. Second, there is the modularity and scaffolding as participants experimented with different collaborative tools in their own projects. *Outils-Réseaux*'s modular approach accentuates the malleability of collaborative ICT spaces and highlights the active role of individuals, groups and communities in shaping innovation to fit their needs and according to their constraints. In assembling tools to meet the needs of their individual projects, AnimaCoop participants became designers in their own right. This supports the observation that with Web 2.0 platforms and collaborative tools in particular, the conventional distinction between designers and users tends to dissolve (Mackay et al. 2000; Millerand and Baker 2010).

> **Practical Tip**
>
> A modular approach allows for multiple combinations that can be adjusted to fit the needs of individual situations.

Finally, the AnimaCoop training reflects a modular structure at a social level. Participants produced local pockets of innovation. In addition to providing an opportunity for group facilitators to reflect on their practices and explore collaborative tools, AnimaCoop was designed to take advantage of the multiplicity of locally initiated projects in the municipality of Brest. It explicitly brought these individuals together and provided a space for them to meet and discuss common interests. This is in keeping with the City of Brest's strategy of creating synergies between projects and individuals. Local pockets of innovation are the starting point, but there is a multiplier effect in networking them.

6.4 Cross-Case Analysis

Our three success stories have several things in common. First, they all illustrate the active role of ordinary users in appropriating the collaborative tools that are proposed. Despite their expertise in software development, *Outils-Réseaux* has made a conscious choice to strive for simplicity in the tools it proposes. Users are viewed as active participants who are trying to accomplish something, and the tools are just that—tools. They are there to serve a purpose, whether it is for entering naturalist observations, encouraging discussion or developing a feeling of belonging in a group. The tools should not get in the way. Keeping things as simple as possible has two important implications for open innovation. First, it enlarges the basin of potential contributors to innovation by minimising the technical challenges they may face. Second, users who feel in control of the platforms and tools will also feel capable. Feelings of empowerment should encourage adhesion to community projects at the same time that the range of possibilities for individual participation is enlarged.

In the garrigues and AnimaCoop examples, we observe *Outils-Réseaux*'s keen attention to group dynamics and its desire to be led by the group's needs and rhythm. This runs counter to much of the literature on user/developer interactions where developers tend to take control and lead, if not control, the process. The *Outils-Réseaux* developers and trainers try to fade into the background. They strive to be attentive and reactive, but the appropriation/use process is squarely in the users' hands—either individually or as a group. This is reflected in the attitude of proposing and then waiting to see what happens. No one knew in advance what would happen when they began to work with the garrigues debates, or how the participants in the training programme would react to the different tools proposed. In fact, different working groups picked up on different tools and combinations, and they used them to different ends. Coherence within a user-driven approach implies that different rhythms and selective appropriation of tools are expected and accepted.

Selective appropriation and use would be much more difficult to manage were it not for *Outils-Réseaux*'s modular approach. In a building block approach, bricks can be assembled in different ways without compromising the integrity of whatever structure results. Different packages of tools can be assembled into a customised whole. What is more, when combined with a user-driven approach, the users themselves can do the customising. The user/developer divide tends to dissolve as users take up tools, improve upon them and pass them on. This is precisely what has been happening in the AnimaCoop programme, as the participants return to their roles as local community organisers and implement some of the things they have learned. In terms of implications for open innovation, when the possibility for evolution is designed into the process and the system, it increases the ability to deal with incremental changes in a situation. This opens the possibility for viewing innovation as an ongoing phenomenon rather than one of radical rupture. Providing the flexibility needed to deal with evolution may, in turn, further enable innovative behaviour.

Finally, *Outils-Réseaux* is working on two fronts that, together, encourage open innovation. The infrastructural support for collaboration (the tools and the way they are assembled) that it promotes reflects values of openness and transparency, and make both direct (*Saga pedo* inquiry, garrigues debates) and indirect (AnimaCoop) reference to the collaborative, constructed nature of knowledge. *Outils-Réseaux* also accords much importance to reflecting on experiences with its client organisations. Contacts are frequent and often informal. This sharing of experiences helps anchor knowledge as well as to multiply it.

6.5 Implications for Research: From Modularity to Open Community Innovation

Open collaborative innovation projects involve users and others who share both the work of generating a design and the results of their individual and collective efforts openly. Each contributing user innovator does some fraction of the work, but can rely on others to do the rest. Everyone involved obtains the value of the entire design.

Baldwin and von Hippel (2009) note that modularity is important for collaboration in design because separate modules can be worked on independently and in parallel, without intense ongoing communication across modules. When projects are small, each contributor's activities are relatively "transparent" to his or her collaborators. Larger projects can be divided up and reassembled. Quick, low-cost communication as enabled by the Internet, and ease of use—as enabled by the Wikini and the simple technologies promoted by *Outils-Réseaux*—are essential for ensuring coordination in open collaborative innovation. This is in fact the pattern observed in successful open source projects and other forums of open collaborative innovation (Raymond 1999; Franke and Shah 2003; Baldwin et al. 2006). Using the modular design architecture as a means of coordinating their work, a collaborative group can develop an innovative design that is many times larger in scale than any single member of the group could manage alone. The *Saga* inquiry clearly illustrates the possibilities of many people working together in a loosely connected way to produce something of value to the entire group. It also illustrates the importance of innovation by ordinary users.

Innovations by users form an important aspect of open innovation and in some respects the most radical part of it. While user innovation has been systematically examined for some time, much of the research has focused on lead users (von Hippel 2005) and on asymmetries in information and power between developers and users. A focus on lead users and widely recognised inventions may only address part of users' relevant innovativeness, however. The success stories presented in this chapter illustrate the collective, collaborative nature of open innovation. They also show how innovation may emerge from local, everyday practices that produce incremental changes, rather than major inventions. *Outils-Réseaux*'s goal is to put collaborative tools, and thus power, in the hands of ordinary users. In the case of the *Saga* inquiry, individual users produced not only a considerable body of knowledge, but also a community through their actions. In the garrigues debates, participants became aware of new ways of organising themselves as they experienced collective intelligence. In the AnimaCoop training, participants became designers as they assembled collaborative tools for their groups' use.

We suggest that the concept of *community innovation* (van Oost et al. 2009) can be useful in describing the type of emergent, user-initiated project in which the community itself is an essential element of the innovation. *Outils-Réseaux* leads the groups they accompany to understand their project as an evolving entity, shaped by the activities of a community of actors who, with collaborative tools, are simultaneously users and producers. *Outils-Réseaux* mediates between the social world of users and the technical world of software developers. The concept of community innovation addresses the interrelation between social actors and the technical tools and contextual elements surrounding them. It also focuses attention on the evolving nature of a project. Outils-Réseaux aims at training and accompanying users so they can be autonomous. Empowering the user clients is at the heart of *Outils-Réseaux* approach.

Merkel et al. (2005) suggest that collaborative tools may be particularly appropriate for the types of activities carried out by community groups. In promoting conceptual and technical tools that enlarge the range of possibilities and give communities greater control over the use of technology in their organisations, *Outils-Réseaux* is working towards the sustainability of community innovations. The process is dynamic in the sense that a group's composition, expectations and priorities evolve as they experience collaboration and gain experience (and confidence) with collaborative technologies. *Outils-Réseaux*'s accent on simplicity, its toolkit approach (Franke and Schreier 2002), its actions in a boundary spanning between users/developers (Fleming and Waguespack 2007) and its leadership/animation activities thus position it as facilitator of community innovation at the local level. The ultimate goal remains to encourage an emerging civil society in which ordinary citizens become more and more actively involved in shaping their technical and social environments.

Acknowledgments This research was funded by the Social Sciences and Humanities Research Council (SSHRC) of Canada.

References

Baldwin, C. Y. & von Hippel, E. (2009) Modeling a Paradigm Shift: From Producer Innovation to User and Open Collaborative Innovation. MIT Sloan School Working Paper 4764-09 Retrieved from http://ssrn.com/abstract=1502864 (May 10, 2010)

Baldwin, C. Y., Hienerth, C., & von Hippel, E. (2006). How user innovations become commercial products: A theoretical investigation and a case study. *Research Policy, 35*(9), 1291–1313.

Beck, K. (2000). *Extreme programming explained: Embrace change.* Boston: Addison-Wesley.

Chesbrough, H. W. (2003). *Open innovation.* Boston, MA: Harvard Business School Press.

Dittrich, Y. (2002). Doing empirical research on software development: Finding a path between understanding, intervention, and method development. In Y. Dittrich, C. Floyd, & R. Klischewski (Eds.), *Social thinking-software practice.* Cambridge, MA: MIT Press.

Fleming, L., & Waguespack, D. M. (2007). Brokerage, boundary spanning, and leadership in open innovation communities. *Organisation Science, 18*(2), 165–180.

Franke, N., & Schreier, M. (2002). Entrepreneurial opportunities with toolkits for user innovation and design. *International Journal on New Media Management, 4*(4), 225–234.

Franke, N., & Shah, S. (2003). How communities support innovative activities: An exploration of assistance and sharing among end-users. *Research Policy, 32*(1), 157–178.

Mackay, H., Carne, C., Benyon-Davies, P., & Tudhope, D. (2000). Reconfiguring the user: Using rapid application development. *Social Studies of Science, 30*(5), 737–57.

Millerand, F., & Baker, K. S. (2010). Who are the users? Who are the developers? Webs of users and developers in the development process of a technical standard. *Information Systems Journal, 20*(2), 137–161.

Merkel, C. B., Clitherow, M., Farooq, U., Xiao, L., Ganoe, C. H., Carroll , J. M. & Rosson, M. B. (2005) Sustaining computer use and learning in community computing contexts: Making technology part of "who they are and what they do." *Journal of Community Informatics, 1(2).* Retrieved from http://ci-journal.net/index.php/ciej/article/view/215/173 (May 10, 2010)

Perrenoud, P. (1983) La pratique pédagogique entre l'improvisation réglée et bricolage. *Éducation & Recherche*, n° 2, 198-212 (republished in Perrenoud, P. (1994) *La formation des enseignants entre théorie et pratique*, Paris, L'Harmattan, 21–41).

Raymond, E. (1999). *The cathedral and the bazaar: Musings on Linux and open source by an accidental revolutionary*. Sebastopol, CA: O'Reilly.

Schuler, D., & Namioka, A. (2003). *Participatory design: Principles and practices*. Hillsdale, NJ: Lawrence Erlbaum Associates.

Van Oost, E., Verhaegh, S., & Oudshoorn, N. (2009). From innovation community to community innovation: User-initiated innovation in wireless Leiden. *Science, Technology and Human Values, 34*(2), 182–205.

von Hippel, E. (2005). *Democratizing innovation*. Cambridge, MA: MIT Press.

Further Reading

Hyssalo, S. (2009). User innovation and everyday practices: Micro-innovation in sports industry development. *R&D Management, 39*(3), 247–258.

von Hippel, E. (2001). Innovation by user communities: Learning from open-source software. *MIT Sloan Management Review, 42*(4), 82–86.

von Hippel, E., & von Krogh, G. (2003). Open source software and the 'private-collective' innovation model: Issues for organisation science. *Organisation Science, 14*(2), 209–223.

Chapter 7
Open Source Technology in Intra-Organisational Software Development—Private Markets or Local Libraries

Juho Lindman, Mikko Riepula, Matti Rossi, and Pentti Marttiin

Abstract This chapter explores how two organisations have changed their software development practices by introducing Open Source technology. Our aim is to understand the institutional changes that are needed in, and emerge, from this process. This chapter develops a conceptualisation building on the insights of entrepreneurial institutionalism, concentrating on the changing relationships of organisational groups in the areas of decision-making, rewarding and communication. We identify the links between the (1) emerging, yet embedded technology and (2) the underlying institutional decision-making, reward and communication structures. We move the Open Source 2.0 research agenda forward by concentrating empirical work on the nuances of institutional change that open source brings about in large hierarchical organisations. We will discuss the appropriateness of internal accounting organised according to the principle of an open market vs. a local library. We believe that both of these metaphors can support innovation, but different groups will find different approaches more appealing.

J. Lindman (✉)
Hanken School of Economics, Helsinki, Finland
e-mail: juho.lindman@hanken.fi

M. Riepula
Aalto University School of Economics/CKIR, Helsinki, Finland
e-mail: mikko.riepula@aalto.fi

M. Rossi • P. Marttiin
Aalto University School of Economics, Helsinki, Finland
e-mail: matti.rossi@aalto.fi; pentti.marttiin@nsn.com

J.S.Z. Eriksson Lundström et al. (eds.), *Managing Open Innovation Technologies*,
DOI 10.1007/978-3-642-31650-0_7, © Springer-Verlag Berlin Heidelberg 2013

7.1 Introduction

The topic of this chapter is how *open innovation technology,* rather than *open innovation* as such, changes an organisation. We study the institutional transformation caused by the introduction of Open Source Software (OSS) technology (practices and tools) within traditional software development organisations.[1] OSS literature often assumes a "bazaar" of development in a virtual organisation characterised by loose control, openness and community orientation. However, inside a single large organisation, where contributions come from employees or subcontractors, the setting is different. The companies introduce OSS practices and foster the creation of communities to serve their business needs, that is, to create quality products. Such arrangements often imply a looser structure, more open documentation, feedback from the user community and the introduction of agile practices. These developments are corroborated by business arguments of partial outsourcing to the developer community, cost savings from using common (sometimes external OSS) platforms and the possibility of creating industry standards through a wide availability of the finished products.

The phenomenon is important because open source technologies (1) are adopted in large organisations based only on a partial understanding of the nature of the institutional change they enable, drive or necessitate, and (2) are not adopted in organisations because their consequences are seen to include unnecessary or unknown risks. We believe that building a conceptualisation based on extensive fieldwork will enable a better evaluation of these technologies and their contextual appropriateness.

Therefore, our research questions are:

- How can the introduction of open innovation technologies, such as OSS technologies, be leveraged to improve development practices?
- What are the institutional effects of these changes?

To answer these questions, we analyse two cases of OSS technology being introduced within a large corporation. Our goal is to build a conceptualisation of what happens in a hierarchical systems development organisation when OSS

---

[1] We use the terms "OSS-style development" and "OSS practices" synonymously, encompassing "OSS technologies" as a form of open innovation technologies. Our main interest is how these can be used within companies developing products, not necessarily OSS as such. By "OSS technologies" we do not mean the licence of the developed software, but the common infrastructural tools used in OSS communities. The tools include concurrent versioning systems, issue trackers, email-driven and archived communication, and web presence, which all support software development practices similar to OSS in creative commons, but in our cases within a single organisation.

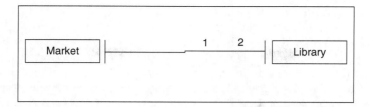

Fig. 7.1 Relative positions on continuum between a market and a library

technology is adopted.[2] Based on institutional theory (Scott 2001; Greenwood and Hinings 1996), we seek to identify the inertia caused by old institutional forces and the changes in reward structure and the developer and manager mindset needed to realise the benefits of more open development.

This chapter is organised as follows. In the second section, we review relevant literature on OSS technology in commercial organisations. In the third section, we develop a conceptualisation to explain the transformation. The fourth section is about the research approach used. Case findings then demonstrate the links between the embedded technology decision-making and communication and reward structures. In the final section, we conclude how OSS technology is leveraged in the case companies' systems development and identify the accompanying institutional changes.

7.2 OSS Technologies in Commercial Organisations

OSS technologies have been successfully implemented in different organisations and OSS-style development based on distributed and global practices has gained industrial credibility (Fitzgerald 2006). OSS as such is used more and more as an integral part of all kinds of products. OSS development is often characterised by a modular software architecture, distributed global development teams, meritocracy, voluntarism, often elaborate decision-making mechanisms and the technical and legal openness of the code which enables code inspection, bug reporting and maintenance (Fitzgerald 2006). OSS as such is traditionally defined as software licenced under an OSI-approved software licence (Välimäki 2005). OSS practices are practices that emulate development in an OSS community (technical infrastructure enabling communication, reward structures, supporting work and knowledge transfer). OSS practices often include the use of email (and the archives thus

---

[2] One of the main reasons for companies to adopt OSS technology is their interest in improving software reuse. At the same time, companies are adopting distributed and virtual teamwork practices and changing their software development processes from waterfall to iterative, thus adopting agile practises (about traditional, agile and open source practises in Barnett 2004). These two changes favour the adoption of OSS tools, but failed to address the challenge of reuse.

available) as the primary communication tool, availability of the code from a source code repository via concurrent versioning system (CVS) or similar, web presence (e.g. SourceForge) and some kind of issue tracker. The main difference between traditional (closed source) and OSS development is that the latter can sustain non-commercial communities as the source code is available to all. The source code might belong to its developer or the community in a way that prevents traditional software licence sales (Dahlander and Magnusson 2005). However, the availability of the source code outside the organisation is not a prerequisite in implementing practices similar to OSS, which are limited to inside a company (Fitzgerald 2006).

Inner source (van der Linden et al. 2009; Lindman et al. 2008) and corporate source (Dinkelacker et al. 2002) as terms refer to OSS practices limited inside companies. Often the introduction of OSS-style development starts with these tools, but as "tools are not only tools" their productive application might require fundamental changes in software development (Sharma et al. 2002). Inside a large organisation (Wesselius 2008; Gurbani et al. 2010) or in a business-to-business setting (Fink 2003) the fundamental differences between OSS and traditional software are smaller than inside small software companies. The licence and corporate policies and processes define how software is acquired, procured, installed, used, maintained and discarded. Furthermore, company guidelines, contracts and/or licences also define how software is developed, remuneration acquired and benefits divided (Välimäki 2005).

In the first phase of OSS commercialisation, companies were interested in ways to directly benefit from the revenue stream created by OSS (Rajala et al. 2006). OSS research has traditionally focused more on individual motivations of the developers and community-driven development than OSS in hierarchical organisations (Stol and Babar 2009). Now in the second phase of OSS commercialisation, the use of OSS-style development processes is gaining a foothold in large commercial organisations (Gurbani et al. 2010; Fitzgerald 2006; Santos 2008).

7.3 Conceptual Framework

Organisations are struggling to balance the possibilities offered by OSS technology, but research efforts have only recently started to focus more on organisational issues in large hierarchical organisations. We draw on literature streams of institutional theory and focus on entrepreneurial institutionalism to understand the phenomenon in organisational context.

7.3.1 Institutional Theory

Institutional theory views institutions as *"multifaceted, durable social structures, made up of symbolic elements, social activities, and material resources"* (Scott

2001, p. 49). Institutional structures, such as reward and communication structures, are set up by regulative, normative and cultural elements or pillars (Scott 2001). Institutional theory (Powell and DiMaggio 1991) has been accommodated to explain change (Greenwood and Hinings 1996), even though it has been criticised for mainly focusing on "convergence" (similarity). It should be noted that institutional theory is far from a monolithic tradition (for a more thorough discussion about "old" and "new" institutionalism, see Powell and DiMaggio 1991; Greenwood and Hinings 1996).

Institutional theory underlines the "relationship" between an organisation's normative context and the varying interests of the groups (stakeholders) within the organisation. Functionally, different groups in organisations are not neutral towards each other, but instead the technical boundaries of the groups are reinforced cognitively (Greenwood and Hinings 1996). Our conceptual framework draws on institutional theory (Scott 2001) and social constructionism by analysing the concept of an "organising vision" (Swanson and Ramiller 1997). There are tensions between the traditions of institutionalism and social constructionism, but as Scott (2001) notes "choice [in organisations] is informed and constrained by the ways in which knowledge is constructed..." We posit that while normally the actors and proponents of organisational change truly subscribe to OSS inspired values for the better, "the OSS spirit", they are also renegotiating the exact meaning of OSS to fit the organisational context. These negotiations can be understood better by analysing the term "OSS" as a justification for organisational change. The exact meaning of adapted OSS is renegotiated and implies changes in the allocation of resources and the division of work between units.

7.3.2 Entrepreneurial Institutionalism

Research in institutionalism, which focuses on change, is called entrepreneurial institutionalism. It is a response to the call for institutional theory to focus more on agency and organisational change (Garud et al. 2007). Work on institutions has traditionally focused on continuity (Garud et al. 2007, p. 960). In contrast, work on entrepreneurship has focused on change. In institutional theory, this contrast of structure and agency has been identified as the paradox of embedded agency (Dimaggio and Powell 1991). One solution to this paradox is to view structures as platforms for change rather than constraints (Garud and Karnøe 2003).

Any new technology is a change in the status quo, with winners and losers. The meaning of organisational visions (Swanson and Ramiller 1997) is renegotiated within the boundaries of a certain language community and draw on local discursive resources. OSS technology is an organisational tool that stresses local issues regarding software production in the context of a certain organisation. OSS also provides ways of addressing these issues. It can be seen as a metaphor used in an organisation that is making sense of its changing business environment so that it is able to operate in it. OSS often offers a promise of a more agile development approach, more contribution, more open discussion and less hierarchy in software development. In short, it gives certain justifications, reasoning and opportunities to a decision-maker faced with difficult decisions concerning reorganisation or introducing a new organisational innovation (Van de Ven 1993).

We use the institutional entrepreneurship lens to identify how the meaning of OSS technology changed during implementation and how our two organisations evolved when OSS technology was institutionalised. We aim to provide insight on the process of OSS technology institutionalisation and the underlying changes. In order to explain the institutionalisation of OSS technology, we focus on three structures within the companies: the reward, decision-making and communication structures. However, we do not claim that these would be easily separated entities.

We chose the different organisational groups to highlight their different interest and incentives in the process. The different selected groups (stakeholders) are (1) the technology provider unit (the central group), (2) the technology user unit (business unit) and (3) the developer/users.

7.4 Research Approach

The nature of our research problem, human behaviour and interaction led us to use a qualitative research approach (Seaman 1999; Klein and Myers 1999). We chose a case study approach and adopted the principles of interpretive case studies.

> **Practical Tip**
>
> When planning organisational changes, understanding the current situation makes transitions processes smoother. This is especially true when a specific technology related to innovations is being adapted. Identifying and mobilising the different stakeholders require on-site research of the different organisational groups involved.

We applied semi-structured thematic interviews as the main data collection method. Two to three people per case organisation were interviewed on three occasions over two-year intervals to better capture the nuances of the changing organisation. We stopped interviewing after the 14th interview, because recent interviews did not convey additional information regarding the actual events. Research design can thus be considered longitudinal. The first interviews were gathered in 2006 and the second round of interviews was conducted in 2008. The final round took place between 2010 and 2011. Most interviews lasted about 1 h.

The interviewees represented three different organisational groups, one person from the service provider group, one from the service user group and—except for the last round—one from the developer/user group. We chose managerial respondents from the business and central groups to gain an understanding of the management rationale for introducing OSS technology. The developers were included to bring in the user viewpoint.

One of the researchers works in one of the case companies and was therefore able to provide access to the organisation and, as a "native", reflect on the organisational context. We were very careful to eliminate any bias this connection might bring to the setting. In addition, we used secondary data obtained in the course of the industry research project, such as project descriptions, manuals, portal usage data, documentation and visits to the sites to familiarise ourselves with the setting.

In the first two rounds, we analysed the interviews by first recounting the organisational history and change as described by the respondents. We circulated the transcribed interviews back to the respondents, so they could correct the views should they have been misinterpreted. The last round mainly focused on what had changed since the previous rounds of interviews.

The systematic analyses were based on pattern matching recurring themes between different interviews and then categorising the data according to the themes.

The themes we focused on were how the respondents talked about (1) instituting new technology, (2) changes in the communication media and the reward structures between units and individuals and (3) changes in the different ways the respondents described their group involvement. The authors extracted all the instances where the respondents talked about the themes and reported their findings.

We classified the findings into three areas: (1) how OSS technology is renegotiated to fit the organisational context and how OSS infrastructural tools are used inside companies, (2) how the respondents saw the change between business units and central unit and (3) how the respondents described the reward, decision-making and communication structures as both a platform and driver of change.

7.5 Cases

The two cases were selected among the partner companies of the ITEA-COSI project, which also set the context and enabled access to the case companies. ITEA-COSI was a joint academic and industrial project focused on software commodification.

7.5.1 Philips Inner Source

The offering of Philips Healthcare (PH) consists of a wide variety of medical systems, for example, X-ray technology, ultrasound, magnetic resonance and information management. The factory-pre-installed software is customised and configured, but not sold separately. PH normally maintains the software for 10 years, which often leads to a large installed base and makes large changes very complicated. PH is maintaining and developing a large software base including a set of software components reused in all business units.

Historically, components were developed in a central software group (Wesselius 2008). In this configuration, it was difficult to manage the different development activities and unaligned roadmaps. Lack of required domain knowledge in the central group made asset reuse difficult.

To solve these two issues, the business units started to contribute to developing new software assets. This would enable the business unit with the best domain knowledge to develop the software and then add it to a shared portfolio. Business units would not have to wait for the central group to develop the (often rushed and high priority) asset. OSS technology (tools and practices) was introduced in PH to legitimate the change.

The division of work was based on the idea that the central group was responsible for the common platform and business units to develop add-ons, customise and configure the software. Components are distributed via intranet, email, ftp and CD. Business units choose the components for use, customisation and configuration. Different groups offer services to each other (e.g. support and maintenance) based on agreements between internal customers. Developed software was also made available to other business units. One of the main benefits of a common platform is that it would avoid duplicate work and promote the reuse of software. Co-development activities with business units and central group were favoured in order to benefit from organisational learning.

There were also certain risks involved mainly dealing with the distributed setting. The central group would become more dependent on several business units at the same time. The overall quality would be more difficult to control, if business units only made stand-alone add-ons. Business unit incentives were also un-aligned, as it seems that there is no guarantee that units would actually contribute back and not only use the resulting code. This applies also to the maintenance of the software asset and balancing the maintenance between business units. The scenario where one business unit is putting a lot of resources and effort into development and maintenance, but all the business units would use the outcome was considered problematic.

The communication plan was to be as explicit as possible and share information with all the interested parties. Co-development activities required informal discussions between developers, but broader issues were decided in formal settings, such as steering groups and operational teams. There were also formal architect meetings and a monthly platform group meeting in which all interested parties could participate. Information was also posted on the intranet and PH mailing lists. Marketers who were chosen per business unit acted as a back channel of communication to gather feedback in case of problems. Development work is somewhat controlled by steering groups and operational meetings, but development was mainly driven by business groups which need new functionality.

A few years ago, a new scheme was developed for sharing the development costs. The old model was based on centralised component development and a component tax where the central group did not have profit targets (Wesselius 2008). The central group performed maintenance of the components. The component tax levied from business units was based on component development and maintenance activities and on an agreed upon roadmap on a yearly basis. Based on the relative amount of component usage and the size of the unit's external sales, the estimated costs were then distributed among the business units. Users of old component versions paid more for maintenance to offset the burden of maintaining many old versions.

When moving to an inner source approach, the component tax model is not ideal since it does not promote contributing to the shared component base. A business unit that contributes a reusable component has to make an extra effort to make the component reusable. Business units have profit targets, and investing resources to make components reusable is conflicting with these targets. It was not clear which group was expected to perform maintenance for the contributed component or allocate the maintenance resources. If the contributing business unit has to do the maintenance, this will again add costs to the unit. However, making the central component group responsible for maintenance would require this group to build competences for maintaining software components developed by other groups. The central group would be enlarged and take away the domain experts from the business units.

7.5.2   Nokia iSource

Nokia is one of the leading mobile communications companies. It is a publicly held company with listings in five major exchanges and in 2004 (prior to the merger of its Network unit with Siemens to form Nokia Siemens Networks or NSN) its net sales totalled EUR 29.2 billion. We study the organisational changes from the viewpoint of technology adoption and focus on the role of the source code portal called iSource.

The idea to adopt collaborative development utilising open source software practices was presented to Nokia in the early 2000s. It was encouraged by the positive experiences when adopting open source practices in a company context (Dinkelacker et al. 2002). The aim was to tackle the challenges of reuse and cost-effective re-development of software with multiple parties. These challenges are typical of centrally developed platforms that multiple services use for a long period. At a time of the study, Nokia had several application platform concepts. Several research projects contributed to MITA (Mobile Internet Technical Architecture), Mobile Platforms unit delivered platforms to mobile phones and Nokia Networks had worked with, for example, DX200, NMS, NEMU, Flexi- and TSP platforms.

The iSource portal, meant to support collaborative development, was piloted in research projects and promoted company wide. A corporation-wide iSource service was established in 2003 by the Nokia IT department to support infrastructure and to promote the portal tool. A service level agreement was made between the IT department and the business units. Creation of the iSource service adds the third organisation group which we use in our analyses, in addition to the perspective of business unit and individual developer.

iSource is a corporation-wide source code portal for agile, fast cycle, multi-site software development (Lindman et al. 2008). The main idea behind iSource is to provide a portal enabling visibility of software and the source code inside the company. The goals are to increase engineers' awareness of software developed inside the company and to boost innovation by avoiding the problem of reinventing the wheel. iSource's origins are in the free version of SourceForge that has been later upgraded to GForge. The web portal integrates a set of tools for use by projects, including version control tools (Subversion, CVS), issue tracker, mailing lists (Mailman), forums and file management. Today both Nokia and NSN have their own corporation-wide instances of iSource.

The adoption of iSource can be divided into two phases: "bottom-up" adoption (2001–2006) and "top-down" introduction (2007-). These phases also reflect the need for portal tools, the maturity of the environment and the company's trust in open source software.

First adopters of the portal have been leading edge research projects that were co-working with universities and research institutes. iSource has been easy to implement in small projects, especially if co-workers were using the same tools. The iSource service released projects from the need to manage their own tools and infrastructure. The portal also provided a controlled way to work with external parties. Several projects that were first developed inside a company were open sourced later (e.g. Maemo and Python for S60).

Since the joint merger of Nokia and Siemens in 2007, the focus of the service has been on launching subversion for company-wide use. During the "top down" phase the iSource portal was deployed for traditional software development driven by cost optimisation and simplification needs. Business units started to make their decisions to transfer to iSource from more complex and expensive commercial tools.

7.6 Analysis, Findings and Discussion

On examining the cases in our study, it seems that OSS *technology* has become institutionalised in both organisations, even if detached from the classical style of developing OSS as an open endeavour. New tools have gained acceptance, provided inspiration and become familiar to the developers. Both case companies use OSS tools and processes as a way to promote software projects inside the organisation.

7 Open Source Technology in Intra-Organisational Software Development

Table 7.1 Renegotiating the term "OSS"

	Classical "OSS"	Renegotiated "OSS" both at NSN and PH
Reward structure	Mostly voluntary task assignment, peer-recognition, occasionally sponsored development.	Designated projects, contributions based on employment contracts and task assignment, development costs shared based on negotiation between actors, if at all.
Decision-making structure	Meritocracy, loose command structures, debates sometimes leading to crises; developers walking away from poorly functioning projects and contributing to the more attractive ones.	Hierarchical, traditional corporate chain of command, partly based on technical expertise. Some signs of seeking more consensus, though. Resources assigned to projects in project/matrix organisations.
Communication structure	Open discussion email-lists, open message boards, web-presence of projects, open documentation, open training materials. Email and instant messaging.	Intranet, visibility to selected partners who share the development costs. Use of modern *de facto* corporate communication tools such as email, instant messaging, voice calls, video conferencing etc. Some constraints due to not all information being public.

7.6.1 The Meaning of the Term "OSS" Is Re-negotiated Locally

In retrospect, we can see a process of implicitly renegotiating the meaning of the term "OSS" to suit the organisational context. The adopted practices do not resemble OSS as understood by the "classical OSS movement", which was based on voluntarism, peer recognition and public discussion. Instead, the OSS technology institutionalised in these two cases supports designated projects based on employment contracts. Costs are made visible and cost sharing between units is based on agreements between units. The differences are summarised in Table 7.1.

As summarised by Table 7.1, the reward and decision-making structures are quite different, whereas the communication structure remains largely the same when we compare the two cases to pure-form OSS projects.

In one of the two case companies, promotion of OSS technologies was a way to sell the organisational innovation—the inner source approach—to the affected parties by aligning the change process to fit the agendas, and to serve the interests of three key groups: the business units, the central unit and developers. As a result, the changes needed for the new software development processes seem to have been easier. Despite this, some groups are interested only in the tools per se and ignore the opportunity to share components on the inner source platform. One of the interviewees suspected that the main reason for such reluctance to share the results is in the traditional project resourcing: if a group's task is, and its success is measured by, the delivery of projects in a given time, budget and scope, then this gives no time or money to maintain or support the components in the library.

Oncethe component projects have already been finished, the resources will have been moved on to new projects and support is no longer available from the developers most familiar with the component.

> **Practical Tip**
>
> How "OSS" is renegotiated locally emphasises how important it is to reserve enough time to go through the change related to the local practices in any innovation technology. The process of learning related to the new technical infrastructure and in the way of working is likely to take some time and organisational effort.

In the other case company, the promotion of the inner source approach was done more explicitly as a process change: a rationale for enabling easier reuse. Along with this process change came the technologies that are now de facto standard corporate tools (such as SVN as the version control tool). Their challenges have been on a higher level as the organisation has grown through acquisitions and thus the development practices have been quite heterogeneous to start with.

7.6.2   The Market Versus Library Metaphors

The inner source approaches were specifically geared towards enhancing reuse, but they present the management with an incentive issue: basically, why would a business unit contribute its developments to the inner source platform?[3]

We saw that bundling attractive tools to the platform is a way to sell the proposition of sharing. Nevertheless, the issue of support and maintenance remains—what is in it for the contributing group? We identified the metaphors of a private market and a local library to highlight two very different ways in which these technologies become institutionalised.

In a private market, the internal units can place their components on sale in the inner source system, and see who, if anyone, is willing to buy the component at the given terms addressing use, support and maintenance. Unlike in a public market, we'll assume that in a private market there is no (or at least much less) fraud, and therefore the components can be posted openly for anyone to view, inspect and try out, but as soon as the component ends up in another group's product, this will have an internal accounting implication as per the terms and conditions agreed between the buyer and seller units. This can solve the basic incentive issue, but still leaves

---

[3] In the classic, pure-form OSS development the motivational factors are quite well known, including fun and enjoyment, peer recognition and so on, but these do not directly transfer into the corporate setting where business unit leaders make such decisions.

the resourcing problem with support and maintenance: typically, a contributing unit would move on in its product development and the resources previously allocated to a given component will be reallocated to another project and other components, not allowing much time to be spent on support and maintenance of the old components. However, the currently prevailing model is still far from a marketplace and closer to a local library model. The old component tax model is still effectively in use and brings in a price element from the market metaphor, since at least the heavy users need to pay more.

The practical difficulties of adopting such a model aside, if a particular group's components are in such high demand that others are willing to buy them at a premium, seen from the perspective of overall efficiency, it would make sense for this group to focus on maintaining these components instead of starting new projects. Additionally, in hopes of more revenue, units would be promoting their components and their development on the intranet (if not globally and for all on SourceForge, for example) already before they are finalised, and thus one could expect the search costs of the users to be lowered.

The library metaphor is closer to the classic OSS licensing model: use of components is free; someone just needs to develop and contribute the components to the library. In a corporate development hierarchy, one can find platform units that get their annual budget irrespective of the *actual* and immediate use of their components in the library. This obviously does away with the time and effort needed to negotiate between the contributor and user, but the main issue is now in central decision-making: How much should be budgeted to what kind of development, and who are the people that will get the budget to perform the job? And who should make that decision?

Perhaps we should view the private market arrangement as a promising one for highly differentiating and value-adding components, whereas "corporate commodity" components could be freely distributed in a library without complicated negotiations. If the market and library metaphors are seen as extremes of a continuum, then the two cases could be placed on that continuum roughly as follows. (1 = PH, 2 = NSN).

The private market metaphor is an appealing one—although it is in contradiction with the classical OSS spirit—and it is not surprising that in the other case company this was seriously considered. After all, it does present some benefits of open innovation (ideas flowing freely, quick diffusion of inventions to enable incremental innovation, reuse) while addressing the appropriation in a fairly practical manner.

7.7 Conclusions

In this chapter, we have identified and described different ways in which OSS development practices can become institutionalised in a commercial organisation. The literature emphasises the changes brought by OSS-style development when compared to traditional development approaches in hierarchical organisations, but our data suggests that the introduction of OSS technologies and development practices has changed the two case organisations surprisingly little. However, the meaning of the term OSS has undergone considerable changes. We identified the metaphors of private markets and local libraries as to how resources should be allocated inside organisations. Our respondents explicitly used both these metaphors when they made sense of the organisational change.

These two development organisations are embracing OSS technology in a way suitable for them: more tools, components and terminology are being adopted little by little, but the basic mode of operations still remains the same. There is no radical shift to the OSS mindset, but a slow one towards a more open and collaborative working style, coinciding with more open communication (and, simply, more communication) and a more democratic, consensus-seeking decision-making. Rather than claiming that OSS as such or OSS technologies would have changed everything in the organisational ways these corporations do software development, we would argue that the same technological and societal developments that have contributed to the proliferation of OSS are now becoming institutionalised in hierarchical businesses.

The organisational inertia—most notably the one resulting from the way budgeting and project management are performed within a large development organisation—can be used to explain how large development organisations mould and redefine "OSS" to fit their old trajectory. It seems that companies have considerable leeway and interpretive flexibility in determining what their processes are like, even if they were labelled as open.

References

Dahlander, L., & Magnusson, M. (2005). Relationships between open source software companies and communities: Observations from Nordic firms. *Research Policy, 34*, 481–493.

DiMaggio, P., & Powell, W. (1991). Introduction. In W. Powel & DiMaggio (Eds.), *The new institutionalism in organisational analysis* (pp. 1–38). Chicago: University of Chicago Press.

Fink, M. (2003). *The business and economics of linux and open source*. Upper Saddle River, NJ: Prentice Hall PTR.

Fitzgerald, B. (2006). The transformation of open source software. *MIS Quarterly, 30*(3), 587–598.

Garud, R., Hardy, C., & Maguire, S. (2007). *Organisation Studies, 28*, 957–969.

Garud, R., & Karnøe, P. (2003). Bricolage vs. breakthrough: Distributed and embedded agency in technology entrepreneurship. *Research Policy, 32*, 277–300.

Greenwood, R., & Hinings, C. R. (1996). Understanding radical organisational change: bringing together the old and the new institutionalism. *Academy of Management Review, 21*(4), 1022–1054.

Klein, H. K., & Myers, M. D. (1999). A set of principles for conducting and evaluating interpretive field studies in information systems. *MIS Quarterly, 23*(1), 67–94.

Powell, W. W., & DiMaggio, P. J. (Eds.). (1991). *The new institutionalism in organisational analysis*. Chicago: University of Chicago Press.

Rajala, R., Nissilä, J. & Westerlund, M. (2006). Determinants of Open Source Software Revenue Model Choices. In Proceedings of the 14th European Conference on Information Systems (ECIS 2006), 12–14 June, Gothenburg, Sweden.

Seaman, C. B. (1999). Qualitative methods in empirical studies of software engineering. *IEEE Transactions on Software Engineering, 25*(4), 557–572.

Scott, W.R. (2001). *Institutions and Organisations*, 2nd ed., CA, Thousand Oaks.

Stol, K. & Babar, M. (2009). Reporting empirical research in open source software: the state of practice, in Boldyreff, C., Crowston, K., Lundell, B., Wasserman, A. (eds.) *Proceedings of the 5th Conference on Open Source Ecosystems*: Diverse Communities Interacting, June 3rd–6th, Skövde, Sweden, IFIP Advances in Information and Communication Technology 299/2009, Springer 2009, 156–169

Swanson, B., & Ramiller, N. (1997). The organizing vision in information systems innovation. *Organisation Science, 8*(5), 458–474.

Van de Ven, A.H. (1993). Managing the Process of Organisational Innovation in Huber, G.P. & Glick, W.H. (Eds.). Organisational Change and Redesign: Ideas and Insights for Improving Performance. Oxford University Press, New York.

Wesselius, J. (2008). The bazaar inside the cathedral: Business models for internal markets. *IEEE Software, 25*(3), 60–66.

Further Reading

Barnett, L. (2004). Applying Open Source Processes in Corporate Development Organisations. (http://www.forrester.com/rb/Research/applying_open_source_processes_in_corporate_development/q/id/34466/t/2, Forrester Research.

Dinkelacker, J., Garg, P., Miller, R. & Nelson, D. Progressive open source. Proc ICSE 2002, 177–184.

Gurbani, V., Garvert, A., & Hersleb, J. (2010). Managing a corporate open source asset. *Communications of the ACM, 53*(2), 155–159.

van der Linden, F., Lundell, B., & Marttiin, P. (2009). Commodification of industrial software—a case for open source. *IEEE Software, 26*(4), 77–83.

Lindman, J., Rossi, M., & Marttiin, P. (2008). Applying Open Source Development Practices Inside a Company. *In Proceedings of the 4th International Conference on Open Source Systems.* 7–10 September 2008, Milan, Italy.

Santos, C. (2008). Understanding partnerships between corporations and the open source community: A research gap. *IEEE Software, 25*(6), 96–97.

Sharma, S., Sugumaran, V., & Rajagopalan, B. (2002). A framework for creating hybrid-open source software communities. *Information Systems Journal, 12*(1), 7–25.

Välimäki, M. (2005). *The rise of open source licensing. A challenge to the use of intellectual property in the software industry.* Helsinki, Finland: Helsinki University of Technology.

Chapter 8
Open Innovation in Practice: The Development of the IT Capability Maturity Framework

Brian Donnellan and Gabriel J. Costello

Abstract This chapter describes the IT Capability Maturity Model (IT-CMF), a high-level process capability maturity framework for managing the IT function within an organisation. The framework identifies a number of critical IT processes and describes an approach to improving maturity for each process. The design environment of the IT-CMF is challenging as the processes are based on "open innovation" principles. An example of the application of the IT-CMF to the Intel Corporation Information Technology organisation is outlined. The practical usefulness of the framework lies in its potential to organise and structure a complex portfolio of IT innovation activities in a manner that enabled continuous improvement.

8.1 Introduction

The case study reported in this chapter has been developed in the context of the IT Capability Maturity Model (IT-CMF), a high-level process capability maturity framework for managing the IT function within an organisation (Curley 2004; Curley 2006a, b, c). The framework identifies a number of critical IT processes and describes an approach to improving maturity for each process. We find the design environment with the IT-CMF in particular challenging and interesting as the design and review processes are based on "open innovation" principles. "Open innovation" as presented by Chesbrough (2003) offers an innovation model where organisations leverage both external and internal resources to generate value. This concept challenges the view of

B. Donnellan (✉)
National University of Ireland, Maynooth Innovation Value Institute, South Campus, Maynooth, Kildare, Ireland
e-mail: brian.donnellan@nuim.ie

G.J. Costello
Department of Mec/Ind Engineering, Galway-Mayo Institute of Technology, Bublin Road, Galway, Ireland
e-mail: gabrielj.costello@gmit.ie

J.S.Z. Eriksson Lundström et al. (eds.), *Managing Open Innovation Technologies*,
DOI 10.1007/978-3-642-31650-0_8, © Springer-Verlag Berlin Heidelberg 2013

closed innovation where innovation processes are restricted to experts within the organisation. By leveraging the collective intelligence of experienced practitioners in the Innovation Value Institute community, the information quality of the design artefacts in the IT-CMF is established and enhanced.

The objective of this chapter is to provide insights into how the open innovation community has successfully implemented open innovation principles to develop a new IT Management framework.

8.2 The Evolution of Open Innovation: Changing Innovation Paradigms

Chesbrough (2003) argues that in many industries the centralised approach to R&D which he terms "closed innovation" has become obsolete. This paradigm, he contends, must be replaced by "open innovation" which adopts external ideas and knowledge in conjunction with the internal process. A number of factors are influencing this change such as the mobility of skilled people, the increasing presence of venture capital, emergent high-tech start-ups and the significant role of university research. Companies such as Cisco and Intel have adopted the new paradigm in contrast to Xerox which has lost many innovations due to its closed systems. One of his principles is that "not all the smart people work for us" and he advocates that the smart people within an organisation connect with the smart people outside. Embracing the ideas and inspiration in these external links, he contends, will actually multiply the advantage of internal efforts. However, connecting external innovation to internal innovation requires a new business model.

The growing significance of the open innovation paradigm has prompted West, Vanhaverbeke and Cloodt (2006) to propose a research framework with the following classifications: individual, organisational, value network, industry/sector and national institution (p. 288). In a related work, Vanhaverbeke and Cloodt (2006) suggest that emerging forms of value networks must be examined at the level of different nested layers. These diverse layers span the spectrum from the individual to firms–organisations; through Dyads; onto inter-organisational networks and ultimately reaching to national/regional innovation systems. von Hippel (2005) speaks about the democratisation of innovation where products and services users increasingly have the ability to innovate for themselves with the resulting move from manufacturer-centric to user-centric innovation processes.

8.3 Open Innovation and the IT-CMF

Open innovation is central to the development of the IT-CMF for two reasons. Firstly, the IT-CMF is being developed under the aegis of the Innovation Value Institute which is a consortium designed and operated under the guidance of open innovation principles. The consortium is made up of over 60 organisations drawn from Industry, Academia and Government institutions. These organisations have been successfully collaborating for a number of years in the development of the IT-CMF. A noteworthy feature of the consortium is that its memberships include companies which are in direct competition in industry, yet work very productively together in the open innovation environment in the IVI. Secondly, a key characteristic of the Innovation Management maturity model is that at higher levels of maturity, companies exhibit innovative behaviours that extend beyond their own organisational boundaries to include innovative activities with customers, suppliers, external agencies, etc. This dimension of innovative behaviour is captured under the parameter "reach" in the IT-CMF.

8.4 Open Innovation and IT Innovation

A so-called resource-based view of IT innovation has been popular in the literature (Feeney and Wilcocks 1998). This view sees the ability to leverage IT in new ways as being a core competence of an organisation and a source of sustainable competitive advantage. Resources that might lead to competitive advantage may include proprietary IT technology, unique IT technical and/or management skills. This stream of research has shifted its focus towards "open innovation" (Chesbrough 2003). Today's economic landscape has been characterised as having many features associated with open innovation, e.g. mobile knowledge workers, globally distributed development teams, greater linkages between academia and industry, the emergence of new locations for innovation and a propensity to go beyond organisational boundaries to identify and collaborate with innovators. There has been a growing awareness of the importance of combining internal and external sources of innovative capacity to create a "portfolio approach" to the development of intellectual capital. In the academic context, more attention is being paid to the potential for technology transfer, innovation incubators and entrepreneurial spin-offs.

8.5 The Focus of the Problem: Realising the Value of IT Investments

A particular challenge facing IT managers is how to evaluate the value of IT investments. Bannister's (2005) review of approaches to IT evaluation identifies three strands in the literature:

– Studies that focus on the long-term historical economic impact of investments in IS. Examples include Brynjolfsson and Hitt (2003) who explored the so-called productivity paradox and the cumulative effect of investments in IT on organisations, and Strassmann (1985) who has argued that such effects are only really assessable over long periods, maybe as long as half a century.

- Studies of whether specific investments made over shorter periods have yielded value. These vary from the application of innovative methods to measure value realised to use well-established methodologies, such as return on investment, comparison of how different metrics report or combinations of measures, such as the balanced scorecard (Kaplan and Norton 1992) or the Prudential Appraisal Method (Coleman and Jamieson 1994).
- Studies assessing whether or not a potential investment in IT is worthwhile. The time horizon here is typically fairly short, usually 5–10 years, though from time to time studies will contemplate a more distant time horizon. Almost all such studies are at the level of the organisation, be it a firm or a public sector body.

A novel approach to IT Innovation Effectiveness realisation has been proposed by Peppard et al. (2007). The "IS benefits management" approach advocated by the authors is defined as "the process of organising and managing so that the potential benefits from using IT are actually realised" where "benefits management" emphasises that benefits arise only from changes made by individual users or groups of users, and these changes must be identified and managed successfully. "Benefits realisation" and "change management" are therefore inextricably linked. This is the case when the project is explicitly an IS-enabled or "techno-change" program. A noteworthy aspect of the Benefits Management approach is the application of a Benefits Dependency Network (BDN). The BDN provides the framework for explicitly linking the overall investment objectives and required benefits with the business changes necessary to deliver these benefits and the essential IT capabilities that enable these changes. This approach is an example of a general trend towards a "capability"-oriented view of IT as opposed to the "resourced" based view described in Peppard et al. (2000).

8.6 The IT Capability Maturity Framework

The Innovation Value Institute has developed a framework for managing IT for business value—the IT-CMF and this framework is being tested with leading organisations around the world. IVI's approach leverages existing frameworks and complements them with a comprehensive value-based model for organising, evaluating, planning and managing IT capabilities. An example of the application of the framework in a real-world context is provided in Donnellan et al. (2011).

The IT-CMF proposes a high-level process capability maturity framework for managing the IT function within an organisation. The framework identifies a number of critical IT processes and describes an approach to designing maturity frameworks for each process. By comparison, other IT process frameworks including COBIT, ITIL and CMMI do not explicitly provide a mechanism to address the topic of IT innovation. A sub-group of Innovation Value Institute has been concerned with building and testing the CMF for the IT innovation critical process.

The IT-CMF accepts that innovations arising from both linear sequential processes and complex social processes co-exist within the same firm. The framework unifies a single approach to address the manageability of both classifications of IT innovation. For linear sequential processes, the innovation capability describes the ability or capacity to execute in a manner that increases the probability of a positive outcome in an IT innovation. For complex social processes, and non-sequential activities, the innovation capability describes the pre-conditions required to increase the probability of innovation outcomes.

The IT innovation Capability Maturity Framework describes the IT innovation capability through a five-level capability maturity framework. The maturity approach has been used successfully in the IT industry to describe specific stages of progression to an optimal mode of operation.

Potential advantages of the capability maturity approach include its ability to present a structured, sequential stepwise function. Due to the simplicity of the model, maturity frameworks have seen wide adoption in the IT industry by large organisations (e.g. CMM) and have strong uptake amongst the community of practitioners. The approach is useful in describing a manageable approach to improvement, and therefore preserves the simplicity and direct-acting approaches presented by the linear sequential process innovation frameworks. Each level of the capability maturity framework also describes a set of contextual descriptions, and therefore preserves the approach presented by the non-linear school of frameworks.

Potential disadvantages of the capability maturity approach include its tendency to adopt a somewhat instrumental, doctrinaire and mechanical approach to problems that may be quite complex. The IT Innovation CMF addresses this shortcoming in two ways. Firstly, the maturity framework is augmented with additional dimensions for each of the five levels. The maturity approach chosen introduces a set of innovation capabilities at each level. Each capability is assigned characteristics, attributes and descriptions of representative outcomes on an organisation. Secondly, the IT Innovation CMF is augmented by linking the maturity levels to a supplementary overarching IT capability maturity framework (IT-CMF). Therefore, the IT innovation CMF is divided into four strategies, mirroring directly the strategies of the IT-CMF. Strategies describe the four primary activities associated with managing innovation, funding innovation activities, executing the innovation capability and assessing the value of innovations.

Broadly defined, the innovation capability is a set of actions undertaken to prepare an organisation to be more innovative. This is achieved by increasing the organisation's ability to enact defined innovation processes and by increasing the effectiveness and relevance of non-linear activities on innovative outcomes. Preparation in the linear sequential sense involves the creation of tools and artefacts within the firm. Artefacts may be tangible, such as systems, devices and templates, or intangible, such as activities, roles, processes and methodologies. Preparation in the complex social sense involves affecting change on the environmental context of the firm to increase the probability of an organisation to innovate.

Table 8.1 The IT innovation critical process in the IT CMF

	Managing IT innovation	Funding the innovation portfolio	Executing the IT innovation capability	Assessing the value of IT innovation
5. Systemic innovation	Business transformation and agility	Self-sustaining	Culture drives continuous business innovation	Confidence in value return
4. Managed innovation	Aligned to strategic business needs	Co-funded with business	Routinely delivers innovative operational improvements	Reliable, consistent measurement
3. Defined innovation	Defined IT innovation strategy	Justified business spend	Tools, processes, organisation supports value-chain innovations	Defined value assessment
2. Sporadic innovation	Emerging innovation strategy	One-time spend	Occasional product improvements	Informal value measurement
1. Initial / ad hoc innovation	Undefined innovation strategy	Not explicitly budgeted	Limited impact and scope of innovations	No recognised value

Specifically defined, the innovation capability consists of a description of the core capability and its primary characteristics. Each characteristic is described by observable attributes exhibited by the firm, measurable metrics of attribute existence and performance and expected impact on the firm's ability to increase the probability of innovative outcomes.

The IT Innovation Management Critical Process, the first maturity level describes the IT innovation capability in its most immature form. The capability is initial, linear processes are unmanaged and there is a poor understanding of the nonlinear capabilities and social processes. In practice, there will be a limited adoption of new technologies, and IT managers are in general unaware of the potential or existing benefits of IT innovations.

The second maturity level describes a sporadically managed innovation capability. An emerging capability is characterised by a small group of IT managers who recognise the value of IT innovation and act in an uncoordinated manner to increase IT innovations.

The third maturity level describes a defined innovation capability with a high degree of coordination. Linear processes are defined and are executed upon to increase levels of innovation. Non-linear activities are encouraged through contextual investments.

The fourth maturity level describes an actively managed innovation capability. IT and executive managers promote and coordinate innovation across the enterprise.

The fifth maturity level describes a systemic innovation capability. IT innovations are recognised by the firm to contribute value to the enterprise, and the organisation is active in encouraging innovation (Table 8.1).

Table 8.2 Application of the IT CMF in Intel

Managing IT innovation	Funding the innovation portfolio	Executing the IT innovation capability	Assessing the value of IT innovation
Prior to the initiative, innovation activities were defined as isolated, specific projects. The initiative was an attempt to contextualise and coordinate the projects under a single strategic initiative. If successfully executed, this initiative would represent a move from maturity level 3 to 4.	Prior to the initiative, projects were funded on a sporadic basis. This initiative attempted to provide a coordination mechanism to justify innovation spend. Consequently, this initiative reflected a move from maturity level 2 to 3.	A major component of the initiative included the standardisation of an innovation toolkit, website, and guidelines to formalise the innovation process. This reflected a sustained level 3 innovation capability.	The initiative involved the measurement of 9 innovation metrics across the processes, inputs, and outputs of the innovation activities. These metrics were to inform management in setting new project priorities. This reflected a maturity level of 4.

8.7 The Application of the IT-CMF in Intel Corp

In this section, we present an example of the IT Innovation Capability Maturity Framework applied to the Intel Corporation Information Technology organisation. We demonstrate the innovation framework as a mechanism to structure the set of innovation activities pursued by the Intel IT managers in their attempts to improve efficiency and performance of IT operations through innovation.

Curley has described in some detail the transformation of IT in Intel (Curley 2006a, b, c). In 2005, the Intel Information Technology organisation formalised an initiative to foster and encourage innovation throughout the firm. The focus of the new initiative was to supplement and encompass existing innovation activities with a perspective on the direct financial value generated by each activity. The approach was novel to Intel at the time, who had previously regarded innovation activities as unmanageable and unquantifiable. Existing IT innovation activities included dedicated innovation hiring programs, projects to increase recognition of innovation, innovation rewards and incentives and a set of activities to deploy IT innovations in the organisation. Innovation in IT was recognised as imperative to maintain Intel's competitive edge, through investment in programs to foster long-term systemic innovation.

The IT Innovation CMF describes the set of specific initiatives as a coordinated attempt to improve the maturity of the innovation capability. The maturity framework serves both to structure the set of activities in a mutually exclusive, collectively exhaustive perspective on innovation management, and to assess the performance and potential of the activities. In Table 8.2, the set of Intel IT

Innovation-related activities is summarised and structured into the four strategies of managing innovation, funding innovation activities, executing the innovation capability and assessing the value of innovations. Each set of activities is compared in principle with the description of each maturity level.

8.8 Summary and Conclusions

This chapter reviewed the trends in open innovation and focussed on one particular new development in this area—the IT Capability Maturity Framework (CMF). Among its 60+ members, the Innovation Value Institute has many leading exemplars of IT Innovation practice, including Intel, Microsoft, SAP, etc. This collaborative community of like-minded peers is committed to investigating and advancing tools and best practices associated with IT-enabled innovation. The consortium provides an ideal opportunity to examine the practice of open innovation across a range of innovative organisations. We found the IT innovation critical process to be a novel and practical mechanism for structuring the set of IT innovation activities within a firm. The practical usefulness of the framework lies in its potential to organise and structure a complex portfolio of IT innovation activities in a manner that enabled continuous improvement.

> **Practical Tip**
>
> The application of "open innovation" principles are usually concerned with products and services. The IT-CMF demonstrates that the "open innovation" approach can be successfully applied to business processes in the IT sector.

References

Bannister, F. (2005). When paradigms shift: IT evaluation in a brave new world. *The Electronic Journal of Information Systems Evaluation, 8*(1), 21–30.

Brynjolfsson, E. & Hitt, L. (2003) "Computing Productivity: Firm-Level Evidence", *MIT Sloan Working Paper No. 4210-01*, June 2003.

Chesbrough, H. W. (2003). *Open innovation: the new imperative for creating and profiting from technology*. Boston: Harvard Business School.

Coleman, T., & Jamieson, M. (1994). Beyond return on investment: evaluating ALL the benefits of information technology. In L. Willcocks (Ed.), *Information management* (The evaluation of information systems investments, pp. 189–206). London: Chapman Hall.

Curley, M. (2004) *"Managing Information Technology for Business Value"*. January 2004, Intel Press.

Curley, M. (2006) "IT Innovation, a new Era" *In the Proceedings of the International Conference of Computational Science, Reading*, UK. (2006).

Curley, M. (2006b). *A value based IT capability maturity framework*. Ireland: Intel EMEA Academic Forum.

Curley, M. (2006c). The IT transformation at Intel. *MIS Quarterly Executive, 5*, 109–122.

Curley, M. (2006d). The IT transformation at Intel. *MIS Quarterly Executive, 5*, 109–122.

Donnellan B., Sheridan C. & Curry, E. (2011) "A Framework for Sustainable Information and Communication Technology", *IEEE IT Professional*, January/February 2011.

Feeney, D. F., & Wilcocks, L. P. (1998). *Core IS capabilities for exploiting information technology* (pp. 9–21). Spring: Sloan Management Review.

Kaplan, R. S., & Norton, D. P. (1992). The balanced scorecard—measures that drive performance. *Harvard Business Review, 70*, 71–19.

Peppard, J., Lambert, R. & Edwards, C. (2000) Whose job is it anyway? Organizational Information Competencies for Value Creation, Information Systems Journal, *10*(4), 291–322.

Peppard, J., Ward, J. & Daniel, E. "Managing the Realisation of Business Benefits from IT Investments" , *MIS Quarterly Executive* Vol. 6 No. 1, Mar 2007.

Strassmann, P. (1985). *Information payoff: The transformation of work in an electronic age*. New York: Free Press.

Vanhaverbeke, W., & Cloodt, M. (2006). Open innovation in value networks. In H. Chesbrough, W. Vanhaverbeke, & J. West (Eds.), *Open innovation: Researching a new paradigm* (pp. 258–284). Oxford: Oxford University Press.

von Hippel, E. (2005). *Democratizing innovation*. Massachusetts: The MIT Press.

Chapter 9
Voluntary Contributors in Open Innovation Processes

Anna Ståhlbröst and Birgitta Bergvall-Kåreborn

Abstract There is a trend among many organisations to open up their innovation processes and invite more stakeholders to contribute to it. One of these stakeholders is the voluntary contributor. Few studies have documented the motivation and value of participating in these processes from their perspective. The purpose of this chapter is thus to explore the motivation behind these contributors' participation in open innovation activities and the benefits it has. This study shows that the strongest motivation for their participation is to stimulate their curiosity. The involvement also leads to increased knowledge and a pronounced eagerness to start using innovations.

9.1 Introduction

In this chapter, we choose to explore open innovation from the perspective of private persons who participate in innovation processes because the majority of the literature on open innovation focuses on how an open strategy can be implemented in organisations, especially firms, and the benefits they can gain from this (Chesbrough 2006). Open innovation shifts the focus from ownership to partnership by opening up the borders of the organisation and perforating the innovation and development funnel to enable a constant in- and outflow of resources between the organisation and its environment. Inspired by the open source software movement, Chesbrough and Appleyard even state that in its purest form, *"the value created through an open process would approach that of a public good"* (Chesbrough and Appleyard 2007, p. 60).

A. Ståhlbröst (✉) • B. Bergvall-Kåreborn
Department of Innovation & Design, Luleå University of Technology, Luleå, Sweden
e-mail: anna.stahlbrost@ltu.se

J.S.Z. Eriksson Lundström et al. (eds.), *Managing Open Innovation Technologies*,
DOI 10.1007/978-3-642-31650-0_9, © Springer-Verlag Berlin Heidelberg 2013

Open innovation can be achieved through three core processes (Enkel et al. 2009). The first process, *outside-in*, focuses on how an organisation can bring knowledge resources from the environment into the organisation. Traditionally, this has focused on integration activities with external stakeholders, such as customers and suppliers. Today, it is important to broaden the definition of stakeholders to include innovation networks and new forms of customer integration. Innovation intermediaries, customer communities and crowdsourcing are examples of this broader view. The second process, the *inside-out*, centres its attention on how an organisation can share its knowledge and innovations with the environment. Selling or licensing intellectual property and multiplying technology are common ways of doing this. Finally, the third process, the *coupled process*, combines the other two and refers to co-creation among complementary partners through alliances, cooperation and joint ventures. Here, a mutual give and take between the partners is crucial for success. In this chapter, we concentrate on the *outside-in process*, but instead of following the common path and studying how organisations can collect, absorb and integrate new ideas from the environment (Chesbrough 2003), we study why external stakeholders in the form of private persons choose to contribute to open innovation activities and how this participation affects them.

In "The Future of Open Innovation", Gassmann et al. (2010) identify nine research perspectives of open innovation. One of these, the *user perspective*, centres on integrating users into the innovation process. Even though this is one of the most thoroughly researched perspectives of open innovation including studies on lead users, toolkits and mass customisation, there is still a lack of studies when it comes to broadening the definition of stakeholders and studying private persons' involvement in innovation activities organised by innovation intermediaries.

Understanding what motivates private persons to participate in open innovation projects and the values this participation produces from their perspective is important knowledge for strengthening the "democratising" features of open innovation (von Hippel 2005). It is also important knowledge for organisations that wish to strengthen their relations with their consumers, since attracting and sustaining some kind of relation to present and future consumers is a challenging but crucial task of an open business strategy (Chesbrough and Appleyard 2007). As with open innovation, the value of involving users in innovation and development processes within an organisational context has been well documented in earlier research (e.g. Bergvall-Kåreborn and Ståhlbröst 2008), while the motivation and value created from the individual's perspective remains somewhat unexplored. In this chapter, we focus on *voluntary contributors* in order to emphasise that these private persons contribute to open innovation processes voluntarily in their spare time and that their contributions can take many forms, such as rendering ideas for new innovation, co-designing concepts or evaluating innovations. This concept is therefore inherently broader than concepts such as lead users (von Hippel 1986), creative consumers (Berthon et al. 2007) and early adopters (Rogers 2003). Voluntary contributors participating in innovation intermediary communities are loosely linked to each other compared to communities such as brand communities, open source software development communities and social networks. The main reason for this is the broad variety and number of projects included in the intermediaries' project portfolio. For this reason, project members rarely work together in more than one project.

The purpose of this chapter is thus to explore the motivation behind these voluntary contributors' participation in open innovation activities and the benefits it creates for them. With this as our starting point, this chapter answers two research questions: (1) what motivates private persons to participate in open innovation activities? and (2) how do these voluntary contributors believe that their participation influences them?

In the following, we present different types of contributors, including their characteristics, and argue for the need of yet another definition, that of the *voluntary contributor*. To put the voluntary contributor in a context, we will present our open innovation activities in the Botnia Living Lab. We will then present the results from an online self-reporting opinion survey that we administered to the respondents: "Your participation in innovation activities". The chapter ends with a discussion of our findings and with a presentation of the practical and theoretical contributions of our work.

9.2 Users, Communities and Voluntary Contributors

Involving users or customers of a product or service in the development process is not a new phenomenon. There are many ways to conceptualise these groups of people, and each concept represents certain characteristics linked to their role, relation to the product or service, personal characteristics and contribution to the development process (Bergvall-Kåreborn and Ståhlbröst 2008; Enkel et al. 2005). Thanks to Internet-based technologies, it is also becoming common to interact with these groups of private persons through a platform or portal; users or customers can also interact with each other, if they so desire. This has given rise to several types of innovation communities, such as brand communities, beta-test communities, developer communities, user-content communities and innovation intermediary communities (Ståhlbröst and Bergvall-Kåreborn 2011).

However, as with the user and consumer concepts, these community types represent a great variety and not all would stand the test of communities as environments in which its members share, construct and learn together. In some cases, it is more correct to say that companies interact with large amounts of loosely coupled contributors as a resource in innovation and development processes, rather than as a community. Idea competitions are often examples of this type of relation. By arranging these competitions, companies hope to bring forth new trends, ideas for new products or services or feedback on some artefact by engaging a large group of contributors. However, the interaction between the contributors is usually very sparse or non-existent.

The studies within this area emphasise motivational factors in contributing to specific communities (Ståhlbröst and Bergvall-Kåreborn 2011) but do not follow up with the values actually attained by the contributors. However, they do identify a rather broad range of intrinsic and extrinsic motivational factors that organisations can experiment with when recruiting and sustaining a community of contributors. Intrinsic motivation occurs when an individual engages in an activity, such as a hobby, without being influenced by obvious external incentives (Leimeister et al. 2009). This type of motivation refers to the desire to feel competent and self-determined. External motivation is activated by external incentives, such as direct or indirect monetary compensation, or recognition by others (Hars and Ou 2002). Both these motivational factors might be of importance to the contributors' decision to take part in innovation activities. For example, some users might be motivated by the competitive factors if the community arranged an ideas competition; other users might be externally motivated by the chance of winning a prize of monetary value, or be intrinsically motivated by the opportunity to have fun while competing (Stepanikova et al. 2010). Some examples of motivators are altruism, knowledge exchange and learning, desire for status, satisfying a general interest in innovation or a specific need, or receiving a reward (Antikainen et al. 2010).

We define contributors of loosely coupled communities as *voluntary contributors* to highlight the fact that they usually contribute as private persons on a voluntary basis, rather than as community members. They share an interest in a particular study, rather than a common purpose and a set of community values. The type of loosely coupled community that we focus on in this chapter is initiated by an innovation intermediary called Botnia Living Lab (BLL). The people constituting the community are loosely coupled and heterogeneous individuals who participate as private persons without any significant financial compensation. Their contributions can take many forms, but is always linked to at least one phase of the innovation and development process in a specific project. BLL supports innovation for a diversity of stakeholders in order to produce innovative ICT-based products or services. Hence, no specific brand, product or service strongly connects the participants to each other and to the BLL. We therefore refer to this group of people as *voluntary contributors*.

BLL is an innovation intermediary milieu where private companies, public organisations, researchers and end-user representatives work together to create, validate and test a variety of new services, business ideas and technologies in real-life settings (Bergvall-Kåreborn and Ståhlbröst 2009). The BLL environment, launched in 2003, has an online community in which voluntary contributors have signed up. The aim of the community is to gather private persons who are willing to volunteer for innovation activities and hence, support the process user involvement for BLL. From this community, BLL invites contributors to participate in innovation processes based on the characteristics that are suitable for a specific project. The endeavour of BLL is to involve private persons in their natural environment by means of technology, with the objective to gain access to their needs, ideas and attitudes as they appear in the contributor's everyday situation. This means that the voluntary contributors can be involved, for example, in their homes, when they walk around in the city, when they are out for a drive or when they are at work.

9.3 Methodology: Data Collection

To effectively and efficiently manage open innovation processes in which voluntary contributors are involved repeatedly, it is important to understand the characteristics of the private persons involved in these processes. Hence, a study of the private persons involved in the open innovation activities was carried out at BLL. In this study, we used an online survey to collect data from these voluntary contributors. The respondents invited to answer the survey were directed towards contributors who had been, or wanted to be, part of BLL's innovation activities. A link to the survey was sent via email to 2,545 potential contributors in Sweden during the spring of 2010. This study was introduced to the contributors as a self-reporting opinion survey called, "Your participation in innovation activities". The survey drew responses from 270 users, which gave us a response rate of 10.6 %. One plausible reason for the low response rate can be that many of the invited contributors are only occasionally involved in BLL activities and thus might not feel qualified to answer. Obtaining answers from all of these sporadic contributors could have been valuable since their perspectives might have rendered a different view on motivation to participate in innovation activities. However, the aim of the study was to obtain responses from those who want to be, have been or are involved in innovation activities; thus, the non-respondents might be outside our scope of interest.

In this study, the question framework was based on the literature study concerning users and motivators in different types of online communities (Ståhlbröst and Bergvall-Kåreborn 2011). The framework has not been tested and validated in other studies; hence, the results from this study need to be validated in additional studies. Our survey consisted of six question areas: background questions (e.g. demographic characteristics such as gender, education), Internet usage habits, type of technology adoption, motivation for participating in innovation activities and their experience of how their participation influenced them. In this chapter, we explore both voluntary contributors' motivation for participating and their view of its impact on them.

9.4 Characteristics of Voluntary Contributors

In order to understand the characteristics of the private persons who want to take part in the innovation activities, we analysed their background data (see Table 9.1).

Two-thirds of the respondents are male and one-third female. The respondents range in age from 15 to 68 years, with 29 % of the respondents between 21 and 30 years and 29 % between 31 and 40 years. Seventy-one per cent of the respondents are between the 26 and 50 years of age.

Almost half of the respondents have a university degree and nearly 70 % are employed. We therefore conclude that the community consists of a rather young population that is employed and quite well educated.

Table 9.1 Demographic characteristics

Demographic characteristics	Frequency (n)	Per cent (%)
Age		
15–20	4	1.5
21–30	78	29.0
31–40	78	29.0
41–50	66	24.5
51–65	32	12.0
66–	4	1.5
Unusable data	7	2.5
Gender		
Male	178	66.0
Female	92	34.0
Education		
Elementary school	14	5.0
2 years of education	49	18.0
3 years of education	74	28.0
University education	124	46.0
Research education	8	3.0
Main occupation		
Senior high school student	4	1.5
University student	30	11.0
Employed	183	68.0
Company owner	15	5.5
Retired	11	4.0
Unemployed	14	5.0

9.4.1 Community Use Characteristics

To increase our understanding of the people involved in innovation community activities, we considered it important to gain insights into their community usage and habits in the BLL innovation community to elicit their participation in forthcoming activities. To start with, we wanted to understand how they take part in the community. We found that even though the community at BLL is mainly directed towards private individuals whose involvement is voluntary, only 4 % of the respondents state they participate as part of their work (see Table 9.2).

We also wanted to know the respondents' current usage patterns of the BLL community. Here we found that the majority of the respondents, almost 60 %, have been community members for several years, which indicates a strong loyalty and commitment to the community. What was unanticipated was the large percentage of respondents, almost 20 %, who do not know how long they have been members. Linking this to gender, we see a clear divide in relation to the long-time members; 28 % of all women and 68 % of all men have been a member for several years. That is, for the male respondents, the majority has been part of the community for several years, while only a third of the female respondents are long-time members. For all

9 Voluntary Contributors in Open Innovation Processes

Table 9.2 Community use characteristics

Community use characteristics	Frequency (n)	Per cent (%)
Duration of participation in the community		
A few weeks	10	4
A few months	26	10
Approximately one year	28	10
Several years	155	57
Do not know	50	18
Amount of user innovation involvement activities		
None	36	13
1–2	50	18
3–5	41	15
6–10	30	11
More than 10	44	16
Do not know	68	25
Involvement role		
As a part of one's job	11	5
As a private person	256	95

other categories, the women are in majority. This indicates that the number of new female members has increased over the last years, and if this trend continues, the balance between male and female members in the community can be expected to slowly even out. There can be many reasons for women's interest in innovation activities related to IT development. One possible external reason can be the maturity of technology in general; for instance, online communities are no longer considered high-tech and directed towards "geeks", but are rather directed to the everyday Jane and Joe. This could be compared to mobile phones whose usage has spread to the majority of the Swedish population. Hence, technology is becoming a natural part of our lives and thus, more people are attracted to actively take part in its development.

The figures for respondents' involvement in the community activities are relatively evenly spread out between none to more than ten. Around 40 % have participated in three or more activities, while just over 30 % have participated in up to two activities. The largest single group consists of respondents who do not know how many studies they have participated in. This might be because many of the respondents have been involved in the community for several years and cannot remember how many innovation activities they have taken part in. The nature of the innovation activities in which the respondents have been involved is also diverse; some of the activities span an extended period of time (e.g. field trials in their homes for several months) and others are short and direct (e.g. answering an online questionnaire). Based on that, it might be difficult for the respondents to know what does and does not count as an innovation involvement activity.

The data also show that the majority of the respondents have participated in more than one study and as such can be seen as returning voluntary contributors to the community.

9.4.2 Technology Adoption Types

In this study, we also want to learn about the kind of technology adopters the contributors involved in our community are. It can be expected that most private persons involved in these communities are very interested in new technology. We found that most contributors in our community are, to some extent, interested in technology and its development. When we clustered our contributors, nearly 5 % stated that they usually develop the technology they need for themselves or others in their immediate surroundings; these can be viewed as *innovators*. Sixteen per cent of our respondents stated that they often have ideas or discover that they need a new product before they enter the market; these users are referred to here as *visionaries*. The largest group of contributors (38 %) are *technology enthusiasts*; they want to use a new technical product or service as soon as it is available on the market. The second largest group (36.5 %) are the contributors who view themselves as *utility users*: those who start using a product when some people around them have verified that the technology is useful. The second smallest group (5 %) of contributors are the *technology conservatives* who start to use a technology after it has been well established on the market and most people in their surroundings use it. We had an additional group which none of the respondents associated with: the *technology sceptics*. This refers to those who usually take a long time before starting to use a new technology.

9.4.3 The Voluntary Contributors' Internet and Social Media Use

The voluntary contributors that are involved in BLL's innovation activities should not only be *contributors*, they should also be *qualified contributors*. This means that for each case, voluntary contributors are invited to participate based on fulfilling certain criteria. This process is usually carried out by use of a qualifying questionnaire where the contributors answer a small number of screening questions to make sure that they have the required background. For instance, most innovation activities at BLL are focused on IT innovations; hence, the voluntary contributors must represent that group in general and sometimes with an additional scope, such as being interested in writing or shopping.

This provides situational information that must be considered in the development of the innovation. Based on that, it is important to understand the respondents' use of the Internet as well as their social media usage. When it comes to the respondents' use of the Internet, they show a very high level of use (see Table 9.3). Almost all respondents (96 %) have the technical ability to use the Internet either 24/7 (43 %) or several times a day (53 %); these two groups are almost equal in size. However, viewing the two use levels from a gender perspective, 51 % of the men use the Internet 24/7 while only 25 % of all women do.

9 Voluntary Contributors in Open Innovation Processes

Table 9.3 The users' Internet and social media use

Users' personal characteristics	Frequency (n)	Per cent (%)
Internet usage		
Online access 24/7	113	43.4
Several times/day	139	53.4
Once/day	6	2.3.0
A few times/week	0	0
A few times/month	2	0.76
Members of social networks (like Facebook)		
Yes	217	83.5
No	42	16
Do not know	1	0.5
Number of social networks		
1–3	181	81
4–6	35	15.5
7–9	5	2
>10	3	1.5
Frequency of use of social network		
24/7	34	15
Several times a day	103	46
Once a day	35	15.5
A few times a week	37	16.5
A few times a month	11	5
More seldom	5	2

All contributors are also members of at least one social network, such as Facebook. Of these, 81 % are members of one to three social networks, while 15 % are members of four to six. More than three-quarters (76.5 %) visit their social networks on a daily basis, and only 2 % visit their social networks less than once a month.

In terms of social media use, this number would probably have been even higher if the study had been carried out today due to the continuous increase in the popularity of these social media and social networks.

The data regarding the contributors' social media behaviour (Table 9.4) indicate that the factor that attracts most users of social media is the opportunity to socialise with other people in their network. This includes activities such as catching up and communicating with friends, in addition to sharing experiences and pictures with their personal network.

What can seem surprising is that activities that are closely related to BLL activities, such as answering questionnaires and testing new products and services, are ranked relatively low.

9.4.4 Voluntary Contributors and Their Motivation

When it comes to factors that motivate private persons to contribute voluntarily to innovation activities, our focus is based on a literature review regarding motivation factors when participating in innovation communities (Ståhlbröst and

142
A. Ståhlbröst and B. Bergvall-Kåreborn

Table 9.4 Social media behaviour

Social media behaviour	Frequency (n)	Per cent (%)
Read about what friends do or have done	192	71
Look at people's pictures	137	51
Communicate directly with friends (like chat)	129	48
Comment others pictures, logs, etc.	108	40
Search for information	102	38
Show personal pictures	78	29
Write in a personal log	58	22
Test new products and services	54	20
Answer questionnaires	52	19
Participate actively in discussion forums	52	19
Play games	51	19
Carry out different tests	49	18
Search for new friends	44	16
Create or participate in groups	39	14

Table 9.5 Contributors' motivational factors

Users' motivational factors	Mean	Low (1-2)	High (6-7)
Get a needed innovation	4.87	11.5	41
Stimulate curiosity	5.63	2.8	**59.1**
Contribute with ideas to innovations	4.86	10.3	36,9
Give vent to creativity	4.98	7.5	39.7
Be considered as innovative by others	4.95	13.9	34.2
Be the first to test an innovation	4.91	11.5	44
Be entertained	5.26	6.4	**50.6**
Feel that my opinion is important	4.64	11.1	32.2
Make a better society	4.77	7.9	34.1
Test innovative products and services	5.56	3.6	**59.2**
Test technical solutions that are new to me	5.42	6	**55.2**
Learn something new	5.83	2.4	**69**
Feel social belonging	4.18	**17.9**	22.6
Share experiences with others	4.57	10.3	27.8
Get to know new people	4.01	**22.6**	21.4
Win something	4.56	**21.7**	**53.5**

Bergvall-Kåreborn 2011). The question was formulated as: *How important is it that your participation in innovation activities gives you an opportunity to...* and then the motivational factors were presented. In these questions, the factors were measured using multiple items, which were gathered in the survey using a seven-level Likert scale, where 7 represents *very important*, and 1 represents *not at all important*. The factors were adapted primarily from the previous literature, such as Antikainen et al. (2010), but modified to fit into the specific innovation intermediary community. Table 9.5 depicts the motivators and the response rate.

The result of this question revealed six motivators that respondents considered most important. Here we discuss the motivators with the highest means, above and close to 5. The motivations for the respondents to contribute in innovation activities are to learn something new, to stimulate their curiosity, to test innovative products and services, to test products and services that are new to them as individuals and to be entertained. The motivators they consider least important for their participation in innovation activities are to get to know new people, to acquire a sense of social belonging, to share experiences with other participants and to win something. These motivators had a mean score close to 4; hence, they are not considered unimportant but they have been classified as the least important motivators in this study.

9.4.5 Experienced Influence of Contributing

In this study, we also want to gain insights into how the private persons contributing to innovation processes experience and how their participation influences them. Hence, questions related to the influence experienced, questions starting with *How do you experience that your participation in innovation activities affects your...* were asked of the respondents, who answered on a scale from *increased* to *decreased*. The results showed that 63 % of the contributors reported that their interest in buying the innovation they have helped to develop increased. Sixty-six per cent stated that their desire to market the innovation increased, and 72 % of the respondents stated that their desire to use the innovation increased (Table 9.6). Sixty-three per cent of the respondents stated that their willingness to give feedback on other innovations increased when they participated in open innovation activities. Fifteen per cent of the respondents did not answer this question.

One noticeable result from this study is that involving contributors in the innovation processes has many benefits, since these contributors state that their willingness to buy and use the innovation increased when they were involved in innovation activities. It is also noticeable that the contributors' willingness to give feedback on other innovation, to learn new things and to test new technology, increased.

In terms of the contributors' experience of how their participation affected their willingness to use innovations and to contribute to innovation activities, we asked about their understanding and knowledge about innovations. The question was formulated as: *To what extent do you agree that your participation...* and then they were given different alternatives reported on in Table 9.7. The respondents graded their answers to these questions on a seven-level Likert scale, where 7 represented *I agree totally*, and 1 represented *I disagree totally*.

The answers to these questions show that the majority of the respondents think that their insights about what to expect from innovations increased when they participated in innovation activities. They also state that their understanding of how innovations are developed increased, as did their knowledge of which innovations they wanted and could use. Based on that, involving contributors in innovation activities is beneficial both in the short term, during a specific activity, and in the long term, and after a specific innovation activity has been finalised, since the contributors' attitudes towards innovations are positively affected.

Table 9.6 Experienced influence of participation in innovation activities

How do you experience that your participation in innovation activities influences your willingness to…	Answers	Per cent (%)
…buy the innovations you co-create or test	Increased	63 %
	Unaffected	16 %
	Decreased	1 %
	I do not know	5 %
	No answer	15 %
…market the innovation to others	Increased	66 %
	Unaffected	15 %
	Decreased	1 %
	I do not know	4 %
	No answer	15 %
…learn new things	Increased	69 %
	Unaffected	16 %
	Decreased	0 %
	I do not know	1 %
	No answer	15 %
…try new technology	Increased	69 %
	Unaffected	16 %
	Decreased	0 %
	I do not know	1 %
	No answer	15 %
…use the innovation you have been part of developing	Increased	72 %
	Unaffected	10 %
	Decreased	1 %
	I do not know	2 %
	No answer	15 %
… to give feedback on other innovations	Increased	63 %
	Unaffected	19 %
	Decreased	1 %
	I do not know	2 %
	No answer	15 %

9.5 Discussion and Managerial Implications

The objective of this chapter is to understand what motivates private persons to participate in open innovation activities and to understand how these voluntary contributors find that their participation influenced them. To date, the benefit of involving contributors in open innovation processes has concentrated on the benefits for the company that involve the contributors in innovation processes. In our study of contributors, our most important finding was that involving contributors

9 Voluntary Contributors in Open Innovation Processes

Table 9.7 Participation in innovation activities

To what extent do you agree that your participation in innovation activities...	Per cent (%)
...increase your insights regarding what to expect from new products and services?	
1	1 %
2	1 %
3	4 %
4	11 %
5	23 %
6	34 %
7	25 %
...increase your understanding of how innovations are developed?	
1	1 %
2	2 %
3	6 %
4	15 %
5	28 %
6	26 %
7	22 %
...increase your knowledge regarding which innovations you want to use?	
1	2,5 %
2	0,5 %
3	4 %
4	13 %
5	18 %
6	37 %
7	25 %
...increase your knowledge about which products and services you can use?	
1	1.5 %
2	1.5 %
3	4 %
4	12 %
5	20 %
6	31 %
7	30 %

in innovation processes leads to more knowledgeable and educated contributors with great opportunities and to a pronounced eagerness to start using innovations. The contributors who are involved in innovation activities report that their willingness to buy, market, try or use innovations increased. Furthermore, we found that the contributors' understanding of innovation processes and innovations was enhanced when they engaged in innovation processes.

In this section, we discuss the managerial implication of our findings for innovation managers who have already employed open innovation processes in their organisation. These implications are threefold. First, voluntary contributors have a variety of motivations. Second, building long-term relations with voluntary contributors is important since it increases their interest and knowledge in innovation activities. Third, not all contributors are users or customers.

Considering the first implication, we found that the strongest motivators for the contributors to participate were to learn something new, to stimulate their curiosity, to test innovative products and services, to test products and services that are new to them as individuals, to be entertained or to win something. Viewing the other top-ranked motivators, some of them are linked to learning, such as stimulating curiosity, or testing products or services that are new to them as individuals. Hence, to motivate voluntary contributors to participate in innovation activities, it is essential to stimulate their learning and curiosity. Among the top six motivational factors, only one divides the group into two camps: the potential to win something. While the majority of the users state that they are strongly motivated by the chance of winning something, more than 20 % of the users also state that this is not important at all. According to our study, learning can be an overarching motivator, but the voluntary contributors are also motivated to participate in innovation activities by, for example, being entertained, by the chance to win something or by being the first to test an innovation. This can also be related to intrinsic and extrinsic motivation (Leimeister et al. 2009) where, for example, learning new things is intrinsically desired and being the first to test an innovation is extrinsically desired. Therefore, focusing on a single motivator is unlikely to stimulate different contributors. Instead, an innovation manager might be well advised to offer a variety of motivational incentives to stimulate the users to contribute.

> **Practical Tip**
>
> To attract a large group of voluntary contributors it is important to offer a range of incentives. These incentives can take the form of ideas, competitions, contact and interaction with field experts or celebrities, monetary compensation for their time or contribution or recognition to high performers by electing and announcing the contributor of the month to the community.

With regard to the second implication, building long-term relations, we found that the contributors' participation in innovation activities influences their willingness to buy, market, try, use and give feedback on new innovations. In this study, we found that the motivation to learn was to some extent satisfied for the voluntary contributors since they stated that their knowledge about innovations and innovation processes had increased because of their participation. Being involved in these activities also made them want to learn even more and to lower their resistance to new innovations through increased knowledge and understanding. This can be seen in the results showing that the voluntary contributors' willingness to try new technology, to use innovations and to give feedback on other innovations increased when they participated in innovation activities. Their involvement in innovation activities also increased the contributors' understanding of innovation processes and what to expect from innovations. This implies that involving voluntary contributors might even strengthen the democratising of innovation, a situation where users of innovations gradually acquire the ability to innovate themselves (von Hippel 2005). This finding is in line with previous studies of user participation (Bergvall-Kåreborn and Ståhlbröst 2008; Preece et al. 2007).

Building a long-term commitment between voluntary contributors and innovation managers is therefore valuable for the society, companies and for the voluntary contributors themselves. The users are unique in that they alone benefit directly from innovations to which they contribute (von Hippel 2005). This is also reflected in our study where the voluntary contributors experience an increase in their willingness to use and buy the innovation they have been part of developing. The added value for the contributors is also linked to their motivation since they want to learn new things and thus participate in innovation activities. Hence, the contributors can see an added value of participating in innovation activities since they learn more about innovation processes and about the kind of products and services that might be suitable for their needs. Through their improved understanding of innovations, the step towards innovating themselves is shortened. This possibility is also enhanced by the nature of the contributors, the majority of whom are innovators (5 %), visionaries (16 %) or technology enthusiasts (38 %).

> **Practical Tip**
>
> To increase the likelihood that the contributors will buy and use the innovation once it is available on the market, it is essential to keep them enthusiastically involved throughout the process. This can be done in many ways, such as having an open process to ensure that the contributors are aware of what is happening in the project, to ensure that the contributors realise that their ideas and feedback influences the innovation, but also understand why some of their contributions are not integrated; manage their expectations on both the development process and on the finished innovation; build trust, and respect the contributors' integrity.

The third implication recognises that not all contributors are users or customers.

> **Practical Tip**
>
> Remember that even non-buyers or non-users can contribute greatly to your innovation process by helping you to improve and develop your innovation. As such, voluntary contributors should be a more heterogeneous group of people than the potential customer base of a product or service. It is therefore important for you to be creative when identifying and recruiting these people. For example, identify people who have a range of qualifications and can contribute in the different phases in the innovation process. Customer support is a good channel for gathering feedback on products or services. Trendsetters, for example, within social media such as blogs, need to be identified since these trendsetters both identify and set future trends.

In this chapter, we have defined a new concept, *voluntary contributors*. These contributors usually contribute to open innovation processes as individual private persons rather than as community members. They have a common interest in a particular study, rather than in a common purpose and a set of community values. They participate on a voluntary basis without significant financial compensation and represent a highly heterogeneous group of loosely coupled people.

In relation to the early phases of innovation process, the concepts of user and consumer have been discussed. It is hard to know the users or consumers of a product or service that does not yet exist. Further, by limiting the perspective of possible participants to expected users or customers, companies are limiting the group of people that they can engage in their innovation activities. This could hamper the innovation power since the value of an open process increases with the number of people involved in two ways (Chesbrough 2003). Firstly, a larger group of people contributes a larger volume of ideas, content and feedback with the potential to improve the quality and variety of the product or service in focus, as seen in Wikipedia, YouTube and Google Maps. Secondly, a larger number of people have the potential to generate a more noticeable momentum behind the product or service, leading to a situation where more people draw others to the product or service.

While much literature within the open innovation area tends to focus on the need for a specific product or service as the main motivator for customer contribution, our study illustrates a wide range of motivational factors that can explain why people choose to contribute to open innovation processes. Hence, the democratisation of open innovation and user-centric approaches goes beyond enabling people to design their own products and services. For the voluntary contributors in our study, there is a close relationship between the motivational factors and the values achieved, which indicates that most of the contributors satisfied their need to learn new things. Considering that learning is important for voluntary contributors in general, innovation community managers need to reflect on how they can stimulate the learning aspect for the contributors. One way of doing this is to facilitate community interaction that builds on exchanging knowledge and experiences linked to technology and innovation, rather than on social belonging and relationship building. Hence, these innovation communities need to resemble developer communities and forums, rather than social networking sites, such as Facebook and MySpace.

References

Antikainen, M., Mäkipää, M., & Ahonen, M. (2010). Motivating and supporting collaboration in open innovation. *European Journal of Innovation Management, 13*(1), 100–119.

Bergvall-Kåreborn, B. & Ståhlbröst, A., (2008). Participatory design- One step back or two steps forward. Paper read at *Participatory Design Conference, at Bloomington*, Indiana, 821, Simonsen, J. Robertson, T. & Hakken, D. 102–111

Bergvall-Kåreborn, B., & Ståhlbröst, A. (2009). Living lab—an open and citizen-centric approach for innovation. *International Journal of Innovation and Regional Development, 1*(4), 356–370.

Berthon, P., Pitt, L. F., McCarthy, I., & Kates, S. M. (2007). When customers get clever: Managerial approaches to dealing with creative consumers. *Business Horizons, 50*(1), 39–47.

Chesbrough, H. W. (2003). The era of open innovation. *MIT Sloan Management Review, 44*(3), 35–42.

Chesbrough, H. W. (2006). *Open innovation—The new imperative for creating and profiting from technology*. Cambridge, MA: Harvard Business School Press.

Chesbrough, H. W., & Appleyard, M. (2007). Open innovation and strategy. *California Management Review, 50*(1), 57–76.

Enkel, E., Gassmann, O., & Chesbrough, H. W. (2009). Open R&D and open innovation: Exploring the phenomenon. *R&D Management, 39*(4), 311–316.

Enkel, E., Javier, P.-F., & Gassmann, O. (2005). Minimizing market risks through customer integration in new product development: Learning from bad practice. *Creativity and Innovation Management, 14*(4), 425–437.

Gassmann, O., Enkel, E., & Charles, C. (2010). The future of open innovation. *R&D Management, 40*(3), 213–221.

Hars, A., & Ou, S. (2002). Working for free? Motivations for participating in open-source projects. *International Journal of Electronic Commerce, 6*(3), 25–39.

Leimeister, J., Huber, M., Bretshneider, U., & Helmut, K. (2009). Leveraging crowdsourcing: Activation-supporting components for IT-based ideas competition. *Journal of Management Information Systems, 26*(1), 197–224.

Preece, J., Rogers, Y., & Sharp, H. (2007). *Interaction design: Beyond human-computer interaction* (2nd ed.). New York, NY: John Wiley & Sons, Inc.

Rogers, E. M. (2003). *Diffusion of Innovations* (5th ed.). New York, NY: Free Press.

Stepanikova, I., Nie, N. H. & He, X. (2010). Time on the Internet at home, loneliness, and life satisfaction: Evidence from Panel time-diary data. *Computers in Human Behaviour, 26*(3), 329–338.

Ståhlbröst, A., & Bergvall-Kåreborn, B. (2011). Exploring users' motivation in innovation communities. *International Journal of Entrepreneurship and Innovation Management, 14*(4), 298–314.

von Hippel, E. (1986). Lead user: A source of novel product concepts. *Management Science, 32*(7), 791–805.

von Hippel, E. (2005). *Democratizing innovation*. Cambridge, MA: The MIT Press.

Further Reading

Bacon, J. (2009). *The art of community: Building the new age of participation*. Cambridge: O'Reilly.

Chesbrough, H. W. (2011). *Open service innovation—Rethinking your business to grow and compete in a new era*. San Francisco, CA: Jossey-Bass.

Ke, W., & Zhang, P. (2010). The effects of extrinsic motivation and satisfaction in open source software development. *Journal of the Association for Information Systems, 11*, 784–808.

Muhdi, L., & Boutellier, R. (2011). Motivational factors affecting participation and contribution of members in two different Swiss innovation communities. *International Journal of Innovation Management, 15*(3), 543–562.

Schweisfurth, T., Raasch, C., & Herstatt, C. (2011). Free revealing in open innovation: A comparison of different models and their benefits for companies. *International Journal of Product Development, 13*(2), 95–118.

Chapter 10
Creating Value Through Open Innovation in Social E-Learning

Per Andersson, Pierre Jarméus, Simone Masog, Christopher Rosenqvist, and Carl Sundberg

Abstract This chapter discusses how to create value in the network, which is critical since social media-based E-learning can be seen as a network of actors interacting with each other. The more value a network can potentially accrue, the richer the learning experience is for the participants. Value in this instance is defined as the network's ability to generate and aid the construction of social knowledge. Further, the chapter discusses the implementation of social media-based E-learning and finally some practical advice is presented about how to implement social media-based E-learning.

10.1 A New Learning Landscape

A new breed has been born under the banner of Digital Natives. Digital Natives are not only familiar with handling digital technology, but they are more likely to be highly efficient users (The Institute for Corporate Productivity 2010). Furthermore, this, in combination with the development of the experience economy as outlined by Pine and Gilmore (1998) and the increased digitalisation of society, gives rise to new learning opportunities. Moreover, according to Normann and Ramírez (1998) the construction of new mental concepts can lead to value creation. This is seen happening today as the traditional definition of a teacher and student increasingly becomes blurred in higher education. Teachers rather take the important role of a guide and facilitator in the interaction process. Learners engage in discussions and socially construct knowledge.

P. Andersson (✉) • S. Masog • C. Rosenqvist • C. Sundberg
Department of Marketing & Strategy, Stockholm School of Economics, Stockholm, Sweden
e-mail: per.andersson@hhs.se; simone.masog@alumni.hhs.se; christopher.rosenqvist@hhs.se; carl.sundberg@alumni.hhs.se

P. Jarméus
Accenture AB, SOLNA, Stockholm, Sweden
e-mail: pierre.jarmeus@accenture.com

J.S.Z. Eriksson Lundström et al. (eds.), *Managing Open Innovation Technologies*,
DOI 10.1007/978-3-642-31650-0_10, © Springer-Verlag Berlin Heidelberg 2013

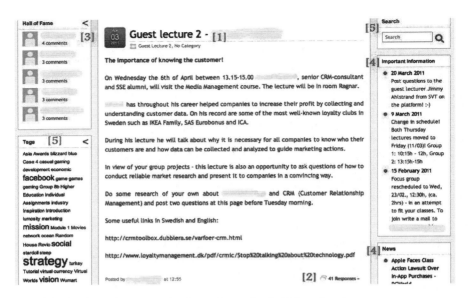

Fig. 10.1 The figure is an example of open innovation in higher education

Socially constructed knowledge is defined as two or more parties coming together, and through interaction create knowledge, as for example, Wikipedia and its various contributors. This social construction of knowledge is facilitated by social media technology. Thus, the traditional teaching concept is questioned as the one-directional flow of knowledge from instructors to learners is replaced by various two-directional flows from information distributors to information receivers. Incorporating social media and other Web 2.0 technologies into the learning environment opens up for experimenting and gives rise to new teaching concepts.

Using technology, such as social media for learning and the social creation of knowledge, is an example of E-learning 2.0. However, there is currently a lack of knowledge, which seems to generate resistance to innovation because of the fear of not realising the value of E-learning 2.0 investments (Ram and Sheth 1989). Therefore, a project was started at the Stockholm School of Economics (SSE) to further explore E-learning 2.0. The project had two phases, which in itself can be seen as a form of open innovation by combining the efforts of students, teachers and external parties. The first phase established a general level of understanding regarding E-learning 2.0 and the market, while the second phase focused on two primary issues: value creation and implementation, in relation to social media. The project involved the construction and administration of an E-learning 2.0 platform (see Fig. 10.1), conducting 30 interviews with industry experts and practitioners, two focus groups and two quantitative studies. The research was done in accordance with academic standards, e.g. semi-structured interviews following well-known research guidelines and taking an objective stance. The project resulted

10 Creating Value Through Open Innovation in Social E-Learning 153

in three reports and multiple insights. One of these insights, the focus of this chapter, is that open innovation is a natural part of E-learning 2.0, which can serve as a platform for open innovation in an organisation, thus creating long-term value.

10.2 Chapter Disposition

This chapter is divided into three sections. Section 10.1 discusses how to create value in the network, which is critical since social media-based E-learning can be seen as a network of actors interacting with each other. The more value a network can potentially accrue, the richer the learning experience is for the participants. Value in this instance is defined as the network's ability to generate and aid the construction of social knowledge. Section 10.2 discusses the implementation of social media-based E-learning and is divided into two parts: the acceptance process and implementation strategies. User acceptance of the network is highly dependent on the value of the network, and at the same time value can only be created when users decide to accept the network. This loop represents a significant obstacle and which is why the acceptance process, along with the implementation strategies that can affect it, is important to understand. Section 10.3 provides practical advice about how to implement social media-based E-learning.

Section 10.1 is based on the theories and findings by Masog (2011). Similarly, Sect. 10.2 is based on the theories and findings by Jarméus and Sundberg (2011). Davis (1986) especially provided valuable inspiration. Both Sects. 10.1 and 10.2 draw significantly from the theories of Normann and Ramírez (1998). Section 10.3 is inspired by the experiences and reflections of the authors in implementing social media-based E-learning. It is also worth noting that throughout the sections the authors use the term 'network' and 'social media-based E-learning' interchangeably.

10.3 Open Innovation and Sustainable Value

As a platform, social media-based learning can give rise to different types of open innovation, in particular, continuous improvement of the solution by means of user co-production as well as newly derived forms of networking, business opportunities and changed behavioural processes. However, to create sustainable open innovation in the long term, clear value must be visible to all actors in the value constellation of Web 2.0 technologies. Therefore, areas of open innovation in social media-based learning are identified and linked to sources of value creation based on value creation theory (Normann and Ramírez 1998).

10.3.1 New Ways to View Learning

Social media-based E-learning emphasises the social construction of knowledge and thereby questions the traditional teaching concept. Thus, new innovative ways of how to view learning can arise. The authors argue that these viewpoints once combined with the powerful method/mindset of open innovation, using social media as the tool, can result in new methods of learning. These new methods of learning can be linked to value creation through new mental concepts and increased liquidity. Liquidity refers to the value creation driven by the removal of barriers of time and space. Social media can enhance the service quality of a course by reducing existing barriers of space. The barriers of a traditional classroom interaction are removed and can be extended to the online space. Virtual conferences can overcome geographical distances. The authors' studies show that social media can also assist to eliminate the compartmentalisation of single courses from a learning perspective and thereby overcome traditional course systems.

The distance of different employees in different geographic locations can be reduced by, e.g. communicating instantaneously through social media. Social media can also create value by reducing the distance between different hierarchical levels within a company. In an academic context, the gap between the academic world and practitioners can be narrowed. This type of interaction can increase the value and relevance for students of a certain subject and at the same time also increase the professionals' understanding of academic work and the differences inherent in the working style, giving rise to new forms of networking and collaboration.

10.3.2 New Ways of Networking

Innovative forms of training can emerge, the authors believe, by new types of cooperation and networking. Teachers around the world can collaborate and engage in new joint teaching approaches. Virtual office hours or email support can be provided basically 24/7. This can ultimately lead to higher quality and added value for the learner. Experts and practitioners can hire out their expertise and knowledge to universities or in corporate training. For instance, a practitioner in the field of e-commerce can answer questions in a forum or give virtual lectures in the frame of an online marketing course for a contracted amount of hours per month. While this already exists in a decentralised manner, a platform-based online service can arise, in which universities and corporate training departments can search online for, e.g. a practitioner in web design for 10 h a month. Similarly, experts and practitioners can voice their offers. As a result, a transparent and accessible market for hiring out single practitioners and expert hours can be created on a worldwide scale.

These opportunities can be strongly linked to network-related value creation. New actors, e.g. experts, alumni or practitioners, can be added, who were not available before because of financial, space or time constraints. Social media represents a tool, which allows individuals to cultivate larger networks at lower costs. The mere size of the network can be value creating as indicated by Metcalfe's law which states that the overall value of the network increases exponentially for every additional user that joins. Other network-related value creation mechanisms are represented by activity reconfiguration, in particular by the concept of relieving and enabling actors. Enabling and relieving represent *"opportunities based on the better utilisation of the joint resources of both parties, [. . .]"* (Normann and Ramírez 1998, p. 59) and it is also about discovering *"new ways to create more value through more effective means of matching shared activities"* (Normann and Ramírez 1998, p. 60). From a more macro-level perspective view on learning, the concept of engaged partiality can also be connected to the mechanism of relieving and enabling. While one single individual is relieved of knowing everything about a specific subject area, as this is not possible any longer, a network of actors is empowered to become specialists in a subfield. Previously sequential executed actions can now be carried out simultaneously. Thus, time is saved as actions are carried out at the same time.

10.3.3 New Behavioural Processes

The application of open innovation in learning situations can comprise new behavioural processes which replace traditional ones. Actors, other than students, encourage the use of social media technologies, e.g. Twitter or wikis. As there is not one established way of how to use social media in learning situations, there is a lot of room for experimentation and innovation.

The emergence of new behavioural processes can be connected to density-related value creation; more specifically, value is created by an increase in the number of options in a certain time period or space. Social media can increase the amount of interaction in a given time period and allows for more communication. Specific social media channels, such as microblogs, are especially useful in improving the communication of time sensitive information. Beyond that, microblogs, such as Twitter, can be applied to communicate comments and questions on a separate screen to a presenter during a presentation. Being able to store information in a wiki or forum can assist users to assess the existing knowledge base and avoid the duplication of work. Beyond that, social media can free the time of employees, who represent information hubs in companies. Parts of the knowledge of these employees can be internalised and made accessible by wikis, for example. Thus, new working flows can arise as information is increasingly accessed in different ways.

To assess which specific functionalities are valuable to users in a specific learning situation, an ongoing process of user co-creation of a Web 2.0 technology learning platform should take place. This in itself represents a form of open innovation since the users take an active part in the process in contrast to the traditional learning approach where the instructor alone determined it. Thus, new behavioural processes arise, as a result of user co-creation being a part of open innovation. The utilisation of co-creation will be further discussed in the section 'Starting the Open Value Creation Process'.

User co-creation to assess which functionalities are valuable for learners in a learning situation can be linked to offering related value creation. Different social media channels possess different functionalities and thereby different benefits. These should therefore be bundled. For instance, a Twitter channel can be used for instant and time-sensitive communication, while a wiki's best application is for the accumulation and internalisation of knowledge over a longer time horizon. Value can additionally be generated by giving the user the possibility to integrate or aggregate different systems in a seamless way to achieve a one-stop shop for information. The bundling of social media functionality with search functionality is one of the most important value drivers in the integration of different functionalities, as individuals become more efficient in finding information faster.

10.3.4 Changing and Facilitating Corporate Workflows

Social media provides the infrastructure to grow idea markets in a corporation and let everyone participate in order to contribute to new innovations. This is an example of how social media tools innovate the innovation process within a company, which represents a type of intra-organisational change and open innovation. Traditionally, the task to innovate has been reserved to scientists, engineers, designers, lead users or employees in the R&D department. Open innovation creates value in the way that it can reduce costs and at the same time increases the number of profit generating innovations. The innovation process within a company can become more transparent and inclusive by means of social media. This transparency has the potential benefit to reward everyone who contributed to the generation of an innovative idea and not only the one who finally published it or picked it up in a project. New networks with new actors can be formed to foster the innovation process in a company. This is in line with Birkinshaw et al. (2007) who say that especially for discontinuous innovation, companies should create new networks not in existence before, e.g. idea networks, cross-industry alliances or communities of practices. Two of the obstacles identified to finding prospective partners, geographical and institutional, can potentially be overcome by means of social media (Birkinshaw et al. 2007).

Social media-based learning can foster and actively support new business development, where new employment models and new corporations can arise and traditional work processes are radically altered. Different social media tools are seen as a cost-efficient way to connect with internal and external experts and facilitate interaction on a global scale. This finding can be connected to the trend, which is illustrated by Manyika et al. (2007, p. 3) as follows: *"As more and more sophisticated work takes place interactively online and new collaboration and communication tools emerge, companies can outsource increasingly specialised aspects of their own work and still maintain organisational coherence."* Thus, social media tools play a central role in driving this trend further as Web 2.0 technology lays the foundation for the cost-efficient interaction with experts.

Organisational learning is often accelerated by dialogue, shared experiences, personal relationships and other forms of informal learning. Social media can therefore help facilitate the trend, which according to Manyika et al. (2007) can be described as gaining more value from interactions. Furthermore, they claim that companies in developed countries offshore transformational activities as production to a greater extent, as well as transactional work, consisting of clerical work. The remaining tasks within developed countries require conversation, interaction, negotiation and collaboration, which are labelled as tacit interaction. This in itself represents a form of innovation of work processes. Social media tools can assist employees who mainly interact tacitly to become more effective, by creating an environment in which knowledge is more accessible, timely and relevant. Ultimately companies will engage in managerial innovation in creating more value in their interaction, which potentially gives a company the competitive edge as networks of people and talents, as well as processes, are hard to copy (Manyika et al. 2007).

10.4 Starting the Value Creation Process

The 'the value in use' concept is central, according to the authors, for a functioning social media-based solution in learning. The concept means that the participants only receive value from the network when they are actively using it. Therefore, the implementation stage is critical to attract a sufficient number of users and keep them engaged in the long term. If the implementation of the social media-based information system is not done correctly, a sufficient number of users will not be engaged in the long term, and as an effect no long-term value can be achieved. This section will therefore discuss the implementation as the first step towards long-term value and how open innovation can assist in this process.

10.4.1 The Acceptance Process

The technology acceptance process of social media-based E-learning 2.0 can be depicted as a snowball initially standing still on a slope with two inclinations. At first, the snowball is small and not moving. However, once the snowball starts moving, it will start growing in size by adding even more snowflakes. Furthermore, the slope has two inclinations. At first, it is relatively flat, and one has to push hard (assuming that the weight is constant no matter the size of the snowball) to make it roll at all. However, after a while, the slope starts to have a high level of downwards inclination and pushing the snowball becomes quite easy. This is actually how the acceptance process appears to work. At first, there are no people in the system, and since people (actors) mean value, the value network is small. This leads to a problem, since new users may not see/understand the value of the system. However, as more and more people (snowflakes) join, the value network grows. At a certain point the ability to demonstrate the system's value to new users becomes easier, and a 'tipping point' is reached upon which the technology acceptance process takes off. What drives the acceptance itself is an interrelation between various external variables and the corresponding experience. In other words, when a person uses the system he or she will have an experience that is affected by, and affects, the system and its related activities. Depending on how the technology then is perceived, the user will decide when and how to use it. Furthermore, once a person does decide to use the system, that person is added to the systems network of users. In other words, when a person accepts the system, the system's value is likely to go up. A person's acceptance in turn affects the system and its social activities, which in turn will affect the experience. We can thereby see how the acceptance process will 'pick up speed' as more people become users of the technology due to its social nature.

10.4.2 The Enhanced Acceptance Process

The acceptance process, or 'snowball of acceptance', is in a sense built up by people. However, in this process, the people have had a relatively passive role in affecting the acceptance process since they only affect existing activities and parts of the system. This is an inefficient use of resources since if we consider the situation we will see that we have a pool of skilled professionals or ambitious students, joined together in a social web built for the creation of knowledge. The authors believe that one should be able to utilise this pool of human resources, through open innovation, to drive the acceptance process forward. Since the process relies on the system, the activities and the experience itself, people could make contributions by making these three areas function better. For example, building a proper system and designing perfect activities is a difficult task. In this instance, user co-creation would be useful to improve the current system and design new activities.

There are multiple reasons why an open innovation infused acceptance process is viable. Firstly, extensive open source projects take place around the Internet today. These projects sometimes build solutions that directly rival big and expensive alternatives. To imagine a group of people designing a social media-related platform aimed specifically for E-learning 2.0 is feasible. Secondly, the employees and customers of an organisation often have some understanding of their own needs, but lack sufficient ability to pinpoint them. To share information between the users and experienced developers could facilitate a better implementation process. For example, instead of letting five to ten people sit and try to imagine all the current and future uses of the system and then start building it, you can start by asking the actual users and ensure that the system can be consistently upgraded and adapted to new input as it is built. Finally, once the system is up and running, users of the system, both inside and outside the organisation, could continue to bring advice for how to improve it (or even build the improvements themselves). The result, the authors assume, would be a flexible and 'organic' E-learning 2.0 solution. Not only would the solution have the potential to fit the users better, but the sense of 'ownership' and 'belonging' with the system among the users would likely be greater since they helped build it.

10.4.3 Designing the System

Beyond understanding the basics of the acceptance process, depicted earlier like a snowball on a slope, one needs to understand what the user group wants from the system. If the system is designed so that it is optimised towards the user group then they are more likely to accept it, i.e. the snowball starts rolling. Generally, some key areas to focus on are perceived usefulness and ease of use of the system, as well as other motivational factors relating to the nature of social media. However, knowing in detail what the optimal system will look like is not always clear. This is due to the previously mentioned inability of users to pinpoint in detail what features they want or need from a system. Therefore, open innovation can help since it can provide options that the users would not have considered initially but are essential in reaching the optimal system. If the system is developed internally in accordance to a single round of user feedback, instead of continuous co-creation, there is a lesser chance that an optimal system can be reached. The users sometimes need to be provided with readymade features and try them before they can judge if it should be implemented in the system. The cost of developing a feature that might not be implemented is a needless cost and makes little economic sense. It is likely that by utilising open innovation in the design process, the development time and associated costs of these features can be avoided.

10.4.4 Gaining Insights for Strategy Formation

As the system deals with the socially constructed knowledge, strategies should be aimed at influencing individuals to use the system in a social way. Therefore, a need exists to understand the individuals in order to form strategies that can effectively influence them. The authors want to argue that to fully understand the users they need to be examined beyond that of the internal formal setting, expanding the use of open innovation to the informal setting and thereby taking a holistic approach. Generating strategies that are based on insights gained from looking internally, in the formal learning environment, can be considered insufficient. This is because they only draw from a partial understanding of the user. Having an open innovation approach and looking at behaviour and strategies formed outside of the formal environment can provide additional insight into forming acceptance strategies.

Therefore, strategies that work in the outside formal environment should be able to be transferred into the formal one.

Additionally, it is worth noting that the majority of the online interaction occurs in an informal environment and not within closed systems. Therefore, it is more likely that strategies will organically develop in the informal environment in order to guide and control the interaction occurring, e.g. chat room hosts overseeing interaction. However, strategies that are transferred to the formal environment might need some configuration in order to fit the conditions present in the system as they might differ from the informal ones.

By identifying the three aspects, managerial, social and technical, the authors have gained a critical insight, namely that to successfully implement and attract enough users to the system, and thus be able to achieve long-term value, a holistic approach to the strategy and implementation is necessary. This is important to consider when utilising open innovation in the implementation process, since it is a good idea to apply this mindset to several aspects of the implementation.

10.5 Some Final Practical Advice

As the implementation of social media-based E-learning represents a continuous cycle, it can sometimes be difficult to locate a starting point. However, the authors hope that by providing some practical advice, potential implementers will more easily identify a starting point and initiate the implementation process.

Firstly, and most importantly, to increase the chances of starting the continuous cycle and achieving long-term value, the authors recommend that you ensure that you have an in-depth knowledge regarding E-learning 2.0, as well as strong leadership and management.

> **Practical Tip**
>
> Ensure that you have an in-depth knowledge regarding E-learning 2.0, as well as strong leadership and management.

Secondly, Fig. 10.1 demonstrates some general advice for a social media-based E-learning platform:

> **Practical Tip**
>
> 1. The platform provides a meeting ground where external and internal parties can interact. This is a good way to improve liquidity, which in turn, can facilitate open innovation.
> 2. The platform provides an efficient way to communicate by providing structure for desynchronised multi-user interaction.
> 3. It motives an exchange culture by rewarding active users.

4. Social media features, such as Twitter and RSS feeds, can be used to streamline the information flow and more easily allow multi-device accessibility.
5. The platform should be easy to navigate. The authors especially recommend a powerful and easy-to-use search function.

Finally, we strongly advocate following these three pieces of practical advice based on our own experience:

Practical Tip

Clarity of vision and information: Have a clear vision so that the efforts pull in the same direction and make sure you have a structured approach to information management to avoid clutter.

Gather a broad set of knowledge and confirm its usability: Make sure that you take in advice from outside your own organisation to assure a broad perspective on how the system can, and should be able to, function. Furthermore, make sure that the ideas and suggestions work when contrasted with current E-learning 2.0 knowledge.

Assure proper support and resources: Ensure that you have the proper support and resources before starting the journey, since it may take longer than you think.

References

Birkinshaw, J., et al. (2007). Finding, forming and performing—creating networks for discontinuous innovation. *California Management Review, 49*(3Spring 2007), 67–84.

Davis, F. D., Jr. (1986). *A technology acceptance model for empirically testing new end-user information systems: theory and results*. MA, USA: Massachusetts Institute of Technology.

Hallberg J, Masog S, Jarméus P & Sundberg C (2010) *E-learning 2.0—The Phenomenon and the Future*. Stockholm School of Economics.

Jarméus P & Sundberg C (2011) *Social Media for Learning—A qualitative and quantitative study regarding the implementation process, strategic issues and utilisation of Web 2.0 technology for formal learning*. Stockholm School of Economics.

Manyika, J. M., Roberts, R. P., & Sprague, K. L. (2007). Eight business technology trends to watch. *The McKinsey Quarterly, 20*, 1–9.

Masog S (2011) *Social Media Driven Value Creation in a Corporate and Academic Learning Context—An Explorative Study*. Stockholm School of Economics.

Normann, R., & Ramírez, R. (1998). *Designing interactive strategy: From value chain to value constellation* (2nd ed.). Chichester, GB: John Wiley & Sons Ltd.

Pine, B. J., II, & Gilmore, J. H. (1998). *Welcome to the experience economy* (pp. 97–105). Boston, MA: Harvard Business Review.

Ram, S., & Sheth, J. N. (1989). Consumer resistance to innovations: The marketing problem. *The Journal of Consumer Marketing, 6*(2), 5–14.

The Institute for Corporate Productivity. (2010) The Rise of Social Media: Enhancing Collaboration and Productivity Across Generations. ASTD Press.

Further Reading

Bradley, A., & Mcdonald, M. (2011). *The social organization*. Boston, MA: Harvard Business Review Press.

Koulouvari P. (2001) *Organizational learning in dynamic environments: case studies from the media industry,* Ph.D. thesis. KTH – Royal Institute of Technology, Stockholm, Sweden http://kth.diva-- - -portal.org/smash/record.jsf?pid=diva2:8870

Rosenberg, M. (2001). *E-Learning: strategies for delivering knowledge in the digital age.* New York: McGraw-Hill.

Rosenberg, M., & Chichester, J. (2006). *Beyond e-learning: approaches and technologies to enhance organizational knowledge, learning, and performance.* New York: Wiley.

Theme III
Moving Forward

The Future Use of Open Innovation in Theory and Practice

Innovation never takes place in a vacuum. As Leonard-Barton, among others, reminds us, innovations happen at the boundaries between disciplines or specialisations. It is novel or incremental changes that induce processes that might be addressed as an innovation.

Chesbrough has, for good reason, suggested that many contemporary firms have shifted to an open innovation model. However, this shift to "openness" can be studied from many different perspectives and be linked to many different forces in society. In the following five chapters, in Chap. 11, Lindman et al. start by identifying and investigating the basic requirements for creating open innovation technologies. However, companies have a myriad of different (knowledge) sources to exploit and take advantage from, requiring different tools and practices. To help with this matter, in Chap. 12, Corvello et al. present a paper in which they single out the requirements associated with different sources linked to devices to maintain open innovation practices. Seven strategies are presented to facilitate the knowledge exchange that might propel and generate innovations. These two chapters are followed by three concrete outcomes of enacting open innovation technologies. In Chap. 13, Fähling et al. shed light on how open innovation technologies are used as platforms where companies offer small, highly structured paid tasks to be solved by crowdsourcing. By doing this, they illuminate the potential of open innovations technologies and give advice about how they can be used to its full potential. In the following chapter, Chap. 14, Hürlimann and Yakhlef explore the role of IT in all the different phases of a user innovation process and point to the importance of complementing the use of IT with more traditional modes of interactions and communications with their customers and users. Chapter 15 by Keller et al. is about an explorative study that focuses on how open innovation technology is put into practice in the healthcare sector and highlights both its potential and some of its intriguing obstacles. Finally, in Chap. 16, Ridell et al. remind us that practising open innovation process also strikes back and forces us to confront the important issue of how open, open innovation really is. By doing this they summarise the comprehensive theme of all the papers; we need to identify and understand both the barriers and drivers to practice open innovation.

Mats Edenius

Chapter 11
Overcoming Industrial Inertia by Use of Open Innovation Technologies

Juho Lindman, Tuija Heikura, and Petra Turkama

Abstract Industries develop at different paces. The constant environmental flux of information and communication technology companies becomes especially clear when comparing them with more traditional industries, in our case, the Finnish construction industry. The sector is dominated by a number of large industrial actors with established positions operating predominantly in the domestic or Scandinavian market. Based on our literature review and a round of key person interviews, this chapter categorises the different sources of institutional inertia in this particular industry. We build a research framework for defining the requirements for creating open innovation technologies that could accelerate structural changes in a traditional industry. First, sources of inertia are identified empirically. Second, we discuss a set of requirements for an open innovation technology which would be needed to overcome this inertia.

11.1 Introduction

Our aim is to provide a set of requirements to overcome industrial inertia using more participatory innovation technologies. In this chapter, we show how industrial inertia operates at the level of the Finnish construction industry. The construction industry offers an interesting contrast to sectors such as information and

---

J. Lindman (✉)
Hanken School of Economics, Helsinki, Finland
e-mail: juho.lindman@hanken.fi

T. Heikura
Suomen Teknologiakeskusten Liitto TEKEL, Helsinki, Finland
e-mail: tuija.heikura@tekel.fi

P. Turkama
Aalto University School of Economics/CKIR, Helsinki, Finland
e-mail: petra.turkama@aalto.fi

J.S.Z. Eriksson Lundström et al. (eds.), *Managing Open Innovation Technologies*,
DOI 10.1007/978-3-642-31650-0_11, © Springer-Verlag Berlin Heidelberg 2013

communication technologies, which are more often researched in the context of innovation. We build on the insights of open innovation in order to investigate the complex web of relationships between legal, commercial and social aims concerning the built environment. Our level of analysis is that of an organisational field (i.e. an industry). For the purposes of this framework, we include the construction and renovation of residential and office buildings.

Analysing industrial inertia is not only important because it offers feedback to the actors of the Finnish construction industry, but also because it highlights the difficulties in changing an interlinked network of interdependencies in many sectors. Furthermore, it offers a reality check for those who want to use the same approaches to innovation technology across various sectors neglecting their structural characteristics. First, we empirically identify the different types of inertia, then we build a framework categorising the sources of inertia and finally we discuss a set of requirements for an (open innovation) technology, which would overcome these barriers.

We do not endorse the view that different industries are separated and never communicate with each other. Instead, we see that different industries and national states are interlinked. We limit our research to a single country mainly for the purposes of analysis and to reduce the complexity which would emerge if more than one national political and juridical system needed to be taken into account.

The chapter is structured as follows: First we show how literature on open innovation and entrepreneurial institutionalism come together to build a research framework used in analysing industrial inertia and categorising their institutional sources. Then we proceed to an empirical inquiry on the Finnish construction industry. Finally, we report our findings followed by discussion on the requirements for (open innovation) technology followed by conclusions.

11.2 Construction Industry and Open Innovation

The market structure of the construction industry has been claimed to inhibit innovation. For example, Lutzenhiser and Biggart (2003) conducted analyses on how the market structure affects the diffusion of energy efficiency. They even remark that the industry actors seem to have a "separate social world with its own logic, language, actors, interests and regulatory demands" (p. 47).

The residential building industry was the topic for Eccless' (1981) classic study on how the industry field was structured. Eccless' (1981) research was on entities he coined as "quasi-firms". They were groups of companies from the (construction) industry, which could not easily be viewed in terms of either market or hierarchy. These entities were later further researched under the term inter-organisational networks (Taylor 2005). For example, Gann and Salter (2000) describe how the problems in learning and feedback loops resulted in poor innovation rates in the context of the construction industry.

The process of innovation is increasingly driven by open networks of cooperation and involves dynamic interrelationships between technological transformations, organisational capabilities of firms, public policy and supportive regulatory structures. Collaborative networks of companies enable systemic innovations through strategic pooling of resources, sharing risks and leveraging. These collaborative networks usually have a strong industry partner as a driver, and the objective is to extend the ecosystem towards the customers, and focus on creating a consortium with a wider pool of expertise. The trends towards participatory approaches have been explained by various theoretical traditions and approaches, including social action theories (Etzioni 1967), transaction cost economists (Teece et al. 1997) and a resource-based view on the firm (Wernerfelt 1984).

The economic rationale for open innovation is emphasised in the much cited works of Von Hippel (2005) and Chesbrough (2006). Von Hippel's view on open innovation builds on the basic assumption that current demand and consumer needs are too complex for a single organisation to fulfil, and thus require external resources for finding new ideas and developing new products or services. In practice, this means multidisciplinary participation with complementing actors (organisations, users). Reflecting this, Chesbrough (2006) states that open innovation networks build on the assumption that the network will result in improved sustainability of partnerships, a comprehensive offering, increased success rate and greater user satisfaction. We recommend the use of open innovation technologies as a means to advance and reinforce this sharing and collaboration, and thus accelerate industry development and structural changes also in traditional, asset-heavy industries such as the construction industry. The use of open innovation technologies opens up informal, low threshold channels for employees and customers to voice their opinions and ideas. The process would arguably have several direct benefits in terms of new ideas from experts and lower costs of obtaining information, as well as indirect benefits through increased job satisfaction and commitment to the company.

11.3 Overcoming Inertia and Entrepreneurial Institutionalism

The culture of knowledge sharing among partners and collaborators is yet to be developed in the case of the Finnish construction industry. Companies are increasingly beginning to engage employees in innovation activities and introduce less hierarchical forms of organisational structures. However, the scale of operations is significantly lower than in less established industries. For example, ICT companies are already deriving business value from Web 2.0 tools—such as blogs, RSS, wikis, podcasts, peer-to-peer, mashups and the like—and are already shifting from using them experimentally to adopting them as part of a broader business practice. This implies that the process has accumulated economic value to the companies. The mechanisms underlying this value creation process have been developed in an evolutionary process, and thus cannot be transferred directly to more traditional industries. The development starts with small-scale pilots and trials, and can gradually develop into industry-level practice.

Our theoretical understanding of sociotechnical change is based on Geels (2004). In his framework, Geels (2004) advanced the systems of innovation theory by providing an increased focus on the user side. The elements of the framework can be categorised into systems, actors and *institutions*. The novelty of the approach is in its focus on the change and transformation of systems rather than taking a snapshot of the environment and analysing it as though it were static.

Scott (1995) analyses organisational environments by using three pillars of institutions which exert influence on individual organisations: regulative, normative and cognitive. Often research has started from the focus on institutional environments "*characterised by the elaboration or rules and requirements to which individual organisations must conform if they are to gain support or legitimacy*" (Scott 1995, p. 132). Entrepreneurial institutionalism is a recent research stream, which focuses on how organisations change these institutional environments, rather than focus on how institutional environments constrain organisations. In more detail, we start with Scott's pillars of institutions, but view them as something which should be changed, rather than something which is a given structure that constrains actors. In other words, we view these pillars from an entrepreneurial institutionalism viewpoint. We empirically investigate inertia at the industry level in a single country. We analyse our data using the classification proposed by Scott and divide the responses between the three pillars: regulative, normative and cognitive. We build our analyses on the three pillars of institutions with an eye on what kind of challenges would need to be met in order to bring about change. To summarise our argument, we claim that institutional entrepreneurship is a good approach for setting the requirements for open innovation technology.

11.4 Research Methodology

Our data are derived from interviews of 38 experts, chosen from a wide variety of backgrounds in order to form a clearer picture of the factors contributing to industrial inertia. The respondents were representatives of companies (e.g. construction companies, architect firms, property investors), public organisations (e.g. cities and public development and housing organisations), members of parliament, members of academia, finance experts and representatives of various non-governmental organisations, i.e. associations that represent construction companies, construction workers, commercial building owners and operators. We chose the respondents to make sure that the viewpoints regarding technology, market, finance and legal framework were also covered by the experts.

Our methodology was not geared to find which views are most common so as to make a statistical generalisation. Instead, the aim was to find a sufficient number of different viewpoints on the same theme to form an informed view based on different stakeholder views. Our underlying assumption was that some critical issues are not necessarily readily acknowledged or obvious to the majority of respondents, but that such lesser known issues nevertheless play a part in deciding what kind of hurdles needs to be overcome. Another underlying assumption was that for a solution to work in such a complex and widely connected context such as the built environment, it must consider a large number of intertwined issues.

> **Practical Tip**
>
> When identifying a comprehensive group of perspectives regarding the topic under discussion, it may be helpful to consider which representatives need to be involved from, e.g. academia, companies and public organisations; which groups of people or their representatives (e.g. NGOs) need to be contacted; whether the interviewee set include people who possess legal, financial, market and technology expertise. Also, it may be a good idea to complement the group of people interviewed based on the input from interviewees as data gathering process proceeds.

We transcribed the interviews and analysed them using pattern-matching techniques as follows. In the analyses we were interested in the "rules" (Scott 1995) which guide perceptions regarding industry change. We started off with Scott's three pillars of institutions and divided them further as explained below. We manually coded all the instances in which the respondents were talking about industrial change barriers. There were two ways in which the inertia was approached in the interviews. We asked the respondents to name challenges, needs and threats which call for the industry to change but which had not to date been met. In addition, we asked about the obstacles that stand in the way of industry development. Both forms of inquiry provided insight regarding inertia sources.

Individual entries from the interviews, i.e. reasons for a comparatively slow pace of development and low level of innovations within the Finnish construction industry, were originally classified into five categories (see Table 11.1). A sixth category, education, was added when it became evident that a number of entries concerning education and training needs did not fit any of the five categories.

11.4.1 Legal Inertia

The entries falling into the category of legal inertia were issues that relate to laws, the legal system and the practical interpretation of laws as barriers for development. It was pointed out that the legal framework plays a role in hindering the achievement of the desired state (for example, an eco-efficient city), but as there are many factors involved, it is difficult to accurately estimate the weight of an individual factor. The laws regulating city planning and construction are very complicated and therefore raise the competence requirements very high. The officers implementing the laws may be inclined to give negative decisions if the case is complex and novel, as the incentive to avoid mistakes is quite strong. Even if laws change, the

Table 11.1 Industry-level inertia

Institution	Type of inertia	Prominent example entry
Regulative	**Legal** Regulation concerning, for example housing, energy, safety and laws enforcing public procurement policies	-regulations (i.e. actions of public sector) do not support low or zero energy buildings -increased regulation has added total costs and responding to the changes has required resources -the legal framework as one of many factors plays a role in hindering the achievement of the desired outcome, but as there are many factors involved, it is difficult to know the role of one factor -the processes related to urban planning and construction are very complicated thus elevating the competence requirements too high
Normative	**Political** Large public investment and planning at the different levels (communities, municipalities, state), links to larger cities	-the requirement of transparency and the public procurement process make it difficult to choose innovative proposals -protecting cultural heritage is standing in the way of making energy-efficient solutions; cultural heritage protection regulations should be relaxed -[the construction companies] have not paid attention to changes in society, more specifically, the environment and the market -the cycles regarding urban planning are long; the outcomes of decisions may take as long as twenty years to emerge
	Commercial Size of the Finnish market, strong incumbent companies, streamlined processes and existing clientele, customer demands for mass-produced solutions rather than modifications.	-a buyer is found for all new buildings; therefore, the construction companies have fewer incentives to interact with their customers - industry is profitable: it does not have the need to innovate -using a new material is risky; it could lead to a new wave of dampness problems -risk avoidance; old and tested solutions are less risky than new ones; construction projects can cost tens or hundreds of millions so risk management is important; the more complicated the solutions the more one has to allocate resources for risk management and the handling of realised risks; in such cases the profitability of the project may be poor; risks should somehow be reduced and the ability to afford risk increased

Cultural		
Artefact New construction work takes time, limited options to modify, long life cycle of products, risks related new products.		-the Finnish climate is more challenging than the rest of Europe
		-using a new material [e.g. for insulation] is risky; it could lead to a new wave of dampness problems;
		-buildings are made to last for decades; once a building has been built it constitutes quite a permanent change to the landscape; one cannot therefore apply a quick pace of change in, e.g. urban planning as one could in some other area such as health services
Technology Technological solutions relatively simple, long product development lead times.		-there is scarcity of technologies for decreasing energy consumption on renovations for existing buildings
		-there is scarcity of techniques and materials that are thought to be well tested and safe
		-a building that would be extremely flexible in terms of changing user needs would cost more than customers are willing to pay
Education Need to raise awareness of the issues of the industry		-attitudes; conservative nature of people in the business
		-there is a gap between current and required know-how
		-there is perhaps a lack of know-how regarding the assessment of life cycle costs and impacts as well as communicating this to customers and developing products and services with life cycle costs and impacts in mind
		-culture and behaviour of people changes slowly

group that interprets them remains the same, so the application of a new law may be quite similar to the application of the previous law. A part of this phenomenon could also stem from the need to avoid making mistakes, but it could also indicate certain reluctance to change.

A view more popular among the construction companies, but also noted by members of the public sector, was that increased regulation has added to the total construction costs. Responding to the changes has consumed resources. Whereas a company may see that too much of their resources are consumed in a race to respond to ever changing regulations, a lawmaker criticised the companies of failure to develop on their own initiative. The voices of construction company representatives are not, however, unanimous: some even say that the regulations should be taken much further in the direction where they would really, for example, protect low or zero energy buildings. This way, the lack of certain kinds of laws and regulation was identified as a barrier for development. Existing regulations were also felt to hinder development as they all too often were thought to stand in the way of using new materials and techniques needed to reach the low energy consumption requirements.

11.4.2 Political Inertia

It should be noted that the line between legal and political issues can be rather blurred in some cases. For example, buildings, their appearance or original use may be protected due to cultural heritage. Some protection choices have their foundations in laws, while others are more clearly political. The planning permission choices are partly grounded in laws and partly regulated based on, e.g. aesthetic values. Several interviewees felt that cultural heritage protection often stands in the way of introducing desirable energy-saving solutions to existing buildings or to buildings in close proximity to the protected ones. Some of the interviewees called for relaxing cultural heritage regulation, because the majority of the total energy consumption is caused by existing buildings.

City representatives felt that the requirement of transparency and the public procurement process make it difficult for public officials to choose innovative proposals. Comparing prices per unit is much simpler than comparing qualitative descriptions or artistic impressions. Non-city respondents do not see the issue as one related to difficulty or competence, but rather blatantly blame cities for a sheer lack of willingness to consider qualitative aspects of bids. The prices of work in the lowest bids are even suspected by one interviewee to be too low to include the mandatory social security costs. As the hourly rates mentioned were 30 to 35 € an hour and the lowest wages permitted in the construction industry were just above 9 € an hour (plus employer paid social costs), the lower bids could theoretically accommodate the legal requirements. However, generally expected profit levels and the increasing use of unregistered foreign subcontractors linked to tax evasion on the other hand strongly back up this suspicion.

In addition, there was suspicion of coercion or corruption in cases where city officials keep accepting the bids of companies that have time and again delivered poor quality work. The poorly delivered work needs to be fixed and the cost of the work rises significantly thus making the other bids more economical.

As the cities and municipalities collect tax from their inhabitants, some people actually choose where they want to live based on tax rates. The cities and municipalities therefore compete. According to an interviewee representing academia, this inhibits coordinated and efficient city planning efforts regarding land use, traffic, housing and the placement of commercial services.

A point worth mentioning is that the cycles of city planning are long. As predicting the impact of city planning is just as difficult as predicting the future in general, one must wait for as long as 20 years to see the outcomes. Such long cycles include significant market, legal framework and technology changes, which makes the assessment of an individual cause–effect relationship difficult.

11.4.3 Commercial Inertia

The commercial category received more entries than the other categories. One phrase was heard from many interviewees: "A buyer is found for all new buildings" from which can be concluded as being the reason why construction companies do not really have a genuine desire to develop. Others said that for this reason companies do not need to talk to their customers, find out how consumer behaviour has changed and realise how they should develop the industry. A third conclusion was that consumers are to blame for the slow pace of development in the construction industry as they keep buying whatever is "thrown" their way.

A problem recognised by many interviewees was centred on the fact that consumers are unable to estimate the cost of living especially related to energy use and are thus reluctant to pay more money for an eco-efficient house. One respondent expressed it as always being a dilemma when the one who pays for a solution (the construction company) is different from the one that benefits from it (the buyer and the low energy consumption of the house). The reason why low energy houses do not appear to sell for a higher price was thought to possibly result from consumers making the purchase decision primarily based on location. The long-time favourite phrase in real estate backs up this assumption: "Location, location, location".

A problem experienced on the public procurement side was that, for several reasons, the construction companies do not make the life cycle costs and impacts explicit to the purchaser. If these were made more explicit then the higher cost of eco-efficient buildings would be more justified in the buyer's eyes.

In order to respond to the energy consumption goals associated with low energy or zero energy buildings, new materials (e.g. for insulation) and techniques must be used. As the materials are new, there is no consensus that the material is safe for the construction workers to handle or for the inhabitants living in the houses built from them. There are also concerns regarding how the materials function over time and under the influence of the harsh elements. In addition, there were concerns how the building as a whole functions when the new materials are used, e.g. for insulation: whether there would be a build-up of dampness in some part of the building and if the ventilation would be sufficient. Furthermore, low energy and zero energy buildings need to be built in a very specific, high quality manner in a time when the quality problems in new builds are experienced quite widely.

In Finland, a construction company has a 2-year guarantee period which is followed by a 10-year responsibility to fix construction errors that could not be observed during the guarantee period. This is perceived by companies to be a risk with new materials and techniques. Old and tested solutions are less risky than new ones. Construction projects can cost tens or hundreds of millions so risk management is important. The more complicated the solutions, the more resources must be allocated for risk management, which may have a negative impact on the profitability of the project. This problem is in a way heightened in the case of companies with high brand value.

11.4.4 Artefact Inertia

Not much was said about the artefact itself, i.e. the building. New materials could potentially cause health hazards and additional costs. The health hazards concern the workers and/or users of the building, whereas the additional costs could affect construction companies and home owners (e.g. in the situation that the construction company has gone bankrupt or the 10-year responsibility to fix construction errors has passed) as well as insurance companies. Both the potential health and renovation costs would also eventually flow into the domain of public spending as, for example, health care costs, loss of income tax and increased pension costs are ultimately covered by public funds. Also home owners burdened by overwhelming renovation costs could become eligible for social benefits. The potential impact of health and renovation costs could be wide.

It was also noted that buildings are made to last for decades. Once a building has been built it constitutes quite a permanent change in the landscape. One cannot therefore apply a quick change of pace in city planning as one could in some other area.

11.4.5 Technological Inertia

The technology related barriers for change were mainly focused on the lack of low energy and zero energy building techniques, or on how to increase the energy efficiency of existing buildings. Several interviewees pointed at the lack of research and testing regarding the long-time durability and performance of new materials and building techniques. An issue partly associated with the low level of the development of energy efficient renovation techniques was that they do not pass economic cost–benefit analyses. The latter point implied that such decisions are made on an economic, not ecological basis.

What made the technology category stand out from the other categories was that the entries implying lack of technology or techniques were very few in number and that technology was most commonly seen to be a part of the solution to the challenges related to the built environment.

11.4.6 Education Inertia

There was a very high number of entries that can best be categorised as ones relating to education. Different kinds of learning related issues were mentioned. A lack of knowledge, know-how or awareness was identified among construction workers, construction and design companies, public officials and consumers. The construction workers were said to lack knowledge and know-how in low energy and zero energy building; neither did they know how to deliver good quality. Construction and design companies were said to lack know-how in the calculation, assessment and communication of qualitative features, life cycle costs and life cycle impacts. Also, they were seen to lack the capacity to innovate. Shortcomings associated with public processes were discussed in the legal category (i.e. public officials are not up to the challenge of handling novel and innovative planning permission issues as they do not understand the complex regulation of the built environment). The consumers are suspected of not being knowledgeable about their unrealised role as drivers of change or the long-term benefits of paying a higher price for an eco-efficient house.

Other related causes of inertia were attitudes, the conservative nature of people, lack of willingness to change, fear (that a solution may not work or fear of making mistakes) and risk avoidance. Some believed that a "wait-and-see" attitude was adopted by many in the construction industry because of the previous hype regarding issues that were claimed to revolutionise the industry but didn't (e.g. knowledge engineering). "Who says that climate change isn't one of these false alarms"—is how one interviewee believes that many others may feel. This shows that there is no consensus on basic drivers and challenges, which lays a very clear foundation for a slow pace of development.

11.5 Conclusions and Discussion

We set out to identify a set of requirements to overcome industrial inertia using more participatory innovation technologies. Our unit of analysis was a single industry and our scope was that of a single country. We assumed that there would be linkages to other industries, but the results of the empirical inquiry are pointing towards the need for a much wider collaboration and participation than that found in more common examples of open innovation, i.e. open innovation between companies or companies and user groups. This revelation has significant consequences as it adds a source of complexity to the open innovation technology requirements.

The sources of inertia that cause a slower pace of development were found to represent each pillar of institutions. Inertia sources falling into the regulatory pillar were further defined as containing legal aspects. The normative pillar was further divided into political and commercial categories, while the cultural pillar was divided into artefact, technology and education categories. As the empirical data contained elements of such a variety of categories, it is clear that addressing a single facet is not likely to be enough to overcome such things as climate change or scarcity of natural resources as the themes link to several, if not all, pillars and categories.

Our findings support the idea that public intervention is important in facilitating change. In the knowledge intensive organisational structures of businesses, institution setting and culture need to undergo substantial changes. In the case of the construction industry, this involves identifying the relevant policy frameworks that impact and contribute to structural changes and proposed development instruments. The empirical inquiry reveals that the strongest drivers for change in the industry are related to policies and regulation. Thus, proactive, innovation prone policies have the highest potential for sustainable industry-level changes in the field, provided they address the challenges in way that all stakeholders can relate to. Linking participatory policy making to the kind of wide-ranging open innovation processes suggested here is therefore advisable.

Innovation, especially demand-driven innovation, is a process where challenges, needs and threats perceived in the operational environment are met with such development processes that lead to new ways of responding to demands. Open innovation implies that the innovation process extends over organisation boundaries. Often the process extends to two or more business organisations, but when the demands in question deal with issues that cannot be solved solely within the private sector, open innovation means that there is a need to cross organisation type borders as well. This is the case regarding the construction industry and the wider built environment. Meeting currently perceived demands of the operational environment requires the collaboration and participation of both public and private sector organisations, investors, associations, the academia, lawmakers and consumers. When a change process needs to be facilitated for a wide variety of organisations and a variety of different kinds of experts, it is clear that a set of requirements for the supportive open innovation technologies rise.

1. The individuals participating in the process are geographically dispersed. For this reason, support for participation over distance must be possible.
2. The individuals participating in the process are sometimes participating as representatives of an organisation and sometimes as citizens (who are employed in organisations that do not participate in the process). For this reason alone, the technology must support asynchronous participation.
3. The individuals have different kinds of educational and work experience related backgrounds. In most cases, acquiring certain knowledge from another participant's areas of expertise is a prerequisite for reaching a state where collaborative, reality-based problem solving becomes possible. This implies a need for knowledge depositories regarding, e.g. materials, techniques, processes, principles, interests, etc.

11 Overcoming Industrial Inertia by Use of Open Innovation Technologies

4. Issues relating to land use and the artefacts, not to mention statistics regarding many key aspects, can be presented in a form that is easier for all participants to understand. Therefore, visualisation of data (including 3D and animations) would cater to the need to reach a common understanding of the issue at hand so that a reality-based solution can be achieved.

5. As the participatory, open innovation process incorporates numerous situations where a large group of participants partake in decision making, there will, in all likelihood, be the need to orchestrate non-binding polling processes.

6. Finally, as the purpose of the approach is to facilitate dialogue, the technology must include a supportive function. The current dialogue is often short and fragmented, meaning that a representative of one group expresses a statement (e.g. in a newspaper article) and a representative of another group gives a response. Dialogue participants need to commit to and engage in longer dialogue processes if solutions that are acceptable and well functioning in all aspects are to be found. This places certain demands on the technology, i.e. it needs to support long dialogue processes which are useful in current discussions and serve as introductory materials for those joining the process at later stages.

Finding solutions to overcome the influence of the inertia sources will no doubt require the collaboration of actors who represent very different kinds of organisations (e.g. companies, public sector organisations, such as city planning offices, or ministries, associations, finance and development organisations, academia, and so forth). The individuals representing these organisations form an equally diverse group regarding roles, experience and education. The analysis points to an obvious tendency of members of one group to propose that the actors of another group should take the initiative and pay the investment costs. Needless to say, this is an uneasy basis for collaboration and the diversity and tensions between the groups need to be addressed in the open innovation technology which is to support the collaboration.

References

Eccles, R. (1981). The quasifirm in the construction industry. *Journal of Economic Behaviour and Organisation, 2*(4), 335–357.

Etzioni, A. (1967). Mixed scanning: A third approach to decision making. *Public Administration Review, 27*, 387–392.

Chesbrough, H. W. (2006). *Open business models: How to thrive in a new innovation landscape.* Boston, MA: Harvard Business School Press.

Gann, D., & Salter, A. (2000). Innovation in project-based, service-enhanced firms: The construction of complex products and systems. *Research Policy, 29*(7–8), 955–972.

Geels, F. (2004). From sectoral systems of innovation to socio-technical systems: Insights about dynamics and change from sociology and institutional theory. *Research Policy, 33*(6–7), 897–920.

Lutzenhiser, L., & Biggart, N. (2003). *Market structure and energy efficiency: The case of new commercial buildings.* Pullman, WA: California Institute for Energy Efficiency.

Scott, R. (1995). *Institutions and organisations*. Newbury Park, CA: Sage.

Taylor, J. (2005). Three perspectives on innovation in interorganisational networks: systemic innovation, boundary object change, and the alignment of innovations and networks. Doctoral dissertation. Stanford University.

Teece, D. J., Pisano, G., & Shuen, A. (1997). Dynamic capabilities and strategic management. *Strategic Management Journal, 18*(7), 509–33.

Von Hippel, E. (2005). *Democratizing innovation*. Cambridge, MA: MIT Press.

Wernerfelt, B. (1984). A resource-based view of the firm. *Strategic Management Journal, 5*(2), 171–80.

Further Reading

Chesbrough, H. W. (2003). The era of open innovation. *MIT Sloan Management Review, 44*, 35–41.

Cohen, W., & Levinthal, D. (1990). Absorptive capacity: a new perspective on learning and innovation. *Administrative Science Quarterly, 35*(1), 128–152.

KTI. (2010). *The Finnish property market*. KTI: Helsinki.

Kohvakka, A. (2007). *What is wrong with real estate and construction productivity*. Helsinki: Helsinki University of Technology.

Pittaway, L., Robertson, M., Munir, K., Denyer, D., & Neely, A. (2004). Networking and Innovation: systemic review of the evidence. *International Journal of Management Reviews, 5*(3–4), 137–168.

Rosenberg, N. (1994). *Exploring the black box. Technology, economics and history*. Cambridge: Cambridge University Press.

Steinbock, D. (2009). *The Vital Cluster: Globalisation, Urbanization and Finland's Real Estate and Construction Cluster. RAKLI*—The Finnish Association of Building Owners and Construction Clients: Helsinki.

Van de Ven, A. H. (1993). Managing the process of organisational innovation. In G. P. Huber & W. H. Glick (Eds.), *Organisational change and redesign: Ideas and insights for improving performance*. New York: Oxford University Press.

Chapter 12
Using Information Technology to Manage Diverse Knowledge Sources in Open Innovation Processes

Vincenzo Corvello, Davide Gitto, Sven Carlsson, and Piero Migliarese

Abstract Companies adopting an open approach to innovation aim at exploiting as many sources of knowledge as possible to create new products or services. Communities of customers, networks of experts or other organisations are all considered sources of valuable knowledge. However, to be managed effectively, each source requires different tools and practices. Managers responsible for the implementation of a technological system supporting open innovation should be able to single out the requirements associated with each source and devise customised strategies to facilitate the knowledge exchange. This chapter: (1) provides a framework which enables managers to analyse each specific source of knowledge and elicit the associated requirements, (2) suggests seven strategies to facilitate the knowledge exchange and (3) shows how these seven strategies can be adapted to different sources of knowledge.

12.1 Introduction

For a company, an open approach to innovation consists, on the one hand, in exploiting external sources of knowledge to create new products, services or processes. On the other, it consists of external channels to exploit the knowledge it owns. Knowledge can be sourced from groups of individuals such as customers (Nambisan 2002; Carlsson 2004), lead users (von Hippel 2005), external experts or even an anonymous crowd. But it can also be obtained from universities, consultants, intermediaries, other companies or impersonal sources such as

---

V. Corvello (✉) • D. Gitto • P. Migliarese
Dipartimento di Scienze Aziendali, Università della Calabria, Rende (CS), Italy
e-mail: vincenzo.corvello@unical.it; davide.gitto@unical.it; piero.migliarese@unical.it

S. Carlsson
Informatics, School of Economics and Management, Lund, Sweden
e-mail: sven.carlsson@ics.lu.se

J.S.Z. Eriksson Lundström et al. (eds.), *Managing Open Innovation Technologies*,
DOI 10.1007/978-3-642-31650-0_12, © Springer-Verlag Berlin Heidelberg 2013

scientific publications and patents. Knowledge can be exploited in the form of patents (Gambardella et al. 2007), licences, spin-offs or it can be strategically used in alliances (Lichtenthaler and Ernst 2008).

Managing open processes, however, is far more complex than managing innovation within the boundaries of a single organisation. One important difficulty is that many diverse actors are involved in open innovation processes. In a closed innovation approach, for example, concepts of new products are mainly generated by employees in the marketing department. In an "open" company, they can be generated by customers, expert users or consultants. The problem is that the interactions with different sources of knowledge require different practices and competences.

In particular, different technological systems are needed to interact with different partners. Several authors studied the role of Information Technology in open innovation initiatives. Most of them, however, took a very specific point of view, considering interactions with a specific source or a specific recipient of knowledge and studying systems designed for those specific interactions. For example, there are information systems to interact with employees, like the ones implemented by Procter and Gamble (Huston and Sakkab 2006); with experts, like those involved by intermediaries such as InnoCentive (Chesbrough 2006) or with customers, like in the cases of Fiat, Cisco or Microsoft (Nambisan 2002).

In our opinion, the fit between technology and type of interacting actors is a fundamental criterion to implement an effective system. But what features should be different in systems implemented to interact with different partners? There is a lack of research in the literature addressing the issue of the technology-partner fit when designing or implementing information systems for open innovation.

The aim of this chapter is to propose a framework to support companies in implementing information systems suitable for each specific partner.

The starting point for our framework is the Relative Absorptive Capacity (RAC) theory (Lane and Lubatkin 1998). Building on Lane and Lubatkin's ideas we suggest that when the source/recipient of knowledge is different, also the difficulties in exchanging knowledge change. For example, when the company interacts with a scientist it will be easier to exchange scientific knowledge, but it will be more difficult to exchange product-related knowledge. The opposite holds true when the interacting parties are the company and a customer. Following this line of reasoning, it is possible to give directions on the design and implementation of information systems for open innovation suitable for different partners.

The remainder of the chapter is organised as follows: in Sect. 12.2 we briefly discuss the Relative Absorptive Capacity theory; in Sect. 12.3 we present our framework consisting of seven strategies to facilitate knowledge exchanges in open innovation processes; in Sect. 12.4 we discuss how the seven strategies can be adapted to different sources of knowledge, using as an example of possible sources a community of customers and a network of experts; in Sects. 12.5 and 12.6, respectively, we discuss the implications for practice and the implications for research.

12.2 Relative Absorptive Capacity

In this chapter, we draw on the Relative Absorptive Capacity (RAC) theory to build a theoretical framework aimed at supporting companies in designing and implementing information systems for open innovation.

RAC theory, proposed by Lane and Lubatkin (1998), is an extension of the Absorptive Capacity theory (Cohen and Levinthal 1990). Absorptive capacity is a firm's ability to acquire new knowledge in a certain domain. It increases with the firm's level of prior related knowledge. For example, if a software company employs personnel who have already worked in the field of grid computing, it will be easier for that company to keep up to date with innovations in this technological field.

Building on this idea, Lane and Lubatkin (1998) observed that the ability to acquire new knowledge also depends on the source of knowledge. In particular, the more the provider and the recipient of knowledge are similar, the higher is the recipient's absorptive capacity. Absorptive capacity, then, is not an absolute capability of companies or individuals: it depends on the partner they interact with. It is better called Relative Absorptive Capacity. In our view, RAC is not only a structural characteristic of the dyad of companies, but a "temporary capability" the two partners can build as a part of the exchange process. In other words, even if two companies or individuals are dissimilar, the recipient's RAC can be increased through the use of suitable procedures and organisational and technological tools (Carlsson et al. 2009). Lane and Lubatkin (1998) also suggest that two firms are more likely to effectively exchange new knowledge if they have similar (1) knowledge bases, (2) knowledge processing systems and norms, (3) organisational structures and (4) dominant logics.

In open innovation processes a company and its counterparts in a knowledge exchange are inevitably "different". For example, the knowledge bases, procedures, structure and logics of a community of customers are very different if compared with those of a marketing department. Our hypothesis is that the processes and tools a company implements when adopting an open innovation approach should increase the company's RAC. In particular, since we focus on technology, Information Systems should be designed and implemented in order to fit the specific provider/recipient dyad. In fact, different counterparts in the innovation exchange imply different levels of RAC for different knowledge domains. As a consequence, Information Technology should provide different kinds of support when the interlocutor changes.

12.3 How Information Technology Can Increase RAC in Open Innovation Processes

When the RAC between two partners is not sufficiently high, exchanging knowledge becomes difficult. However, technological tools and organisational procedures and structures can be put into place in order to increase RAC. Building on previous works (Carlsson et al. 2009), we propose seven strategies to increase RAC (see Table 12.1).

Table 12.1 The seven strategies to substitute for RAC

Strategy	Example Applications
Create shared resources to diffuse domain specific knowledge	Use Databases, Portals and Web 2.0 to share knowledge related to the problem at hand
Create shared resources to diffuse complementary knowledge	Use Databases, Portals and Web 2.0 to share knowledge related to complementary aspects (IP management, company policies, etc.)
Accelerate knowledge transfer	Create rich communication channels for knowledge transfer
Develop standard methods and rules	Use wizards, procedures and structured virtual workspaces to coordinate the interacting parties
Act as an intermediary organisational structure for innovation transfer	Create liaison roles such as gatekeepers and community managers
Manage relations with knowledge source	Introduce differentiated access rights
Build a company/network culture	Use reputation, recommendation and reference mechanisms

The seven proposed strategies have been obtained by expanding Lane and Lubatkin's (1998) framework through the integration of ideas derived from a review of the literature on open innovation. In particular, we reviewed the literature on open innovation looking for ways in which companies that adopted an open approach to innovation changed one or more of the dimensions which, according to Lane and Lubatkin (1998), influence RAC. As a result, we obtained the seven strategies, each of which is related to one of the four dimensions of RAC, namely knowledge base (strategies 1 and 2), knowledge processing systems and norms (strategies 3 and 4), organisational structure (strategy 5) and dominant logic (strategies 6 and 7).

12.3.1 Compensating for Differences in the Knowledge Base

Open innovation implies the direct or indirect interaction between employees in a company and external actors. For example, the knowledge from customers or lead users will be used by the marketing department. External experts will provide knowledge used by the R&D department. The transfer of knowledge will take place directly if an internal department directly manages the process, or indirectly if another office, task force or external intermediary manages the exchange.

In any case, the exchange will be easier if the interacting parties share a common knowledge base. Companies implementing an open innovation approach should foster the rapid creation of such shared knowledge bases if they do not already exist.

A non-negligible part of the transferred knowledge is not specific of an exchange, but is needed in several exchanges. An evident example is the knowledge related to IP protection issues which is involved in every exchange (at least in part). Storing and organising the knowledge which is needed repeatedly in open innovation exchanges would facilitate the interaction between partners.

A knowledge exchange usually implies more than one type of knowledge to be exchanged in both directions. For example, in the case of the intermediary InnoCentive, both scientific knowledge and knowledge related to IP issues has to be transferred from the intermediary to the solver, while knowledge related to the product/market is transferred from the seeker to the solver. In each exchange we can distinguish between the knowledge related to the specific technological or scientific area (e.g. knowledge about programming techniques in the case of interactions regarding software) and the knowledge related to complementary issues (e.g. knowledge related to IP or project management). We call the first type of knowledge *domain-specific knowledge* and the second one *complementary knowledge*.

As a consequence, the following two strategies can be adopted to increase RAC:

1. *Create shared resources to diffuse domain-specific knowledge*: the team, office or intermediary managing the open innovation process can collect, organise and package knowledge related to each specific domain. These knowledge packages can be provided to the partners in order to speed up the development of a common, domain-specific knowledge base.
2. *Create shared resources to diffuse complementary knowledge*: the team, office or intermediary managing the open innovation process can collect, organise and package knowledge related to interdisciplinary (i.e. issues common to several technological domains) or complementary aspects (e.g. issues related to problems such as intellectual property rights, regulatory issues, technological infrastructures) useful in more than one exchange.

Information systems can significantly contribute to the implementation of these two strategies. Knowledge can be packaged, organised and made available through document management systems, knowledge repositories and portals (Robey et al. 2000; Kane and Alavi 2007) and tutorials. Wikis, forums and blogs can support the collaborative creation of knowledge resources. Hypertext and hypermedia technologies support the retrieval of knowledge available on the web, in intranets or in knowledge repositories (Robey et al. 2000). Applications for knowledge representation (Robey et al. 2000) help users to gain understanding of a set of concepts. Virtual learning environments help users to make sense of contextual knowledge.

> **Practical Tip**
>
> Face-to-face meetings are powerful knowledge transfer mechanisms. If possible, in the early phases of innovation exchanges, face-to-face meetings should be organised to facilitate the exchange of tacit knowledge. Once the partners know each other, then the subsequent exchanges of knowledge become easier. Besides, it is important to increase the level of trust towards the system. Personal, direct and face-to-face communication increases the reciprocal trust of the interacting parties.

12.3.2 Compensating for Differences in Knowledge Processes and Norms

In open innovation, the interacting parties use different work procedures and comply with different norms. This phenomenon has been studied in the interactions between companies (Lane and Lubatkin 1998), companies and universities, companies and public administrations. The phenomenon is even more evident in the case of interactions with customers, lead users or external experts. The practices and norms of customers when participating in open innovation processes are certainly different from those of employees in the marketing or R&D departments. Besides, the practices of customers are expected to be different from those of experts or lead users.

These differences in the way of working can easily yield inefficiencies, misunderstandings, conflicts and overall poor results. Open innovation systems can increase RAC both by facilitating and accelerating knowledge transfer and by defining methods and norms of interaction to be adopted by the recipient and the provider of knowledge. As a consequence, the third and fourth strategies to increase RAC are the following:

3. *Accelerate knowledge transfer*: the team, office or intermediary managing the open innovation process can implement tools, structures and procedures to facilitate knowledge flows between the interacting parties.
4. *Develop standard methods and rules*: by using standard methods and rules (including standard documents, procedures and technologies) provided by the team, office or intermediary responsible for the open innovation process, the participants can partially overcome the problem of different organisational processes.

While the two strategies 1 and 2 imply the need for well organised, easy to use databases, maybe integrated with Web 2.0 collaborative systems, the third strategy requires rich communication channels and collaborative spaces.

Information Technology provides several tools to support communication and discourse. As a consequence, it is able to speed up knowledge transfer (Robey et al. 2000). Collaboration tools such as Lotus Notes support intra- and inter-organisational learning. Web 2.0 technologies provide further possibilities to cooperate and exchange knowledge. In general, communication tools such as instant messaging facilitate the transfer of tacit and explicit knowledge (Kane and Alavi 2007).

User toolkits (von Hippel 2005) and tools for product or concept testing and simulation incorporate knowledge from the company. They are also a way for the company to acquire users' knowledge.

As concerns the fourth strategy, Information Technology is often used to create standard working methods. Also in the field of open innovation there are several examples of tools used to standardise interactions. For example, the open innovation intermediary InnoCentive provides solvers with interaction procedures consistent with the expectations of the seekers. The interaction takes place in a structured virtual room dedicated to the specific challenge. Standard methods also reduce the need to exchange knowledge. User toolkits, for example, guide lead users in incorporating their knowledge into the product. Stock markets for innovation allow customers to express their preferences without explicit communication. Several companies implement open innovation strategies that include tools to standardise interaction procedures. A popular example is IBM's Connect and Develop.

Also the use of wizards, which consist of tools helping users to perform a certain task more effectively, can reduce the possibility of errors or misunderstandings when interacting with external knowledge sources.

Another example of a suitable tool is the quick poll and survey tool for reducing differences in knowledge processes and norms, especially when the knowledge exchange consists of acquiring external users' opinions or ideas concerning a new product or service.

> **Practical Tip**
>
> International standards provide a shared language and common procedures to organisations. Knowledge exchanges are facilitated if the partners adopt the same international standard. From a pure IT perspective, ensuring the full compatibility of the software application with the most common web protocols and mobile operating systems will increase and facilitate knowledge exchanges.

12.3.3 Compensating for Differences in Organisational Structures

When conceptualising RAC, Lane and Lubatkin (1998) considered organisational structure a key factor in knowledge processing systems. Organisational structure embodies organisational knowledge. As a consequence, similar organisational structures imply similar organisational knowledge and, thus, an easier knowledge exchange. In open innovation processes, the source of knowledge is often a community or a network of individuals. Lane and Lubatkin's (1998) argument holds also in this case. Communities or networks have their roles, their (weak or strong) relations and even their hierarchical systems. That is, a community or a network has an organisational structure which embodies organisational knowledge. Obviously a company's and a community's organisational structure are very different and this could hinder knowledge exchange. So, the fifth strategy to increase RAC is:

5. *Act as an intermediary organisational structure for innovation transfer*: the team, office or intermediary managing the open innovation process can develop tools, roles and relations able to limit the problem of different organisational structures.

The intermediary organisational structure is often virtual. Organisational structures are virtual when they are reconfigurable, geographically dispersed and based on electronic communication (Corvello and Migliarese 2007). These organisational units mainly operate on the web. They collect dispersed individual knowledge and distribute it to organisations after organising and elaborating it to support innovation (Verona et al. 2006). Virtual knowledge brokers are an example of this kind of structure. According to Verona et al. (2006), virtual knowledge brokers are "the virtual manifestation of knowledge brokers (KBs)—third parties who connect, recombine, and transfer knowledge to companies in order to facilitate innovation".

> **Practical Tip**
>
> Several web-based intermediaries exist that act as intermediary organisations in innovation exchanges. Organisations which do not consider it economically convenient to develop internal structures to manage innovation exchanges (e.g. small firms) can exploit the services of such intermediaries. In general, different organisational structures imply different communication, collaboration and decision-making procedures. Accordingly, for each type of OI partner, it is important to identify its dominant organisational structure (i.e. peer-open-community vs. hierarchical-closed community) and then develop a flexible "interface" structure able to manage the interaction with different communication, collaboration and decision-making styles.

12.3.4 Compensating for Differences in Dominant Logics

According to Grant (1996), a firm develops preferences for projects of a given type, size and risk level, and favours strategies dependent upon certain key success factors, stages of product life cycle or product-market positions. This set of preferences is called dominant logic. When two companies exchange knowledge the dominant logic influences the effectiveness and efficiency of the knowledge transfer. Also a community of customers or a network of experts has their dominant logics. For example, customers are likely to be interested in functional aspects of a product while experts are likely to be interested in a product's technology.

The differences in dominant logics affect the interaction. For example, customers or experts could be interested in solutions which are not the ones the company is interested in. To some extent, this phenomenon is unavoidable and even positive since it can increase creativity. If not controlled by the company, however, it can easily yield inefficiencies and information overflow. As a consequence, the sixth and seventh strategies we propose are:

6. *Manage relations with knowledge sources*: the team, office or intermediary managing the open innovation process can develop tools, rules and procedures which differentiate the roles of the participating actors according to their dominant logic.

7. *Build a company/network culture*: in the long run the company can select among the external actors the ones that will become partners in open innovation processes and build together with them a shared culture to support the interactions.

Relations can be managed by introducing processes of progressive inclusion of external actors in a company's network (Migliarese and Corvello 2010). That is, the relation with an external actor becomes more intense as the two parties interact repeatedly. Information technology can support the implementation of these processes by introducing differentiated access rights for old-timers and newcomers in a community/network.

The Internet enables the creation of virtual customer environments—platforms for collaboration that allow companies to tap into individual and social customer knowledge through an ongoing dialogue (Verona et al. 2006). Kane and Alavi (2007) suggest the concept of Electronic Communities of Practice to indicate those virtual milieus able to create and sustain communities online. These environments can be used to create a shared culture, shared ethics and to build trust.

> **Practical Tip**
>
> The participation in virtual communities of practice or communities of interest can be useful to discover potentially useful inventions but also to create links with potential partners in innovation exchanges or in joint innovation projects.

12.4 Supporting the Management of Diverse Knowledge Sources Through Information Technology

The framework we provided, consisting of seven strategies to substitute for RAC, can be used as a tool to adapt a company's open innovation approach to the specific knowledge source. In particular, it can be used to specify a differentiated approach to the management of Information Technology for each source.

When the source of knowledge is a community of experts, a community of customers or another organisation, RAC varies because the knowledge bases, knowledge processing systems and norms, organisational structures and dominant logics of the source are intrinsically different.

The seven strategies of our framework are a blueprint to be customised for the specific kind of source. For example, the tools to be used to "accelerate knowledge transfer" are different when the knowledge source is another organisation or when it is a community of customers. In the first case, the interlocutors know each other and have defined roles and rules of interaction (e.g. they know the respective working hours). Rich, synchronous communication channels are needed which facilitate the exchange of information. In the second case, the company interacts with a semi-anonymous crowd. Customers interact when they choose and mainly asynchronously. Interaction rules are much more blurred. Appealing or even entertaining tools are needed, which allow the consumer an easy interaction while allowing the company to collect and organise data in a structured way.

To exemplify how our framework can be used, we consider in this chapter two possible sources of knowledge: a *community of customers* and a *network of external experts*. To the first category belong communities such as those promoted by FIAT or Microsoft (Nambisan 2002), while to the second belong the networks managed by web-based intermediaries such as InnoCentive or Ninesigma.

Before going on to explain how the seven strategies can be practically implemented in the case of a community of customers or a network of experts, it is useful to reflect on some main differences which characterise these two types of knowledge sources.

12.4.1 Two Examples of Knowledge Sources: Customers and Experts

Communities of customers and networks of external experts represent sources of valuable knowledge for the firms. However, these two kinds of knowledge sources show some important differences relevant to the scope of this chapter.

First, communities of customers are reasonably expected to be more numerous than typically restricted and specialised networks of experts. This difference will have practical implications in terms of architectural sizing of the information systems to be implemented.

Another difference consists in the fact that, typically, large communities of customers comprise anonymous users who are presumably totally unknown to the firm. Networks of experts, instead, being much more limited, will be made up of technical and scientific experts whose identity can also be known to the firm they are interacting with. This difference allows the firm (1) to (potentially) understand the specific needs and requirements of expert users and, accordingly, (2) to take these needs into account when designing interaction and communication tools. The same does not easily hold in the case of anonymous customers.

From a demographic point of view, furthermore, customers' communities are typically expected to be more variated than experts' ones. This implies that when designing a technological system for interacting with customers, particular care should be given to the development of tools and interfaces suitable for users of different ages, different expectations and different mental and psychological attitude.

Also, the cultural and educational backgrounds of the two types of knowledge sources are critical factors affecting the development of proper interaction tools and procedures. Experts, by definition, will exhibit a higher level of scientific and technical knowledge than customers. This entails that different kinds of knowledge can be acquired from these distinct sources: complex and product-related knowledge from experts, simple and market-related knowledge from customers.

Finally, customers differ from experts also in terms of motivation driving them to contribute and collaborate in the open innovation processes. Some customers could be generally attracted by the opportunity to actively participate in the product development process, thus expressing their own tastes, preferences and ideas, some others could be simply interested in the rewards offered by the company.

Experts, on the other hand, are interested in collaborating with the company, solving its technical and scientific problems and acquiring notoriety and reputation within their community.

Understanding the motivations in each case allows the company to implement proper tools, rules, procedures and organisational mechanisms (e.g. rewarding systems) to effectively manage, nourish and strengthen external communities.

In the following section, we will see how the distinct characteristics of the two knowledge sources turn into tangible and practical differences in terms of systems, tools and procedures to be implemented to effectively interact with them.

12.4.2 An Application of the Framework to Customers and Experts as Knowledge Sources

The objective of this section is to show an exemplified application of the proposed framework to the development of proper open innovation systems for two distinct knowledge sources: a community of customers and a network of experts.

We will discuss how to *tailor* each of the seven suggested strategies to the specific knowledge source to be managed.

12.4.2.1 Create Shared Resources to Diffuse Domain-Specific Knowledge

Customers are usually involved either in the earlier stages of open innovation processes, like idea generation and selection of potential new products, or in the final stages, like product testing and promotion.

In these stages, exchanged knowledge is related to products' functionalities and market characteristics more than to technical or scientific aspects. At these stages, the company is interested in maximising the circulation of new ideas, so it should develop appealing or even entertaining collaboration tools which stimulate intuitive, easy and fast interaction with customers, and at the same time, triggering viral mechanisms and allowing integration with social networking platforms.

Networks of external experts, instead, are involved in the innovation process mainly to solve technical issues arising during the design and engineering phases. Domain-specific knowledge here includes technical and scientific knowledge about products or processes. The exchanged knowledge can be of great importance to the firm. As a consequence, knowledge protection features have a central role in collaboration tools design and selection.

Moreover, external experts, being highly professional, skilled persons, typically self-motivated to collaborate in open innovation projects, need reliable and effective collaboration tools more than user-friendly and entertaining interfaces. Effective tools to manage this kind of interaction are, for example, databases and knowledge repositories shared on virtual private networks (VPN) or protected extranets.

12.4.2.2 Create Shared Resources to Diffuse Complementary Knowledge

Similar considerations could be made about the creation of complementary knowledge bases.

Since the role of customers in open innovation processes is primarily bound up with creative and innovative idea generation, customers will primarily need complementary knowledge concerning product functionalities (e.g. features of the product/service to be designed), interaction rules (terms and conditions of the relationship) and involved collaboration tools (e.g. software the customers have to use to interact with the OI system). Other examples of complementary knowledge to be diffused within communities of customers, especially in the software industry, are the licensing mechanisms regulating the use and development of software products (e.g. free software licences and open source licences). Forums, blogs and FAQ sections are suitable tools for this purpose. They support the rapid and efficient diffusion of knowledge resources within a community.

As to external experts, the support they provide often implies the exchange of innovative scientific and technological knowledge and solutions that could be protected by patents or licences. Accordingly, a fundamental aspect to be managed when interacting with networks of external experts is the complementary knowledge concerning intellectual property rights, regulatory issues and contractual norms regulating the knowledge exchange.

Document management tools which allow the efficient and secured transmission of legal documents and information like MOUs (Memorandum Of Understanding), NDAs (Non-Disclosure Agreements), patents and confidential product designs, especially if combined with certified electronic mail, are an effective way to increase the source's and recipient's knowledge exchanges.

12.4.2.3 Accelerate Knowledge Transfer

Information technology supports more efficient and effective communication and information exchanges. However, it is useful to differentiate between systems and tools for large, heterogeneous crowds of amateur customers and tools for smaller communities of skilled and professional experts.

When the knowledge source is a community of customers, the company usually deals with a multitude of distinct users from which it expects to receive simple and possibly codified information about product preferences, market expectations, new product development ideas, and so on. Customers can interact at any point and knowledge exchanges normally do not require personal or direct interaction between the users and the company's employees. Accordingly, interaction tools can be designed in the form of simple and asynchronous communication interfaces integrated with Web 2.0 systems. In order to accelerate the knowledge transfer, there could be quick poll and survey applications and tools for product or concept design, testing or simulation among the functionalities to be provided.

Conversely, when a company means to accelerate and foster knowledge exchanges with a network of external experts, it has to develop a different kind of communication tools. As previously said, external experts provide a company with scientific and technological knowledge that can be highly complex to transfer on the one hand, and highly difficult to acquire on the other. The knowledge transfer requires a close, direct and sometimes synchronous interaction between the source and the recipient of knowledge. As a consequence, to speed up this kind of communications, companies should design rich communication channels that provide rapid feedback. These channels can include: Web 2.0 tools, instant messaging, chats, web conferencing and virtual workspaces.

12.4.2.4 Develop Standard Methods and Rules

To normalise the knowledge processing procedures and norms between two communicating parties (thus overcoming the problem of different organisational processes), the solution advanced in this chapter consists of developing standard methods and rules of interaction.

Standardising interaction patterns basically implies developing common interfaces by means of which a company is able to internally convey external inputs coming from collaborating partners. Standard interfaces also mean communicating through standardised documents, procedures and technologies.

Communities of customers will primarily need user-friendly interfaces which do not hinder creativity and participation. Interaction tools have to be intuitive and easy to use. Accordingly, the main focus when implementing such tools is more on design and usability issues than developing complex functionalities. Particular attention must be placed on maintaining these virtual collaboration spaces as entertaining and appealing, even integrating them with social networking platforms (e.g. Facebook, Twitter, Myspace). The language used should not be too technical or domain specific.

Experts, instead, are more likely to appreciate professional interfaces, structured virtual rooms that provide more functionality to the user. A professional expert who collaborates within an OI project is driven by a mix of intrinsic motivation (i.e. passion for an area of expertise) and extrinsic motivation (i.e. reputation, notoriety, monetary rewards). Appealing and entertaining user-friendly interfaces can be useful but they are not essential. Rather, it is important for experts to express their full competences and knowledge, in the case of gaining reputation within their community. Collaboration interfaces, accordingly, have to support expert users thoroughly; technical language is the norm; there are fewer requirements in terms of ease of use.

12.4.2.5 Act as an Intermediary Organisational Structure for Innovation Transfer

Communities of customers and networks of experts are typically characterised by different structures. Usually in a network of experts technical competence is recognised as a source of legitimate influence. The same does not necessarily hold for communities of customers. When interacting with a network of experts, the company should introduce roles as *knowledge brokers* or *gatekeepers*. In the case of a community of customers, the role of the *community manager* should be introduced. Such a role is typically marketing oriented and is familiar with social networks.

12.4.2.6 Manage Relations with Knowledge Sources

In the previous paragraph, it has been highlighted how partners who share different dominant logics could find it difficult to exchange knowledge. In order to prevent this pitfall, companies should implement OI systems that differentiate users according to their dominant logic.

One possibility is to differentiate access rights and categorise customers and experts in different profiles depending on their status (customer or expert), experience in the community (old-timer or newcomer), capabilities or interests (area of expertise). Effective OI systems should also promote and encourage different levels of involvement between users: the system should discriminate between coordinating or leading users, active users, peripheral users and outsider.

12.4.2.7 Build a Company/Network Culture

Another strategy to overcome the differences in terms of partners' dominant logics consists in creating a shared community or network culture with external actors.

Regarding technological aspects, social networking platforms can be developed to foster and support interactions and relationship-building processes among users (customers or experts). Instant messaging tools, forums and blogs can be implemented to encourage communication and the building of a common identity.

Finally, reputation, recommendation and references mechanisms, along with competences profiles can be activated within networks of experts in order to satisfy their needs for reputation and notoriety.

Table 12.2 summarises some relevant features that differentiate communities of customers from networks of external experts for each of the seven strategies suggested to increase RAC and gives examples of the suitable information technological tools to be implemented in order to successfully manage the two different kinds of knowledge sources.

The tools listed in each cell of Table 12.2 are clearly not exclusive of the each kind of source. However, we deem each tool to have a specific value for the source it is associated with.

12.5 Practical Advice

By adopting an open approach to knowledge sourcing for innovation companies, aim at exploiting as many sources of ideas and knowledge as possible. The external environment provides many different sources: communities of customers and users, networks of experts, universities and other companies. All these sources are able to provide valuable knowledge.

However, as multiple flows of knowledge are activated through the involvement of all these sources, the management of knowledge becomes more and more complex. Information technology can support the management of these knowledge flows, but companies need guidelines on how to implement the correct system for problems they may encounter.

This chapter focuses on one specific problem: how to adapt the technology to the specific source of knowledge?

As a matter of fact, the interaction between the company and each of its sources requires technological systems with specific features. In this chapter, we provided a framework which supports decisions related to the technological system to be implemented.

Building on Lane and Lubatkin's (1998) RAC theory, which considers four characteristics (knowledge base, knowledge processing systems and norms, organisational structure and dominant logic) as being crucial in influencing the ability to transfer knowledge between a source and a recipient, we suggest that a company has to analyse these four dimensions in the source it intends to exploit before starting to implement a system for the external sourcing of knowledge.

For each of the four dimensions, we suggest strategies which can support the transfer of knowledge and ideas. We propose seven strategies in total. When the difference in one dimension is especially relevant, then a suitable technological system should be designed in order to reduce the difficulties created by this difference.

In practical terms, we suggest that, to design an effective open innovation system, the following "checklist" should be considered:

- Firstly, a firm should identify *who* the main knowledge sources are it intends to exploit

Table 12.2 The seven strategies for different knowledge sources

	Community of customers	Network of external experts
Create shared resources to diffuse domain specific knowledge	• Portals, document management tools • Forums, blog and RSS Focus on: − Entertainment and appealingness − Usability	• Database and knowledge repositories • Virtual private networks, extranets Focus on: − Reliability − Security
Create shared resources to diffuse complementary knowledge	• Forums, blog and wikis • FAQ. (frequently asked questions) Focus on: − Firm expectations and product func. − Contribution terms and conditions (rewards, Intellectual Property rights)	• Document management systems • Certified and secured email Focus on: − Confidentiality agreements − IP rights and licensing agreements − Complementary tech. information
Accelerate knowledge transfer	• Asynchronous comm. channels • Quick poll and survey tools • Product design and testing tools Focus on: − Simple and impersonal comm. − Inputs codifiability and analysability	• Rich comm. channels, rapid feedback • Instant messaging • Video/audio and web conference Focus on: − Rich and personal communication − Flexibility and complexity of inputs
Develop standard methods and rules	• User-friendly interfaces and wizards Focus on: − Appealing design − High usability − Compatibility with users systems	• Structured workspaces • User toolkits Focus on: − High functionality and performance − Less emphasis on ease of use
Act as an intermediary organisational structure for innovation transfer	• Community managers Focus on: − Marketing competences	• Gatekeepers and Knowledge brokers Focus on: − Technical competences

(continued)

12 Using Information Technology to Manage Diverse Knowledge... 195

Table 12.2 (continued)

	Community of customers	Network of external experts
Manage relations with knowledge source	• Differentiated access rights by: − Interests and capabilities − Driving motivation − Involvement level Focus on: − Customers profiling − Segmentation of tools	• Differentiated access rights by: − Competences and area of expertise − Driving motivation − Experience Focus on: − Competences and expertise profiling − Different contributions management
Build a company/network culture	• Social networks and user profiles • Instant mess.ing, discussions, forums Focus on: − Appealing and usable design − Socialisation capabilities	• Social nets and competences profiles • Reputation mechanisms Focus on: − Selective access and membership − Communication capabilities

- Secondly, for each knowledge source, the existing differences between:
- Source's and firm's *knowledge base*
- Source's and firm's *knowledge processing systems and norms*
- Source's and firm's *organisational structure*
- Source's and firm's *dominant logic*

should be analysed and measured

- Finally, for each difference in one of the four dimensions, and for each identified knowledge source, one of the seven suggested strategies should be implemented and proper information systems and tools should be designed to fill that difference.

Managers should take into account the fundamental principle that no technical system is suitable and sufficient to interact and to exchange knowledge with multiple and variegated knowledge sources.

12.6 Implications for Research

Two aspects need to be further investigated from the point of view of scientific research:

1. To manage inbound open innovation effectively, it is necessary to take into account the differences between the recipient and the source of knowledge. RAC's theory provides a framework to study these differences and their impact on open innovation processes. In this chapter, this framework has been expanded and used to draw guidelines for managers. However, empirical studies to evaluate the impact of RAC on open innovation are still needed.
2. This chapter suggests that technology can support the creation of RAC. The effectiveness of different tools in increasing relative absorptive capacity is another topic which deserves further investigation: which tools are more suitable for which situations? What environmental conditions influence the relationship between technology and effectiveness of innovation processes? What other competences and capabilities, together with technology, are needed to implement effective open innovation processes?

Overall, this chapter proposes a promising framework to study an aspect of open innovation, which is important but still under-investigated.

References

Carlsson, S. A. (2004). Knowledge managing and knowledge management systems in inter-organisational networks. *Knowledge and Process Management, 10*(3), 194–206.

Carlsson, S.A., Corvello, V., Migliarese, P. (2009). Enabling Open Innovation: proposal of a framework supporting ICT and KMS implementation in web-based intermediaries. In *Proceedings of the 17*th *European Conference on Information Systems*. Verona, June 8–10.

Chesbrough, H. W. (2006). *Open business models: How to thrive in the new innovation landscape*. Boston, MA: Harvard Business School Press.

Cohen, W., & Levinthal, D. (1990). Absorptive capacity: A new perspective on learning and innovation. *Administrative Science Quarterly, 35*, 128–152.

Corvello, V., & Migliarese, P. (2007). Virtual forms for the organisation of production: A comparative analysis. *International Journal of Production Economics, 110*(1–2), 5–15.

Gambardella A., Giuri P., Luzzi A. (2007). The market for patents in Europe. *Research Policy, 36*(8), 1163–1183.

Grant, R. M. (1996). Toward a knowledge-based theory of the firm. *Strategic Management Journal, 17*, 109–122.

Huston, L., & Sakkab, N. (2006). Connect and develop—inside P&Gs new model for Innovation. *Harvard Business Review, 84*, 58–66.

Kane, G., & Alavi, M. (2007). An investigation of exploration and exploitation processes. *Organisation Science, 18*(5), 796–812.

Lane, P. J., & Lubatkin, M. (1998). Relative absorptive capacity and interorganisational learning. *Strategic Management Journal, 19*, 461–477.

Lichtenthaler, U., & Ernst, H. (2008). Intermediary services in the markets for technology: Organisational antecedents and performance consequences. *Organisation Studies, 29*(07), 1003–1035.

Migliarese, P., & Corvello, V. (2010). Organisational relations in organisational design and engineering. *International Journal of Organisational Design and Engineering, 1*(1), 55–68.

Nambisan, S. (2002). Designing virtual customer environments for new product development: Toward a theory. *Academy of Management Review, 27*(2), 392–413.

Robey, D., Boudreau, M., & Rose, G. M. (2000). Information technology and organisational learning: a review and assessment of research. *Accounting, Management and Information Technologies, 10*(2), 125–155.

Verona, G., Prandelli, E., & Sawhney, M. (2006). Innovation and virtual environments: Towards virtual knowledge brokers. *Organisation Studies, 27*(6), 765–788.

von Hippel, E. (2005). *Democratizing innovation.* Cambridge, MA: MIT Press.

Further Reading

A previous version of the framework discussed in this paper was proposed in the cited paper by Carlsson, Corvello and Migliarese (2009). For readers interested in Open Innovation, besides the two by now classic books by Henry Chesbrough, we suggest the paper by *Chesbrough and Kardon Crowther "Beyond high tech: early adopters of open innovation in other industries", R&D Management, 36(3): 229–236, 2006.* We also recommend two special issues of international journals dedicated to the topic: *Technovation (2011, 31(1))* and the *European Journal of Innovation Management (2011, 14(4)).* For more information about RAC two papers are particularly interesting: the already cited paper by Lane and Lubatkin (1998) and *Lichtenthaler "Relative capacity: Retaining knowledge outside a firm's boundaries", Journal of Engineering and Technology Management, 25, 200–212, 2008.* The importance of the specificity of the different sources of knowledge is also considered in the paper by Abecassis-Moedas and Mahmoud-Jouini *"Absorptive capacity and source-recipient complementarity in designing new products: an empirically derived framework, Journal of Product Innovation Management, 25(5): 473–490, 2008.*

Chapter 13
Pico-Jobs as an Open Innovation Tool for Utilising Crowdsourcing

Case Study of a Leading Manufacturer of Light System Solutions

Jens Fähling, Ivo Blohm, Jan Marco Leimeister, Helmut Krcmar, and Jan Fischer

Abstract The Internet enables new forms of crowdsourcing by electronic platforms. Companies can use these platforms for opening up their innovation processes and for integrating customers by small, highly structured paid tasks. We call these tasks Pico-Jobs and illustrate them as an open innovation tool for systematically utilising the creative potential of customers for activities during the innovation process. The characteristics of Pico-Jobs are elaborated by reviewing leading crowdsourcing platforms and the Pico-Jobs offered on these platforms. Overall, companies can use Pico-Jobs for three different purposes: (1) Crowd Wisdom, which allows users of these crowdsourcing platforms to share their knowledge and perceptions with the company, (2) Crowd Creation, which encourages the creation of new content or artefacts on these platforms and (3) Crowd Voting, which involves platform users for the evaluation of product ideas, prototypes or designs. Our real-world case with OSRAM pinpoints these application patterns of Pico-Jobs and their potential for speeding up customer integration for generating and evaluating ideas for innovations.

J. Fähling (✉) • I. Blohm • H. Krcmar
Technische Universität München, Munich, Germany
e-mail: faehling@in.tum.de; ivo.blohm@in.tum.de; krcmar@in.tum.de

J.M. Leimeister
Universität Kassel, Kassel, Germany
e-mail: leimeister@uni-kassel.de

J. Fischer
Innosabi GmbH, Munich, Germany
e-mail: jan.fischer@innosabi.com

J.S.Z. Eriksson Lundström et al. (eds.), *Managing Open Innovation Technologies*,
DOI 10.1007/978-3-642-31650-0_13, © Springer-Verlag Berlin Heidelberg 2013

13.1 Introduction

In order to improve their innovativeness, more and more companies in various industries are changing their traditional approach of developing innovations (OECD 2009). Opening up the closed innovation development paradigm in order to utilise external resources for innovation activities becomes increasingly important. For this emerging competitive strategy of open innovation, customers are frequently seen as having enormous potential for creativity (Kristensson et al. 2002) and generating innovations (von Hippel 2005).

In conducting open innovation, firms aim to integrate customers along the entire innovation process for various activities. Hence, companies can consider different perspectives of their customers and develop innovative products and services tailored to the specific needs of their customer base more effectively. Thus, utilising the "collective intelligence" or "wisdom of crowds" is an underlying principle of customer integration into innovation processes (Liber and Spector 2007; Surowiecki 2005a, b). Therefore, companies increasingly begin to exploit this phenomenon of collective intelligence in order to change the traditional way R&D departments used to function (Blohm et al. 2010b). Figure 13.1 illustrates the differences between the closed and open innovation paradigms.

Open innovation intermediaries such as InnoCentive, provide platforms on which companies can post R&D problems as challenges that are open to solve for anyone. Further, prediction markets such as the Iowa Electronic Markets capture collective wisdom by creating networks of individuals with special knowledge and thus help companies to solve their most sophisticated scientific problems or provide accurate predictions. For instance, Boeing, DuPont and Procter and Gamble regularly use the InnoCentive platform to find solutions for some of their most ornery product development issues (Dushnitsky and Klueter 2011). On average, more than 30 % of the posted tasks are being solved, which is "30 % more than would have been solved using a traditional, in-house approach" (Howe 2008).

A new type of marketplace for crowdsourcing has evolved on the Internet in order to make the collective intelligence of Internet users usable to companies. Platforms like Amazon's Mechanical Turk (mturk) install a member base third party that can offer small and structured tasks which cannot be solved automatically (i.e. Pico-Jobs) (Blohm et al. 2010b). In this context, we use the Latin term "pico" because it means "small" and emphasises one of the core characteristics of Pico-Jobs. In this chapter, a new method for systematically utilising the creative potential of the users of these platforms for activities along the innovation process is illustrated on the basis of a real case.

This chapter addresses two prevalent research questions in order to investigate the application of Pico-Jobs as a new tool of open innovation. Firstly, what are the characteristics of Pico-Jobs and how can they be used to integrate customers into

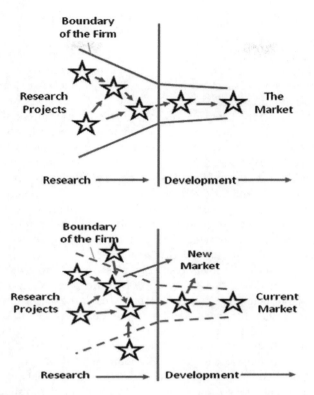

Fig. 13.1 Closed and open innovation. Source: Following Chesbrough (2003)

the innovation process? In the first instance, leading crowdsourcing marketplaces in the German and English-speaking Internet such as mturk have been analysed regarding their size, the offered jobs, the characteristics of task solvers and providers as well as the process of offering jobs. The platforms have been identified by conducting expert interviews and doing Internet research in the German and English-speaking Internet. Included were all platforms that offer paid jobs and act as an intermediary between job providers and solvers. For each platform, 30 randomly selected Pico-Jobs were content analysed and categorised regarding their structuredness, variability and complexity.

Based on this analysis, a case study at OSRAM was conducted in order to analyse and examine the application of Pico-Jobs in an organisational context. OSRAM is a leading manufacturer of light system solutions. In the scope of this case study, several interviews with a German innovation consultancy, Innosabi, were conducted. Innosabi is specialised in open innovation and conducted a workshop for developing new applications of LED light bulbs using Pico-Jobs together with OSRAM. Moreover, the artefacts of this workshop as well as the Pico-Jobs used in this case study were content analysed.

13.2 Integrating Customers and Their Creative Potential

In literature and practice, four core practices for integrating customers into the early stages of the innovation process, where ideas for innovations were generated, are discussed. These are the Lead-User-Method, Toolkits, and Idea Competition and Innovation Communities.

The Lead-User-Method implies systematic identification of single innovative customers, so-called lead users, and their integration into workshops in order to generate ideas and concepts for new products or services together with companies' employees (von Hippel 1988, 2005).

Toolkits encourage users to think about problems with current products or offer applications to modify and configure existing products. They support customers to externalise their ideas and guide interaction between customers and manufacturers (von Hippel and Kats 2002; Jeppesen 2005). Thus, toolkits structure the process of customer integration and provide various means for providing feedback and enabling learning-by-doing (Piller and Walcher 2006).

By conducting Ideas Competitions, companies attempt to collect innovative ideas from customers (Leimeister et al. 2009; Blohm et al. 2010a, b). Ideas competitions is an emerging approach in practice, in order to capture the voice of the customer that becomes manifested in the customer ideas. Therefore, manufacturers reduce their attempts to understand user needs in favour of transferring need-related aspects of product and service development to users themselves.

Innovation communities are a very similar approach to ideas competitions, but are not restricted by time. They build on the principle of user collaboration. Whereas ideas competitions build on the premise of competition in order to stimulate participation and motivation among participants, ideas communities animate customers to collaborate with each other. In such communities, initially developed ideas are picked up by other community members and these ideas are elaborated step by step (Bretschneider 2011). Not only can each participant contribute his/her own ideas but also connect with idea contributors that submitted similar or complementary ideas, and elaborate on ideas in collaboration. Thus, the various networks or teams collaboratively elaborate ideas that might be better, more meaningful and more relevant than those initially submitted (Bretschneider et al. 2008).

In the following, we introduce Pico-Jobs as a new method for integrating customers and their creative potential via crowdsourcing marketplaces over the Internet.

13.3 Pico-Jobs and Their Characteristics

In this section, leading crowdsourcing marketplaces are compared on the basis of their size, the type of tasks offered, the characteristics of task solvers and providers as well as the process of offering jobs in order to work out the characteristics of Pico-Jobs. Table 13.1 gives a brief overview of the platforms.

13 Pico-Jobs as an Open Innovation Tool for Utilising Crowdsourcing 203

Table 13.1 Investigated crowdsourcing marketplaces

	Origin	Online since	members	Team for job solver	#jobs
Mturk	USA	2005	>400,000	Mechanical Turk Worker	>100,000
Clickworker	Germany	2009	>4,000	Clickworker	>1,500
Bitworxx	Gremany	2008	>10,000	Bitworker	n.a.
Shorttask	USA	2009	>20,000	Solver	>15,000
Liveops	USA	2009	>53,000	Agent	>50,000
Klickwork	Austria	n.a.	n.a.	Webworker	<100

Source: http://www.mturk.com; http://www.clickworker.com; http://www.bitworxx.com; http://www.shorttask.com; http://www.liveops.com; http://www.klickwork.com (retrieved on February 22, 2012)

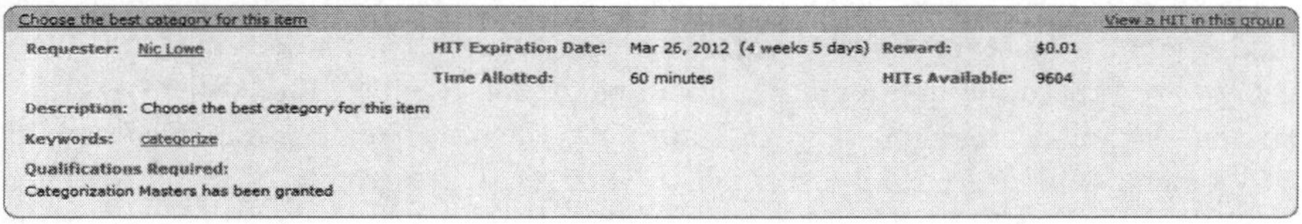

Fig. 13.2 Exemplary task posted on Mturk. Source: http://www.mturk.com (retrieved on February 22, 2012)

The jobs on these marketplaces comprise a high thematic variability ranging from tagging and categorising photos, any kind of content creation, market research and translations to responding surveys. Tasks can generally be characterised by their structuredness (degree to which tasks can be broken down into independent solution steps required to solve a task), variability (amount of changes required to solve a task) and its complexity (amount of decision problems and decision variables that have to be taken into account in solving a task). A typical job that can be found on the crowdsourcing marketplaces is categorising content such as products (cf. Fig. 13.2).

As shown in this example, most jobs consist of only one or very few steps in order to get successfully completed: the jobs are therefore highly structured. Moreover, the job solvers have to repeat the same task very often to accomplish the job. Thus, variability of the jobs is rather low. The results of the jobs are generally well defined because of the high structuredness and the low variability. The task's target groups vary vastly. Whereas some tasks address only a single person or a small group of persons with very specific skills (e.g. in the case of English–Chinese translations of technical manuscripts), others address a large crowd of task solvers (e.g. in the case of tagging photos). Task complexity is strongly depending on the platform on which the jobs are posted. On mturk most tasks have a low degree of complexity. However, on platforms such as liveops, task specificity and complexity are higher with tasks from auditing, healthcare or legal domains.

The *process* of solving jobs is quite similar on all platforms. Generally, all job solvers can pick the jobs they like to process from a central ideas pool in which all

Table 13.2 Characteristics of the jobs posted on crowdsourcing marketplaces

	Structuredness	Variability	Complexity	Type
Mturk	high	high	low – medium	market based
Shorttask	Medium	Low	Low	market based
Klickwork	medium	low	low – medium	market based
Clickworker	medium -high	low	medium – high	service based
Bitworxx	medium -high	low	low – medium	service based
Liveops	high	low	high	service based

Source: http://www.mturk.com; http://www.clickworker.com; http://www.bitworxx.com; http://www.shorttask.com; http://www.liveops.com; http://www.klickwork.com (retrieved on February 22, 2012)

open jobs are stored. The same tasks are generally processed simultaneously and independently by several job solvers. For each successful completion, job solvers get money or points equalling money credited to their user accounts. When a certain amount is reached, e.g. US$10 in case of mturk, the money can be transferred to the user's bank account. Usually, the job solvers receive a couple of cents for each task—money is earned due to repeating the same tasks very frequently. In the above-mentioned example in Fig. 13.2, the job solver receives US$0.01 for each item that has been categorised correctly.

All platforms employ a quality assurance system consisting of an approval rate and qualification tests. Job providers can require job solvers to have certain qualifications that are needed in order to process a job. On mturk there are 3,088 different qualifications that job solvers can achieve such as *automotive categorisation qualification test, BTTS English/French fluency—L1 translator or audio transcript verification* that is defined as "a qualification for correctly rating the quality of an audio clip and its transcript for use in speech recognition training" (mturk 2010). Job solvers have to pass well-defined qualification tests in order to achieve these qualifications. Job providers can rely on already existing qualifications or define new qualifications they want their job solvers to have. Moreover, job providers can reject the results of the job solvers after job completion in case the work is of poor quality. An approval rate that is usually defined as the ratio of successful job completions is calculated for each job solver. Besides qualification tests job providers can require a minimum approval rate for the employed job solvers.

Table 13.2 summarises the characteristics of the jobs posted on different crowdsourcing marketplaces. On each marketplace we analysed the 50 most recent jobs and evaluated them according to their structuredness, variability, complexity as well as type (cf. Sect. 13.2). By structuredness we mean the variance of the task solving process. The lower the variance of the steps required for solving the job, the higher the structuredness of the job. Variability was evaluated by the variability of different jobs on the marketplace. The complexity of a job is defined by the number of different steps that are required in order to finish the job and by the requirements on the job solvers' qualifications.

Regarding posting jobs, two major types of crowdsourcing platforms can be identified (cf. Fig. 13.3). Some platforms offer forms which contain a job

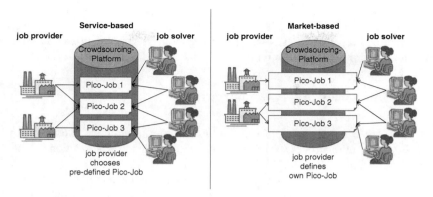

Fig. 13.3 Two types of crowdsourcing platforms

description, required qualifications, the job solver's remuneration and other job-related information. This type is called market-based because the platform is organised as a marketplace. On these platforms job providers have no constrained solution space so that the task can be defined totally freely by the job providers.

In contrast, other platforms offer a set of well pre-defined tasks to job providers. In this regard, this platform is more comparable to a traditional service company that sells pre-defined services that are delivered by the job solvers. This type is called *service-based* because job providers can only choose from pre-defined jobs of the platform.

The *job solvers* are usually private persons. According to Villaroel and Andrei Tucci (2009), mturk members are predominantly female (about 59 %), employed (about 71 %) and well educated: 64 % of respondents have a college degree or higher. Their professional background spans various industries, e.g. ranging from scientists, to lawyers, engineers and teachers. According to mturk, about 46 % of job solvers are Americans and 34 % are Indians. Most job solvers are motivated by fun and earning money. Another reason for participation is spare time (Villaroel and Andrei Tucci 2009). However, another interested target group is reached by the German platform Bitworxx: besides private persons the jobs are offered to call centre employees in order to utilise over capacities.

The *job providers* mostly comprise enterprises and freelancers. Private persons post jobs only occasionally. The content analysis of the jobs revealed that job providers span various industries, albeit IT-related industries, which are dominating.

Summing up the analysis, three major characteristics of the jobs offered can be defined (Blohm et al. 2010b):

1. The jobs are small, highly structured, repeatable and yield a well-defined result.
2. The jobs are processed asynchronously and distributed for remuneration.
3. An online platform acts as financial and operational intermediary between job solvers (usually private persons) and job providers (usually corporations) and defines the process of cooperation.

Synthesising the three major characteristics of the jobs posted on crowdsourcing marketplaces, *Pico-Jobs* are defined as (Blohm et al. 2010b): small, highly structured and repeatable tasks that are processed asynchronously and distributed for remuneration via crowdsourcing marketplaces on the Internet.

13.4 Categories of Crowdsourcing

Pico-Jobs are a tool for using crowdsourcing in order to integrate external knowledge into innovation processes, from problem definition, ideas generation as well as idea and concept evaluation.

According to Howe (2008), the notion of crowdsourcing encompasses a number of different approaches, which vary according to the nature of contributions made by the crowd. For this reason, the choice of an appropriate model or a combination of models primarily depends on a company's needs and goals to be achieved via a crowdsourcing initiative. Crowdsourcing activities can be subdivided into crowd wisdom, crowd creation and crowd voting.

The major idea driving crowdsourcing and in particular its *Crowd Wisdom* model is that groups of people accumulate more knowledge than single individuals. "The crowd possesses a wide array of talents, and some have the kind of scientific talent and expertise that used to exist only in rarefied academic environments" (Howe 2008). Crowd Wisdom implies that the crowd is a source of creative energy and thus can be highly useful for activities such as articulating needs or experience. The phenomenon of interest in Crowd Wisdom is the job solver as potential customer and knowledge carrier. Pico-Jobs for utilising Crowd Wisdom allow companies to gather customer inputs, consolidate and evaluate these inputs very fast, in order to flow those findings back into further Pico-Jobs. Companies can use Pico-Jobs to react very fast to dynamics in innovation processes by many, short feedback cycles, e.g. for generating an understanding of customer perceptions or identifying applications for new technologies. For improving an existing product, companies can, e.g. ask customers for an emotional evaluation of the existing product, how they actually use the product and for ideas of novel applications. In every step, inputs from the previous step of all participates—the so-called crowd— can be recognised.

While the Crowd Wisdom model focuses on opinions and experiences of the job solvers, *Crowd Creation* "involves cultivating a robust community composed of people with a deep and on-going commitment to their craft and, most important, to one another" (Howe 2008). In this category, job solvers create new content or artefacts, or enrich an existing artefact and deliver it to the job provider via the crowdsourcing platform. Examples of Crowd Creation with Pico-Jobs are language translations, producing effective TV commercials, adding metadata to product descriptions as well as describing and tagging pictures. Phenomenon of interest is the new content or artefact.

Crowd Voting is another category of crowdsourcing, which "uses the crowd's judgments to organise vast quantities of information" (Howe 2008). Evaluations of alternative ideas, concepts or designs represent examples of Pico-Jobs for crowd

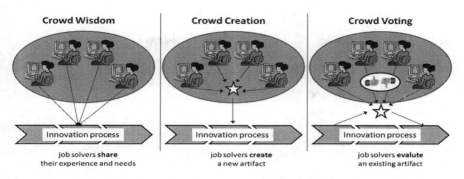

Fig. 13.4 Three categories of Crowdsourcing and related Pico-Job

voting. Compared to Crowd Wisdom, in this category the job solvers evaluate an existing artefact instead of sharing their own experiences or needs. The phenomenon of interest in Crowd Voting is the evaluation of an existing artefact.

In Fig. 13.4, all three categories of crowdsourcing and related Pico-Jobs for integrating customers across the innovation process are illustrated.

13.5 Crowdsourcing-Related Pico-Jobs in the Innovation Process

Crowd Wisdom, Crowd Creation as well as Crowd Voting can be utilised by Pico-Jobs for innovation processes. We suggest analysing each phase of the innovation process in order to identify opportunities of using crowdsourcing with Pico-Jobs. Our analysis is based on the innovation process of Tidd and Bessant (2009), which consists of four phases:

- Search—how can we find opportunities for innovation?
- Select—what are we going to do–and why?
- Implement—how are we going to make it happen?
- Capture—how are we going to get the benefits from it?

In the phase, *Searching*, companies are scanning their internal and external environment for relevant signals about threats and opportunities for change. Pico-Jobs can therefore help to use crowd wisdom to identify these signals by asking corresponding questions about needs, beliefs or change of customers' behaviour. In addition, information about usage of, and experiences with, existing products as well as suggestions for improvement can be used by companies as signals. All information can be gathered by Pico-Jobs. Furthermore, companies can use Pico-Jobs to find people around the world to research for specific, especially local, information. Crowd creation and voting are not yet applicable in this innovation phase because companies do not even know what they will innovate. The main contribution of Pico-Jobs in this innovation phase is to understand the customer.

Table 13.3 Possible applications of Pico-Jobs as a tool for open innovation

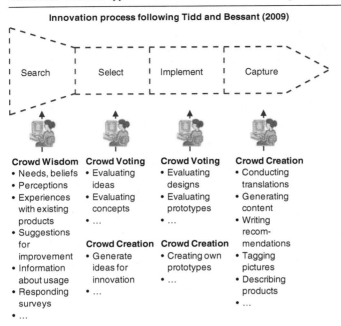

In the next phase, *Select*, companies decide on the basis of their strategic view which of these signals to respond to. Here again Pico-Jobs can utilise collective intelligence for generating and evaluating possible innovations. On the one hand, Pico Jobbers can generate their own ideas for innovations, and on the other hand, they can evaluate or comment ideas. Crowd voting is a great possibility to get feedback from Pico-Jobbers about innovation ideas and concepts, and to support the selection process during the Select phase. The focus is placed on interaction with customers.

Implement is the third innovation phase and contains translating the potential in the trigger into something novel and to launch it. The biggest potential for Pico-Jobs in this phase is crowd voting. Pico-Jobbers can vote and comment on designs and prototypes. In summary, companies can provide customers the possibility to participate in decision making about the solution.

The last phase of the innovation process is called *Capture* and focuses on how companies are going to get the benefits from the innovation. In this phase, Pico-Jobbers can mostly contribute through content creation. The innovation is already launched and must be enhanced continuously. Pico-Jobbers can help, e.g. with translations, generating content on websites or forums, writing recommendations of products or tagging pictures.

Table 13.3 summarises the opportunities of Pico-Jobs across all phases of the innovation process.

13.6 Using Market-Based Pico-Jobs in Practice at OSRAM

In the case, Pico-Jobs were applied for developing new applications for light emitting diode (LED)-based light bulbs at OSRAM, a leading manufacturer of light system solutions (Blohm et al. 2010b). In contrast to traditional incandescent light bulbs, LED bulbs do not create light by a glowing wire. LED light bulbs have a common shape but consist of several LEDs on the inside. The LED technology results in longer lifetimes and smaller energy consumption. Moreover, LED enables wholly new lighting applications such as smart light applications adapting to their environment. However, developing new applications for light bulbs is difficult as customers are very price sensitive and alternative lighting solutions as energy saving bulbs are frequently suffering from a bad image.

For these reasons, OSRAM engaged in integrating customers into the development of new applications for LED-based light bulbs. In the first instance, Pico-Jobs were used to get a deeper understanding of how customers use light bulbs in general and how different types of light bulbs are perceived. Therefore, Pico Jobbers were asked to describe situations in which they directly interact with light bulbs. For solving these Pico-Jobs an approval rate of 98 % was rewired as qualification. In return, Pico-Jobbers earned between US\$0.10 and 0.50 for each completed Pico-Job. Moreover, Pico-Jobbers were rewarded with a bonus of US\$0.50 for outstanding work. Due to this surplus, fast response times and high quality of results could be warranted.

The results of these Pico-Jobs were content analysed and used to deduct assumptions about usage patterns of light bulbs. These assumptions were again translated into Pico-Jobs and placed on mturk. Using this storytelling approach with a magnitude of iterations, a holistic comprehension of the needs and the associations of light bulb users could be gained (Zaltman 1997). Altogether, about 150 Pico-Jobs for Crowd Wisdom were posted and 1,889 responses were gained. A model for explaining usage behaviour and perceptions of lighting bulb customers could be gained by content analysing these responses. Based on this model search areas for new LED applications were defined. For instance, a magnitude of customers stated that they are frustrated with light bulbs breaking, because light is generally needed in the moment the light bulb burns out.

In a second step, these search areas such as "avoiding customer frustration" were used as a starting point for a brainstorming workshop with marketing and R&D employees of OSRAM in order to generate new product ideas that highlight the benefits of LED bulbs in terms of Crowd Creation. For instance, several ideas for light bulbs displaying the light bulbs remaining life time were developed. During the workshops, all ideas developed were instantly evaluated using Pico-Jobs as Crowd Voting, resulting in 50–100 evaluations for each idea. These validated ideas then were used as stimuli for refining the ideas and generating new ones (cf. Table 13.4).

According to OSRAM, the results developed with this Pico Job approach (cf. Fig. 13.5) provided high value for the entire new product development process and allowed an effective integration of a magnitude of customer responses.

Table 13.4 Example of a Pico-Job and corresponding answers

Pico-Job	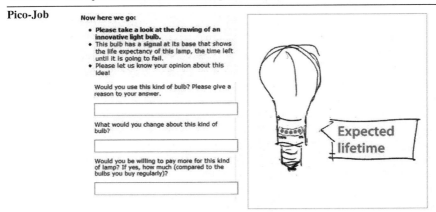
Answers	*"OMG!! I would love this bulb. I am caught without bulbs sometimes and I think this would actually make me remember to get some." (anonymous Pico-Jobber)* *"Maybe a visual change in colour that the light bulb emits when it is getting close to expiration would be better" (anonymous Pico-Jobber)* *"Why would I want to grab a ladder, remove a fixture cover, and check my bulbs on a regular basis when it's much easier to wait until one needs attention?" (anonymous Pico-Jobber)*

Source: following Blohm et al. (2010b)

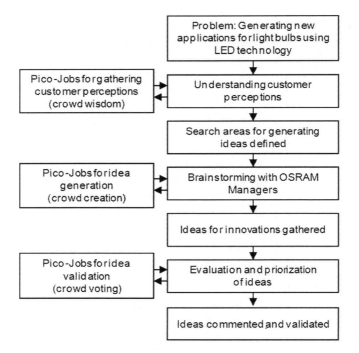

Fig. 13.5 Application of Pico-Jobs at OSRAM. Source: following Blohm et al. (2010b)

This approach combines all three categories of Pico-Jobs—Crowd Wisdom, Crowd Creation and Crowd Voting—in order to define search areas based on valuable feedback from customers, generate appropriate ideas as well as comment and evaluate the ideas.

13.7 Practical Advice

The case illustrates Pico-Jobs as a new tool for open innovation. On the one hand, several advantages emerge for companies and job providers. First, the amount of time used in product development could be radically reduced. In comparison to web-based ideas competitions (Blohm et al. 2010a; Ebner et al. 2009; Leimeister et al. 2009) or surveys, only very little amount of time and costs for pre- and post-processing incur for the job provider. Second, the job provider gets the results quickly due to a very short response time of the job solvers. In our case, more than 100 answers could be gathered within a couple of hours. Third, Pico-Jobs reduce the cost risk to a minimum, because no overhead costs incur for the job provider and one only has to pay for useful inputs exceeding a minimum quality defined by the job provider. Fourth, the job providers do not have to reveal their identity and the single Pico-Jobs are fragmentised so that third persons cannot estimate what subject the job provider is working on. Due to this reason as well as the remuneration, intellectual property can easily be transferred to the job provider. Furthermore, job providers get access to a large group of customers, which results in a variety of inputs from many different perspectives; this is especially interesting since those customers feel an intimacy, which allows a deep understanding of their real needs and pains with a product or service. This could not be achieved with less anonymous methods. On the other hand, a high variance of input quality resulting in high efforts for data analysis and self-selection effects of job solvers seem to be limitations of Pico-Jobs. In particular, Pico-Jobs for crowd wisdom bear the risk of imprudent and untrue answers because, on the one hand, it is difficult to verify them and, on the other hand, Pico-Jobbers are interested in solving as many jobs as possible to maximise their remuneration.

There are also some disadvantages for the job solvers. They often can only choose from simple and click-based tasks and are sometimes poorly paid. On the other hand, Pico-Jobs also offer advantages for job solvers. They get the opportunity to work from home, choose their own working hours, get paid for doing good work and can choose from many different tasks. We could observe high intrinsic motivation to solve product development tasks—despite external motivation by a payment. These kinds of tasks differ from the majority of tasks offered like picture tagging or research of addresses that represent examples of crowd creation. Comments show that product development tasks are more fun for the participants and are therefore chosen over other kinds of tasks.

Table 13.5 summarises the most important advantages and disadvantages for both job providers and solvers.

Table 13.5 Advantages and disadvantages of Pico-Jobs as a tool of open innovation

Advantages for job provider	Advantages for job solver
short preparation time	work from home
Cheap	choose own working hours
fast response time	get paid for doing good work
Anonymity	big variety of different tasks
variety of inputs	earn money "in the meantime" with small tasks
Disadvantages for job provider	**Disadvantages for job solver**
high variance in input quality	sometimes bad paid
limited types of tasks	often only simple tasks
sometimes high effort for evaluation	remuneration is dependent on quality of results (no guarantee)

Bonabeau (2009) emphasised various biases that can be reduced by the use of crowdsourcing applications: On the one hand, people tend to seek information that confirms their assumptions and to maintain those assumptions even in the face of inconsistent evidence by generating solutions. On the other hand, in matters of the evaluation of solutions, people tend to perceive patterns where none exist and to exorbitantly influence by the presentation of the solution. The case shows that Pico-Jobbers mitigated those and further biases, e.g. by obtaining diversity of assumptions, anchors and beliefs.

> **Practical Tip**
>
> We derived some success factors from the case for successfully applying Pico-Jobs for integrating customers in innovation activities:
>
> Define a clear task statement because of limited options for job solvers to ask questions for clarification. Job solvers will not even realise that they do not solve the job in an appropriate way.
>
> Provide examples for valid as well as invalid results to support job solvers with solving the job.
>
> One Pico-Jobs—one task. Offer multiple simple rather than complex Pico-Jobs. That makes it easier for job solvers to find an appropriate job and solve it properly, and for job provider to evaluate the results and calculate the remuneration.
>
> Provide a structured template in order to minimise the variety of result representations.
>
> Use low costs of Pico-Jobs for quality control through the comparison of the same results generated by different job solvers.
>
> Offer fair remuneration. The higher the remuneration, the more job solvers will try to solve the job despite their qualification and ability. The lower the remuneration, the less job solvers will recognise the job in the pool of Pico-Jobs.
>
> Do not underestimate the time for evaluating and post-processing the results so they can be used in the innovation process.

> Design the job as interesting as possible. If suitable and useful, use multimedia or other entertaining elements to motivate the job solvers and support them with generating high quality results.

13.8 Implications for Research

This research shed light on the phenomenon of jobs offered on crowdsourcing marketplaces which we call Pico-Jobs. We also described their application in innovation processes for the first time. The case demonstrated the applicability and practicability of Pico-Jobs as an open innovation tool. However, there are still open issues to be solved. The following research questions refer to some different aspects of Pico-Jobs that are still unsolved and need to be researched in the future:

Which types of task are applicable for Pico-Jobs and why?
How should tasks be broken down for Pico-Jobs?
What may concepts, methods and tools for quality management look like?
What are suitable incentives for motivating customers to participate in Pico-Jobs?
Which theories could be used and extended?
What may an overall management concept for Pico-Jobs look like?

References

Blohm, I., Bretschneider, U., Leimeister, J.M. & Krcmar, H. (2010a) Does collaboration among participants lead to better ideas in IT-based idea competitions? An empirical investigation. *In Proceedings of the 43rd Hawaii International Conference on System Science*. Kauai, Hawaii.

Blohm, I., Fähling, J., Leimeister, J. M. & Krcmar, H. (2010b) Accelerating customer integration into innovation processes using pico jobs. *The XXI ISPIM 2010*, Bilbao, Spain.

Bonabeau, E. (2009). Decision 2.0: The power of collective intelligence. *MIT Sloan Management Review, 50*(2), 44–52.

Bretschneider U (2011) *Ideen Communities sur Integration von Kunden in die frühen Phasen des Innovationsprosess: Theorie und Empirische Analysen. Dissertation*, Chair of Information Systems (I17), Technische Universität München.

Bretschneider, U., Huber, J. M., Leimeister, J. M. & Krcmar, H. (2008) Community for Innovations: Developing an Integrated Concept for Open Innovation, In: León, G., Bernardos, A., Casar, J., Kauts, K., & DeGross, J. (eds.), Open IT-Based Innovation: Moving Towards Cooperative IT Transfer and Knowledge Diffusion, *Proceedings of the International Federation for Information Processing (IFIP) 8.6 Conference*, Madrid, 287, Boston: Springer, 503–510.

Chesbrough, H. (2003). The era of open innovation. *MIT Sloan Management Review, 44*(3), 35–41.

Dushnitsky, G., & Klueter, T. (2011). Is there an e-Bay for ideas? Insights from online marketplaces. *European Management Review, 8*(1), 17–32.

Ebner, W., Leimeister, J. M., & Krcmar, H. (2009). Community engineering for innovations: The ideas competition as a method to nurture a virtual community for innovations. *R&D Management, 39*(4), 342–356.

Howe, J. (2008). *Crowdsourcing: Why the power of the crowd is driving the future of business.* New York: Crown Publishing Group.

Jeppesen, L. B. (2005). User toolkits for innovation: Consumers support each other. *Journal of Product Innovation Management, 22*(4), 347–362.

Kristensson, P., Magnusson, P. R., & Matthing, J. (2002). Users as a hidden resource for creativity: findings from an experimental study on user involvement. *Creativity & Innovation Management, 11*(1), 55–61.

Leimeister, J. M., Huber, M., Bretschneider, U., & Krcmar, H. (2009). Leveraging crowdsourcing—activation-supporting components for IT-based idea competitions. *Journal of Management Information Systems, 26*(1).

Liber, B., & Spector, J. (2007). *We are smarter than me: How to unleash the power of crowds in your business*. New Jersey: Prentice Hall.

mturk (2010) Amazon Mechanical Turk, http://www.mturk.com, retrieved on 21.01.2011

OECD (2009) *Open innovation in global networks*.

Piller, F. T., & Walcher, D. (2006). Toolkits for idea competitions: a novel method to integrate users in new product development. *R&D Management, 36*(3), 307–318.

Surowiecki, J. (2005a). *The wisdom of crowds*. New York: Anchor Books.

Tidd, J., & Bessant, J. (2009). *Managing Innovation: Integrating technological, market and organisational change*. Hoboken, New Jersey: John Wiley & Sons.

Villaroel, J., & Andrei Tucci, C. L. (2009) Motivating firm-sponsored e-collective work. Working Paper Cambridge, MIT Sloan School of Management.

von Hippel, E. (1988). *The sources of innovation*. New York: Oxford University Press.

von Hippel, E., & Kats, R. (2002). Shifting innovation to users via toolkits. *Management Science, 48*(7), 821–833.

von Hippel, E. (2005). *Democratising innovation*. Cambridge MA: MIT Press.

Zaltman, G. (1997). Rethinking market research: Putting people back. *Journal of Marketing Research, 34*(4), 424–437.

Further Reading

Chesbrough, H.W. (2006) *Open Innovation. The New Imperative for Creating and Profiting from Technology*, Boston MA.

Dahan, E., & Hauser, J. R. (2002). The virtual customer. *The Journal of Product Innovation Management, 19*(1), 332–353.

Ebner W., Leimeister J. M., Bretschneider U. & Krcmar H. (2008) Leveraging the wisdom of crowds: Designing an IT-supported ideas competition for an ERP software company. *HICSS 417*.

Malone, T. W., Laubacher, R., & Dellarocas, C. (2010). The collective intelligence genoem. *Sloan Management Review, 51*(3), 21–31.

McAfee, A. P. (2006). Enterprise 2.0: The dawn of emergent collaboration. *MIT Sloan Management Review, 47*(3), 20–28.

Leimeister, J. M. (2010). Collective intelligence. *Business & Information Systems Engineering, 2*(4), 245–248.

Lévy, P. (1997). *Collective intelligence*. New York: Mankinds Emerging World in Cyberspace.

Riedl, C., Blohm, I., Leimeister, J.M., & Krcmar, H. (2010) Rating Scales for Collective Intelligence in Innovation Communities: Why Quick and Easy Decision Making Does Not Get it Right. *In Proceedings of the International Conference on Information Systems (ICIS)*, St. Louis.

Surowiecki, J. (2005b). *The wisdom of crowds*. New York: Anchor Books.

Williams Wolley, A., Chabris, C. F., Pentland, A., Hashmi, N., & Malone, T. W. (2010). Evidence for a collective intelligence factor in the performance of human groups. *Science, 330*(6004), 686–688.

Zwass, V. (2010). Co-creation: Toward a taxonomy and an integrated research perspective. *International Journal of Electronic Commerce, 15*(1), 11–48.

Chapter 14
Open Strengths and Weaknesses of IT User Innovation: Evidence from Three Cases

Matthias Hürlimann and Ali Yakhlef

Abstract The advent of the open innovation approach, together with the increased sophistication of new IT tools, has excited several researchers' interest in user innovation. However, most such research remains fragmented and limited in its scope. The aim of the present study is to explore the role of IT throughout all the different phases of user innovation process and their associated advantages and disadvantages. In doing so, the study draws on material gleaned from three cases of companies in their attempt to integrate users and customers during the different phases of the innovation process. The study shows that IT tools are not enough rather they need to be complemented with more traditional modes of interactions and communications with their customers and users. This is all the more so as customers and users in other parts of the world differ with regard to their preferences, technical maturities and access to IT. The chapter ends with conclusions and some implications for theory and practice of open innovation technologies.

14.1 Introduction

The advent of the open innovation approach, together with the increased sophistication of new IT tools, has excited several researchers' interest in user innovation. Whereas researchers have largely emphasised the role of 'innovation technology' (IvT) to tap external sources at the ideational stage (Dodgson et al. 2006), Desouza et al. (2008) have suggested a framework of customer involvement at the different

---

M. Hürlimann
Zug, ZG, Switzerland
e-mail: matthias.huerlimann@gmail.com

A. Yakhlef (✉)
Stockholm University School of Business, Sweden
e-mail: aya@fek.su.se

J.S.Z. Eriksson Lundström et al. (eds.), *Managing Open Innovation Technologies*,
DOI 10.1007/978-3-642-31650-0_14, © Springer-Verlag Berlin Heidelberg 2013

stages of the innovation process. However, Gassmann et al. (2010) bemoan that most such research remains fragmented and centred on a single dimension, focused on the role of IT in a specific phase of the innovation process (e.g. Ebner et al. 2009; Leimeister et al. 2009), or using specific technologies (e.g. Füller and Matzler 2007; Kohler et al. 2009). More often than not, the role of IT in the innovation processes has been assigned a secondary, supportive or facilitating role (e.g. Awazu et al. 2009; Dodgson et al. 2006).

Although such studies have provided valuable insights, there is more to say about the role of IT in the overall user innovation process. To the authors' knowledge, a critical and comprehensive study of IT in the context of the user innovation process as a whole is lacking so far. For instance, in light of the stickiness and immobility of tacit knowledge (von Hippel 1986), it is usually the case that some tools are more suitable than others in the different phases of customer involvement. More knowledge is required of what and how IT tools are used to capture external in the different phases of the product development process.

The aim of this study is to explore the role of IT throughout all the different phases of user innovation process, focusing on their limitations and advantages. In doing so, the study draws on material gleaned from three cases of companies' use of IT in user innovation. The question guiding this study is: What role do different IT tools play in the various phases of the user innovation process and what are the opportunities and the challenges they present?

This rest of the chapter unfolds in the following way. The next section presents a literature review in order to build a tentative framework to guide us in structuring the empirical material (Sect. 14.3) which we analyse in Sect. 14.5. Section 14.4 outlines the method that we apply. Finally, in Sect. 14.6, concluding remarks, implications and suggestions for further studies are drawn up.

14.2 IT's Role in User Innovation

Open innovation has emerged from its initially limited focus on software, high-tech industries into a topical and widely recognised research field consisting of different sub-areas (Gassmann et al. 2010). The driving assumption is that "ideas for successful product innovations are most likely to come from end-users and customers of the products and not from within the organization" (Desouza et al. 2008, p. 39). As noted earlier, the shift from closed to open innovation presupposes the existence of reliable tools and instruments that firms can use in order to open up their R&D activities (Chesbrough 2003; Gassmann et al. 2010). In this connection, the term 'IT' is used as the umbrella term for different technologies, techniques, soft- and hardware related to the processing of information. Whereas information and communication technology (ICT) is seen as providing the infrastructure for the exchange of digital information, for instance through computers, other communication devices and the Internet (e.g. email, websites and Web 2.0 applications like interactive blogs and social networking sites such as Facebook), IvT is concerned with emergent technologies that build upon

ICT and leverage virtual models, visualisations and simulations in the innovation process (e.g. Internet-based toolkits, virtual environments and interaction platforms) (Dodgson et al. 2006).

The expression 'user innovation' is taken to refer to "an innovation where users have performed a substantial part of the problem-solving process leading to a solution" (Piller and Walcher 2006 p. 308). In this context, users may play a vital role throughout the different innovation stages: defining the problem, coming up with ideas to express novel desires and requirements or by providing valuable insights during the development or use of the solution to an identified problem. Although different terminologies have been used to describe these different phases of the innovation process (e.g. De Moor et al. 2010; Desouza et al. 2008; Füller and Matzler 2007; Lazzarotti and Manzini 2009), in this study we will adopt the three stages suggested by Desouza et al. (2008): (a) idea generation and development; (b) design, testing and refinement and (c) commercialisation. What tools are used in connection with these different stages?

The initial phase of the user innovation process is concerned with the identification and integration of users' ideas into the company (Desouza et al. 2008). In this phase, ICTs provide an infrastructure for a reliable, cheap and fast way to exchange ideas (Dodgson et al. 2006). Hoyer et al. (2010) also point out the ease of communicating ideas over the Internet, e.g. through company websites, email and social media. Furthermore, ICT enables innumerable users to share ideas (Di Gangi and Wasko 2009; Piller and Walcher 2006). A particular way of searching for and attracting ideas on a specific topic takes place in the form of online idea competitions (OIC) (Ebner et al. 2009; Leimeister et al. 2009).

Virtual communities (VCs) are yet another mode of capturing ideas from users, who consist of numerous voluntary participants collaborating with one another over the Internet (Schröder and Hölzle 2010). Schröder and Hölzle (2010) emphasise that VCs constitute a good basis for developing promising ideas for mainly incremental, but also radically new innovations. By studying such online communities in the sports market, Füller et al. (2007) conclude that most innovative ideas stem from users who, driven by excitement, engage and share their thoughts through 3D drawings and designs.

After the early engagement of users in the innovation process to identify and develop ideas into mature ones, the second stage of the user innovation process is concerned with the participation of users in the transformation of ideas into concrete products and services (Desouza et al. 2008). At this point, users become actively involved in business processes and increasingly integrated into a firm's value chain (Desouza et al. 2008). Awazu et al. (2009) pointed out the facilitating role of ICT to link customers into business processes, e.g. by providing information system interfaces to efficiently and effectively exchange product data. Involving users in both the ideation and the product development phase is seen as crucial, as this helps to increase the user acceptance of the finished product as well save costs and time (Hoyer et al. 2010). Users play a significant role at this stage by critically evaluating, refining and improving concepts and prototypes through virtual interaction platforms

(Füller and Matzler 2007). Firms may actively seek users' input in the product development process using interactive web technologies or crowdsourcing (Kleemann et al. 2008).

Moreover, firms make use of simulations and visualisation techniques to explore ideas and prototypes (Awazu et al. 2009; Füller and Matzler 2007; Gordon et al. 2008). Almost two decades ago, Rothwell (1994) pointed out that computer-aided design (CAD) systems are a suitable way to achieve a closer integration of users and to speed up the process of transforming a model into a physical prototype. Rothwell (1994) also emphasised that simulation has the potential to reduce the number of physical prototypes required during the development process.

Although physical prototyping is still seen as necessary in later phases of the innovation process, virtual prototyping enabled by emergent IvT gained importance in earlier stages of the process as it allows companies to effectively overcome uncertainties (Dodgson et al. 2006). Advanced CAD tools enable engineers to build virtual 3D models of products that make it possible to experience virtual products through simulations facilitating the efficient evaluation of impacts resulting from design changes (Gordon et al. 2008). Instead of experiencing virtual products in isolation, CAD tools can be integrated in virtual worlds or virtual realities that simulate the real world on the Internet: "Virtual reality has become pervasive in the engineering, design, simulation, and testing of new products" (Füller and Matzler 2007, p. 380). Leveraging such new virtualisation technologies allows companies to gain invaluable insights as it makes it possible for firms to examine users' reactions and ways of interacting with virtual prototypes (Füller and Matzler 2007; Kohler et al. 2009). Virtual product experience offers firms the possibility to collaborate with users and customers during the innovation process (Kohler et al. 2009).

The final stage of the user innovation process concerns the launch of a product and related interactions with users and customers to learn from their feedback before as well as after purchase (Desouza et al. 2008). Offering pre-release versions that encourage customers to experiment and provide feedback that can be incorporated into subsequent revised versions is a suitable way to gain valuable insights before the launch of a new product or service that is quite common in the software industry (Desouza et al. 2008). Moreover, providing room for customisations and modifications of products can provide critical insights for further innovations, since customers are likely to use products in different ways under such circumstances (Desouza et al. 2008). Internet offers companies new opportunities to collaborate with user and customers in this phase of the process. Hoyer et al. (2010) notice that releasing information through social media can advertise and create buzz around upcoming products. However, as Hoyer et al. (2010) emphasise, issues related to secrecy and intellectual properties may arise in this context. Instant messaging and Wikis are used during and after the release of innovation to monitor users' reactions and gain quick feedback from them.

To sum up, recent leaps in IT have brought along changes in the way companies collaborate with customers and users during the innovation process. ICTs have provided easier access to customer information and transformed customers and users from passive receivers of innovations to active participants in the different

14 Open Strengths and Weaknesses of IT User Innovation: Evidence from Three Cases 219

Table 14.1 User innovation tools

Innovation Process Stage	User Innovation Tools	Advantages	Disadvantages
Idea generation and development	ICT	ease of communication broad reach	information overload problems to identify promising ideas
	OIC & VC	generation of innovative ideas	technical barriers importance of incentives
Design, testing and refinement	ICT	effective data exchange	
	Toolkits	outsourcing of tasks no transfer of sticky information addressing heterogeneous user needs	unsuitable for certain user types
	IvT	overcoming uncertainties efficient evaluation	unsuitable for certain product types concerns about secrecy
Commercialisation	ICT	learning from feedback	concerns about secrecy
Overall limitations			transfer of rich and tacit information issues with intellectual property rights

stages of the innovation process. Relying on sophisticated tools and ways of interacting with users, firms are becoming better positioned to capture tacit knowledge through closer cooperation between companies and customers (Chesbrough 2011). These considerations explored in this section are captured in the following framework (Table 14.1), which will be used to guide our data generation process and the subsequent analysis of the empirical material.

14.3 Method

As noted earlier, the present study draws on case study material gleaned from organisations. According to Yin (2009), case study research offers an overall method covering the design, data collection and analysis to understand real-life phenomena in context. More specifically, Darke et al. (1998) suggest that case studies are particularly suitable to study how and why IT is being used in organisations. Hence, three cases are chosen on theoretical sampling basis (Eisenhardt and Graebner 2007; Silverman 2010). Silverman (2010) pointed out that it makes sense to include cases that are positive and negative instances in relation to relevant theories. Accordingly, Eisenhardt (1989) emphasised that disconfirming cases have the opportunity to improve and extend theory. Case study methodology is often criticised for not being to generate generalised results. However, as Yin (2009) emphasises, case studies are not generalisable to populations, but rather aim to expand and generalise theories. In this connection, Eisenhardt and Graebner (2007) add that exploratory case study aims to develop and make a theoretical contribution to theories rather than testing them. Thus, this study seeks to make analytical generalisations that contribute to theories concerned with the role of IT in the user innovation process.

In examining the use of IT in the user innovation process, we have chosen a multiple-case study design including Sony Ericsson, Volvo IT and 3 M Svenska AB. A multiple-case study approach makes it possible to make comparisons, and hopefully provide varied empirical information that is more likely to yield generalisation than single cases (Eisenhardt and Graebner 2007).

To address the prevalent concern of lacking rigour in case study research, for each of the three cases, a case study protocol was created to support a systematic collection of data. Moreover, empirical material collected for each case was organised in a case study database. According to Yin (2009), such measures contribute to increased reliability of the overall case study as it enables the maintenance of a clear chain of evidence.

Interviews were being conducted in a semi-structured way with informants identified and selected in collaboration with organisations' leading R&D and innovation managers. The informants were prompted to talk freely about the user innovation process. Moreover, specific sub-questions were asked to gain detailed information about the organisation's practice of user innovation and the role IT tools play in that process. The questionnaire used to elicit the bulk of empirical information for this study is in Appendix 1.

In total, 16 interviews consisting of 8 face-to-face (3 with Ericsson, 3 with Volvo and 2 with 3 M Sweden), 3 group (one with each case) and 5 telephone interviews (2 with Ericsson, 2 with Volvo and 1 with 3 M Sweden) were conducted. Face-to-face and group interviews took place at the organisations' premises in Sweden. The average duration of the interviews was 55 min. All interviews were tape-recorded and transcribed in verbatim. To make the cases more convincing and accurate, data generated through interviews were triangulated with information from internal documents and company websites. Moreover, draft versions were sent to the informants for perusal, as a further effort to increase the validity and overall quality of the data.

Studying the use of IT in the user innovation process in three diverse cases requires a general analytic strategy to examine rival explanations. Yin (2009 p. 139) points out that "[t]he use of rival explanations, besides being a good general analytic strategy, provides a good example of pattern-matching for independent variables". The theoretical framework introduced in Table 14.1 was employed as a suggested set of guidelines to support the analysis of the empirical material. In this way, the empirical data were coded based on the use of IT in the various stages of the user innovation process. As the aim of the present research is exploratory in nature, insights gained during the analysis contributed to continuously refine and extend the theoretical framework to better fit the empirical material. Within-case analysis was initially performed to analyse the empirical material of each case separately, followed by a comparison of emerging patterns across the three cases. The report of the analysis concentrates on the cross-case analysis, which according to Yin (2009), is a suitable format of reporting multiple-case studies where the amount of space is limited.

14.4 Empirical Material

14.4.1 Sony Ericsson

In 2001, Sony Ericsson was established as a joint venture between Sony and Ericsson. The company manufactures mobile hand-held devices with a focus on the smart-phone market. As of today, the company employs nearly 8,000 employees worldwide and is headquartered in London, UK. The major part of its R&D activities is located in Lund, Sweden. In order to be responsive and quick in the fast moving mobile phone industry, Sony Ericsson co-creates its products and services with external parties such as consumers, suppliers and operators.

14.4.1.1 Idea Generation and Development

Sony Ericsson is aware that the Internet is a significant way of tapping innovative ideas on a global reach. First, it used a so-called *Innovation Portal* as an easy way for external parties to get in touch with Sony Ericsson. Although individual persons as well as larger companies are invited to submit their ideas, the major target group of this portal was small firms such as start-ups with new ideas that could be used in differentiating features of its future products. Another initiative is the 2010 launch of a platform called *SE-dot* prompting mobile phone end-users to answer the question: "What do you want your phone to do?" After receiving over 1,000 ideas, the company built a Facebook support forum, called *Sony Ericsson Product Blog*.

Sony Ericsson also operates a Consumer Insight Center that engages with end-users of its hand-held devices to listen and learn about ongoing trends in society. Collecting such information is relevant for future improvements of products and services. Face-to-face meetings are seen as the preferred way to interact with people, as body language and all senses can be used during the conversations, which helps reduce misunderstandings. The Internet is used to complement face-to-face conversations to get diverse inputs and a global perspective, which is considered as extremely important. For that purpose, project-specific Internet platforms are set up to enable people from different parts of the world to participate and to share thoughts, findings, relevant materials, etc. In addition, the Internet is seen as an endless source of information that offers new opportunities to collect valuable information. Using a combination of online and offline methodologies is therefore seen as the most promising approach to get valuable consumer insights.

Furthermore, user studies are conducted on-site at the User Experience Design Center where consumers are interviewed and observed when using devices. Technological limitations such as the quality to record conversations in crisp and real-life resolution make it necessary to meet the participants physically and capture small nuances in their answers and expressions that are hard to capture on film. In particular, this is the case when participants cannot express themselves verbally well enough. As a senior user experience designer at Sony Ericsson puts it: "You must almost be in the room to understand what they actually are thinking, because they are not saying anything. And this is where IT fails. It's too cumbersome to set up, it's too cumbersome to consume the information if you are not there".

Moreover, the use of such online channels has also brought with it some challenges, as expressed by an informant: "how to filter out the dust...and find the nice jewels in there?" The company also experienced problems of patents and confidentiality. If users disclose too much information, the origin of an already existent internal idea might become questionable, or it could hinder Sony Ericsson from making a patent out of an idea that got discussed in a public forum.

14.4.1.2 Design, Testing and Refinement

Collaboration with partners takes place in different ways during the development of new products and services. An important channel is Developer World, an online portal where Sony Ericsson engages with consumers to discuss and share thoughts, for instance in the Developer Blog. Moreover, the portal serves as a place to provide users with tools and support that enable them to customise and extend Sony Ericsson's products. Giving users this freedom and opportunity is seen as necessary. Says a member of the strategy team: "I mean they know what they want from the device and we can sit and think about it as much as we want to, but in the end, sometimes we got to just open up a foundation". An application called Themes Creator allows end-users to modify the look and feel of a phone, to better match their custom needs. A more advanced tool provided on Developer World is the Timescape Extension Development Kit (EDK), which enables business-oriented customers to create extensions for Sony Ericsson's signature application, Timescape. Another platform that enables users and customers to engage with Sony Ericsson during the development of software features and applications is the open source mobile operation system Android that is used in Sony Ericsson's latest phones. Providing the users with such tools gives them (users) the feeling of being involved, which also brings them closer to the brand of Sony Ericsson.

In addition, opening up the development process is a fruitful approach, as it allows the company to collaborate and develop products at a higher speed. Sony Ericsson lacks the resources to do everything by itself, and the company also believes that a bigger development community leads to better products and services. However, losing control is a major challenge related to the open development process. User-developed applications might not work well with Sony Ericsson's devices or some external App developers might have bad intentions. Such issues could negatively affect how people perceive the brand of Sony Ericsson.

Users are also involved in other tasks during the development process. For instance, people are invited to test concepts and prototypes in user labs. They are observed while performing tasks with prototypes or asked about their opinions. Besides developing physical prototypes, Sony Ericsson also creates prototypes for computer displays. This allows users to test simulated prototypes on devices such as touch screens or tablet computers. Such simulations enable Sony Ericsson to evaluate the user interface of future products at an early stage, long before the physical device is available. In addition to usability tests with end-users, Sony Ericsson has a customer acceptance system in place to test final prototypes before the release. Factory-produced prototypes of hand-held devices are provided to customers such as telecommunication operators to run a wide range of technical validation tests in their local environments. A database system supports the partners to report problems that need to be addressed before releasing the finalised products to the market.

However, making use of the Internet to share such prototypes is not an option for Sony Ericsson as such prototypes are considered as secret, as a SENIOR USER EXPERIENCE DESIGNER points out: "We cannot build a phone together with our users on the Internet. Because then we know that all the competitors will use the same information". Besides the problem of confidentiality, the potential lack of internal maturity is another reason that hinders the company from engaging in simulated online environments such as Second Life to get feedback on prototypes.

14.4.1.3 Commercialisation

Sony Ericsson does not announce future visions and information about upcoming products on the Internet. Releasing such information would enable competitors to adjust their strategy to better compete with Sony Ericsson. "We don't do that because we want to keep it secret until the very end, if we manage" (Senior User Experience Designer). On the other hand, so-called application programming interfaces (APIs) are made available on Developer World prior to the launch of certain products, to allow the community to start early in developing for upcoming products.

When a new product is on the market a range of digital channels are used to engage with users and customers. Twitter, YouTube and the Sony Ericsson Product Blog are ways to distribute information such as recently released products, coming updates and other useful information. Having a Facebook site is, moreover, seen as necessary to reach out to the younger generation of Sony Ericsson's target group. In addition to showcase new products, Facebook also serves as a channel to get valuable input and feedback from users. Developer World is also doing a good job after the release of products, as it serves both as a channel to support the developer community as well as to learn from it. Using a big variety of Web 2.0 technologies enables Sony Ericsson to get all kinds of information. Both online and offline communication channels are important to engage with consumers. Technology is suitable for dealing with the 'easy stuff', but face-to-face interactions are seen as more suitable to interact with users for more complex discussions. Furthermore, different generations and different kinds of users desire different types of communication channels.

14.4.2 Volvo IT

Volvo Group is a global company with approximately 90,000 employees worldwide. Volvo IT, a subsidiary of Volvo Group, employs around 5,000 employees to support its customers with various IT solutions. The main customers are other parts of the Volvo Group, but Volvo IT also develops IT services for a number of selected external customers. Service global development process (S-GDP) is a novel Volvo Group standard process for developing service projects that is going to be adopted within Volvo IT in the near future.

14.4.2.1 Idea Generation and Development

Workshops are a common way for Volvo IT to generate interesting ideas for new services, where TechWatch & Business Innovation and different parts of Volvo IT meet customers from specific functional areas to conduct brainstorming sessions. Quite often, the workshops take place virtually. Microsoft Live Meeting, a web meeting technology that is used in such cases, is seen as a great way of connecting people from different parts of the world. Virtual workshops reduce the time and cost of travelling and have a positive impact on the environment. However, it was also emphasised by the informants that online meetings cannot replace face-to-face meetings entirely: "When you have a creative workshop or creative meeting, it is difficult to reach the same level of interaction via IT tools". The major channel of tapping new ideas is through face-to-face workshops together with the customers.

The initial phase of the Volvo Group S-GDP standard is concerned with capturing customers' explicit as well as implicit needs. Interviews are seen as an important way of getting customers' ideas and of identifying their problems and challenges. Face-to-face interaction is the favoured way of performing the interviews to get input from selected participants, as an informant points out the limitations of IT-based communication: "I mean you are not only interested in what the customer says, you are interested in how they react on different questions. And you are interested in observing how they act. And you can't capture all these elements through IT tools". In some cases, surveys are used to complement and cross-check the interviews, where IT is seen as a feasible method to reach many people in different geographical regions. In service development projects, gathering customer insights and ideas through online forums or social media is not seen as a suitable approach. Firstly, because of the uncertain amount of time it takes to collect input, and secondly, because of the difficulties in engaging with the right target group to ensure the validity of input.

About a year ago, TechWatch & Business Innovation initiated an online platform that serves as a place for customers to submit and build upon one another's ideas on selected topics within a certain period of time, so-called Innovation Jams. So far, it is a minor but growing channel for capturing customers' ideas. Innovation Jams enable Volvo IT to reach out to the global community within the Volvo Group and to get novel perspectives from people with diverse backgrounds and across different functions. Besides the generation of new innovative ideas, Volvo IT also expects to get a better understanding of local markets as people participate from different regions. However, attracting participants is seen a challenge for the Innovation Jam concept, as people need to find time outside their usual work duties to participate. Hansson at Volvo IT emphasises that such an online tool needs to be engaging. Giving the users the opportunity to vote is seen as an incentive, as it involves the participants in the selection process of the ideas. From a Volvo IT perspective, this also makes the idea selection process simpler, cost- and time-efficient. Another aspect which might prevent people from participating in Innovation Jams is the familiarity with online media, where, as Hansson points out, the maturity required of people to interact online via blogs and social media may be seen as a hindering factor. Moreover, he emphasises that "not everyone dares to input their ideas and make that visible throughout the entire organisation". To lower this barrier, building trust is seen as important so that people open up and actively share their thoughts to the community in online idea portals such as Innovation Jams.

14.4.2.2 Design, Testing and Refinement

Innovative ideas to better support customer's business processes through novel IT solutions are usually vague. To test the feasibility of new technologies in a real context, the TechWatch & Business Innovation team initiates prototypes together with customers. An online SharePoint platform called TeamPlace is used to share relevant project data during the prototyping phase. Testing prototypes or so-called IT demonstrators together with end-users in as real a context as possible is seen as crucial, as Hansson points out: "The most important part is to be out there, in the workshops, testing this together with the mechanics, together with the end-user and just seeing the reactions from their perspectives". TechWatch & Business Innovation previously evaluated the applicability of Second Life for use within the Volvo Group, but as Hansson states: "We saw that it [Second Life] was too cumbersome for us at that time and it could not really measure up to the existing solutions that we had in place".

Visualisations of services are seen as important during service developments, because of the intangible and abstract nature of service. An informant asserts that simple drawings or animations do a great job of illustrating how a service is delivered, but he raises concerns regarding the time- and cost-effectiveness of building more advanced 3D visualisations. Exposing a visualised concept to the public, for instance in Second Life, is not suitable for the Volvo Group. The problem is how to capture the desired inputs from the right target group without jeopardising confidentiality: "The projects you are working with involve company secrets. So you don't want to expose too much of it to your competitors before you launch the product. So that's another reason why you don't want to make it public on the Internet".

When a prototype turns out to be feasible and customers desire such a new service, Volvo IT initiates a service development project. Ongoing interactions with the customer take place through a steering committee that involves project managers from both the customer side and Volvo IT's side. TeamPlace serves as an online platform to share data and project information. According to another informant, meetings in steering committees constitute the primary channel for exchanging information and gaining customer feedback during the development of services. Consistent with this view, another informant says that formal meetings are the preferred way to get comments and feedback from customers, as it enables the company to get the attention and commitment of involved people for a specific period of time, which would not be the case in interaction over online media. Because Volvo Group is a global company its meetings often take place in the form of video and telephone conferences. Face-to-face interaction is required for longer meetings or during creative workshops.

Providing customers with tools to develop certain parts of the service differs from project to project. When a customer explicitly asks for it, they can be given the opportunity to customise the service via an interface, in order to fine-tune and integrate it well with existing processes. X recognises the potential of such an approach: "Do-it-yourself is usually good. When you do it you get what you would like to have". Based on this view, the complex technical and functional skills required to develop a service in his area of expertise make this approach unsuitable. S-GDP considers different methods to collaborate with customers during the development phase of a service. However, this is not driven by IT tools, but takes place in workshops where customers are taught different, creative methods. One such method aims to involve customers by giving them a set of questions tailored to the scope of a specific project, as Y explains: "Basically you ask the customer to fill in a diary on how they experience a certain service and what kind of improvements or changes they would like to propose. And in that case, they create parts of the service themselves". Of crucial significance are cost-efficiency, the required maturity level from end-users and consideration of customers' needs when choosing a method for interaction. Even though Z mentions that interactive web forums, social media or mobile phone applications might be suitable to get feedback from customers such as truck drivers, a paper-based diary is seen as a cheap and effective way to reach the customers.

14.4.2.3 Commercialisation

Before the final release of a service, pilots are launched to a number of users during a trial period. To gather feedback and comments for final service adjustments, TeamPlace serves as a platform where blogs are set up and surveys published. X emphasises the efficiency of using a blog in this phase of the project, given that project members are dedicated and available to engage in spontaneous discussions with pilot end-users. TeamPlace enables the project team to quickly and easily spread information. In addition, information on upcoming services gets published on Violin, a Volvo Group Intranet portal. Using such a portal makes it easy for Volvo IT to announce a service and broadcast information within the Volvo Group to potential customers. For instance, easy to understand videos or so-called webcasts are published to demonstrate how a service works in the real world.

After the launch of a service, user manuals, guides and FAQs are made available on a Support Forum. Y as well as X emphasise the point that customers and users cannot provide feedback via this forum. Volvo IT is currently not organised to handle such a channel, but the potential of getting truly natural end-user and customer feedback is recognised. X mentions that maintaining a forum or social media as a feedback channel would require people and manpower to moderate and keep it alive. X adds that the challenge of not being overwhelmed with a lot of irrelevant questions and feedback that need to be filtered. Van Parys, moreover, highlights that the types from users and customers need to be considered for the use of interactive web applications. In a project he was previously involved in, users of the service were blue-collar workers who did not have daily access to IT communication systems: "They do not have an email address because they are the workforce in the warehouse. So this is an obstacle". So far, Volvo IT has not given priority to an interactive online forum in the post-release phase of a service to engage in discussions with customers and users.

End-user feedback is collected in other ways than interactive web forums. For instance, online surveys are conducted on a quarterly basis. End-user surveys enable Volvo IT to gather feedback from a large number of people spread among different countries. A back-end IT system supports the analysis of the results. Furthermore, users can call a service desk or contact local representatives of Volvo IT via email.

Customer feedback and requests on services are normally received in customer work groups that are regular meetings where service roadmaps and issues regarding current services are discussed. J mentions that "important meetings are always face-to-face, especially when you meet customers". C supports this perspective, highlighting the importance of meeting customer representatives in person, "to really keep the contact and to have a face to put on a voice. Because if you just have voice or virtual meeting conferences, it's not so efficient and it's harder to get the trust and the good connection".

14.4.3   3 M Svenska AB

In 2004, the multinational conglomerate 3 M took over Hörnell, a former Swedish producer of welding shields. Since then, 3 M's excellence centre for welding has been operating in Gagnef, Sweden, where the welding shields of the Speedglas product lines are produced. LF is the leading manager of the R&D department. Senior Specialist MW is working in the global Technical Service organisation and also is the chairman of the Voice of Customer (VoC) group that stays in close contact with welders from all around the world.

14.4.3.1 Idea Generation and Development

The VoC group engages with welders from different parts of the world to understand their needs. The primary method to get the voice of customers for new product innovations is through personal interviews. VoC group members personally meet welders at their workplaces in different parts of the world. A personal dialogue is the preferred way to interact with welders. Face-to-face interaction enables interviewers to get a clear understanding of their needs, as body language is involved and because the opportunity to ensure the quality of the interview exists. The appropriateness of using IT to perform such qualitative interviews is rather limited, as MW points out: "Because there's so much between the lines that you cannot pick up when you do it [the interview] over web-based media". Video conferences are not seen as a suitable way of interacting with end-users, as conference rooms or computers are usually not available at welders' workplaces and a set up would be quite complicated.

VoC group enables the company to engage through face-to-face meetings with welders, instead of utilising web-based media. Firstly, in certain regions, an average welder is over 50 years old. Even though LF acknowledges that many older people are familiar with computers nowadays, he believes that most welders are not that versed in the use of computers. Furthermore, 3 M also serves markets in less developed countries, where access to computers is rather limited. Hence, the use of IT is not the first choice of interacting with welders, as LF states: "It is not so easy to reach the end-users. And in my opinion, it is a generation issue". MW believes that company-owned welding equipment, which is quite common in Europe, makes welders less interested in engaging in discussions and talk about welding shields in their free time. In addition, he points out that a low social status of welders in certain countries might as well impact on their willingness to share insights in public. Therefore, personal interactions to engage with welders at their workplaces are seen as necessary to get their feedback. However, MW emphasises that the situation is quite different in the USA: "A big difference between Europe and the US is that in the US, they [the welders] sometimes need to buy their own equipment and they are more dedicated to tell other people about how it is working. And also, they are willing to discuss product-related issues in their spare time, because they own the product personally".

This unique situation in the USA, where welders are proud of their work and interested in sharing feedback about their Speedglas welding shields, enables 3 M to successfully run a Facebook site. Facebook is seen as a valuable tool to engage with welders to quickly and easily collect their needs and feedback for future innovations. LF and MW mention potential issues related to intellectual property rights, as welders can easily share information on channels such as Facebook. 3 M is interested in getting insights into customers' needs. However, problems arise when welders disclose detailed information about ideas for solutions instead, as such information cannot be used by 3 M without a previously signed disclosure agreement. MW emphasises that this could even "destroy our ideas. I mean we

14 Open Strengths and Weaknesses of IT User Innovation: Evidence from Three Cases 229

might have that idea already, but we haven't been using it. And that could stop us from using that idea when listening to that welder, because then he could claim that we have stolen it from him".

14.4.3.2 Design, Testing and Refinement

Insights into customer needs gained from personal interviews are translated into new products through an iterative process. VoC group members visit welders at their local workplaces several times during the construction phase in field trials, where welders evaluate the latest prototypes. Field trials enable the VoC group to receive direct feedback and opinions from end-users. Because welders can expect that a certified and approved welding shield is protecting them appropriately, focus is put on comfort. MW points out that welders are mostly interested in issues like: "How big, how heavy is it? Can I breathe, can I talk when having that on? Can I fold it up easily?" Welders want to touch, feel and try on the product. Giving them the chance to experience real prototypes is therefore seen as crucial for getting the best and most accurate feedback. On the other hand, drawings or visualisations of prototypes are seen as a limited approach to gain welders' insights during the construction phase.

Because visualisations of prototypes are seen as inappropriate for gaining feedback, 3 M does not make use of the Internet to share simulations with end-users during the construction phase. Likewise, 3 M does not disclose such information online for two other reasons. Issues related to intellectual property hinder the company from doing that, as MW mentions: "Many of the things we are doing cannot be shared without a disclosure agreement. You don't know today if something is going towards something that could be patented in the future". Furthermore, prototypes are kept secret because they are treated as confidential. Disclosing them to the public is not desired, as 3 M tries to stay ahead of competition. "You cannot have it on the web because you never know who will get that information. The risk is that it may fall in the wrong hands" (MW).

3 M Speedglas welding shields are equipped with auto-darkening welding filters that protect the eyes and skin from radiation. A company internal tool enables the adjustment of certain filter parameters to make the product appropriate for different welding situations. This tool is employed during the development process in close collaboration with welders, to come up with an appropriate range of filter settings for the final products. 3 M does not provide users with such a tool to make custom adjustments by themselves because legal restrictions prevent the company from doing so. Protecting equipments such as welding shields need to be certified and approved if they are to be used.

When purchasing a 3 M Speedglas welding shield, customers have the opportunity to select a graphical design from a range of predefined graphics. The predefined graphical design options take the form of a web-based survey. End-users could vote for their favourite graphical design via an online platform. Conducting an online survey was seen as an easy and cost-efficient way to check the opinion of many people. Enabling customers to create their own graphical design for welding shields was being considered as a future possibility.

14.4.3.3 Commercialisation

When a product is released, the Internet is used to publish product information and training material, for instance on the company website or on Facebook. Using the web to provide users with film clips, for example on YouTube or 3 M's website, is seen as an easy and good way to explain how products work. However, MF points out that online media is not the usual way to distribute such information, as printed manuals and user instructions are still demanded for every product.

A common way for welders to report issues or to provide feedback on products is by contacting their local dealers. Dealers, on the other hand, contact regional 3 M staff members who enter problems and feedback into a Customer Feedback Resolution (CFR) system. CFR serves as a kind of database where all product-related issues and problems are collected. MW acknowledges that it is hard to get an "'undestroyed' voice of customers" through the CFR system, because welders do not fill out the reports by themselves. Direct feedback from welders is received through other channels. For instance, the VoC group conducts surveys where welders are asked clear and specific questions about 3 M's products. Using online questionnaires is seen as an efficient way to get users' feedback. However, the questionnaires are made available both online and in paper form because of the varying access to computers in different regions.

In addition, Facebook serves as a valuable source of feedback from welders. MW states that: "if you look into the US Facebook group, you can find a lot of interesting feedback and needs, positive and negative things. And I spend time reading those reports, and you can learn a lot from doing that". Even though Facebook is global, more than 80 % of 3 M's Speedglas Facebook group members come from the USA, where English as a language of the website is seen as a barrier for welders in non-English speaking countries when taking part in the discussions. "I think if you talk to Swedish welders, not many of them are willing to write a sentence in English, explaining what they think about the product. To have them really confident, you should have it [Facebook] in Swedish". In addition, having resources available to support such an online feedback channel is seen as crucial. In the USA, some employees are dedicated to take care of the Facebook page. So far, however, setting up and taking care of similar web forums have not been prioritised and pushed outside the USA.

14.5 Discussions and Concluding Remarks

Although advances in IT have made it somewhat easy to codify tacit information (Yakhlef 2005), the technology still suffers from significant limitations. The use of face-to-face interactions remains the favoured way to capture and transfer rich and tacit information from users and customers (Di Gangi and Wasko 2009; Lettl 2007; Yakhlef 2005). The case of 3 M provides instances that support this line of argumentation. After the release of a new product, 3 M uses IT in the form of online questionnaires to get customer feedback about specific issues. However, 3 M's VoC group prefers to make use of face-to-face interviews in the earlier phases of the innovation process because of high levels of uncertainties, which require unstructured dialogues rather than interactions based on specific questions and answers. To emphasise the necessity of face-to-face interactions, Wiederkehr pointed out the limitations of IT to capture information 'between the lines' that are seen as important to gain a clear understanding of the customers' needs. Such limitations were furthermore corroborated in the case of Sony Ericsson. Observations and face-to-face dialogues are the preferred methods to engage with users and customers in consumer insight studies and tests in user labs, in order to gather information and relevant details that IT is not able to capture and transfer. The ability to use all senses and body language seems to be a crucial aspect of face-to-face interaction in order to get a better understanding of users and customers. A global insight analyst at Sony Ericsson, moreover, emphasised that human interactions are favoured for complex discussions, whereas IT is suitable for more straightforward interactions. In addition, the case of Volvo IT revealed aspects which further strengthen the perspective that face-to-face interactions are required for the transfer of rich and tacit information. Hansson and Johansson highlighted that ICT cannot replace face-to-face interactions when a high level of creativity is required and Larsson moreover emphasised that virtual interactions are not suitable to replace face-to-face interviews with customers as ICT cannot capture relevant aspects besides the pure verbal conversation. In addition, Hansson emphasised the need to evaluate prototypes in a real context in order to capture end-users' reactions. Thus, it emerges from all three cases that face-to-face interactions are favoured over the use of IT to collaborate with users and customers during the innovation process when rich and tacit information needs to be transferred.

As pointed out by Hoyer et al. (2010), concerns about the ownership of intellectual property rights could hinder a company from collaborating extensively with user and customers during the innovation process. They emphasised that "[a] lack of consistency in intellectual property policies might create perceptions of unfairness among consumer contributors. They may also create legal entanglements" (Hoyer et al. 2010, p. 289). Accordingly, the case of Sony Ericsson revealed potential issues with intellectual property rights from the use of Web 2.0 application during the ideation phase. A strategy analyst at Sony Ericsson pointed out problems when users and customers reveal confidential information in public online forums: "If they disclose too much and they see this in our product at a later stage, we perhaps would have worked on it long before, but just because they displayed us the information they could claim that well you got this idea from me, it's my idea, and that's a problem even though we didn't really listen". Problems with intellectual property rights got moreover highlighted in the case of 3 M. Both Fredriksson and Wiederkehr delineated issues resulting from detailed solutions suggested by users and customers in Web 2.0 applications without a disclosure agreement, as future claims could be made when such information is used by 3 M in new innovations. Therefore, potential issues with intellectual property rights seem to be a hindering

Table 14.2 The use of user innovation tools

Innovation Process Stage	User Innovation Tools	Sony Ericsson	Volvo IT	3 M
Idea Generation and Development	ICT	Innovation Portal, Facebook, Product Blog, Virtual Interaction Platforms	Virtual Workshops, Online Surveys	Online Surveys, Facebook
	OIC		Innovation Jams	
	VC	SE-dot		
Design, Testing and Refinement	ICT	Developer World, Developer Blog	TeamPlace	Online Survey
	Toolkits	Android Platform, Themes Creator, Timescape EDK	Customisation of services	
	IvT	Virtual Prototypes		
Commercialisation	ICT	Developer World, Facebook, Product Blog, Twitter, YouTube	Blogs, Online Surveys	Facebook

factor for the extensive use of ICT to capture users and customers' ideas, which strengthens Hoyer et al.'s (2010) proposition.

Sony Ericsson employs both traditional channels such as call centres and online channels to engage with customers and users, as "different generations, different kind of users have different kinds of needs and are familiar and comfortable with different kinds of channels" (global insight analyst). Accordingly, it seems to emerge from the case of Volvo IT that ICT is not appropriate to interact with all types of customers and users. Van Parys highlighted the restricted access to IT for some customers and end-users such as blue collar workers in warehouses. This aspect seems to prevent Volvo IT from prioritising the use of ICT to gather feedback from users and customers after the release of a new innovation. Hence, it seems to emerge that both traditional as well as IT-based channels are required to engage with various types of customers and users. The case of 3 M moreover corroborates this line of argumentation. Low technological developments of certain countries and the lack of computers at a typical welder's workplace prevent customers and end-users to engage in IT-based initiatives. In addition, a majority of welders are not expected to be versed in the use of IT, which furthermore seems to hinder 3 M from making extensive use of IT to collaborate with them. Thus, different needs and preferences, restricted access to computers and a low technical maturity of certain types of users and customers may constitute barriers for the use IT in the user innovation process.

To sum up, Table 14.2 illustrates how the three cases differ in the extent to which IT is used during the user innovation process. In addition, Table 14.3 provides an overview of the vices and virtues of IT to innovate with users and customers. Certain aspects are shared among multiple cases regardless of the diverse use of

Table 14.3 Advantages and disadvantages of user innovation tools

Innovation Process Stage	User Innovation Tools			Sony Ericsson	Volvo IT	3 M
Idea Generation and Development	ICT	Advantages	ease of communication	X	X	X
				X	X	
			broad reach			
		Disadvantages	information overload	X		
			problems to identify promising ideas	X		
	OIC & VC	Advantages	generation of innovative ideas	X	X	
		Disadvantages	technical barriers		X	
			importance of		X	
			incentives		X	
			transparency			
Design, Testing and Refinement	ICT	Advantages	effective data exchange	X	X	X
	Toolkits	Advantages	outsourcing of tasks	X	X	
			no transfer of sticky	X		
			information	X		
			addressing heterogeneous user needs higher quality and speed	X		
		Disadvantages	unsuitable for certain	X	X	X
			user types			X
			legal requirements			
			lack of control			
	IvT	Advantages	overcoming	X		
			uncertainties	X		
			efficient evaluation			
		Disadvantages	unsuitable for certain	X	X	X
			product types			X
			concerns about			
			secrecy			
Commercialisation	ICT	Advantages	learning from feedback	X	X	X
		Disadvantages	concerns about	X	X	X
			secrecy		X	
			required resources			
Overall Limitations		Disadvantages	transfer of rich and	X	X	X
			tacit information	X	X	X
			crucial conversations	X	X	X
			issues with			X
			intellectual			
			property rights X			
			cultural aspects			
			unsuitable for certain			
			user types			

IT, whereas others seem to be case specific. On the one hand, the present piece of research exemplifies that ICT facilitates the ease of communicating ideas, an effective exchange of data during the design, testing and refinement of products as well learning from customers and users' feedback in the commercialisation phase. On the other hand, all three cases revealed that the use of IvT for sharing virtual prototypes on the Internet is hindered by concerns about secrecy and that face-to-face interactions are required because of limitations of IT to transfer tacit information. Furthermore, it seems to emerge from the case study that wrong incentives and a high transparency could hinder people from participating in OIC, that the use of toolkits may increase the development speed and lead to better solutions, but that a lack of control over the development efforts of users and customers as well as legal requirements might hinder its use. In addition, it becomes apparent from the study that the amount of resources required to maintain Web 2.0 applications could hinder its use after the release of an innovation and that IT is not suitable to engage with all types of customers during the user innovation process.

The aim of this is to explore the significance of IT in the different phases of the user innovation process. The theoretical framework introduced in Table 14.1 presented relevant theoretical concepts and propositions that suggested both pros and cons for the use of IT to engage with customers and users for the development of new products and services. The framework turned out to be highly valuable to fulfil the aim of the study, as it facilitated the analysis of the extent to what IT is used in the different phases of the user innovation process and reasons for and against the use of IT in this process. On the one hand, the empirical material confirmed and strengthened the theoretical assumptions. The study exemplified that ICT facilitates the ease of communicating ideas, an effective exchange of data during the design, testing and refinement of products as well as learning from customers and users' feedback in the commercialisation phase. Moreover, all three cases revealed that the use of IvT for sharing virtual prototypes on the Internet is hindered by concerns about secrecy and that face-to-face interactions are required to handle the limitations of IT to transfer tacit information. On the other hand, however, the exploratory nature of the present piece of research revealed that theory only explains reasons for and against the use of IT at different stages of the user innovation process to some extent. Pros and cons that go beyond the theoretical propositions emerged from the three cases, which contribute to the development of theory.

The case of Volvo IT indicated that the wrong incentives and a high transparency could hinder people from participating in OICs. Even though anonymity might be suitable to address the latter challenge, hiding people's identity might not be desirable for company internal OICs.

Moreover, Sony Ericsson revealed that the use of toolkits may increase the development speed and lead to better solutions, but that a lack of control over the development efforts of users and customers could possibly harm an organisation. One could argue that the more freedom and empowerment is given to users and customers by the use of toolkits, the more benefits a company can reap from the shared development efforts but the higher the risk that problems emerge due to an increased lack of control. In addition, it became apparent from the case of 3 M that legal requirements can prevent a company from using toolkits, as in the case of protective equipment which needs to be certified and approved. Another emerging aspect which might constitute a barrier for the use of Web 2.0 applications to engage with users and customers after the release of a new innovation was the amount of resources required to maintain such interactive online communication channels. At Volvo IT as well as in non-US regions at 3 M, priority has not been given to use ICT for interacting with users and customers in the post-launch phase of an innovation. Hence, one could put into question the cost-efficiency of such initiatives or it could be argued that company internal capabilities required to leverage Web 2.0 applications for that purpose are missing. Finally, it emerged from all three cases that IT is not suitable to deal with all types of customers and users throughout the innovation process. One could conclude that utilising both traditional and IT-based communication channels is of special importance for organisations that target a wide range of customers and users in various parts of the world who vary in their preferences, technical maturities and access to IT.

> **Practical Tip**
>
> The main lesson to take home from the chapter is that managers should not believe that IT tools can be a substitute for face-to-face interaction in the innovation process. For instance, the use of IvT for sharing virtual prototypes on the Internet may be impaired by concerns about secrecy, therefore face-to-face interactions are required in order to make up for the deficiency of technology to transfer tacit information and to facilitate the development of trust among the parties. At Volvo IT, for instance, the use of IT, such as online video conferences, is considered inappropriate for important meetings where trust is important for people to share valuable information for new innovations.

14.6 Implications and Further Research

The study concluded that IT is not suitable to interact with all types of customers and users. However, one aspect highlighted both at Sony Ericsson and 3 M has not been given much attention to, due to the limited scope of the present study. It was indicated that different generations of people might desire different interaction channels. Whereas Web 2.0 applications are seen as appropriate to reach out to younger generations, informants highlighted that this is likely not the case for older generations. Hence, a call for additional research is made that focuses on the suitability of IT to integrate different generations of people in the innovation process.

At Volvo IT, the use of IT such as online video conferences is considered as inappropriate for important meetings where trust is important for people to share valuable information for new innovations. Further research should investigate to what extent emerging technologies are able to substitute face-to-face interactions when trustful relationships are crucial.

In addition, the case of 3 M indicated that a low social status of users' professions could hinder them from sharing insights about products in public. Moreover, informants suspected that users who privately own products have a higher interest in sharing comments and providing feedback about products compared to users who make use of but do not personally own the products. Further studies are desired to investigate these two issues, which could provide valuable insights about users' motivations and interests to actively participate in the innovation process.

One of the limitations of this study lies in its exploratory nature. Even though a multiple-case study approach was chosen and the theoretical framework turned out to be useful for the analysis of the cases, it could be argued that the representativeness of the present study consisting of three cases is rather limited and that further research is required to confirm the findings and usability of the framework in different fields and domains.

References

Awazu, Y., Baloh, P., Desouza, K. C., Wecht, C. H., Kim, J., & Jha, S. (2009). Information–communication technologies open up innovation. *Research Technology Management, 52*(1), 51–58.

Chesbrough, H. W. (2003). *Open innovation: The new imperative for creating and profiting from technology*. Boston, MA: Harvard Business School Press.

Chesbrough, H. W. (2011a). *Open services innovation: Rethinking your business to grow and compete in a new era*. San Francisco, CA: Jossey-Bass.

Darke, P., Shanks, G., & Broadbent, M. (1998). Successfully completing case study research: combining rigour, relevance and pragmatism. *Information Systems Journal, 8*(4), 273–289.

De Moor, K., Berte, K., De Marez, L., Joseph, W., Deryckere, T., & Martens, L. (2010). User-driven innovation? Challenges of user involvement in future technology analysis. *Science & Public Policy (SPP), 37*(1), 51–61.

Desouza, K. C., Awazu, Y., Jha, S., Dombrowski, C., Papagari, S., Baloh, P., & Kim, J. Y. (2008). Customer-driven innovation. *Research Technology Management, 51*(3), 35–44.

Di Gangi, P. M., & Wasko, M. (2009). Steal my idea! Organizational adoption of user innovations from a user innovation community: A case study of dell ideastorm. *Decision Support Systems, 48*(1), 303–312.

Dodgson, M., Gann, D., & Salter, A. (2006). The role of technology in the shift towards open innovation: The case of Procter & Gamble. *R&D Management, 36*(3), 333–346.

Ebner, W., Leimeister, J. M., & Krcmar, H. (2009). Community engineering for innovations: The ideas competition as a method to nurture a virtual community for innovations. *R&D Management, 39*(4), 342–356.

Eisenhardt, K. M. (1989). Building theories from case study research. *Academy of Management Review, 14*(4), 532–550.

Eisenhardt, K. M., & Graebner, M. E. (2007). Theory building from cases: Opportunities and challenges. *Academy of Management Journal, 50*(1), 25–32.

Füller, J., Jawecki, G., & Muhlbacher, H. (2007). Innovation creation by online basketball communities. *Journal of Business Research, 60*(1), 60–71.

Füller, J., & Matzler, K. (2007). Virtual product experience and customer participation–a chance for customer-centred, really new products. *Technovation, 27*(6–7), 378–387.

Gassmann, O., Enkel, E., & Chesbrough, H. (2010). The future of open innovation. *R&D Management, 40*(3), 213–221.

Gordon, S., Tarafdar, M., Cook, R., Maksimoski, R., & Rogowitz, B. (2008). Improving the front end of innovation with information technology. *Research Technology Management, 51*(3), 50–58.

Hoyer, W. D., Chandy, R., Dorotic, M., Krafft, M., & Singh, S. S. (2010). Consumer cocreation in new product development. *Journal of Service Research, 13*(3), 283–296.

Kleemann, F., Voß, G. G., & Rieder, K. (2008). Un(der)paid innovators: The commercial utilization of consumer work through crowdsourcing. *Science, Technology & Innovation Studies, 4*(1), 5–26.

Kohler, T., Matzler, K., & Füller, J. (2009). Avatar-based innovation: Using virtual worlds for real-world innovation. *Technovation, 29*(6–7), 395–407.

Lazzarotti, V., & Manzini, R. (2009a). Different modes of open innovation: A theoretical framework and an empirical study. *International Journal of Innovation Management, 13*(4), 615–636.

Leimeister, J. M., Huber, M., Bretschneider, U., & Krcmar, H. (2009). Leveraging crowdsourcing: Activation-supporting components for it-based ideas competition. *Journal of Management Information Systems, 26*(1), 197–224.

Lettl, C. (2007a). User involvement competence for radical innovation. *Journal of Engineering and Technology Management, 24*(1–2), 53–75.

Piller, F. T., & Walcher, D. (2006a). Toolkits for idea competitions: a novel method to integrate users in new product development. *R&D Management, 36*(3), 307–318.

Rothwell, R. (1994). Towards the fifth-generation innovation process. *International Marketing Review, 11*(1), 7–31.

Schröder, A., & Hölzle, K. (2010). Virtual communities for innovation: Influence factors and impact on company innovation. *Creativity and Innovation Management, 19*(3), 257–268.

Silverman, D. (2010). *Doing qualitative research: a practical handbook* (3rd ed.). London: Sage.

von Hippel, E. (1986). Lead users: A source of novel product concepts. *Management Science, 32*(7), 791–805.

Yakhlef, A. (2005). Immobility of tacit knowledge and the displacement of the locus of innovation. *European Journal of Innovation Management, 8*(2), 227–239.

Yin, R. K. (2009). *Case study research: Design and methods* (4th ed.). London: Sage.

Further Reading

Chesbrough, H. W. (2011b). *Open services innovation: rethinking your business to grow and compete in a new era.* San Francisco, CA: Jossey-Bass.

Lazzarotti, V., & Manzini, R. (2009b). Different modes of open innovation: A theoretical framework and an empirical study. *International Journal of Innovation Management, 13*(4), 615–636.

Lettl, C. (2007b). User involvement competence for radical innovation. *Journal of Engineering and Technology Management, 24*(1–2), 53–75.

Lindič, J., Baloh, P., Ribière, V. M., & Desouza, K. C. (2011). Deploying information technologies for organizational innovation: Lessons from case studies. *International Journal of Information Management, 31*(2), 183–188.

Piller, F. T., & Walcher, D. (2006b). Toolkits for idea competitions: a novel method to integrate users in new product development. *R&D Management, 36*(3), 307–318.

von Hippel, E. (2001b). Perspective: User toolkits for innovation. *Journal of Product Innovation Management, 18*(4), 247–257.

Chapter 15
Open Service Innovation in Health Care: What Can We Learn from Open Innovation Communities?

Christina Keller, Mats Edenius, and Staffan Lindblad

Abstract The purpose of the chapter is to describe and discuss how principles from open innovation, which are primarily derived from commercial product development, could be applied to open service innovation in non-profit health care organisations. To evaluate the drivers, barriers and prerequisites of such innovation, we performed an explorative study consisting of interviews with two rheumatologists, engaged in a Swedish research project on open innovation in health care. According to the interviews, the main driver was considered to be "the empowered patient", holding a good knowledge of his or her disease. Barriers to open innovation were the lack of meeting places for patients, a strong local variation in how health care services are delivered and an organisational culture which does not promote learning and innovations. It is necessary for health care organisations to change their current culture of closed innovation, implying that only physicians have valid knowledge about patients' diseases. Other necessary prerequisites for implementing open innovation principles are support from management and structures of financial control which encourage innovations. This explorative study is, to the best of our knowledge, the first to combine principles of open innovation and health care services.

C. Keller (✉)
Högskolan i Jönköping, IHH, Informatik, Jönköping, Sweden
e-mail: kelc@jibs.hj.se

M. Edenius
Department of Informatics and Media, Uppsala University, Uppsala, Sweden
e-mail: mats.edenius@im.uu.se

S. Lindblad
Karolinska Institutet, Solna, Sweden
e-mail: staffan.lindblad@ki.se

J.S.Z. Eriksson Lundström et al. (eds.), *Managing Open Innovation Technologies*,
DOI 10.1007/978-3-642-31650-0_15, © Springer-Verlag Berlin Heidelberg 2013

15.1 Introduction

Currently, in open innovation communities, new or improved services are produced daily by their users. Similarly, we argue that health care needs to especially open its service innovation systems to users, i.e. the patients. The purpose of the chapter is to describe and discuss how principles from open innovation, which are primarily derived from commercial product development, could be applied to open service innovation in non-profit health care organisations.

Chesbrough's classic model of open innovation from 2003 focused primarily on product development in companies large enough to have their own department of research and development (R&D). Chesbrough concluded that the old model of closed innovation implied that successful innovation required strict control of development, manufacturing, marketing and distributions of innovations. In the new model of open innovation, firms should commercialise external (as well as internal) ideas by deploying outside (as well as in-house) pathways to market. The contrasting principles of closed and open innovation are presented in Table 15.1.

Furthermore, open source software development performed by Internet-based communities of software developers who voluntarily collaborate has become an important economic and cultural phenomenon (von Krogh 2003), even if open source software development with time has become more institutionalised (Ågerfalk and Fitzgerald 2008). The initial vision of the open source software development is also shared by the user innovation community, as exemplified by this quotation:

"I imagine product development without manufacturers. Today's user innovation communities are making that idea increasingly real." (von Hippel 2001, p. 82).

Is it possible to imagine health care service development without medical expertise? Probably not. Health care organisations are complex and knowledge intensive (Chu and Robey 2008). There are a number of areas where open innovation could be employed in a classical manner, for example, drug development and development of information systems and software. But there is also the core of health care; the interaction between the patient and the physician in order to cure, alleviate or comfort. In the next section of the chapter, we will review some of the initiatives of open innovation in the health care sector.

15.2 Open Innovation in Health Care

The use of open source software seems to be generally scarce in health care, although the US government 2007 supported efforts to promote the use of WorldVistA, a free and open source software (Vetter 2009). On the other hand, a gradual switch from closed innovation principles to open innovation is taking place in the business of drug discovery (Talaga 2009). During the 2000s, a new kind of organisation called public–private partnerships (PPPs) have combined open

15 Open Service Innovation in Health Care: What Can We Learn from Open... 241

Table 15.1 Contrasting principles of closed and open innovation (Chesbrough 2003)

Closed innovation principles	Open innovation principles
The smart people in the field work for us.	Not all the smart people work for us so we must find and tap into the knowledge and expertise of bright individuals outside our company.
To profit from R&D, we must discover, develop and ship it ourselves.	External R&D can create significant value; internal R&D is needed to claim some portion of the value.
If we discover it ourselves, we will get it to the market first.	We do not have to originate the research in order to profit from it.
If we are the first to commercialise an innovation, we will win.	Building a better business model is better than getting to market first.
If we create the most and best ideas in the industry, we will win.	If we make the best use of internal *and* external ideas, we will win.
We should control our intellectual property (IP) so that our competitors do not profit from our ideas.	We should profit from other's use of our IP, and we should buy others' IP whenever it advances our own business model.

sourced R&D with outsourced R&D. PPPs have been particularly successful in the discovery of new treatment for so-called neglected diseases, such as AIDS/HIV, tuberculosis, malaria, dengue fever and other tropical diseases (Munos 2006).

When it comes to the development of health care services, the formal interaction between patients and health care, open innovation principles, to the best of our knowledge, have not been used before. To be able to describe what a health service really is, we sought assistance from a patient-flow model, which is presented in Fig. 15.1.

The primary process of a health care service could be described as the patient's flow or pathway throughout the service system over time (Ovretveit 1992). The patient's pathway starts with a selection of service. The choice is dependent on what symptoms the patient has, the severity of the symptoms and the local health care policy on where or in which facility the patients should be treated, for example, primary care or at hospital clinics. The point of entry is when the patient contacts the service and makes a request. This is often done by a telephone call or by entering the physical site of the service. The first contact could be the same thing as the point of entry, but sometimes there is a time lag between them. The first contact with the service is critical:

"...this is the first time the client meets a person representing the service. For a client who has a set of expectations, and who is anxious and uncertain about how they will be treated, this member of staff represents the service. They provide the client with the first real evidence about what the service is like, and what might happen to them." (Ovretveit 1992, p. 55).

After the first contact, a staff member receives the patient and assesses the patient's needs. In this phase, the interaction between patient and staff is extremely important, as the patient must trust the staff and feel secure enough to speak freely about the needs, and the staff member should possess the necessary skills to handle the needs of the patient. Next, the health care organisation attempts to meet the

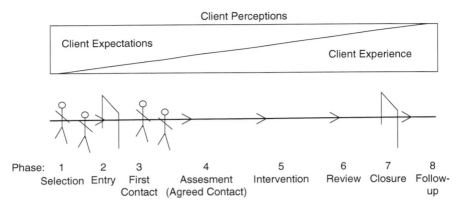

Fig. 15.1 A patient-flow model of a health care service (Ovretveit 1992)

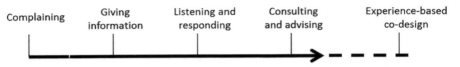

Fig. 15.2 Continuum of patient influence (Bate and Robert 2006)

needs of the patient by offering one or more treatment interventions, for example, medication, physiotherapy or psychotherapy. In the review phase, the patient's needs are reassessed and interventions re-planned to achieve the best effect possible. In the phase of closure, the patient leaves the service, either by recovering or by being transferred to another service (Ovretveit 1992). The final follow-up phase is not always fulfilled in health care services due to lack of resources, but ought to be a significant activity in health care service development and quality improvement work.

In health care services, there is an emerging movement of "empowering the patient", by e.g. web-based health portals and the development of patient communities. The empowered patient is supposed to take an active part in making informed choices in treatment and care (Hasselbladh and Bejerot 2007). Within the British National Health Services (NHS), the method of so-called experience-based design has been used in redesigning health care services to better fit patient needs. Evidence-based design focuses on patients' experiences of the health care service along the three dimensions of performance/functionality (how well the service does its job or fits it purpose), engineering/safety (how safe, well engineered and reliable it is) and aesthetics of experience/usability (how the whole interaction with the service "feels" or is experienced) (Bate and Robert 2006; Pickles and Hide 2008). In particular, it is important to explore the so-called "touch points" where patients meet staff members and subjective experiences are shaped (Bate and Robert 2007). On a continuum of patient influence, starting from the points of "complaining" and "giving information", experience-based design is a step towards engaging the patient as a co-designer of health care services (Bate and Robert 2006). The continuum of patient influence is presented in Fig. 15.2.

15 Open Service Innovation in Health Care: What Can We Learn from Open...

Table 15.2 Contrasting principles of closed and open service innovation in health care (adapted from Chesbrough 2003)

Closed service innovation principles in health care	Open service innovation principles in health care
The physician is the sole expert on the patient's disease.	The patient is an expert on his or her disease.
Only health care professionals have access to knowledge about the disease.	Patients have access to knowledge about the disease via, for example, Internet and patient communities.
Evidence-based knowledge from randomised controlled trials is the only valid knowledge in health care.	Patients' perceived experiences from health care services, treatment and lifestyle changes (patients' intellectual property) are valid knowledge and are complementary to evidence-based knowledge.
The patient is a passive consumer of health care.	The patient is a co-designer and an innovator of health care services.

In Chesbrough's (2003) terminology, health care organisations are so-called "innovation missionaries", not creating service innovations for profit, but to serve a cause. However, traditions and organisational culture in health care has appointed the physician as the expert on the patient's disease with full control of knowledge, treatment and services. In this sense, health care organisations clearly employ closed innovation principles. These principles have only recently been challenged by, for example, the patient empowerment movement (Hasselbladh and Bejerot 2007) and approaches like evidence-based design (Bate and Robert 2006, 2007, Pickles and Hide 2008). We argue that "classic" open innovation principles could also be applied to open service innovation in health care. In Table 15.2, the contrasting principles of closed and open service innovation principles in health care are presented. Table 15.2 is based on Table 1 in Chesbrough (2003), and the contents have been adapted to a health care context by the authors.

In the paradigm of open service innovation, every patient is an expert on his or her disease and should be perceived as such by physicians and professions in health care. Patients have access to knowledge about the disease from, for example, patient guides on the Internet or patient communities engaging in interaction via social media. Not only should evidence-based knowledge be valued in health care but also patients' "subjective" experiences from health care services, and effects from treatment and lifestyle changes. Accordingly, the patient should not be regarded as a passive consumer of health care, but as a co-designer and innovator.

15.3 Patient Innovation System

Since 2009, the research project "Patient Innovation System for Better Health by Evidence-Based Knowledge" at Karolinska Institutet, Sweden, aims at enabling open innovation systems in health care, particularly for patients with the chronic

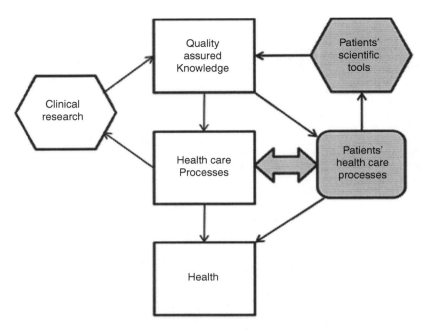

Fig. 15.3 The innovation system of the patient in interplay with health care

disease of rheumatoid arthritis. The leading idea of the project is that patients are able to introduce, spread and develop innovations for development of quality assured knowledge, while simultaneously improving their health. When patients are offered to use knowledge about their disease and support to manage their own health care process, an innovation system owned by patients is created in parallel and in collaboration with health care. The interplay between the patients' innovation system and health care is described in Fig. 15.3. The interplay between the patients' health care process and the process of the health care organisation is depicted by a thick two-way arrow to show that this is the most common interplay. But patients can also, by means of their own scientific tools, look for, find and use quality assured knowledge about their chronic disease. This knowledge is used in patients' own health care processes in their lifelong undertaking of managing a chronic disease, and it is hypothesised to have a positive impact on patients' health.

One of the objectives of the project is to design and evaluate a so-called "lifestyle website" on the Internet, where patients can get advice from other patients and physiotherapists on how to increase their physical activity. The website is designed in collaboration with rheumatoid arthritis patients, who meet with researchers in focus groups. Earlier examples of co-design in health care, for example, experience-based design, are based on the assumption that the health care organisation takes advice from its clients/patients in order to develop services and improve service quality. The lifestyle website adds another dimension to open innovation; social networks where patients support each other in taking part of knowledge about a chronic disease and develop ways of disease management.

But is it possible to employ open innovation principles in an organisation such as health care, which is known for its hierarchies, boundaries between research and medical practice and inertia to change? We performed an explorative study consisting of interviews with two rheumatologists, involved in the research project, on this matter. Their thoughts are presented in the next section of the chapter.

15.4 Rheumatologists' Thoughts on Open Innovation

We gave the two rheumatologists the opportunity to reflect on the principles of "classic" open innovation (see Table 15.1) and its translation to open service innovation principles in health care (see Table 15.2). In addition, they were asked to respond to five questions:

- Chesbrough's terminology of closed and open innovation includes the concepts of "Intellectual property" (IP) and "Research and development" (R&D). What would IP and R&D be in a healthcare context?
- What are the drivers of implementing open service innovation principles in healthcare?
- What are the barriers of implementing open service innovation principles in healthcare?
- Which are the necessary prerequisites of implementing open service innovation principles in healthcare?
- What would happen if you implemented open service innovation principles at your clinic today?

The interviewed rheumatologists were employed at two different clinics at Karolinska University Hospital, Stockholm, Sweden. One of the rheumatologists, with the pseudonym of Xerxes, was male, born in 1949, and had worked as a rheumatologist since 1987. The other rheumatologist, Ylva, was female, born in 1967, and had worked as a rheumatologist since 2003. As Xerxes and Ylva participate in the research project "Patient Innovation System for Better Health by Evidence-Based Knowledge", they hold a generally positive view of open innovation and patient empowerment. The findings from the interviews should be interpreted with this in mind.

15.4.1 IP and R&D in Health Care

The reflections of the rheumatologists on IP in health care revealed that it could be several things. It could be intellectual property rights of medical researchers of research articles and patent rights of medication and medical technology. It could also be source codes of computerised health care information systems owned by system suppliers. However, regarded as the most significant kind of IP in health care was medical specialist knowledge coupled with the ability to expediently translate it into what must be accomplished in health care:

"This is what generates revenues and cures patients—specialist knowledge and the ability to use it in medical practice." (Rheumatologist Ylva).

Hence, the translation of scientific findings and knowledge into medical practice is the most important intellectual property in health care.

R&D was primarily considered as research in service innovations and change work. Drug development and clinical research were not regarded as R&D in an open innovation context as the gap between research and medical practice is considerable:

"R&D is medical research, but not in these circumstances, because medical research is so extremely separated from health care practices. I think that quality improvement work in health care more represents what is called R&D in enterprises." (Rheumatologist Ylva).

It takes a long time to translate evidence-based knowledge from research into medical practice and improved patient health. Thus, the gap between medical research and medical practice is perceived to be very wide.

15.4.2 Drivers, Barriers and Necessary Prerequisites of Open Service Innovation in Health Care

Although considered as "innovation missionaries" in Chesbrough's terminology, health care organisations sometimes take on the same behaviour as organisations striving solely for financial profit:

"I think that the most powerful driver in health care innovation in general is the reduction of costs." (Rheumatologist Ylva).

However, the "empowered patient" was considered as the prime *driver* of open innovation by the two rheumatologists. These patients search for information about the disease on the Internet and share their experiences with other patients by means of social media. As a result, they have taken on some of the behaviours of members of open innovation communities. The problem is that health care organisations are not yet ready to use, or even value contributions from patients in innovation processes as health care is still perceived to be too closed and hierarchical.

Not surprisingly at this stage, the *barriers* to open innovation in health care were perceived to be more powerful by the rheumatologists than the drivers. Patients do not always have the strength and willingness to engage in open innovation. They may be tired or suffer pain because of their chronic disease. As a result, it is easy to surrender to the traditional passive patient role, rather than being an active and outgoing innovator. Patients are also in general isolated from each other, as there are few places where they can meet. Disease-specific patient associations are a quite powerful patient arena:

"But also patient associations need to work "around" health care rather than "together with" health care in initiatives of improving the living conditions of the chronically ill." (Rheumatologist Xerxes).

Another barrier is that care providers, clinics and even individual physicians might deliver the same health care service differently. Medical practice and work routines vary between hospitals and clinics, and the transparency of how services are actually delivered is low. In a health care system with strong local variation, innovations are particularly hard to implement, as every individual perceive the service differently. Care providers are also, according to the interviewees, in general, tired of innovations as the rate of organisational changes has been high in Swedish health care in recent years.

Characteristics of professions were also perceived to provide barriers. Physicians are supposed to have served their apprenticeship when the medical training is completed. Because of that, to learn new things is not regarded as something natural. However, physicians are forced to learn continuously in order to keep up with research discoveries. In spite of this, quality improvement work and changes in medical practice are often regarded as threats. There is no formal organisational learning structure in health care when it comes to improvement work. Every single physician is solely responsible for his or her knowledge development. There is also a perceived general inertia to change. Health care staff is used to following old work routines, and if they are changed it is regarded as being disruptive.

A number of *necessary prerequisites* for enabling open innovation in health care were pinpointed by the two rheumatologists. The organisational culture of health care must change into a culture of collaboration between patients and health care providers. The health care innovation system must be closely connected to the innovation system of the patient (see Fig. 15.3). Health care organisations must be prepared to handle patients' suggestions for improvement and to manage and spread innovations. An organisational culture is needed where mistakes are allowed and not punished, as occasional mistakes are necessary in order to improve. In this respect, it is extremely important to perform more research on implementations of clinical and organisational innovations in health care.

Support from management and structures of financial control which encourage the will of staff to continuously do things better and improve quality of health care services is also needed.

15.4.3 What Would Happen If Open Service Innovation Was Implemented at Your Clinic Today?

According to the interviewees, it would be hard to implement open service innovation in health care as the local variation in work routines is large. Quality registers, which are information systems where patient and treatment data of different diagnoses are stored, might be helpful in creating a process structure and common work routines:

"If care providers of the same speciality take on the same work routines, it would probably be easier to implement innovations in general, also open innovation initiatives." (Rheumatologist Xerxes).

If open innovation principles were implemented today most things in medical practice would change. Hospital and clinic premises would be adapted for interacting with patients, instead of being tailored for performing administrative tasks. Patients would be allowed to speak their mind freely and take up more space than today. Open innovation principles in health care service development would free the power and knowledge of patients. It would also free the power and knowledge of professions other than physicians:

"It is quite probable that the nurse of the rheumatology clinic has more knowledge about the patient, than the senior professor who perhaps hasn't met patients in years." (Rheumatologist Ylva).

Patients hold incredible amounts of specialist knowledge about their chronic disease and are able to discover and understand things that physicians do not notice or regard as important.

15.5 Practical Advice

The findings of this explorative study pinpointed some barriers and necessary prerequisites of open service innovation in health care. To overcome these barriers, we need to accomplish the following:

- The creation of places for patients to meet and exchange experiences. Online communities offer opportunities of interaction with fellow patients without feeling the pressure of social restraints.
- To enhance the implementation of innovations in general, but also open innovation, care providers need to standardise work routines on a national level in each medical specialty.
- The organisational culture of health care needs to allow and respect learning about improvement of health care services in the same way as knowledge of biomedical research is allowed and respected.
- Support from hospital and clinical management, as well as financial incentives is needed in promoting open innovation initiatives.

Health care organisations are, in Chesbrough's terminology, "innovation-missionaries", not driven by the creation of profit but by serving a cause. So are most open software communities. But there is one significant difference between health care and the open software community. The latter is an open culture which appreciates contributions to innovations from others; the former is a closed and hierarchical culture. What can health care learn from open innovation communities? According to von Hippel (2001), user communities of innovation are most likely to thrive when at least some users have sufficient initiative to innovate and voluntarily reveal their innovations, and when user-led innovation can compete with what is produced in the corresponding closed innovation system. Regarding the care of the chronically ill, many patients hold an immense knowledge about their own disease and their reactions to different kinds of treatment. If these patients perceive that their knowledge is valid and important and that physicians and other patients listen to them, there will probably be a strong incentive to innovate and voluntarily share innovations. However, patients' knowledge about the chronic disease might never be able to compete with or exceed the importance of evidence-based medical knowledge. On the other hand, patients' knowledge could be a valid complement to traditional medical knowledge. This way, the innovation system of health care and the patient's innovation system are more closely tied together.

Then, where in the patient flow of health services (see Fig. 15.1) could open innovation be most useful? Principally, in all phases from selection to follow-up, but we think that patients' innovations in the chronic care context might be most valuable in the intervention phase, where patients can bring knowledge to health care about effects of treatment and lifestyle changes in a larger extent than what is common today.

> **Practical Tip**
>
> To be able to understand chronically ill patients' experiences of health care services, it is important to identify the main areas, the so-called "touch points", where patients come into contact with the service. Touch points stand out as moments where patients have been emotionally or cognitively touched in some way and are events that patients repeatedly recall when telling their stories. In redesigning health care services, patient volunteers can be invited to interviews or conversations, with the aim of telling the narrative of their disease and experienced touch points. Then health care staff can be asked to describe their experienced emotions at each touch point. As a result, a joint map is created of "critical points" in the health care process, being particularly significant to focus on in redesigning the process. As a result, the joint map is the point of departure for the continuing redesign of the health care service.

15.6 Implications for Research

As open innovation in health care is a comparatively rare phenomenon, so is research on open innovation initiatives in health care. In the medical research tradition, different research approaches are ranked with the randomised controlled trial as the most scientifically rigorous study, with concealed allocation of the medical intervention and absolute control of the contextual factors. The least

Table 15.3 Typical structure of a hierarchy of evidence (Pawson 2006)

Level 1	Randomised controlled trials (with concealed allocation)
Level 2	Quasi-experimental studies (using matching)
Level 3	Before-and-after comparisons
Level 4	Cross-sectional, random sample studies
Level 5	Process evaluation, formative studies and action research
Level 6	Qualitative case study and ethnographic research
Level 7	Descriptive guides and examples of good practice
Level 8	Professional and expert opinion
Level 9	User profession

rigorous research approach is considered to be the opinion of users. Process evaluation, formative studies and action research, which are all appropriate research approaches for studies of innovation implementation, fall somewhere in between (Pawson 2006). This hierarchy of research is presented in Table 15.3.

The argument from health care professionals states that:

"After all. . . we should not embark on using a new clinical intervention such as a drug or a surgical procedure without solid experimental evidence of its effectiveness, so why should we have a lower threshold for the adoption of organisational interventions. . .?" (Walsh 2007, p. 57).

Hence, there is a long way for research on health care services to achieve the same status as biomedical research. However, discoveries from basic biological science too often fail to reach patients in a timely fashion (Dougherty and Conway 2008). For that reason, more research on how to accelerate the pace at which innovations in health care are implemented might also be justified by health care professionals. According to the findings of our explorative study, research on open service innovations in health care deserves to be recognised as a significant contribution.

This explorative study is, to the best of our knowledge, the first to combine principles of open innovation and health care services. As such, the chapter fills a gap in the existing literature. It is important to perform research on changes in health care service development and delivery applying open innovation principles. Significant research questions in this context might be, for example, how patients' experiences can contribute to the redesign of health care services and to what extent open innovation principles is compatible with the organisational culture of health care.

References

Ågerfalk, P., & Fitzgerald, B. (2008a). Outsourcing to an unknown workforce: Exploring opensourcing as a global sourcing strategy. *MIS Quarterly, 32*(2), 385–409.

Bate, P., & Robert, G. (2006). Experience-based design: From redesigning the system around the patient to co-designing services with the patient. *Quality and Safety in Health Care, 15*(5), 307–310.

Bate, P., & Robert, G. (2007). Toward more user-centric OD: Lessons from the field of experience-based design and a case study. *The Journal of Applied Behavioural Science, 43*(1), 4–66.

Chesbrough, H. W. (2003). The era of open innovation. *MIT Sloan Management Review, 44*(3), 35–41.

Chu, T. H., & Robey, D. (2008). Explaining changes in learning and work practice following the adoption of online learning: A human agency perspective. *European Journal of Information Systems, 17*(1), 79–98.

Dougherty, D., & Conway, P. H. (2008). The "3 T's" road map to transform US health care: The "how" of high quality care. *Journal of American Medical Association (JAMA), 299*(19), 2319–2321.

Hasselbladh, H., & Bejerot, E. (2007). Webs of knowledge and circuits of communication: Constructing rationalized agency in Swedish health care. *Organisation, 14*(2), 175–200.

Munos, B. (2006). Can open-source R&D reinvigorate drug research? *Nature Reviews Drug Discovery.* doi:10.1038/nrd2131.

Ovretveit, J. (1992). *Health service quality: An introduction to quality methods for health services.* Oxford: Blackwell Scientific Press.

Pawson, R. (2006). *Evidence-based policy: A realist perspective.* London: Sage Publications.

Pickles, J., & Hide, E. (2008). Experience based design: A practical method of working with patients to redesign services. *Clinical Governance: An International Journal, 13*(1), 51–58.

Talaga, P. (2009). Editorial: Open innovation: share or die. *Drug Discovery Today, 14*(21/22), 1003–1005.

Vetter, G. R. (2009). Slouching toward open innovation: Free and open source software for electronic health information. *Journal of Law & Policy, 30*, 179–259.

von Hippel, E. (2001). Innovation by user communities: Learning from open-source software. *MIT Sloan Management Review, 42*(4), 82–86.

von Krogh, G. (2003). Open-source software development. *MIT Sloan Management Review, 44* (3), 14–18.

Walsh, K. (2007). Understanding what works—and why—in quality improvement: the need for theory-driven evaluation. *International Journal for Quality in Health Care, 19*(2), 57–59.

Ågerfalk, P., & Fitzgerald, B. (2008b). Outsourcing to an unknown workforce: Exploring opensourcing as a global sourcing strategy. *MIS Quarterly, 32*(2), 385–409.

Chapter 16
How Open Is Open Innovation? Considering, Adapting and Adopting User Knowledge and Competence in the Solution Space

Oscar Persson Ridell, Jimmie G. Röndell, and David Sörhammar

Abstract This chapter presents a longitudinal study of an open, co-created, innovation—ICA Student. It illustrates some of the challenges inherent in the consideration, adaptation and adoption of user knowledge and competence throughout an open innovation process, demonstrating the involvement of users both during the phases of content generation and commercialisation. Findings from the study illustrate five important issues for managers and practitioners to address when co-creating an innovation with future users: (1) the framing of an open innovation; (2) the identification of suitable participants; (3) the absorption and use of diverse inputs; (4) innovation entails both content generation and commercialisation and (5) the realisation that consideration, adaptation and adoption of knowledge and competence will affect the solution space. We conclude the chapter with a discussion on the relative openness of open innovation.

16.1 Introduction

Recently, one of northern Europe's largest food retailers—ICA—launched ICA Student, the result of an innovation project conducted together with the targeted segment of the innovation (students). As ICA had no prior understanding about the wants and needs of this specific segment, the decision was taken at the outset to source knowledge from students by employing an open innovation approach.

Managing innovation that includes input not only from intra-organisational actors—that is, open innovation (Chesbrough 2003)—is considered complex due to the heterogeneity of those involved. The different knowledge they draw on, the diverse competences and experiences they bring to and impose upon an innovation, create a dispersed set of innovators with possibly different innovation-related wants

---

O.P. Ridell (✉) • J.G. Röndell • D. Sörhammar
Uppsala University, Business Studies, Uppsala, Sweden
e-mail: oscar.persson_ridell@fek.uu.se; jimmie.rondell@fek.uu.se; david.sorhammar@fek.uu.se

J.S.Z. Eriksson Lundström et al. (eds.), *Managing Open Innovation Technologies*, 253
DOI 10.1007/978-3-642-31650-0_16, © Springer-Verlag Berlin Heidelberg 2013

and needs. As an initial step to handle this complexity, the managing organisation can use a firm-constructed design limit (Jeppesen and Molin 2003) in order to define the solution space (von Hippel and Katz 2002) in which, for instance, users have the possibility to apply their knowledge and competence. The solution space thus determines the openness of a specific innovation project, defining the possibility for users to provide input to, and influence on, an innovation. There is, however, a lack of research addressing possible intricacies managers meet in terms of what user knowledge and competences are to be *considered*, *adapted* and *adopted* during the extension of an open innovation process.

This chapter offers insights from a longitudinal study of an open innovation process at ICA that was investigated throughout its entire extension. Based on these insights, we evaluate and critically discuss the actual openness of open innovation. It is illustrated that the solution space is affected throughout the entire extension of the process; the opportunity for users to influence a solution space is dynamically reduced during the innovation process by the managing organisation's consideration, adaptation and adoption of user knowledge and competence. Thus, from an individual user's perspective the actual openness of open innovation is relative. Further, whereas the study is focused on the dyadic interaction between a managing organisation and future users of the innovation, it however also shows indications of many other influential internal and external stakeholders—such as IT systems, organisational norms, legal regulations and different suppliers—affecting the progression of the innovation process.

In order to show evidence in support of the above claims, the remainder of the chapter is structured as follows: (2) the fundamental challenges with innovation are briefly discussed, and a short overview of literature on co-creation of innovation, the solution space and user involvement is provided. We argue that literature on innovation, especially with regards to user communities and users as innovators, is maturing, whereas literature considering possible intricacies with adopting user knowledge by a managing organisation, and literature explicitly discussing user involvement during commercialisation of innovation, is still nascent; (3) a succinct description of the longitudinal data collection is presented; (4–4.2.4) the research object (the development of ICA Student) is divided into two parts—content generation and commercialisation—and it is illustrated how the solution space is dynamically reduced due to the adoption of users' knowledge and competence within each of these parts; (5) we provide five points of practical advice that have been deducted from the longitudinal study of ICA Student and (6–6.1) we conclude the chapter with discussions on implications for future research. We point to the need for further theorising the openness of open innovation.

16.2 Co-creation of Innovation

Stories of innovative endeavours frequently paint an exciting and victorious picture of the arduous effort that often is required in order to manage the development and commercialisation of an innovation. Innovating involves considering what users want and need, and for many organisations simply hoping that the market will help by providing an answer when asked directly might be expecting too much; most users might not have a clear understanding of their own wants and needs (cf. von Hippel 1988), and if they do, it can be difficult for them to explicate those wants and needs in any somewhat lucid manner. Put differently, users' wants and needs tend to be "sticky" (von Hippel 1994). Additionally, if the initial hurdles in the user context are somehow traversed, the predicament of matching the elucidated wants and needs with the managing organisation's prerequisites still remains.

Organisations are thus faced with a conundrum with regards to innovation: simply asking users about their wants and needs can lead to not getting any answers at all, or, conversely, getting answers that cannot be met with a proper response. Because of this, a necessity for continuous interaction during innovative endeavours is stressed by researchers (Jeppesen and Fredriksen 2006); interaction between an organisation and users is necessary if value is to be co-created for both (see e.g. Prahalad and Ramaswamy 2004). Co-creation of innovation places, however, puts a demand on the managing organisation to construct an appropriate solution space in which users can apply their knowledge and competence (von Hippel and Katz 2002)—similar to how value co-creation is preceded by the organisation offering users a value proposition (e.g. Ballantyne et al. 2011). A solution space, which can be presented to users via a computer mediated toolkit (Thomke and von Hippel 2002), represents the limitation to user involvement that is initially established by the managing organisation (Jeppesen and Molin 2003). The solution space thus affects—both enabling and delimiting—the managing organisation's consideration, adaptation and adoption of user knowledge during the entire innovation process.

The literature on co-creation of innovation has become considerable, not least through studies of user-to-user knowledge and innovation sharing in communities (Franke and Shah 2003; Wasko and Faraj 2005), and the open source movement (Lerner and Tirole 2002). We argue, however, that literature on the co-creation of innovation is still in its infancy as regards two aspects: (1) there is a lack of studies addressing the reason why some user knowledge and competences are, and some are not, included in an innovation. Research addressing the underlying decision process (see Dahlander and Gann 2010a, b) is of interest to managers in that it can illustrate possible intricacies and challenges when using an open innovation approach. (2) As discussed by Bogers et al. (2010a, b), the role of users during commercialisation of an innovation has only been meagrely studied. Accounts of user involvement during the commercialisation of an innovation could reveal organisational problems that might be inherent in the innovation process, and can hence possibly aid organisations in explaining why innovations that appear to be a hit during stages of design do not go on to become a commercial success.

In an attempt to contribute to the innovation literature, the following account of an open, co-created, innovation intends to illustrate some of the intricacies inherent in the consideration, adaptation and adoption of user knowledge and competence during an innovation process, and it also aims to demonstrate and discuss user involvement during the commercialisation of an innovation.

16.3 About the Study

The data collection started early February 2010 and was completed in early September 2011, representing the entire extension of the innovation process. During this time, period data were collected through interviews, participant observation as well as project documentation. All methods described below were used in order for us to holistically capture the study object, the innovation process.

Five employees, who constituted the project group at ICA (representing ICA Banken or the CRM department), were formally interviewed and informally met with on several occasions throughout the process. The formal interviews were recorded, and they followed a semi-structured interview guide. They all lasted between one and two hours each. The informal meetings took place in relation to innovation-related activities, before and after a case competition and three separate concept presentations.

Participant observations were conducted on occasions when representatives from ICA and representatives from the segment of young adults (students) had innovation-related meetings during the process; the case competition in the stage of content generation (see Sect. 4.1.4) and three separate concept presentations in the stage of commercialisation (see Sect. 4.2.2–4.2.4). Also, participant observations were conducted at four of the project group's decision meetings during which decisions were taken for the innovation and innovation process. All observations were made unobtrusively; we did not take any active part in discussions in order to limit the effects of our presence.

Project documentation was put at our disposal throughout the entire extension of the innovation process. This second-hand data consisted of policy documents and e-mails correspondence, students' essays and case reports (see Sect. 4.1.4), PowerPoint presentations from meetings (see Sects. 4.1.1, 4.1.3, 4.1.4, 4.2.2, 4.2.3), briefs about progression (see Sects. 4.2.1 and 4.2.4) as well as focus group reports and survey data (see Sect. 4.1.3).

In the illustration of the development and commercialisation of ICA Student, all quotes are taken from the collected data, which are kept anonymous as required by the informants.

16.4 The Development and Commercialisation of ICA Student

ICA Student was launched as an offering containing a customer debit card on August 17, 2011. Already two weeks after it had been launched it had gained a market share of 8.4 % and had generated positive response in the form of 15,000 "likes" on Facebook. It was thus, according to ICA, on its way to becoming a huge success. So, how did they do it? Before we go into details, a short note on the managing organisation of this open innovation, the ICA Group, is called for. They are one of northern Europe's leading food retailers with 2,150 stores in Sweden,

Norway, Estonia, Latvia and Lithuania, also including a commercial bank—ICA Banken. The ICA Group is a joint venture; 40 % is owned by Hakon Invest AB of Sweden and 60 % is owned by Royal Ahold N.V. of the Netherlands.

The initial purpose with the offering was to create loyalty among young adults in Sweden. However, during the innovation process, voices were raised about narrowing the target to the sub-segment of students under 30 in higher education, as they were considered more easily identifiable and reachable.

ICA Student is, however, not the first loyalty scheme that ICA has launched; already in 1992 a customer loyalty card was introduced—ICA-Kort. This card has today a market penetration of 50 % of the Swedish population in most age categories, with an average cardholder age of 58. This rather high mean age illustrates that the scheme has not been as successful within younger age categories (especially young adults aged 18–30). Even more problematic for ICA is, however, that the penetration rate of this specific age category has increasingly shrunk during the last decade. It was also found that ICA Banken had the same problem with attracting and creating loyalty within the young adults segment.

In April 2010, ICA Banken held an internal workshop during which the issue of attracting young adults to become customer debit cardholders was explicitly discussed: "... it is a somewhat well established conception that people do not often alter their choice of bank during their lifetime, especially when you get older...if we could offer young adults a specifically designed bank service we could become their natural choice of bank". During this time the CRM department at ICA—who is responsible for the loyalty programme ICA-Kort—had also discussed ways to attract the young adults segment of becoming closer connected to ICA's loyalty card programme. Management therefore decided that: "By combining the two parts, bank and food, we could offer something new and really unique to this segment".

During approximately one and a half years, one person from each department was devoted to innovating a joint offering that could attract the segment of young adults. The project immediately encountered a problem as ICA recognised that they did not have any insights about the segment—they knew "families with children"—and had not conducted a single target group analysis of this customer group, ever. As they did not know anything about the wants and needs of this age category, ICA realised that they could not innovate in-house, which is the usual innovation procedure at ICA. Further adding to the challenge, ICA was not only unfamiliar with the wants and needs (i.e. content generation) of young adults, but they were also unclear about how to communicate an innovation to this segment (i.e. commercialisation).

16.4.1 Content Generation

The project commenced in the middle of May in 2010, and the stage of content generation included the phases as outlined in Fig. 16.1. Each phase is discussed at length below.

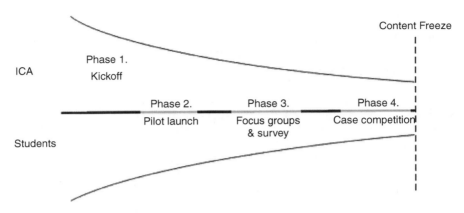

Fig. 16.1 Content generation phases

16.4.1.1 Kick-Off (Phase 1)

On May 10, 2010, a kick-off was held during which the main outline of the innovation project was presented. It was the first one of its kind at ICA to include a combined bank and food offering. The normal procedure at ICA is to develop an offer in-house, do a test run in a small region, adjust the content and then, within a short time period, do an official launch. With the joint project the outset was instead to openly obtain information regarding any specific wants and needs, as specified by the segment itself—"engaging the customer from the very start".

> **Practical Tip**
>
> It is important for organisations to be flexible in their approach to innovation. ICA had no prior knowledge about the wants and needs of the targeted segment, and they therefore felt a need to open up their closed approach to innovation and instead include the targeted customer in an open innovation approach.

At first, the project was intended to be launched already in August 2010, but, considering that ICA had little-to-none previous experience and knowledge about the targeted segment, the decision was taken to commence the project with a pilot launch. However, as time was limited between the start of the project and the planned pilot launch the decision was taken to put together a more generic offering; a free bankcard and insurance combined with a preselected set of discounted groceries—called "startkassen"—that ICA thought would be appealing to the segment of young adults.

16.4.1.2 Pilot Launch (Phase 2)

"We decided to go public as soon as possible [September 16, 2010] ... we had some content that we knew wouldn't end up in the final offering, but some generic stuff—a free bank card and some food offerings—just to be able to go out there and start talking to our potential customers ... not to test the content, just to have something to start the discussion with ... It wasn't that we innovated in-house for 6 months and then went public, not at all; we got things running quickly with an offering, based on generic content, to get users input on it".

> **Practical Tip**
>
> When applying an open innovation approach it is important to have an intermediary—in the case of ICA, a generic offering—to communicate through. Using *boundary objects* is important during open innovation as they enable communication between participants and a joint understanding about what knowledge and competences are sought during an innovation process.

After the summer, the pilot was launched at Stockholm School of Economics, and later at Uppsala University (September 21). In order for ICA to manage the pilot, the limit of participants was initially set to 500 students, but was later reduced to 200 students. The reason for this was that registration of participants had to be executed using a temporary IT solution that demanded a number of manual operations which were outside of the normal routines. Representatives from ICA, including the entire project group, visited the two universities and handed out folders to attract students to participate in the pilot.

One representative from ICA who participated commented; "The first reactions when meeting the students were interesting and offered a great experience ... there were some initial general eye openers in terms of the mind-set of the students ... I remember thinking, aha; yes I guess that's another way of looking at it".

One thing that emerged during the encounters was that the students were quite sceptical towards the ICA customer debit card combining discounts on groceries with banking and insurance services, and also reacted to discounted groceries being preselected and not selectable. Further initial indications concerned the formal demand that students had to transfer their financial aid from the state—called CSN funds—directly to their account at ICA Banken in order to be able to apply for the card. The students perceived this to be very tedious and cumbersome as it would involve bureaucratic paperwork and administration.

Because of limitations within their IT systems, and legislation around bank operations and food purchase registrations, it was not possible for ICA to do any detailed analysis of how participants actually used the generic customer debit card during the pilot. The launch of the pilot did, however, enable the first encounter with the young adult segment, an encounter which later on in the innovation process would prove to be beneficial. "It [the pilot launch] provided us with some fundamental insights regarding the need to continuously, and even further, include the segment of young adults in the development process ... it provided us with arguments to proceed as planned".

16.4.1.3 Focus Groups and Survey (Phase 3)

In early October, the third phase of the process was commenced in order to deepen the insights gained from previous encounters during the pilot launch. ICA decided to involve the young adults segment through a total of four focus groups. The two initial focus groups were conducted lasting two hours each by an external research firm, with both novice (first year) and experienced (second and third year) students from Stockholm and Linköping. Each group had a total of eight students; four second-year students and four final-year students. Representatives from the project group were sitting behind a glass wall listening in on the conversation. The questionnaire used during the sessions was constructed by the project group and was inspired by the insights from the pilot launch encounters. It revolved around participants' attitude towards food, economy and banking, and also what they find themselves missing in their everyday life. And, during the last 20 min of each session the participants were asked to give their input on ICA's evolving concept for young adults.

The focus group sessions provided: (1) a general illustration and understanding of the targeted segment; (2) information about their view on food and economy (banking) and (3) a view of students as a highly heterogeneous segment. The sessions made it clear that the segment of young adults is sceptical about market communication, and often find themselves asking what the catch is. Moreover, ICA found that knowledge about ICA Banken amongst the segment was lower than anticipated and that reservations towards the bank were considerable. In this regard, the conservative nature of the segment became clear; they wanted the old fashioned way of banking with an office, a bank teller and advice about what to do with their money. Also, ICA had the idea about the segment that they would be more short-term oriented. However, rather than focusing on the necessity for discounts and similar offers, students talked about their studies as a transitional phase and were therefore wondering what would happen as they enter the next age segment. "We understood that we had to have a phase of transition, for example, through discounts on mortgage interests ... to show that we believe in the segment, believe in that what is offered will be valuable for them even in the future". In relation to banking, the focus groups also showed that students had thoughts about the design of the customer debit card, and also what would happen with their "accumulated benefits" (such as discounts on interest rates) if they changed their current bank, in which they had been a member all their lives, to ICA Banken.

The subsequent two focus groups were conducted by ICA themselves at two occasions (October 22 and December 9) with a different set of students, using the same procedure as in the first two focus groups. During the first of these focus groups, ICA asked detailed questions about the evolving concept, evaluated each of its parts and addressed whether the students would alter anything in it. The second occasion was more of a brainstorming session in which students were asked about what they would do with the concept if they were given completely "free rein" in terms of, for instance, communication and the banking offer. The two focus group sessions did not lead to any profound revelations: "It was nice to confirm the things that had come up during the initial focus groups, and to be able to discuss this with the students and get their point of view on what had emerged".

The results of both sets of focus groups were presented at ICA before Christmas in 2010, and a number of employees from many different departments within ICA attended the presentation. The presence of higher executives during this meeting was however rather low. One problem that was discussed during the presentation, that students had addressed as fundamental in the focus groups, was the demand ICA was posing with regards to their CSN funds; " ... that their CSN funds would have to be transferred to the account [at ICA Banken] directly we found to be a great hurdle both through the focus group sessions and through the survey".

From mid-December 2010, until the beginning of January 2011, ICA sent out a web-based survey to the 200 students that initially were a part of the pilot in phase 1. The questionnaire contained questions about, for instance, debit cards and virtual banking. Apart from providing yet further input on students' dissatisfaction with the CSN issue, the survey led to one significant revelation. There was a question that asked respondents to choose from three different possible offers on food from ICA. At the outset, ICA was sure that they would go for the option that gave the highest discount (5 % on the whole range), but found instead that most respondents wanted the option that would be cheaper for ICA (50 % discount on three favourite products). ICA thus found through the survey that offers of big discounts do not work on the segment of young adults. Furthermore, it provided information about the preselected set of discounted groceries—"startkassen"—not being as interesting for the segment since they prefer to choose products that they feel are individually right for them.

The result of the survey was, however, not only used in order to gain knowledge about the segment of young adults, but also served as support during negotiations, both internally and with suppliers. For instance, the project group used the information in order to gain acceptance within their own departments and to illuminate important strategic questions for their respective management; "When we [ICA Banken] continued to put our demands internally we could use the survey to motivate decisions ..."

16.4.1.4 Case Competition (Phase 4)

On January 18, 2011, as a final effort to gain insights from the targeted segment, ICA gathered 25 marketing students, who were divided into six teams, from two universities in Sweden at ICA's headquarters. These students had previously gone through a screening process, supervised by their teachers, that contained the assignment to answer the question; "Why don't younger consumers enter into loyalty schemes in the same extent as older consumers?" The reason why they now were sitting at ICA's headquarters was to enter into a case competition, which would put ICA's concept to the segment of young adults.

After a short welcome speech from the project owners the six teams had 24 h to develop an offering based on the generic ICA and ICA Banken concept aimed at the young adults segment. They gave the students three rules for the concept: (1) it should "attract at least 30 % of the target group of young adults"; (2) it should "feel technically fresh in the autumn of 2011, and continue to have that feeling for 5 years on with only small changes" and (3) it should "be rooted in reality both in a technical and economic sense". As a guiding light, ICA gave the eager students the words "be innovative!" The students also got a PowerPoint presentation containing facts and figures about both ICA and the target segment of young adults. For ICA, the aim of the competition was to gain knowledge of how representatives from the segment saw the generic concept, and how they would improve it in relation to young adults.

> **Practical Tip**
>
> Even though it is necessary to set clear delimitations with regards to what knowledge and competences are sought from users, it is equally important to provide users with *creative freedom* during an open innovation process. Striking a balance between openness and delimitation is hence crucial.

Twenty four hours later, on January 19, the six teams presented their concepts to a crowded auditorium and a jury of two senior managers from ICA Banken and one senior manager from the CRM department at ICA's headquarters. After each presentation, the jury, as well as members of the auditorium, asked each team challenging questions that forced them to clarify their statements and ideas. Several of the student teams were "positively arrogant" towards ICA's generic concept, all suggesting radical changes that ICA sometimes agreed to, but often questioned. The dialogue even continued after the six presentations had finished.

There was no case solution that ICA adopted altogether into an offering to the segment of young adults. Instead, they took bits and pieces from several of them. Many of the teams argued for a broader target segment, while recognising that the sub-segment of students is the trendsetter for the entire segment of young adults. ICA acknowledged that, in the short run, only focusing on students would not be profitable as they do not have a lot of money to spend themselves. However, it was considered that the student sub-segment, being easily identifiable and reachable, will be profitable in the long run; if they are approached early on, the chances that they will stay loyal customers increase.

Yet again, ICA found the students reluctant as in the CSN issue. They therefore took the decision to exclude in the offering the demand on students of having to put CSN into their account at ICA Banken. Instead, they incorporated one aspect of a case solution, giving double bonus points every time the customer debit card was used (points that only could be used in ICA's food stores). One of the student teams also suggested giving discounts on more costly food, instead of only on common groceries; "... every student sometimes needs to eat noodles at the end of a month, but that is not something we want to be reminded of ... instead we all want to spoil ourselves with a nice steak, even though we might not be able to afford it ... but if it is on discount, then what the heck". This reasoning—"some everyday luxury"—was something ICA considered and adopted into the offering.

There were also two ideas that emerged during the case competition that ICA considered but rejected for different reasons. First, all teams disliked the colour of the regular debit card, which is pink; "... that is not a card you wave in a bar ...". Several of the teams had designed their own cards, most of them in black. However, ICA argued that there is too much internal administration to change the colour, and also that pink represents some of the core values at ICA. They did, however, consider these opinions from the students, and ICA is planning a three colour option to the card in the near future. Second, another idea that was considered, but not adopted, was "Nickles and dimes". The idea was to let cardholders save up for something they desired, such as a computer or an around the world trip. Practically, the concept meant letting cardholders pay, for example 100 SEK when the groceries only cost 89 SEK, and the pocket change (11 SEK) would then end up in the ICA Banken savings account. This concept was widely acclaimed among the jury and the auditorium as a highly innovative and brave idea, and the jury gave it first prize in the case competition. Still, the concept was not included into the offering, and the reason was because of the IT structures at ICA and regulations in Swedish law. At the moment, all required IT systems—for instance the CRM system, the bank system and the cash registers at the stores—could not be effectively linked in order to make the necessary transactions possible. Also, ICA had found that this type of transaction could be problematic in relation to regulations in Swedish law about connecting personal data between different computerised systems. Still, "Nickles and dimes" was set aside as an innovation for the future. Interesting to note is that "Nickles and dimes" was regarded as immensely innovative, whereas the similar concept "Eat up your loan" was not considered, but rejected immediately. The core of this concept was to amortise loans through consumption. Bonus points gained from shopping at ICA were to be used to repay loans, and the more consumption the greater the amortisation. "Eat up your loan" was regarded as innovative, but the jury rejected it based upon the idea that whereas shopping food should be fun, amortising loans is boring, and the two should therefore never be mixed.

Several of the teams also focused on how to connect with the student segment. Traditionally, ICA has communicated with their customers through their magazine Buffé, big outdoor billboards and TV commercials. Several of the teams stated that ICA needed to be more innovative and proactive on social media platforms, such as Facebook and blogs, and that they also had to develop a mobile app. Their argument was that younger consumers do not easily get attracted by traditional commercials. Instead, they listen to their peers, and that ICA therefore needs a more personal tone. The reason behind the app was that the segment felt a need to be constantly updated of their bonus points and account status, something that an app could provide. ICA agreed with these points, but stated that it represents a new type of dialogue that they are not used to. Therefore, ICA felt a need to get additional assistance in order to be able to communicate in the way preferred by the targeted segment.

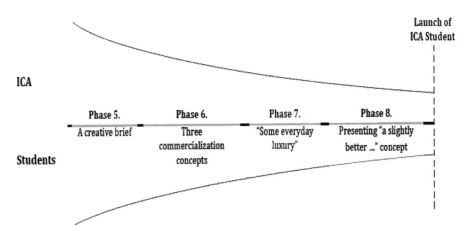

Fig. 16.2 Commercialisation phases

The content of the offer to students, which at this point had been named ICA Student, was hereby decided by ICA to be put into "freeze-mode"; that is, the content outline of ICA Student was wrapped up and closed.

16.4.2 Commercialisation

As realised during the content generation stage, ICA found a need to involve the targeted segment also during the commercialisation stage; "This segment is highly challenging ... if miscommunicated to, things can easily go the wrong way fast". Therefore, in order to achieve a proper tonality in the communication with the segment, the decision was taken to include students also during the commercialisation stage of ICA Student; "It's power by students! ... we wanted to be open to the students' influences during the whole process".

> **Practical Tip**
>
> It is important to recognise that commercialisation can be an equally important part as content generation in an open innovation project. Hence, it is crucial to also involve users during the stage of commercialisation.

The commercialisation stage followed the outline presented in Fig. 16.2, and each phase is elaborately discussed below.

16.4.2.1 A Creative Brief (Phase 5)

The first phase of commercialisation was initiated in early March 2011, when students from Berghs School of Communication were asked to provide input about how ICA should communicate with the targeted student segment. In a similar vein to the phases in content generation, a group of students from Berghs were given a presentation by ICA in the form of a "creative brief", which contained information about the content of ICA Student, the target segment, and general information about ICA. Also included in the brief was a budget, a specification about the available communication channels and an outline on the overall goals regarding ICA Student.

> **Practical Tip**
>
> Just as during the stage of content generation it is important to use boundary objects during commercialisation—in the case of ICA, a creative brief—in order for users to be able to apply their knowledge and competences also in this stage of the innovation process.

The students from Berghs had two weeks to develop a presentation about how to reach the targeted segment. ICA was looking for suggestions about tonality, layout, advertising channels, promotion activities and other vital aspects in order to be able to properly interact with students. "Obviously we expected the students to come up with ideas relating to things we hadn't thought about, otherwise we wouldn't have involved them...this includes communication details but also, or even more so, the overall mind-set of the communication".

16.4.2.2 Three Commercialisation Concepts (Phase 6)

Two weeks after they had been handed the creative brief, the students from Berghs presented three conceptual themes to ICA's project group: (1) "keeping it cheap"; (2) "some everyday luxury" and (3) "ICA—no ordinary bank". A commonality amongst the three concepts was that all focused on a similar IT solution for communicating and interacting with students. Berghs strongly suggested using social media platforms, especially Facebook and Facebook-related blogs and forums, as a hub for interacting with the segment.

The first concept, "keeping it cheap", had a tonality that used handwritten or typewriter written small ads to enforce a sense of not wasting resources on promotion, but rather offering discounts on groceries and insurances. The second concept, "some everyday luxury", embraced the issue of how the small things sometimes can make all the difference in someone's everyday life, focusing on how ICA, for instance could provide "a slightly better" dinner party, weekend or vacation. The third concept, "ICA—no ordinary bank", was an antithesis approach that ironized the general view of ICA Banken as not being a real bank and insurance provider. The idea was hence to turn this unconventional notion into something positive.

During the presentation, which contained overall strategic approaches as well as specific production and copy-related aspects, ICA was able to ask questions to clarify and enable yet further elaboration of the material. This was followed by a discussion in which participants from ICA considered the presented material. The main purpose of the discussion was to evaluate whether the different concepts were adaptable to ICA. "Even though there are some fantastically creative ideas on how to do this we need to keep in mind that some of them might not be doable as we have a number of formal and informal rules, regulations and limitations to consider". The discussion came to focus on if, and if so, how, aspects from the different concepts could be combined and adapted, in order to; "... keep the out-of-the-box mindset while adapting it to our existing profile". While the ironic concept generated a few smiles, it was uniformly rejected as it clashed with ICA's ongoing campaign that focused on establishing ICA Banken as a genuine bank and insurance provider. However, the project group considered the two other concepts, and found them both partly adoptable to ICA and ICA Student. Concerns were raised regarding some of the promotion activities in the concepts, for instance the second concept's idea about installing ICA-labelled vending machines and tables for playing table tennis at student campuses. Even though it was considered feasible as such, questions about procurement processes and legal obstacles led to a rejection of this specific "guerrilla" marketing activity.

Conclusively, the decision was taken that Berghs should continue the development by combining the activities included in the "some everyday luxury" concept with the tonality of the "keeping it cheap" concept. The student group was moreover specifically asked to focus on how the digital communication and interaction should be designed, as well as how ICA Student could be both distinguishable and simultaneously incorporated within ICA's existing digital communication platforms and routines.

16.4.2.3 "Some Everyday Luxury" (Phase 7)

Five weeks after the three commercialisation concepts had been presented to ICA, a meeting was held at headquarters in which Berghs presented their reworked version. The formerly distinctive concepts now had been combined into a single concept that was given the name "some everyday luxury". Facebook was suggested to be the common interaction and communication hub to which all promotion activities were to be directed, and the students argued that ICA Student should have its own Facebook site separate from ICA's general Facebook site. All ads and posters were to have a message clearly stating that ICA Student's Facebook site was the advertiser, and the messages were designed following the "keeping it cheap" concept. For example a newspaper ad was to state: "less money spent on this ad enables us to give you a better discount on breakfast cereals", and a short and cheap ad intended for the music streaming service Spotify read: "less money spent on this spot gives you a better deal on your insurance".

Another idea, following the suggested "guerrilla" marketing approach, was to hand out covers for bike saddles reading "ICA Student—slightly better than a wet saddle". Also, it was proposed that ICA should sponsor tent camps in different university cities, where the lack of student housing was evident at the beginning of the semester, and then to print "ICA Student—slightly better than sleeping out in the open" on all the tents. Further, ice creams were to be handed out in parks around campuses in return for the students filling out the application form for signing up for ICA Student.

Berghs suggested that, early on in the semester, a competition called "Battle of the corridors" was to take place in which students living in student housing were to come up with suggestions about how to improve their student living if they would have 100,000 SEK to spend. Participants had to visualise their suggestions, and write a short motivation, and were subsequently to post their suggestions on ICA Student's own Facebook site. The suggestion with the most "likes" would be rewarded with the suggested sum to spend on improving their student housing situation. Also, in order to generate viral promotion effects on social media, Berghs suggested a concept called "Random acts of love" which consists of ICA Student randomly handing out vouchers on Facebook that only can be used in ICA stores. By handing out these gifts, and simultaneously posting that someone has received a gift on ICA Student's Facebook site, the idea was to virally generate word of mouth about ICA Student.

Provided with the rich and innovative material from the students at Berghs, the task for the project group at ICA was now again to consider and adapt the details and tonality of the hitherto developed concept in order to enable an adoption into the ICA context. Thus, a period followed in which the project group had a dialogue with suppliers, retailers and different internal departments, as to determine the final outline of ICA Student's commercialisation. During this time, the project group also prepared and secured IT resources—for instance access to social network platforms and blogs—along with social website editors and bloggers, and looked at opportunities and limitations in ICA's current graphical and typographical layout portfolio and IT system.

> **Practical Tip**
>
> When applying an open innovation approach it is also important to reflect on the *organisational fit* of the progressing innovation. This requires a continuous dialogue not only with intra-organisational actors, but with suppliers and retailers as well as a consideration of the innovation's fit within current IT structures.

16.4.2.4 Presenting "A Slightly Better..." Concept (Phase 8)

On May 20, 2011, the preliminary outline—content and commercialisation—of ICA Student was presented at ICA headquarters in front of the students from Berghs and several ICA employees from different departments. A number of aspects related to the commercialisation stage were addressed. Motivations were given as to how and why some of the inputs from the students from Berghs were considered, adapted and now adopted into ICA Student, and why some inputs were considered but not fully adopted.

ICA began discussing the essence of the tonality of the "cheap" concept. Commonly known as Sweden's biggest buyer of advertisement, the question was if "cheap" could be trustworthily used by ICA: "Our conclusion is that we cannot fully use the cheap theme, since, even if we could try, the only one fooled would be ourselves ... we cannot communicate ICA Student in isolation ... we must remember that this group will eventually go from being students to becoming regular ICA card holders". Another aspect addressed was that retailers, suppliers and other partners might not be able to respond to the "cheap" concept in a synchronised manner as they do their advertising individually, which then can, or cannot, be perceived as cheap. Consequently, basing commercialisation tonality on the "cheap" concept was considered unachievable.

However, it was declared during the presentation that ICA would adopt the straightforwardness in the communication approach that had been emphasised by the student group in order to properly interact with the targeted segment without losing the ICA touch. A decision had been taken that ICA would embrace a "simple" tonality as opposed to the "cheap" tonality. In this way, as it was explained, the "cheap" tonality was "transformed into something we can feel comfortable with over time". In a similar way, the handwritten or typewriter-style font that was suggested by Berghs was changed to a crayon-like font that already was a part of the established ICA font portfolio.

Berghs had suggested "some everyday luxury" as a foundational concept for the commercialisation of ICA Student. However, ICA was more inspired by the group's "guerrilla" marketing catchphrases "ICA Student—slightly better than a wet saddle" and "ICA Student—slightly better than sleeping out in the open". The decision had been taken to use the "slightly better" wording as the foundational concept of the commercialisation, and it was to be adopted into all ICA Student communication. Moreover, in terms of the suggested "Battle of the corridors", ICA adopted the entire marketing event but with a few adaptations. For instance, the prize was not to be concentrated to a single winner as suggested, but was instead to be spread out over time and was to be more related to the "random acts of love" campaign. The prizes were also to be more related to ICA by using an ICA-led jury who would decide amongst the ten most "liked" postings on the ICA Student Facebook site.

Furthermore, ICA adopted the suggestion to establish a separate Facebook site for ICA Student. It was to be given its own editorial resources as it was considered that "it is important that we allow the ICA Student Facebook site to evolve on its own with its own unique dialogue ... we do not want to risk the specific ICA student offerings getting lost in the ordinary site's flow of more generic offerings and discussions". The "guerrilla" marketing saddle cover event was also to be adopted, but with a slight adaptation of the catchphrase; from "ICA Student—slightly better than a wet saddle" to "there are wet student rears, and then there are ICA student rears".

Handing out free ice creams to get students to sign up for ICA Student, as suggested by Berghs as an important part of the launch, was however not possible to adopt as by the end of the summer there were no available freezers for all the ice cream. Neither could the tent camps be carried out since it had already been taken care of by the major student cities themselves. A plan to adapt this campaign by ICA was addressed at the presentation, and discussions had been initiated to get local retailers to provide the city funded camps with breakfast. But the negotiations had been affected by local rules and regulations, which could turn out to be difficult to circumvent. Also, the suggestion to put commercial spots on Spotify was considered but not adopted since ICA was hesitant because Spotify, during the time, was moving from being financed by advertisement to becoming a surcharged service.

ICA announced that ICA Student was to be launched on August 17, 2011 (about the time the semester starts), and the presentation was concluded with a statement about the importance of having co-created the content and commercialisation together with students. It was the project group's expressed standpoint that, although some of the input from students had not even been considered, whereas other input had gone all the way from consideration to adoption, the end result was the result of a truly interactive process.

16.5 Practical Advice

The above account of the open, co-created, innovation—ICA Student—illustrates several important issues for managers and practitioners working with innovation. The following five points highlight what we find to be the most significant issues that can be drawn from the longitudinal study of this specific innovation process: (1) framing an open innovation; (2) identifying suitable participants; (3) absorbing and using inputs not directly applicable to the specific innovation; (4) innovating is more than just content generation and (5) realising that consideration, adaptation and adoption of knowledge and competence will affect the solution space.

> 1. Our study shows that innovation, especially when not only intra-organisational actors are included, is dependent upon the fundamentals from which it is developed. An important lesson drawn from the study is thus that a managing organisation that invites participants to co-create innovation should enforce constraints on the process. ICA Student was since the offset to become an offer including both food and bank offerings to the young adults segment, and the participants who were involved in the project had to comply with this constraint (i.e. ICA's constructed design limit). However, the development of ICA Student also shows that framing an innovation offers the prerequisites for participants to get involved and apply their knowledge and competence. It is important for a managing
>
> *(continued)*

organisation of an open innovation to also clearly frame and communicate what it wants and needs; not only worry about the wants and needs of future users.

2. Young adults were initially the targeted segment for ICA Student. However, due to the vast heterogeneity of this segment, ICA found a need to identify a sub-segment that would be representative. Students were regarded as suitable because of being in the forefront of the segment in terms of trend awareness and were also considered identifiable and reachable. A revelation for ICA was that students were very skilled at expressing their wants and needs, as it is something that they are trained to do. Organisations employing an open innovation approach ought to keep in mind that it is important to engage participants who do not only have relevant wants and needs, but who also can express those wants and needs efficiently.

3. Throughout the process, ICA gained insights relevant for developing and commercialising ICA Student. However, the innovation process also led to a gain in insights not directly applicable to the specific innovation; insights that were gained through interacting with participants (especially external) and that were used to create "leverage" internally. As commented by a project group member; ". . . the project has led to issues that before were not as prioritised internally by some, have now climbed on the agenda . . . projects have gained acceptance through the students [knowledge and competence], . . . such as modernising the IT platforms". Managers and practitioners ought to be attentive to inputs that are not directly applicable to the specific innovation but that can be used to support their claims about bringing issues up on the board's agenda.

4. In order to be successful with an open innovation, it is crucial to continue involving future users also during phases of commercialisation. The innovation process that has been studied involved the targeted segment both during content generation and commercialisation. ICA Student clearly shows that users can contribute immensely with knowledge and competence not only for generating content, but also in order for an innovation to be accepted and carried within the targeted segment. It is important for managers to acknowledge that innovation is not only about content generation; involving future users in the phases of commercialisation is equally important, as this chapter clearly shows.

5. On the same note as the above advice regarding framing of an open innovation, it is important to realise that *consideration*, *adaptation* and *adoption* of knowledge and competence dynamically affect the solution space. Various inputs were continuously considered, adapted and adopted throughout the innovation of ICA Student until it was launched. This continuous adoption of knowledge and competence meant that participants' possibility to influence the innovation was increasingly restricted

> throughout the process. Practitioners should be aware that adoption of knowledge and competence throughout a specific innovation process affects subsequent considerations, adaptations and adoptions for the managing organisation. Also, adoption of knowledge and competence influences the possibilities for other participants, such as users, to affect an innovation; it progressively delimits the solution space. Practitioners need hence consider the *relative openness*—for both the managing organisation and other participants—when applying an open innovation approach.

16.6 Implications for Research

In the beginning of this chapter it was mentioned that the innovation literature is increasingly maturing, but that certain aspects still remain in their infancy. We argued that the literature has only vaguely considered user involvement in the commercialisation of an innovation. We also argued that it falls short with regards to considerations of the intricacies managers face during the adoption of user knowledge (i.e. why some user knowledge and competence is included in an innovation, and why some is not). This chapter has taken an initial step towards empirically overcoming these shortcomings by illustrating how a managing organisation considers, adapts and adopts user knowledge both during content generation and commercialisation of an innovation.

Our investigation of how a managing organisation considers, adapts and adopts knowledge and competence from users throughout an open innovation process has led us to question *the openness of open innovation* (see Practical advice, point 5). The source of this issue is empirical, and in the final part of this chapter we therefore use abstraction in order to discuss, theoretically, the relative openness of open innovation.

16.6.1 The Openness of Open Innovation

Open innovation necessitates the involvement of at least two distinct participants, and the total number of participants, as well as their heterogeneity, can easily be perceived as a major determinant of the openness of an open innovation. In the development of ICA Student, one participant initiated and managed the process by setting a solution space, and thus enabled, as well as directed, other participants' application of knowledge and competence throughout the open innovation process. Thus, the participant managing an open innovation—in our case ICA—decides what knowledge and competence to consider, adapt and adopt throughout the extension of the process, regardless of the number of participants and their heterogeneity.

Consideration, adaptation and adoption are the successive decision activities through which a managing participant determines the openness of an open innovation; they constitute the activities through which a solution space is progressively reduced. *Consideration* involves a managing participant continuously deciding what is deemed relevant knowledge for a specific innovation. *Adaptation* involves knowledge and competence that has been considered relevant being revised so as to be in accordance with the managing participant's wants and needs. *Adoption*, lastly, means that relevant and revised knowledge is situated into an innovation, and that the solution space is altered and the acting definition of knowledge vis-à-vis the innovation progresses for all participants. Based on this reasoning, the openness of open innovation is relative for all participants; it depends on the managing participant's continuous consideration, adaptation and adoption of knowledge and competence throughout the entire extension of the process. Intriguingly, the more unambiguous a managing participant becomes in defining knowledge in relation to an open innovation process, the more closed that open innovation will become.

However, as the development of ICA Student shows, reality is more complex for a managing participant as regards dealing with the successive decision activities. The possibility to consider, adapt and adopt knowledge and competence throughout an open innovation process is affected by, for instance, laws and regulations, IT systems and organisational norms. Naturally, such aspects will affect a managing participant's progression towards a more unambiguous definition of knowledge. Thus, to enhance the theoretical understanding of the openness of open innovation, we suggest that future studies should aim to include more internal and external participants. Future studies could fruitfully illustrate the influence of, for instance, IT systems and regulations, as well as include other stakeholders, such as suppliers, retailers and other intra-organisational departments, in their discussions about the openness of open innovation.

References

Ballantyne, D., Frow, P., Varey, R. J., et al. (2011). Value propositions as communication practice: Taking a wider view. *Industrial Marketing Management, 40*(2), 202–210.

Bogers, M., Afuah, A., & Bastian, B. (2010a). Users as innovators: A review critique, and future research directions. *Journal of Management, 36*(4), 857–875.

Chesbrough, H. W. (2003). *Open innovation: The new imperative for creating and profiting from technology*. Boston, MA: Harvard Business School Press.

Dahlander, L., & Gann, D. M. (2010a). How open is innovation? *Research Policy, 39*(6), 699–709.

Franke, N., & Shah, S. (2003). How communities support innovative activities: an exploration of assistance and sharing among end-users. *Research Policy, 32*(1), 157–178.

Jeppesen, L. B., & Fredriksen, L. (2006). Why do users contribute to firm-hosted user communities? The case of computer-controlled music instruments. *Organisation Science, 17* (1), 45–63.

Jeppesen, L. B., & Molin, M. J. (2003). Consumers as co-developers: Learning and innovation outside the firm. *Technology Analysis & Strategic Management, 15*(3), 363–384.

Lerner, J., & Tirole, J. (2002). Some simple economics of open source. *The Journal of Industrial Economics, 50*(2), 197–234.

16 How Open Is Open Innovation? Considering, Adapting and Adopting User...

Prahalad, C. K., & Ramaswamy, V. (2004). *Future of competition: Co-creating unique value with customers*. Boston, MA: Harvard Business School Press Books.

Thomke, S., & von Hippel, E. (2002). Customers as innovators: A new way to create value. *Harvard Business Review, 80*(4), 74–81.

von Hippel, E. (1988). *The sources of innovation*. New York: Oxford University Press.

von Hippel, E. (1994). Sticky information and the locus of problem solving: Implications for innovation. *Management Science, 40*(4), 429–439.

von Hippel, E., & Katz, R. (2002). Shifting innovation to users via toolkits. *Management Science, 48*(7), 821–833.

Wasko, M., & Faraj, S. (2005). Why should i share? Examining social capital and knowledge contribution in electronic networks of practice. *MIS Quarterly, 29*(1), 35–57.

Further Reading

For readers interested in the co-creation of innovation and value, we suggest the following work:

Bogers, M., Afuah, A., & Bastian, B. (2010b). Users-as-innovators: A review, critique, and future research directions. *Journal of Management, 36*, 857–875.

Dahlander, L., & Gann, D. M. (2010b). How open is innovation? *Research Policy, 39*, 699–709.

Gidhagen, M., Ridell-Persson, O., & Sörhammar, D. (2011). The orchestrating firm: Value creation in the video game industry. *Managing Service Quality, 21*, 392–409.

Normann, R., & Ramirez, R. (1993). *Designing interactive strategy: From value chain to value constellations* (pp. 65–77). Boston, MA: Harvard Business Review.

Vargo, S., & Lusch, R. (2008). "Service dominant logic: Continuing the evolution". *Journal of the Academy and Market Science, 36*, 1–10.

The Future of Open Innovation Technologies and Its Management

Mikael Wiberg and Jenny Eriksson Lundström

Departing from the book chapters presented, this final section provides an aggregated view of the concepts and phenomena presented in the book. We ponder on the future of Open Innovation and the needs in furthering the understanding of open innovation technologies and their management. What follows in this final section may be considered an intellectual exercise. We conclude the book with some final reflections on the nature of Open Innovation and ask: What is Open Innovation really about?

Open Innovation Today

The book addresses three main themes spanning over contributions all dealing with the challenges of adapting to the new innovation landscape, highlighting the sources of knowledge, issues of learning and new social media, especially in the inter-organisational context. More explicitly, the authors of the chapters deal with modularity as the essence of community building, the governance models and the incentives for participation, as well as issues of organisational and cultural change.

Several studies could be found in the literature that provide evidence to the importance and need for understanding open innovation. However, focus is mainly on success and less on important and systematic knowledge on the underpinnings of these endeavours. To move forward, a more comprehensive take on the practical turn is needed. The maturity of any discipline is largely depending on its ability to make explicit the boundaries to related fields and to define core concepts. This means a continuous endeavour of iteratively investigating the real-world occurrences of the concepts, exploring their use and employing them to the benefit of individuals, organisations and society at large. Maturing the understanding of the phenomenon, this allows for a theory of open innovation to emerge. As time evolves, the theory needs to be further developed. The means of this endeavour is the empirical study as the way to rediscover the meaning and use of concepts.

J.S.Z. Eriksson Lundström et al. (eds.), *Managing Open Innovation Technologies*,
DOI 10.1007/978-3-642-31650-0, © Springer-Verlag Berlin Heidelberg 2013

Hence, the imperative of empirical studies of the phenomenon cannot be underestimated. As they clearly matter, we now turn to matters of practice.

Practical Matters Matter

For any organisation, the alignment of the business objectives and the sustainable realisation of these are important. Open innovation is but one way of strategically addressing this realisation, called for by changes in demographics and technological advances. As any corporate strategy affects the entire organisation, it increasingly becomes important to identify the core competence of the organisation. Many examples on open innovation exploitation have been documented. Organisations draw on open APIs or semi-open business models using various strategies. Often the redefining of open innovation concepts is used instead of rethinking the corporate strategy in terms of needs and challenges. In this way, the degree of openness becomes an issue for constant business repositioning in accordance to an ever-changing global business arena.

One of the important technical imperatives of open innovation is the digital platform of the organisation and the platforming of it including digital maturity and information infrastructure. Equally important is to view the opportunities inherent in the already existing organisational structure. As an example, e-business flourished in organisations, which by building their businesses on flexible solutions, via a general readiness for changes in their field, were able to get first to market by simply taking their stock online. Rather than spending resources on rebuilding their inventory for the new business models, they were able to address valuable learning and first-mover advantages. The equivalent for open innovation could be the readiness of digital infrastructure and maturity of the organisation.

In this endeavour, we find that in the inter-organisational realm, as well as within the organisations at large, the units look coherent and homogeneous at first sight, but taking a second look, the various parts of the unit show their multifaceted structure and individuality. A challenge lies in identifying the boundaries of these units and leveraging these for the future to come. Innovation happens at the interfaces, in the collisions and through dialogue and the negotiations of ideas. Posting good examples provides the starting point for new improved innovations. Hence, it becomes crucial to identify and to break down boundaries posing barriers for a seamless integration of the platforms. In this undertaking, dialogue is the key to accommodate mind-set. Often future innovations are to be found in the needs created by the previous version of practice. In the global connect, meeting those needs just in time has never been as important as it is now.

To reap the benefits requires doing and fostering innovation. It means taking an active stance and leaping into the unknown, across boundaries, into the future. This leap does not, however, have to be undertaken in isolation. Drawing on best practice is to optimise the chance for success. Condensing practice in a comprehensive manner—that is what theorising is all about.

Researching Future Research

As any emerging paradigm, open innovation as a field of research deals with the lack of explicit theoretical constructs for describing, explaining and predicting how open innovation initiatives are to change the preconditions of innovation. Theory provides tools of contemplation or analysis for understanding, explaining and making predictions on a particular phenomenon. Even though the origin of the theory is empirical evidence, a theory is condensed by means of a well-understood method that could be repeated by others. Empirical data is also the ultimate test for theoretical reasoning, making the theory well grounded. Hence, using a well-grounded theory enables us to capture open innovation as it unfolds in practice, study and test the particulars that we find in the empirical data and ultimately add new or improved descriptions, explanations and models for predictions of outcomes to the existing body of knowledge.

While theorising open innovation, we also need to develop and refine the methods that we use for data collection and analysis. The large-scale platforms mean seeing the light of large collections of data. Improving the ways of making such "big data" readily available for analysis, thus becomes a key issue for open innovation.

Any good theory builds on clear definitions. There is an importance in clarifying relevant concepts and in finding better ways of talking about them, the interrelations and the boundaries among them. In many cases, the granularity of concepts is important for the in-depth understanding of complex phenomena. This includes the concept of open innovation itself. While openness seems the lingua franca of innovation, opening up cannot mean selling out. Opening up may also mean the loss of the original context of the data, allowing for misinterpretation or misuse. Naturally, this creates a need for new means of protection and hence, new boundaries.

At the End of the Beginning

Regardless of whether resources are coming from academia or industry, to further invest in open innovation, research is in dire need of well-grounded theories of open innovation. Still, to get to a maturity of any field, experience is required. Taking the field further, leveraging from the end of the beginning, issues of rigor in research and methods and relevance of questions posed become highlighted. A framework, setting the research agenda for the theorising of open innovation, places due focus on these research questions from each of the perspectives of the individual, the organisation and society at large.

For the open innovation research agenda, there are many questions to explore: Does openness really entail boundaries, and if so, does it mean that openness is a transitory process? Does one open innovation model fit all? What are the necessary prerequisites of open innovation in terms of technology, organisational or societal structures?

Although several of these questions remain to be answered, it is imperative to theorise what is already known. The reason for this is that important lessons are not only made in the end of a journey, they are continuously collected over time. Also these findings are essential, as writing what we currently know, is the first step in finding out what there is to know.

Postludium

To edit a book on open innovation is nothing short of attempting first hand to manage the phenomenon itself. In more than one sense, it is an example of opening up to external peers and their understanding of the phenomenon, this with a clear goal, during which, we as editors repeatedly asking ourselves if we have rightfully managed to address the most relevant issues, best practices and challenges of this phenomenon.

Unlike many other books though, a book on open innovation does not have a definite ending. While most books have a closing statement, we should on the contrary open up for continuous dialogue. Giving this direction, this final statement is about pointing at certain aspects rather than arriving at a set of conclusions. At the heart of open innovation lies a process-focus and a focus on democratising innovation. So, instead of concluding a discussion, one of the most important aims with this book has been to demonstrate a few basic objectives through a collection of chapters each adding to our understanding of this phenomenon.

The book's objectives were to advance and disseminate research on systematic practical open innovation and make the research results available to practitioners. Hence, the goal was none other than to communicate the essence of open innovation to the intended target audience. We had to bring forth results meeting the standards of the international academic community, while at the same time clearly communicate the outcome to industry community partners and civil society. Usually this involves issues such as: What is new, what is true, what is relevant and what lies ahead for organisations pursuing open innovation technologies?

We started out with a view of open innovation as communication, providing decentralisation of power, providing empowerment of employees, users and customers. Highlighting the need for practicing openness in order to fully employ open innovation, we have researched motivations, maturity and methods of employing open innovation in organisations. However, no matter which question we choose to address, we should make sure to always return to the fundamental question: What is really the essence of open innovation? In an attempt to fuel this debate, why not make a pastiche of the manuscript of the Pirates of the Caribbean fame. And through this manoeuvre we argue:

J.S.Z. Eriksson Lundström et al. (eds.), *Managing Open Innovation Technologies*,
DOI 10.1007/978-3-642-31650-0, © Springer-Verlag Berlin Heidelberg 2013

-*"This is the blessing and the curse of open innovation. Wherever we want to take openness of innovation, we are able to take it. And the reason for this is that what open innovation is, you know. It's not just the methods, processes or actors involved, neither the passion for innovation or strive for the greater good; that is what open innovation needs. Not what open innovation is. What open innovation really is about, is dialogue."*

- Your call. . .

List of Contributors

Editorial Board

Jenny Eriksson Lundström is Senior Researcher at NITA- the Swedish IT-User Centre and an Associate Senior Lecturer of Information Systems at Uppsala University Department of Informatics and Media, Sweden. She received her Ph.D. in Computer Science in Intersection with Social Science at 2009. In the field of Information Systems, she has been researching issues concerning the domains of information technology, knowledge and management with a particular interest in IT and innovation viewed from a multi-level perspective.

Mats Edenius is a Professor of Information Systems at Uppsala University Department of Informatics and Media, Sweden. He holds a Ph.D. in Business Administration. His research interests lie within the areas of information technology, knowledge and management.

Stefan Hrastinski is Associate Professor in Media Technology at KTH Royal Institute of Technology, Sweden. He is also affiliated with The Swedish IT-User Centre and the Department of Informatics and Media at Uppsala University. His main research interests are online learning, collaboration and innovation in organisational and educational settings.

Mikael Wiberg, Ph.D. is Full Professor at the Department of Informatics and Media at Uppsala University in Sweden where he holds the chair in HCI— Human Computer Interaction. Prior to this position Wiberg has held a position as Research Director for Umeå Institute of Design, Umeå University. Wiberg has published his research in a number of international journals and books (including the book "The Interaction Society", and the newly released book "Interactive Textures for Architecture and Landscaping: Digital elements and technologies"). Wiberg has served as chair, reviewer, organiser, associate editor and session chair for a number of international conferences. Currently, Wiberg is also working as an associate editor for *ISJ—Information Systems Journal, PUC—Personal and*

Ubiquitous Computing journal, Springer Verlag and as associate editor for *International Journal of Mobile HCI*.

Pär J. Ågerfalk is Full Professor at Uppsala University where he holds the Chair in Computer Science in Intersection with Social Sciences. He received his Ph.D. from Linköping University and has held fulltime positions at Örebro University, Lero— The Irish Software Engineering Research Centre, Jönköping International Business School, and University of Limerick. His work has appeared in a number of leading journals in the software and information systems area, including *MIS Quarterly, Information Systems Research, Communications of the ACM* and *Information and Software Technology*. He is currently the Dean of the Swedish Research School on Management and IT, a Senior Associate Editor with the *European Journal of Information Systems*, a Co-Editor of *the Scandinavian Journal of Information Systems* and the founding Chair of the AIS Special Interest Group on Pragmatist Information Systems Research.

Contributing Authors

Mark Aakhus is Associate Professor in the School of Communication and Information at Rutgers University. He earned his Ph.D. from the University of Arizona in Communication with an emphasis in Management Information Systems and an MA from the Edward R. Murrow School of Communication at Washington State University. He investigates the role of communication in managing complex situations through close examination of language, argument and social interaction in professional practice, organisational processes and information systems.

Per Andersson is Professor at the Department for Marketing and Strategy at Stockholm School of Economics. Since 2003 he is also Director of the Center for Information and Communications Research (CIC) at the Economic Research Institute. He has performed research in the field of ICT and mobile communications and services since 1993.

Birgitta Bergvall-Kåreborn is Professor in Social Informatics at Luleå University of Technology, where she also earned her Ph.D. Her current research interests concern participatory design in distributed and open environments; with a particular interest in social media and toolboxes for design and innovation. She has contributed to the field of participatory design with more than 30 conference- and journal publications, has served as a referee in a number of academic conferences and journals and is also a member of the editorial board for the international journal *Information and Management*.

Ivo Blohm is a full-time researcher at the Chair for Information Systems, Technische Universität München, Germany, since he graduated from there and the University of Verona, Italy, in Technology-oriented Business Administration in 2009 (majoring in information systems, marketing and electrical engineering).

List of Contributors 283

His research interests include virtual communities, open innovation and adoption of information systems. He runs the research project GENIE, a project which supports customer-driven development of innovations for software companies, funded by the German Federal Ministry of Research and Education.

Sven Carlsson is Professor of Informatics at Lund University School of Economics and Management. His current research interests include the use of IS to support management processes, knowledge management, enterprise systems and the use of social media in business processes. He has published more than 125 peer-reviewed papers and his work has appeared in journals such as *Journal of Management Information Systems, Decision Sciences, Information Systems Journal, Information & Management* and *Knowledge Management Research & Practice*. Sven has been a visiting scholar/professor at University of Arizona, Tucson, National University of Singapore, University College Cork, USC, Los Angeles, Monash University, Melbourne and Università della Calabria, Rende. He is a regional editor for *Knowledge Management Research & Practice*.

Vincenzo Corvello, Ph.D. is a researcher at the Department of Business Science, University of Calabria. His research interests are in the fields of innovation processes organisation and management; innovation in networks of SMEs; organisational design and inter-organisational information systems. He has published papers in international and Italian journals and chapters in international books such as *International Journal of Production Economics*; *Journal of Organizational Design and Engineering, European Journal of Innovation Management, Journal of Systemic, Cybernetics and Informatics*; *Lecture notes in informatics*; *Sistemi e Impresa*. He is a member of the Editorial Board of the *International Journal of Organizational Design and Engineering*.

Gabriel J. Costello is a Lecturer in Engineering at the Galway-Mayo Institute of Technology (http://www.gmit.ie). Prior to this he worked for 20 years in the telecommunications industry where he held engineering, new product introduction and product line management positions. He completed a Ph.D. in Management Information Systems at the J.E. Cairnes School of Business & Economics, National University of Ireland, Galway in the area of information systems innovation. His publications include: *Journal of Information Technology, International Conference on Information Systems (ICIS), International Federation for Information Processing (IFIP), European Conference on Information Systems (ECIS) and European Academy of Management Conference (EURAM)*.

Aldo de Moor is owner of the Community Sense research consultancy company, founded in 2007. He earned his Ph.D. in Information Management from Tilburg University in the Netherlands in 1999. From 1999 to 2004, he worked as an assistant professor at the Department of Information Systems and Management at Tilburg University. From 2005 to 2006, he was a senior researcher at the Semantics Technology and Applications Research Laboratory (STARLab) of the Vrije Universiteit Brussel in Belgium.

David Delon is a system and network engineer specialised in open source software and project management. He is also a trainer in implementing and using Internet-based tools in collaborative projects and trainer in human network animation methodologies. He works at Outils-Reseaux and is personally committed in ONEM, Obsevatoire Naturaliste as he serves as the president of this organisation.

Jessica Deschamps is an infographist and communications specialist. She works half time for Outils-Réseaux and half time as a freelance graphist. She designs logotypes and graphic standards for Outils-Réseaux's partners.

Brian Donnellan holds the Chair of Information Systems Innovation at the National University of Ireland, Maynooth (http://www.nuim.ie) and is Academic Director of the Innovation Value Institute (http://www.ivi.ie). IVI, through its Open Innovation approach, facilitates a collaborative community of like-minded peers committed to investigating, advancing and disseminating the frameworks, tools and best practices associated with managing Innovation. Prior to joining the IVI he was a lecturer in the BIS Group in the Cairnes Graduate School of Business and Law, NUI Galway. He has spent over 20 years working in industry, most recently as Section Manager in Analog Devices Inc. (Boston, USA), responsible for Computer-Aided-Design and Knowledge Management Systems for New Product Development. He has published over 60 peer reviewed conference and journal papers.

Jan Fischer is founder and head of innosabi. He graduated from Mechanical Engineering at Technische Universität München in 2010. During his study and while working at innosabi he focused on integrating customers into product development processes. At the early stage of innosabi, he and his co-founders coined the concept of Pico-Jobs in order to interact with thousands of people all over the world. The solution information of all participants were condensed and aggregated to solve problems in product development processes.

Jens Fähling is a full-time researcher at the Chair for Information Systems, Technische Universität München, Germany, since he graduated from there in Information Systems in 2008. His research interests include collaboration engineering, customer integration and open innovation. He runs a research sub-project part of the collaborative research centre "Sonderforschungsbereich 768—Managing cycles in innovation processes—Integrated development of product-service-systems based on technical products", funded by the German Research Foundation (Deutsche Forschungsgemeinschaft—DFG).

Matt Germonprez is the Mutual of Omaha associate professor at the University of Nebraska at Omaha. Prior to joining UN-Omaha, he was a faculty member at the University of Wisconsin-Eau Claire, Case Western Reserve University and a Ph.D. student at the University of Colorado-Boulder. His research focuses on theory and method development with particular focus on emerging and tailorable technologies. His work has been funded by the National Science Foundation and accepted in *MIS Quarterly, The Journal of the Association for Information Systems, Information Systems Journal, Information and Organisation* and the *Journal of Information Technology.*

List of Contributors

Davide Salvatore Gitto is a Ph.D. student at the Department of Business Administration, University of Calabria. He graduated with honours in Management Engineering at University of Calabria in 2008. His research interests focus on intellectual capital flows across firms, networks of SMEs and information systems supporting organisations. He is presently involved in an international research project aimed at promoting the development of clusters of SMEs based on intellectual capital and innovation.

Lorna Heaton is Associate Professor in the Department of Communication at the Université de Montréal, Codirector of LUDTIC (Laboratory for uses and design of information and communication technologies) and member of the Centre interuniversitaire de recherche sur la science et la technologie (CIRST). Her research focuses on collaborative work, community innovation and the relationships between the design and use of communication technologies, particularly in Web 2.0 environments.

Tuija Heikura is a researcher at the Aalto University School of Economics in the Center of Knowledge and Innovation Research, while pursuing doctoral studies at the Lappeenranta University of Technology, School of Innovation. Her main research interest is management models for facilitating multi-stakeholder, systemic innovation endeavours.

Matthias Hürlimann obtained his Master's degree in Strategic IT Management from Stockholm University School of Business in summer 2011. Currently, he is working in Switzerland as an expert in software development.

Pierre Jarméus has a bachelor's and a master's degree in business and economics from the Stockholm School of Economics in Sweden. He has also participated in the IMBA program at Tsinghua University in China. He is now a management consultant at Accenture working as an analyst focusing on talent and organisational performance.

Karlheinz Kautz, Dr. Philos is Professor in Systems Development at Department of Operations Management at the Copenhagen Business School, Denmark. His research interests are in information systems development, the diffusion and adoption of information technology innovations, the organisational impact of IT and process improvement. He has published his research in European Journal of IS, the Information Systems Journal, Information, Technology & People, the Scandinavian Journal of Information Systems, Software Process: Improvement and Practice, IEEE Software, Journal of Knowledge Management, the Journal of Information Systems, the Journal of Informing Science, the Journal of Information Technology Cases and Applications, Information and Software Technology and the Journal of Information Technology Theory and Application.

Christina Keller is an Assistant Professor and researcher at Jönköping International Business School and Department of Informatics and Media, Uppsala University, Sweden. Keller holds a Ph.D. in Information Systems and her research interests include information technology innovations in healthcare, online learning and design science research.

Helmut Krcmar, Prof. Dr. is Full Professor of Information Systems and holds the Chair for Information Systems at the Department of Informatics, Technische Universität München (TUM), Germany since 2002. He worked as Postdoctoral Fellow at the IBM Los Angeles Scientific Center, as assistant professor of Information Systems at the Leonard Stern School of Business, NYU and at Baruch College, CUNY. From 1987 to 2002, he held the Chair for Information Systems, Hohenheim University, Stuttgart. Krcmar is founder of Informations- und Technologie-Management Beratungsgesellschaft (ITM) and copartner of several spin-offs. His research interests include Information and Knowledge Management, IT-enabled Value Webs, Service Management, Computer Supported Cooperative Work and Information Systems in Health Care and eGovernment.

Jan Marco Leimeister, Prof. Dr. is a Full Professor of Information Systems and holds the Chair for Information Systems at Kassel University, Germany. He is affiliated to the Business School and the Computer Science Department and is Director of the IS Research Centre ITeG at Kassel University. Jan Marco heads research groups on service, collaboration and IT innovation engineering and manages several large publicly funded and industry funded research projects. His teaching and research areas include IT innovation management, service science, ubiquitous and mobile computing, collaboration engineering and strategic IT management.

Staffan Lindblad holds a M.D. and a Ph.D. in Rheumatology and works as an associate professor at Medical Management Centre, Karolinska Institutet and at Karolinska University Hospital, Sweden. His research interests include quality improvement in rheumatology care.

Juho Lindman is Assistant Professor in the Hanken School of Economics in Helsinki, Finland. Lindman defended his doctoral dissertation focusing on open source software development organisation in the Aalto University School of Economics in Helsinki. In the field of information systems, his current research is focused in the areas of open source software development, open data, open access and organisational change.

Björn Lundell, Ph.D., has been a staff member at the University of Skövde since 1984, and he is a researcher at the University of Skövde's Informatics Research Centre. In a number of projects, he has been researching a variety of issues concerning Open Standards, the Open Source phenomena and other aspects related to the openness movement. He is a founding member of the IFIP Working Group 2.13 on Open Source Software; a founding fellow of the Open Forum Academy (an independent "think-tank" of internationally recognised experts in the area of openness established by Open Forum Europe) and the founding chair of Open Source Sweden, an industry association established by Swedish Open Source companies. He is the program co-chair for the Eighth International Conference on Open Source

List of Contributors 287

Systems (OSS 2012) and was the organiser of the Fifth International Conference of Open Source Systems (OSS 2009), which was held in Skövde, Sweden.

Laurent Marseault is a group leader, trainer and consultant. After brief job experiences in multinational corporations, he became a conscientious objector at "les Ecologistes de l'Euzière" for 15 years where he acquired knowledge on training and network animation, which helped give rise to Outils-Réseaux. Laurent Marseault has specialised in leading cooperative groups.

Pentti Marttiin is a manager at Nokia Siemens Networks and a docent at the Aalto University School of Economics. He has been working in industry with global software engineering environments over 10 years. Marttiin has a Ph.D. in Information Systems from the University of Jyväskylä. He teaches project management and his research interests include OSS practices and tools, collaboration models and domain-specific modelling and metaCASE.

Simone Masog has a bachelor's degree in management and economics from Otto-von-Guericke University Magdeburg in Germany and a master's degree in business and economics from the Stockholm School of Economics in Sweden.

Piero Migliarese is Professor of Innovative Organizational Systems at the Engineering Faculty of University of Calabria. His research activity is devoted to the following areas: business organisation and organisational models; intellectual capital; information and organisational system; knowledge management, networks of SMEs. He is author of more than 100 reviewed journal articles, book chapters and conference papers. He has published papers in the following journals: *Decision Support Systems, Human Relations, Interface, European Journal of Information Systems, International Journal of Production Economics, International Journal of Organizational Design and Engineering, Human Studi Organizzativi, Sviluppo e Organizzazione, Economia e Politica Industriale*. He is Associate Editor for the *International Journal of Organizational Design and Engineering*.

Florence Millerand is an associate professor in the Department of Social and Public Communication at the Université du Québec à Montréal. She is co-director of the Lab CMO (computer mediated communication) and member of the Centre interuniversitaire de recherche sur la science et la technologie (CIRST). Her recherche is at the intersection of communication studies and science and technology studies. She examines the sociotechnical dimensions of technological innovation, particularly collaborative information infrastructures in scientific communities.

Sameen M. Rab holds an MSc in Computer Science and Business Administration from the Copenhagen Business School, Denmark. She is employed as an Advanced Business Consultant at NNIT (Management Consulting) in Denmark.

Oscar Persson Ridell is a Ph.D. candidate and lecturer at Uppsala University, and a member of the Swedish national research school of management and IT (MIT). His dissertation work revolves around exploring the nature of the active customer, consumer and user, with the aim to gain insight into the possibilities and intricacies entailed in collaborating with these active counterparts for organisations. His latest peer-reviewed publication is in Managing Service Quality (MSQ).

Mikko Riepula is a researcher in Information Systems and a project manager at Aalto University School of Economics, Helsinki, Finland. His interests include customer-driven development in both software services and product companies, as well as OSS in particular. Before re-engaging in academic work, Riepula worked internationally in the ICT industry for more than 10 years for companies such as Nokia, Accenture and then as a software entrepreneur.

Christopher Rosenqvist is an affiliated Associate Professor at the Department for Marketing and Strategy at Stockholm School of Economics and at the Center for Information and Communications Research (CIC) at the Economic Research Institute. He has performed research in the field of ICT and mobile communications and services since 2003.

Matti Rossi is Professor of Information Systems at Helsinki School of Economics. He has worked as research fellow at Erasmus University Rotterdam, visiting assistant professor at Georgia State University, Atlanta and visiting professor at Claremont Graduate University. He received his Ph.D. degree in Business Administration from the University of Jyväskylä in 1998. He has been the principal investigator in several major research projects funded by the technological development centre of Finland and Academy of Finland. His research papers have appeared in journals such as CACM, Journal of AIS, Information and Management and Information Systems and over 30 of them have appeared in conferences such as ICIS, HICSS and CAiSE.

Jimmie G. Röndell is a Ph.D. candidate and lecturer in Business Studies at the Department of Business Studies, Uppsala University, Sweden. He is a member of the Swedish national research school of Management and IT (MIT). His doctoral thesis work revolves around the issue of how various activities of consumers as "active counterparts" in an IT enabled exchange environment has affected the nature of marketing as a value creating process. He has published several articles in international peer-reviewed marketing journals.

Florian Schmitt is a Web developer and Web designer. He is a developer of cooperative open source software and collaborative applications like yeswiki. His speciality is graphical integration and javascript user interactions. He is also a trainer on web tools and technical subjects.

Michael Sinnet holds an MSc in Computer Science Administration from the Copenhagen Business School, Denmark. He is employed as Chief Project Manager at Danske Capital, a supplier of IT solutions for the financial sector in Denmark.

Anna Ståhlbröst is Assistant Lecturer in Social Informatics at Luleå University of Technology. Ståhlbröst's research is focused on approaches for user-driven innovation in open and distributed processes, i.e. a Living Lab approach. Ståhlbröst has participated in several international and national innovation and research projects and her work has been published in several scientific journals, conferences as well as in books. Her research has contributed to the creation and development of the Botnia Living Lab milieu as well as its methodology for user-driven innovation. She has also been an active part of the establishment of Living Lab networks on a European (EnoLL), Nordic (EnoLL North) and national level (OLLSE).

Carl Sundberg has a bachelor's degree in applied business management from the Imperial College London in England and has a master's degree in business and economics from the Stockholm School of Economics in Sweden. He has also participated in the IMBA program at Tsinghua University in China.

David Sörhammar is Ph.D. and assistant professor at Uppsala University. He is a member of the Swedish national research school of management and IT (MIT). His main research interests revolve around the issues of IT, consumers and value creation. He has published several articles in international peer-reviewed marketing journals and has participated and presented papers at numerous international conferences.

Petra Turkama has international experience in technology and innovation management both in the corporate sector (Nokia 1998–2009) and academia (Nanyang University of technology, Helsinki School of Economics 2006–2009). Currently, she is heading a research team focusing on systemic innovation through human-centric, demand- and user-driven open innovation ecosystems. Her main research interest is Information Technology Management, Systemic Innovation and Knowledge Networks.

Frank van der Linden works at Philips Healthcare CTO Office. He received his Ph.D. in Mathematics in 1984 at the University of Amsterdam. His main interest is software engineering, emphasising software product line engineering. He was involved in Esprit-projects (FP1, FP2 and FP4) and project leader of the three successive ITEA projects on product line engineering: (ESAPS, CAFÉ, FAMILIES—1999–2005). Successive projects were on distributed development, including open source development (COSI 2005–2008) and on medical image processing. He was member of the organizing committee of a series of workshops on conferences in product lines (PFE & SPLC) and several workshops on open source and product lines. He is editor of several proceedings of these workshops and conferences. He is co-author of several books on Software product lines.

Brian Warner is the operations manager at The Linux Foundation for Tizen project. He assists companies as they create and participate in open source projects hosted by The Linux Foundation and has written multiple papers on the corporate open source development model. Prior to joining the Linux Foundation, Warner worked for IBM on the Linux Strategy team. Warner has an MBA and Masters of Science in MIS from Case Western Reserve University.

Ali Yaklef is professor of business administration at Stockholm University School of Business. His main research areas include organisational knowledge, learning, innovation and the relationship between organisation and information technology.

Scientific Reviewers

Daniel Rudmark Borås Högskola/Viktoria Institute
Matti Kaulio KTH Royal Institute of Technology
Ahmad Ghazawneh Jönköping International Business School
Kieran Conboy, NUI Galway, Ireland
Helena Holmström, IT University of Gothenburg, Sweden
Jonny Holmström, Umeå University, Sweden
Michael Lane, University of Limerick, Ireland
Henrik Agndal, Stockholm School of Economics
Sara Melén Hånell, Stockholm School of Economics

Proof Readers and Typesetters

Carol-Ann Soames, Jönköping
Madelen Hermelin Leidefors, Uppsala

Index

A

Absorption, 253
Absorptive capacity, 180–187, 193, 196
Action research, 38–40, 250
Active pedagogy, 96, 101
AGFA healthcare, 11
Agile programming, 96
Amazon's Mechanical Turk (mturk), 200, 201, 203–205, 209
AnimaCoop, 94, 101–105

B

BDN. *See* Benefits dependency network (BDN)
Benefits dependency network (BDN), 126
Best practice, xi, xiii–xvi, 91–92, 130, 276, 279
BLL. *See* Botnia living lab (BLL)
Bloggers, 267
Blogs, 23, 27, 29, 147, 167, 183, 190, 192, 194, 216–217, 221–223, 225, 226, 232, 263, 265, 267
Botnia living lab (BLL), 135–138, 140, 141, 289
Boundary objects, 259, 265
creative brief, 265
Brainstorm, xiv, 21, 99, 209, 224, 260

C

Changed user requirements, v
Chesbrough, xiii, 6, 18, 19, 27, 39, 40, 53–54, 69–71, 80, 94, 123–125, 133, 134, 148, 163, 167, 180, 201, 216, 219, 240, 243, 245, 246, 248, 253

Citizen science sites, 98
Closed innovation, 18, 69–71, 123–124, 180, 200, 201, 216, 240, 241, 243, 245, 247, 249, 258, 272
Closed source, 10, 110
Co-creation, 134, 155–156, 158, 159, 254–255
places for innovation, 255
value, 134, 255
Co-design in health care, 242–244
Collaboration, xiii, xvi, 2–15, 17, 18, 20, 22–24, 26–29, 31, 36, 74, 77, 79, 87, 91–98, 100–105, 115, 120, 125, 130, 154, 156, 157, 167, 175–177, 183, 184, 186, 187, 189–192, 202, 217, 218, 220, 222, 226, 229, 231, 232, 240, 244, 247
boundaries, 4, 17, 31, 93, 125, 176
Collaboration tools, 31, 184, 189, 190
source code portal, 115
Collaborative, xiii, xvi, 2, 3, 17, 36, 74, 94, 115, 125, 154, 167, 183, 202, 217, 240
communities, xiii, 5, 6, 10, 11, 15, 17, 20, 22, 24, 27–29, 31, 91, 98, 100–104, 130, 186, 187, 190, 202, 217, 222
creation, xiii, 11, 17, 18, 23, 24, 26, 31, 77, 125, 167, 183, 190, 218, 222, 226, 231, 244
development, 3–5, 7–11, 15, 27, 29, 31, 36, 77, 91, 92, 94, 103–105, 115, 120, 125, 130, 157, 167, 176, 177, 186, 189, 191, 202, 222, 226, 229, 232, 240, 244
innovation, xvi, 2, 4, 9, 10, 15, 17, 18, 27, 31, 36, 91, 92, 94, 96, 98, 102–105, 124–125, 130, 154, 157, 167, 175–177, 186, 189, 190, 202, 218, 220, 244, 247
nature, xvi, 104, 105, 287–288

J.S.Z. Eriksson Lundström et al. (eds.), *Managing Open Innovation Technologies*,
DOI 10.1007/978-3-642-31650-0, © Springer-Verlag Berlin Heidelberg 2013

Index

Collaborative (*cont.*)
  networks, 7, 17, 18, 20, 27, 31, 87, 92, 96,
    100–101, 115, 154, 167, 189–191,
    202, 284
  tools, 11, 18, 20, 23, 24, 27, 31, 91, 94–97,
    100–105, 116, 156, 167, 184, 189, 190,
    222, 226, 229, 244
Collective
  intelligence, 105, 124, 200, 208
  memory, 99
Commercialisation stage, 256, 264, 265,
    267–268
Commodification, 1, 4, 7–10, 12, 15, 113
Commoditised software systems, 7, 9, 10
Communication, xiii, 10, 13, 18, 20–23, 25, 27,
    28, 30, 31, 46, 47, 55, 59, 60, 64, 70,
    72–73, 77, 79, 91, 104, 108–115, 117,
    120, 141, 142, 154–156, 160, 163,
    165–166, 171, 175, 182–184, 186–188,
    190–192, 194, 195, 216, 217, 219, 223,
    233–235, 257, 259, 260, 263–266, 268,
    270, 279
  intermediary, 186, 259
  tools, 109–110, 117, 156, 184, 188, 191
  users, xiii, 13, 104, 112, 141, 155, 156, 160,
    163, 188, 191, 192, 216, 217, 223, 234,
    235, 279
Communicative workflow loop, 23, 31
Communities, 5, 17–31, 35–51, 56, 81, 93–105,
    124, 134, 156, 170, 180, 202, 217,
    239–250, 254
  building, 18, 22, 24, 27, 29, 36, 48, 50, 82,
    87, 94, 100, 103, 148, 187, 192, 202,
    224, 225, 275
  expert, xiii, 30, 103, 123–124, 146, 180,
    186–193, 243
  innovation, v, xi, xiii, xv, 1, 6, 10, 17–31,
    35–51, 87, 91–105, 108, 124, 127, 130,
    134–139, 141–142, 148, 156, 180, 181,
    185–187, 189, 190, 193, 202, 217,
    224–225, 239–250, 254, 255,
    275, 279
  manager, 21, 24, 28, 31, 40, 148, 182, 192,
    194, 255
  non commercial, 110
  organisations, v, xiii, 1, 6, 10, 17–21, 23,
    31, 35–51, 92, 100, 105, 108–111,
    123–124, 127, 130, 134, 136, 156,
    185–187, 189, 225, 240, 246, 248, 254,
    255, 275, 279
  sustainability, 15, 21, 28, 105
  user, v, xiii, 6, 11, 13, 30, 37, 50, 91, 95–96,
    102–105, 108, 134–137, 140, 148, 188,

    191–193, 202, 217, 222, 223, 225, 240,
    249–250, 254, 255
Computer mediated toolkit, 255
Confidentiality, 190, 194, 222, 223, 225,
    229, 231
Construction industry, 165–167, 169, 172,
    175, 176
Consumer insights, 221, 231
Contemporary best practices, xiii–xvi, 91
Conversation context, 19, 22, 23, 31
Conversation practices, 22–24, 29
  tool mediated, 23
Conversation purposes, 24
Conversations, 1, 2, 17–31, 57, 157, 221, 231,
    233, 249, 260
Cooperation, 10, 35–36, 68–70, 72, 73, 76, 77,
    79–81, 84–87, 96, 97, 99–102, 134, 154,
    167, 184, 205, 219
  informal agreements, 76, 85
Cooperative ecosystem, 10
Coopetition, 69, 73, 81
Corporate strategy, 276
Corporate work flow facilitation, 156–157
Creative methods, 226
Creativity, xiii, xiv, xv, 6, 17, 35, 57, 67–68,
    102, 108, 125, 133, 151–161, 167, 179,
    200, 218, 240, 253
Crowdsourcing, 134, 163, 199–213, 218
  approval rate, 204
  Crowd Creation, 206–209, 211
  Crowd Voting, 206–209, 211
  Crowd Wisdom, 200, 206–209, 211
  qualifications, 204–205, 209
Crowdsourcing market places, 200–204,
    206, 213
  market based, 204, 205
  service based, 204, 205
Customer
  integration, 54, 134, 189, 191, 200, 202,
    207, 209, 212, 217, 218, 226, 235
  interaction, xiv, 135, 148, 163, 170, 180,
    182, 184–192, 202, 208, 209, 217–219,
    223, 224, 226–228, 230–232, 234, 235
  involvement, 2, 76, 86, 148, 167, 180, 189,
    190, 192, 215–217, 222, 226–228, 259
  work-groups, 227
Customer acceptance system, 223
Customer feedback, 2, 54, 56–61, 86, 148, 202,
    206, 208, 211, 218, 226–232, 234
Customer ideas
  elicitation, 54, 58
Customer insight
  lack of, 231

Index

Customisation, 2, 29–31, 46, 60, 68, 70–72, 74, 79–87, 94, 97, 103, 114, 134, 187, 218, 222, 226, 232

D

Decision-making, 7, 21, 30, 61, 91, 92, 109, 112, 113, 117, 119, 120, 173, 177, 186, 208
Demand-driven innovation, 176
Democratising innovation, 124, 146–148, 279
Design, 1, 7, 17–31, 36, 37, 40, 43, 47, 49, 57, 70, 79, 94, 96, 100, 102–105, 112, 117, 123–126, 148, 154, 156, 158, 159, 175, 180, 181, 188–191, 193–195, 206–208, 213, 217–223, 225–226, 229, 232–234, 242–244, 255, 257, 260, 263, 266, 269
Development costs sharing, 14, 115, 117
Development models. *See* Development practices
Development practices, 4, 7, 8, 15, 91, 108, 118–120
  inner source, 118
  open source, 4, 8, 15, 91
Development process, 7, 54, 109, 110, 117, 134–136, 147, 176, 189, 209, 216, 218, 222, 224, 229, 259
Dialogue, 58–59, 61, 157, 177, 187, 228, 231, 262, 263, 267, 268, 276, 279, 280
Diary, 226
  mobile phone apps, 226
Digital channels, 223
  Facebook, 223
  Twitter, 223
  YouTube, 223
Digital communication platforms, 266
Digital infrastructure, 276
Digital maturity, 276
Digital natives, 151
Digital platform, xvi, 266, 276
Document management systems, 183, 194
Dominant logics, 181, 182, 186–187, 192, 193, 195

E

Ecologistes de l'Euzière, 99
Economic impact, 125–126
E-learning 2.0, 152, 153, 157–161
  benefits, 152–153, 157–158, 160
E-learning 2.0 platform construction, 153, 158
Electronic platforms, 187
Email contact, 57
Empowered user

  patient, 242, 246
Empowerment, 94, 103, 105, 155, 234–235, 242–246, 279
Enterprise 2.0 business models, 18
Entrepreneurial institutionalism, 110–112, 166–168

F

Facebook, 23, 27, 141, 148, 191, 216–217, 221, 223, 228, 230, 232, 256, 263, 265–268
Face-to-face meetings, 30, 183, 221, 224, 228
Field trials, 229
Firm-constructed design limit, 254
Focus groups, 152, 244, 256, 260–261
FOSS, FLOSS, 5
Free software, 4–5, 37, 190
Free software foundation (FSF), 4–5
Frequently asked questions (FAQs), 101, 190, 194, 227
FSF. *See* Free software foundation (FSF)

G

General public licence (GPL), 11, 41–43, 45, 48, 49
GForge, 116
Globalisation, v, 2, 13, 18, 54, 68, 74, 75, 84, 109, 119, 125, 156, 221, 224–227, 230–232, 276, 287
GNU, 11
Governance models, 275
GPL. *See* General public licence (GPL)
Guides, 28, 56, 57, 74, 96, 151, 160, 169, 185, 202, 216, 219, 227, 243, 250, 256

H

Health care, 10–14, 57, 62, 113–114, 163, 174, 203, 240–250, 285–286
Health care service, 242, 243, 247–250
Health care service development, 240–242, 248
  evidence-based design, 242
  experience-based design, 242, 244
Heuristic maps, 99, 102
Hierarchical organisations, 110, 119–120, 167, 245
Hyper-text and hypermedia technologies, 183

I

IBM's Connect and Develop, 185
ICA, 253, 254, 256–271
ICA Banken, 256–257, 259–263, 265, 266

294   Index

ICA Student, 253, 254, 256–272
ICT. *See* Information and communication
        technology (ICT)
Ideas competitions, 136, 202, 211
Improved development practices, 108
Incremental innovation, 91, 103, 104, 163
Information and communication technology
        (ICT), 22, 54, 55, 102, 136, 165–167,
        216–219, 231–235
Information infrastructure, 276
Information systems, 20, 23, 27, 31, 55, 180,
        181, 183, 195, 217, 241, 245–248
Information technology (IT), xiv, 54, 62,
        67–88, 91–92, 115–116, 123–130, 139,
        140, 163, 179–196, 215–236, 259, 263,
        265, 267, 270
    barriers, 232, 246–247
    Capability Maturity Model (IT-CMF),
        91–92, 123–130
    industry, 2, 67–88, 127, 205
    innovation Capability-oriented view, 68,
        127–129
    innovation effectiveness, 126
    Innovation Management Critical
        Process, 128
    innovation resource-based view, 125, 126
    innovations, 54, 62, 67–88, 92, 123–130,
        140, 215–236
    investments-value, 125–126
    Management framework, 124
    in open innovation initiatives, 180
    process frameworks COBIT, ITIL,
        CMMI, 126
    systems, 54, 62, 227, 259, 263, 267, 272
    tools, 54, 215, 216, 220, 224, 226, 235
    tools and organisational learning, 53–64,
        111–112, 157
Infrastructural tools, 91, 104, 113
Infrastructure, xiv, 6, 92, 104, 116, 118, 156,
        183, 216, 217, 276
Innosabi, 201
Innovation, v, xiii, 1, 3, 17, 35, 53, 67, 91, 93,
        108, 123, 133, 151, 165, 179, 199, 215,
        239, 253, 275, 279
    brokers, 81, 92
    challenges, v, xiv–xvi, 19, 38, 47,
        123–124, 176
    commercialisation, 223, 226–227, 230,
        232–234, 254, 255, 257, 264–271
    communities, xiii, 1, 6, 17–31, 35–51,
        91–105, 124, 135, 138–139, 141–142,
        189, 202, 239–250, 255
    content generation, 256–264, 269–271

    managers, 40, 109, 128, 144–148, 220,
        269, 270
    manufacturing centric, 124
    missionaries, 243, 246, 248
    processes, xiii, xiv, 7, 31, 53–55, 58, 62,
        67–71, 73, 80, 81, 87, 92, 123–124,
        126–130, 133–148, 156, 157, 163–164,
        167, 176, 177, 179–196, 200–202,
        206–208, 212, 213, 215–220, 231–236,
        246, 254–257, 259, 262, 265, 269–272
    sharing, 17, 18, 37, 69, 70, 81, 82, 87,
        101, 255
    stages, 189, 202, 215–220, 232–234,
        246, 265
    user centric, 124, 148
    Value Institute, 91–92, 124, 126, 130
Innovation technology (IvT), 215–219,
        232–235
Innovators, 6, 70, 104, 125, 140, 147, 243, 246,
        253–254
Institutional changes, 108
    effects, 108
Institutional inertia
    in industry, 165–177
Institutional structures, 111
Institutional theory, 109–111
Intel, v, 92, 124, 129–130
Intellectual capital
    portfolio approach, 125
Intellectual property (IP), 6, 45, 48, 69, 134,
        182, 183, 190, 194, 211, 218, 219, 228,
        229, 231–233, 240, 243, 245–246
Intellectual property rights
    problems, 231–232
Interactive web technologies, 218
Intermediaries, v, 134–136, 142, 179–180,
        182–188, 192, 194, 200, 201, 205, 259
Intermediary communities, 134, 142
Internal maturity, 223
Internet, 96, 98, 104, 135, 137, 140–141, 158,
        187, 200–202, 206, 216–218, 221, 223,
        225, 229, 230, 234, 235, 240, 243,
        244, 246
Internet technology, xiv, 135
Inter-organisational networks, 2, 67–88,
        124, 166
Interviews, 39, 40, 44, 49, 54, 57–59, 74, 75,
        82, 96, 112, 113, 152, 168, 169, 201,
        220, 221, 224, 228, 229, 231, 245,
        249, 256
Intra-organisational software development, 91,
        107–120
    internal accounting, 118

Index

Invention, v, xiii, 91, 104, 119, 187
Involving contributors, 92, 143–145
IP. *See* Intellectual property (IP)
IS benefits management approach, 126
IT. *See* Information technology (IT)
ITEA-COSI, 113
IvT. *See* Innovation technology (IvT)

K

Karolinska University Hospital, Stockholm, Sweden, 245
KBs. *See* Knowledge brokers (KBs)
Knowledge, v, xiii, xiv, 2, 14, 17, 35, 53, 69, 94, 109, 124, 134, 151, 167, 179–196, 200, 216, 240–241, 253–272
  complementary, 134, 163, 183, 190, 194, 243, 249
  domain specific, 56, 79, 114, 181–183, 189–190, 194
Knowledge brokers (KBs), 186, 192, 194
  virtual, 186
Knowledge diffusion, 82, 190
Knowledge exchange
  strategies, 73, 163, 180, 183–187, 195
Knowledge processes, 2, 53–55, 82, 92, 134, 146, 151, 158, 176, 179–196, 216, 244, 254, 255, 259, 265, 271, 272
Knowledge protection, 182, 190
Knowledge sharing, 14, 17, 37, 38, 55, 56, 69, 70, 81, 82, 87–88, 94–95, 101, 104, 134, 182, 183, 185, 187, 189–190, 192, 194, 249, 255
Knowledge sharing forums, 70
Knowledge sources, 80–81, 163, 179–196, 253
  management, 183, 187–195
Knowledge transfer, 55, 95–96, 109–110, 125, 182–184, 186, 187, 190–191, 193, 194
Kundo, 2, 54, 56–62

L

Lack of control, 233–235
Language barrier, 230
Lead-user-method, 202
Lead users, 62, 63, 104, 134, 156, 179, 182, 184, 202
Learning
  by-doing, 202
  exploitative, 53–64
  explorative, 53–64, 248
  new methods, 154, 202

Legal
  regulations, 170, 172, 175, 176, 254, 266
  requirements, 166, 169, 170, 172, 176, 234, 235
Legislation limitations, 259
Leveraged development, 9, 38, 40–44, 48, 51, 108
Libre software, 5
Lifestyle website, 244
Linux, 1, 5, 6, 36–46, 48–51
Linux open-source community, 50
Long-term commitment, 40, 147

M

Management, 6, 31, 36, 59, 75, 92, 97, 113, 124, 160, 170, 182, 213, 220, 244, 254, 275
Managerial implication, 144–148
Managers, 6–7, 21, 24, 28, 29, 31, 40, 58, 74, 75, 77, 79, 85, 97, 98, 109, 112–113, 125, 128, 129, 145–148, 182, 192, 194–196, 220, 226, 227, 235, 254, 255, 262, 269–271
Managing ideas from customers, 2, 53, 54, 56, 57, 59, 202
Managing innovation, 2, 48, 62, 63, 91–92, 125–130, 137, 147, 148, 157, 179–196, 220, 247, 248, 253–257, 259, 261, 262, 269–272, 275–278
Managing open innovation processes, 137, 183–185
Managing open innovation technologies, 53–64, 275–278, v, xi, xiii–xvi
Managing participant, 271, 272
Managing user innovation, 104, 139, 163, 179–196, 215–220, 232–234, 240, 275–278
Mass collaboration, 18, 28, 31
Maturity, 91–92, 116, 123–130, 139, 223, 225, 232, 235, 254, 271, 275–277, 279, xiv
3M-Customer feedback resolution (CFR) system, 230
Metcalfe's law, 155
Microblogs, 155
Mobile app., 226, 263
Modularity, 83, 91, 93–105, 109, 275
Motivational factors, 13, 118, 136, 142, 148, 159
  extrinsic motivation, 136, 146, 191
  intrinsic motivation, 136, 191

Motivations, 1–2, 5, 10, 11, 13, 36, 38, 47–49, 92, 97, 100, 110, 118, 134–137, 141–148, 189, 190, 195, 202, 205, 211, 213, 236, 261, 267, 268, 279, xvi
  extrinsic, 136, 146, 191
  intrinsic, 136, 146, 191, 211
3M Svenska AB, 220, 227–230
  customer feedback resolution (CFR) system, 230
  voice of customer (VoC) group, 227

N

Network culture, 182, 187, 192–193, 195
Networks, xiii, xvi, 2, 7, 17–20, 23–28, 31, 56, 63, 67–88, 92, 96, 100–102, 115, 124, 126, 153–158, 166, 167, 180, 185–195, 200, 202
New product development processes, 54, 68, 70, 78, 222, 234
New technologies, xiii, 55, 63, 111, 113, 128, 140, 143, 144, 146, 206, 225
Nokia, v, 115–116
Non-profit health care organisations, 240
Norms, 18, 20, 21, 56, 69, 73, 81, 85, 181, 182, 184–185, 187, 190–193, 195, 254, 272
Norms of interaction, 20–21, 184
Not invented here, 54

O

Observatoire Naturaliste des Ecosystèmes Méditerranéens (ONEM), 98
ONEM. *See* Observatoire Naturaliste des Ecosystèmes Méditerranéens (ONEM)
Online
  community, 20, 136, 137, 139, 187, 217, 248
  forums, 81, 83, 224, 227, 231
  surveys, 137, 227, 229, 232
Open API, 276
Open collaboration
  software production, 111
Open community innovation, 91, 93–105
Open innovation, v, xi, xiii–xvi, 1–15, 17–31, 35–51, 53–64, 67–88, 91–105, 123–130, 133–148, 151–161, 163–177, 179–196, 199–213, 215, 216, 239–250, 253–272, 275–280
  barriers, 2, 154, 164, 166, 169, 172, 174, 219, 225, 230, 232, 235, 245–248, 276
  benefits, xi, xv, 36, 48, 50, 67–68, 73, 77, 119, 126, 135, 144–145

challenges, xiv–xv, 19, 47, 86, 115, 176, 225
drivers, 2, 48, 113, 156, 164, 167, 175, 176, 226, 245–247
economic rationale, 167
future use, xi, xvi, 158, 163–164, 253, 270
implementation of principles, xiv, 6–7, 92, 124–125, 240, 243
inter-organisational perspective, 67–88
model, xiii, xv, 4, 7, 9, 10, 18, 31, 39–44, 48, 53, 68, 69, 72, 74, 75, 80, 98, 115, 119, 125, 163, 206, 240, 277–278
network, 24–28, 67–88, 100–102, 115, 141, 153–158, 167, 187, 188, 192–195, 200, 202, 216
potential, xiv–xv, 13, 18, 69, 85, 87, 127, 137, 156, 163, 200, 202, 208, 226, 231–232
prerequisites, xvi, 9, 70, 73, 75, 83–85, 100, 110, 176, 246–247, 278
problems, v, 6, 11, 13, 28, 31, 36, 38–40, 57, 59, 60, 70, 73, 79, 112, 116, 125–127, 173–174, 180, 193, 202, 206, 217, 230, 231, 246, 261
theoretical underpinnings, xi, xvi, 1–2
value, 151–161
voluntary contributors, 133–148
Open innovation and Social e-learning, 151–161
Open innovation as strategy, 10, 159–160, 182–188, 194
Open innovation barriers
  politics, xiv, 2, 7, 22, 28, 166, 172–173
Open innovation communities, 1–2, 5, 17–31, 35–51, 93–105, 240, 248
  benefits, 36, 40, 42, 44, 48–50
  compliance, 37, 42–46, 48, 51
  contributions, 36–39, 42, 44–48, 50, 51
  differentiation, 36, 39, 43–51
  motivations, 36, 38, 47–49
Open innovation core processes, 134
  outside-in process, 134
Open innovation diffusion, 119
Open innovation in inter-organisational networks, 2
Open innovation intermediaries, 179, 183–186, 192
  InnoCentive, 180, 183, 184, 188, 200
  Ninesigma, 188
Open innovation practices
  sources, 125
Open innovation processes, 31, 62, 92, 133–148, 180–187, 189, 190, 196
  governing, 31

Index

management, 137, 180, 187–193
Open innovation roles, 70, 72, 73, 83
Open innovation systems, 55, 124, 184, 189,
    240, 243–245, 247, 249
  in health care, 239–250
Open innovation technologies, xi, xiii–xvi, 1,
    2, 53–64, 91, 92, 108, 163, 166–168,
    175–178, 275–278
  applications, 1, 55, 91, 97, 100, 110,
    129–130, 155, 182, 208–210, 213, 222
  barriers, xvi, 2, 154, 164
  benefits and challenges, xiv–xv
  development, 167–169
  drivers, 164
  enactment, 163
  the future, 275–278
  health care, 163
  overcoming inertia, 167–168
  social factors, 92
Open innovation tool, 199–213
Openness, xvi, 1, 4, 5, 37, 54, 59, 70, 104, 108,
    109, 163, 254, 262, 271–272, 276, 277,
    279, 280
Open service innovation, 239–250
Open source, 1, 3–15, 36, 38, 49, 50, 68, 81, 91,
    97, 104, 107–120, 133, 158, 190, 222,
    240, 241, 255
Open source 2.0, 107
Open source community, 10
Open source development, 4, 7–8, 10, 68
Open sourced R&D, 241
Open source initiative (OSI), 5, 109
Open source movement, 255
Open source software (OSS), 1, 3–15,
    108–120, 133, 240, 241
  management of incentives, 112, 118
Open source software development, 6,
    10–15, 240
Open source technology, 91, 107–120
  adoption process, 4, 6–7, 109, 250, 272
  barriers, adoption process, 154, 246
  contextual appropriateness, 108–109
  reasons for adoption, 272
Organisational and cultural change, 111, 112,
    115, 120, 247, 275
Organisational boundaries, 4, 69, 70, 82, 87, 125
Organisational culture, 39, 243, 247, 248, 250
Organisational fit, 267
Organisational learning, 2, 49, 55, 114, 157, 247
Organisational norms, 254, 272
Organisational structure, xv, 54–55, 167, 176,
    182, 185–187, 192, 193, 195, 276
  virtual, 108, 186

OSI. *See* Open source initiative (OSI)
OSRAM, 201, 209–211
OSS. *See* Open source software (OSS)
OSS licence, 3–6, 11, 49, 108–110
OSS practices, 108–110
  corporate source, 110
  inner source, 10, 110, 113–115, 117, 118
OSS renegotiation of meaning, 111, 117
Outils-Réseaux, 91, 93–105
Outsourced R&D, 241

P

Participants and users
  types, 13
Participants identification, 269
Participation incentives, 44, 234, 275
Participatory design, 96
Participatory innovation technologies,
    165–175
Patents problem, 222
Philips Healthcare (PH), v, 10–12,
    113–114, 117
Philips Medical, 1
Pico-Jobs, 199–213
PPPs. *See* Public-private-partnerships (PPPs)
Prediction markets
  Iowa Electronic Markets, 200
  liveops, 203, 204
Project activity measurement, 11–12
Prototypes, 208, 217–218, 222–223, 225, 226,
    229, 231, 232, 234, 235
Public-private-partnerships (PPPs), 241

Q

Quasi-firms. *See* Inter-organisational networks
Questionnaire, 57, 59, 139, 141, 220, 230–231,
    260, 261

R

RAC theory. *See* Relative Absorptive Capacity
    (RAC) theory
R&D. *See* Research and development (R&D)
Relative Absorptive Capacity (RAC) theory,
    180–187, 193, 196
Relative openness, 271
Reputation among peers, 13
Requirements elicitation, 54, 57, 220
Research and development (R&D), 27, 69–71,
    82, 124, 156, 182, 184, 200, 209, 216,
    220, 221, 227, 240, 241, 245–246

298 Index

Reward, 54, 91, 92, 109, 111–113, 117, 129,
    136, 156, 189, 191

S

Scott's three pillars of institutions, 168, 169
Second Life, 223, 225
Sensemaking, 20, 21, 24
Sense of belonging to the community, 13
Service desk, 227
Shared vocabularies, 102
Simulations, 184, 191, 217, 218, 223, 229
Social action theories, 167
Social capital, 18, 69, 73, 81, 85
Socially constructed knowledge, 151, 152, 159
Social media, 1, 17–31, 92, 140–142, 147,
    152–161, 217, 218, 224, 225, 243, 246,
    263, 265, 267, 275
    platforms, 153, 263, 265, 267
    systems design, 17–31
    technology, 152, 155
    tool system, 1, 23–25, 30, 31
Social media technology benefits, 126, 155
Social networking
    platforms, 189, 191, 192, 267
    sites, 27, 141, 148, 216–217
Social networks, 134, 141, 244
Social phenomena, 55
Social relations, 55–56, 58
Social structures, 31, 73, 84–85, 110–111
Social website editors, 267
Software configuration, 72
Software customisation, 68, 71–72, 74, 75
Software development, 1, 2, 4, 6–15, 79, 91,
    96, 103, 107–120, 134, 240
Software development strategies, 7, 8
Software-differentiating, 7, 9
Software industry, 10, 67, 181, 190, 218
Solution space, 205, 253–272
Sony Ericsson, 220–223, 231–235
SourceForge, 11, 110, 116, 119
SourceForge.net, 11
Sources of knowledge, xvi, 87, 163, 179–196
Spotify, 266, 269
Standardisation, 10–11, 129
Standardization-methods, 184, 185, 191–192
Sticky, 216, 219, 233, 255
Strong leadership and management, 160
Structural change acceleration, 167, 176
Structured methods, 112, 185
Structures, xiv, xv, 31, 38, 39, 46, 49, 55, 57,
    63, 64, 73, 84, 92, 102, 109–113, 117,
    129–130, 166–168, 176, 181, 182,

184–188, 192, 193, 195, 202, 247, 248,
    250, 263, 276
Structures of financial control, 247
Support from management, 247
Sustainable open innovation, 153
Systems of innovation theory, 168

T

Technical challenges, 103
Technical infrastructures, xiv, xvi, 91, 92,
    118, 183
Technical maturities, 235
Technological advances, 54, 167, 276
Technological limitations, 221
    maturity level, 128
    restricted access to IT, 232
Technologies, 8, 18, 35, 53–64, 80, 96,
    107–120, 134, 151, 165–177, 179–196,
    215, 245, 275–278
    instituting new, 113
    partner fit, 180
Technology acceptance process, 157, 158
Technology adoption, 115, 128, 137, 140
Technology and innovation, xiii–xvi, 18, 35,
    36, 53–64, 80, 91, 92, 163, 165–177,
    179–196, 215, 275–278
Technology limitations, 221
Theory of open innovation, 275
The paradox of embedded agency, 111
Toolkits, 97, 105, 129, 134, 184, 185, 194, 202,
    216–217, 219, 232–235, 255
Tools, 6, 18, 54, 70, 94, 108, 127, 154, 167,
    181, 199–213, 215, 244, 277
    cloud based, 30
Transparency
    benefits, 156
Trust, 18, 25, 27, 47, 49, 56, 62, 63, 69, 73, 81,
    85–87, 116, 147, 183, 187, 225, 227,
    235–236, 241
Twitter, 18, 23–29, 37, 155, 156, 161, 191,
    223, 232

U

Usability test, 47, 223
Use and user experience, 97
User empowerment
    students, 94, 105, 234
User innovation, 104, 139, 163, 215–236, 240
    community, 104–105, 240
    processes, 163, 216–218, 220, 232
    strengths and weaknesses, 215–236

Index

User interaction, 94, 160
User involvement, 104, 136, 254, 255, 264, 271
  commercialisation, 254, 255, 264, 271
User knowledge, 253–272
User knowledge adoption
  organisations, 253–272
User manuals, 227
User participation, 147
  development, 146–147
  process, 146–147
  sustainability over time, 21
Users
  collaboration, xiii, xvi, 6, 11, 13, 26, 91, 92,
    102–105, 167, 175, 190, 202, 217, 218,
    220, 222, 226, 229, 231, 232
  communities, 248–249, 254
  co-production, 153
  creativity, xiii, 6, 11, 26, 57, 92, 108, 134,
    147, 151, 153, 155–157, 163, 179, 200,
    218, 222, 226, 231, 248, 262, 265
  developed applications, 222
  driven innovation, 103
  empowerment, 94, 103, 105, 155, 234, 279
  preference, 215, 228, 231, 232, 235
  studies, xiv, 134, 137, 146–147, 163, 216,
    220, 221, 231, 236, 249–250, 255, 270
  toolkits, 97, 105, 134, 184, 185, 194, 202,
    216, 234, 235, 255
Users-as-innovators, 124, 254
User-to-user knowledge, 255

V

Value, xiii, xiv, xv, 5, 18–19, 36, 56, 69, 104,
    111, 123, 134, 151–161, 167, 193, 209,
    217, 240, 255
Value creation, 133, 134, 151–160
  density related, 155
  mechanisms, 155, 167
  process, 133, 134, 151, 155–160
  via networks, 154–155
Value creation theory, 153

Value network, 124, 153, 155, 157–158
VCs. *See* Virtual communities (VCs)
Video and telephone conferences., 226
Viral promotion effects, 267
Virtual communities (VCs), 187, 217, 219,
    232, 233
Virtualisation technologies, 218
Virtual learning environments, 183
Virtual models, 216–218
Virtual reality, 218
Visualisations, 98, 177, 210, 216–218, 225,
    229, 267
Volvo IT, 220, 224–227, 231–236
  innovation Jams, 224–225, 232
von Hippel, xiii, 5–6, 36, 37, 39–41, 70, 73,
    104, 124, 134, 146–147, 167, 179, 184,
    200, 202, 216, 240, 248–249, 254, 255

W

Web 2.0 applications, xiv, 216–217, 231,
    234, 235
Web-based health portals, 242
Web-based survey, 229, 261
Web-casts, 227
Web 2.0 collaborative systems, 184
Web of interactivity, 21, 227
Web 2.0 technologies, 152, 153, 155–157,
    184, 223
Web 2.0 tools, 167, 191
We-think, 18
Wikini, 94, 97, 98, 101, 102, 104
Wikinomics, 18
Wikis, 25, 27–28, 96–98, 100, 155, 156, 167,
    183, 194, 218
Wisdom of crowds, xiv–xv, 200, 206–209, 211
Wizards, 182, 185, 194
Word of mouth, 267
Workshops, 13, 94, 100, 101, 201, 202, 209,
    224–226, 232, 257
  virtual, 224, 232
WorldVistA, 241

Printed by Publishers' Graphics LLC